The National Waterway

The National Waterway

A History of the Chesapeake and Delaware Canal, 1769–1985

Second Edition

Ralph D. Gray

UNIVERSITY OF ILLINOIS PRESS

Urbana and Chicago

Library of Congress Cataloging-in-Publication Data

Gray, Ralph D.
     The national waterway : a history of the Chesapeake and Delaware
Canal, 1769–1985 / by Ralph D. Gray. — 2nd ed.
          p.   cm.
     Based on a dissertation, University of Illinois.
     Bibliography: p.
     Includes index.
     ISBN 0-252-01627-0 (cloth) ISBN 0-252-06066-0 (paper)
     1. Chesapeake and Delaware Canal (Del. and Md.)—History.
I. Title.
HE396.C4G7 1989
386'.47'097511—dc19   88-28321
                                                                                          CIP

Again, happily, to my Mother and Father

Contents

TABLES

Preface to the Second Edition

The Chesapeake and Delaware Canal has grown in usefulness and significance during the two decades since the first edition of this book in 1967. Its major role in the transportation system of the eastern United States has exceeded my sanguine expectations of the 1960s and makes even less problematic a prediction of continuing service and prominence well into the twenty-first century. At the same time, it is unlikely that the canal dimensions—a channel width of 450 feet, a depth of 35 feet—will ever be substantially increased, for both economic and environmental reasons. An issue for future consideration is whether the trend toward larger and larger ocean and coastal vessels, with drafts in excess of those available through the canal, will eventually make the waterway obsolete in terms of commercial activity. For the moment, however, some 10,000 deep-draft commercial carriers transit the canal each year, carrying cargo which seems likely to exceed the 20-million-ton mark in the 1990s, and the canal's value to the thousands of pleasure craft transiting the canal annually is also immense.

One can only speculate about the feelings of gratification and pride, perhaps also of vindication, the early promoters and self-sacrificing officers and investors of the original canal company would experience if they could revisit the canal site, bask in the sunlight reflected from the broad expanse of the waterway, and witness the stream of traffic, much of it in vessels of undreamed size and sophistication, which daily courses between the waters of the Chesapeake and the Delaware. Perhaps too they would understand more fully than I why it took longer to complete the 1954 enlargement project (twenty-seven years) than it did to construct the initial canal after the company was organized in 1803 (twenty-six years). Certainly they would note some parallels in terms of unexpected delays, unanticipated problems and expenditures, and unrelenting public scrutiny.

[xi]

But there are also significant differences between the early and recent history of the canal, particularly in accessibility, navigability, and the absence of tolls. The modern facility, operated under the careful tutelage of the U.S. Corps of Engineers since 1919, has been repeatedly improved, straightened, deepened, widened, and cleared of most obstructions to navigation. The Corps' management of the canal operations, from safe transits by increasingly larger ships to bank stabilization and wildlife protection, has also improved. The latter activities reflect well the new emphasis of the Corps of Engineers, indeed the entire nation, upon environmental issues, and new attention has been given to improving public accommodations along the canal route. Historic structures at either end of the canal—at Chesapeake City and Delaware City—have been preserved for the enjoyment and enlightenment of the public, and roads paralleling the canal on either side give access to fishing piers and interesting vistas.

Three major events mark the recent history of the Chesapeake and Delaware Canal. In 1970, just as environmental concerns emerged into the full consciousness of the nation, a congressional committee hearing injected this new concern into the canal-improvement project, forever modifying and expanding the factors to be examined and evaluated when undertaking such projects. Three years later a ship-bridge collision (technically an allision), tragic in its immediate consequences, ultimately led to much improved traffic control and general operating procedures. The third event was completion, in 1981, of the project authorized in 1954 to expand and otherwise modernize the waterway. This was a gradual development, with the channel becoming progressively deeper throughout after new high-level highway bridges had replaced the previous lift-spans, and some minor relocations of the channel were completed. The result has been both an esthetic and commercial success, and while constant maintenance and operational problems remain, so too does the capacity for solving them equitably and expeditiously.

I am grateful to a number of people for providing me, a landlocked midlander for many years, with the opportunity to reacquaint myself with the Chesapeake and Delaware Canal and its remarkable and exciting recent history. My first and largest debt of gratitude goes to Dr. Martin Reuss, an able and energetic member of the Historical Office staff at the Corps of Engineers headquarters at Fort Belvoir, Virginia. I undertook this updating of the canal story at his suggestion, and he has offered wise and patient counsel at every step of the way. I am also appreciative of the time and effort spent on my behalf by various members of the District Engineer Office in Philadelphia, particularly Roy A. Pirritano and Constance Dean of the Public Affairs staff, several members of the library and reference staff, J. Jeffrey Radley in Environmental Resources, and Walt Staret, Chief of the Navigation and Maintenance Branch. James R. Tomlin, Jr., superintendent of the canal at the Corps of Engineers office in Chesapeake City, was generous and forthright with his assistance, as were Frank L. Hamons, Jr., and David Bibo of the Maryland Port Authority when we talked about the significance of the canal to Baltimore shippers and to the Port of Baltimore in general. The reference staffs at the University Library at Indiana University–Purdue University at Indianapolis (IUPUI) and the Indiana State Library in Indianapolis were also helpful, as was Professor Emeritus John A. Munroe of the University of Delaware. I also benefited from a careful reading of the first draft of the new chapters by Professor Philip V. Scarpino, an environmental historian and new colleague in the Department of History at IUPUI. Neither he nor others, however, are responsible for the interpretations offered or the errors that remain, which are mine alone. My final word of gratitude belongs to my family, beginning with my parents, to whom this book is rededicated, and to Jan, Karen and Greg, David and Melanie, and Sarah. All of them, in special ways, made real contributions.

Preface to the First Edition

The Chesapeake and Delaware Canal, as it exists today, is a sea-level waterway connecting the upper reaches of Chesapeake Bay with the Delaware River and Bay. A ship canal capable of accommodating all except the largest cargo or military vessels, it is an important link in the Atlantic Intracoastal Waterway which extends from New England to Florida and provides sheltered navigation for vessels unsuited to or unwilling to risk the dangers of sailing the open seas. The canal also serves as a convenient route to sea for ocean-going vessels sailing from the port of Baltimore.

Following its completion in 1829, the canal was privately operated for ninety years as a lock canal. Although short (less than 14 miles long) and limited in accommodations, it proved to be of enormous economic and military importance to the region and nation. The peak tonnage of the waterway as a lock canal came in 1872, when 1,318,712 tons of cargo passed through; in ten other years the annual tonnage exceeded 1,000,000.

The federal government purchased the canal in 1919, at which time a series of improvements was undertaken to render the waterway adequate for modern shipping requirements. The initial step was to lower the upper level of the canal to sea level, so that the locks could be eliminated. Subsequently, in a project undertaken and completed in the 1930's, the canal was widened, straightened, and deepened to facilitate transits. The depth of the canal was increased from 12 to 27 feet, and the minimum bottom width was changed from 90 to 250 feet. Five bridges, including one railroad bridge, crossed the canal between Chesapeake City and Delaware City.

Completion of the improvements, by which a small barge canal was transformed into a ship canal, was followed by a dramatic increase in the amount of traffic using the enlarged facilities, particularly during the period of World War II. It became apparent, however, that still further enlargements were needed to meet the increased traffic demands and to make the canal safe and free from obstructions. The growing number of groundings and collisions, either with fixed objects or other vessels, made the need urgent. At least eight accidents between 1938 and 1950 involved bridge collisions, with two of the vertical lift bridges (in 1939 and 1942) being demolished, and there were 200 other accidents during the period.

Consequently, in 1954, Congress authorized a $100,000,000 project of improvement. This called for deepening and widening the channel, to 35 and 450 feet respectively, and for replacement of all but one of the remaining vertical lift bridges with modern high-level structures. Relatively minor projects were undertaken first, with 18 per cent of the whole being completed in 1960. Major construction work awaited additional congressional appropriations, which were eventually made in 1962. It is estimated that the present project will be completed in 1968. Currently, even with the canal's inadequate dimensions, more than 20,000 vessels pass through it each year, carrying commodities bound for all parts of the world. The annual average freight amounts to well over 10,000,000 tons. There is, moreover, a considerable traffic in pleasure vessels and passengers.

The present waterway little resembles the small lock canal originally constructed in 1824–29, some sixty years after the first surveys for it were made and almost two hundred years after the idea was conceived. Indeed, by virtue of its early advocacy and its prominence in the internal improvements movement, the Chesapeake and Delaware Canal has been called "the parent of all the canal projects" in the United States.[1] Not only was it one of the first canals in this country to be surveyed, it was one of the few upon which construction was undertaken prior to the "canal era." Its primacy also rested upon its prominence in national affairs during a twenty-year struggle to obtain federal aid for a project of decidedly national, rather than local, importance. When original construction efforts stopped far short of success in 1805, the promoters of the Chesapeake and Delaware promptly made claim for government support of their national project. Their appeals were unsuccessful, however, until the country was in the midst of a great burst of canal building activity in the quarter-century after 1815. During this period, touched off by the spectacular success of New York's Erie Canal, some 3,000 miles of canal were built in the United States by 1840, and another 1,000 miles were completed

[1] George Armroyd, *A Connected View of the Whole Internal Navigation of the United States, Natural and Artificial; Present and Prospective* (Philadelphia, 1826), p. 80.

the following decade.² Although the Chesapeake and Delaware Canal added only 14 miles to the nation's total, it served to connect two of the most important commercial waterways in the country, and made possible continuous navigation along more than 600 miles of the Atlantic coast without venturing to sea.

In the 1850's, abandonments of canal mileage began to exceed the amount of new construction, primarily as a result of railroad competition. As economic historian Carter Goodrich has pointed out, however, "the major era of canal building did not come to an end until most of the apparent opportunities offered by the American terrain had already been exploited."³ This had involved building canals to connect East and West, to connect the Great Lakes with the Ohio or the Mississippi rivers in the West, and to form links in the chain making an eastern intracoastal waterway. One example of each of the former types remains in use in New York and Illinois (although plans are now under consideration for a new canal between lake and river in Ohio), while the Atlantic Intracoastal Waterway is still in use and undergoing further development.

In the early nineteenth century, the Chesapeake and Delaware Canal was primarily a child of Pennsylvania, whose citizens furnished most of the private capital and administrative leadership to the undertaking. Pennsylvanians saw the canal as one answer to the problem of providing transportation between Philadelphia and the vast hinterland along the Susquehanna River. It would complete an all-water route from the interior of Pennsylvania to the metropolis of the state, thereby diverting from Baltimore to Philadelphia the extensive trade of the Susquehanna Valley. Indeed, throughout most of the nineteenth century after completion of the canal, the Susquehanna River trade was the key to the fortunes of the Chesapeake and Delaware Canal Company; as the one flourished or languished, so did the other.

As other routes westward from Philadelphia were completed in the middle years of the nineteenth century, Pennsylvania's interest in the canal waned, but to Maryland, especially to the port city of Baltimore, the canal became increasingly important. Baltimore, needing an outlet to the Atlantic which would be both shorter and safer than the route down Chesapeake Bay, put herself in the vanguard of a movement as early as 1871 to enlarge the original lock canal into a sea-level canal. Due in great part to the skillful and effective

² Carter Goodrich, ed., *Canals and American Economic Development* (New York, 1961), pp. 6–7.
³ *Ibid.*, p. 7.

work of the Atlantic Deeper Waterways Association, organized in 1907 to promote an Atlantic coastal waterway, this feat was accomplished in 1927, eight years after the canal had been acquired by the federal government. Military considerations were among the foremost reasons prompting this action by the government following the close of World War I, although the military value of a Chesapeake and Delaware canal had long been recognized. The absence of such a waterway during the Revolutionary War and the War of 1812 had been painfully evident, and its potential strategic value in later emergencies accounted in large measure for Congress' willingness in 1825 and 1829 to make liberal subscriptions to the stock of the Chesapeake and Delaware Canal Company. The wisdom of this action was demonstrated during the Civil War, and later during World Wars I and II. Given the heavy annual traffic, and the operations underway to further enlarge and modernize the canal, it is clear that the waterway will continue to play a vital role in the inland navigation of the country.

In the pages that follow, I have attempted to present a comprehensive survey of the history of this important and, in many ways, unique waterway. The emphasis has been placed upon providing a connected narrative rather than an analysis of the economic impact; there has been no attempt, in the words of one economic historian, to analyze "guesswork computed to the fourth decimal place" when necessary statistics are missing. My aim has been to tell the story of the canal's origin, construction, and operation, and to give some estimate of its national significance. The financial problems of the parent company, its efforts at modernization of facilities and services, and the struggles leading to government acquisition are major elements of the book.

There should be no need to justify a history of this canal. Although in some ways it was typical of other canal projects, and was completed during the height of the "canal era," in other respects it has singular importance. Deeper, shorter, and more costly, proportionately, than other contemporary canals, the Chesapeake and Delaware has played major roles in national affairs. It was indirectly responsible for the famous Gallatin "Report on Roads and Canals" in 1808, served as a virtual "test case" in the argument over federal aid to internal improvements, provided indispensable services during the early days of the Civil War, and, finally, figured prominently in the twentieth-century debate over the desirability of a federally sponsored Atlantic intracoastal waterway system. Part of the explanation for this rests in the fact that Delaware, the state in which the canal is primarily located (less than two miles of the original line lay in Maryland), was never enthusiastic about the waterway; major support for it came from areas far removed from the actual line of the canal. This was clearly not merely a "local" project even during the nineteenth century, and in recent decades, in both a figurative and a literal sense, it has become a central link in the inland waterway system along the Atlantic coast.

My debts to those who have assisted me in the course of my study of this subject are legion, and many who have contributed must of necessity go unrecognized here. I am especially indebted to Professor Robert M. Sutton, of the University of Illinois, who directed the dissertation on which this book is based, to Professor John A. Munroe, of the University of Delaware, whose knowledge, constructive criticism, and personal friendship have been most helpful, and to the Department of History, University of Illinois, for courageously selecting this study for its Dickerson Award and underwriting its publication. Dr. Walter Heacock of the Eleutherian Mills–Hagley Foundation and Mr. Peter C. Welsh, now of the Smithsonian Institution, first encouraged me to undertake a study of the canal while I held a fellowship from the foundation. I want to express my thanks to the library staffs at the Historical Society of Delaware, where the Chesapeake and Delaware Canal Company Papers are located, at the University of Illinois, and at Indiana University for innumerable courtesies, and to the personnel of the Corps of Engineers, Philadelphia District, for graciously and promptly meeting my every request. Professor Irene D. Neu, of Indiana University, and Professor James R. Hurt, of the University of Illinois, read an earlier version of this history and saved me from many errors and infelicities of style, and the editorial assistance provided by the University of Illinois Press has greatly improved the book. For the errors and shortcomings that remain, I alone of course am responsible. An Indiana University Faculty Research Grant financed the final stages of research and writing, and expert typing services were performed by Mrs. Sheryl B. Moloch and Miss Marcia Meyers of Kokomo, Indiana. My greatest debt, however, is to my wife, Janice, who has shared in all phases of the work on this book cheerfully and willingly, while performing her manifold duties as wife and mother. I am grateful to the editors of *Delaware History*, *Maryland Historical Magazine*, and the *Pennsylvania Magazine of History and Biography* for permission to reprint portions of articles which previously appeared in their journals.

Ralph D. Gray

Kokomo, Indiana
December 6, 1966

Connecting the Bays:
An Age-Old Dream

1

A canal across the narrow peninsula which separates
the Chesapeake and Delaware bays was the dream of many men before
it became a reality in 1829. It is impossible to state with precision the
man who first envisioned the waterway, for it was a project which
almost suggested itself. The topography of upper Delmarva Peninsula
is essentially flat, with a low-lying dividing ridge, or watershed, which
seldom extends higher than 100 feet above sea level. At the site of the
present canal, the summit is but 80 feet above sea level. Moreover,
this peninsula is narrow and is indented on both sides by numerous
streams, the headwaters of which often come within a few thousand
yards of each other, separated only by the low summit. It was the
natural location for a waterway to connect two great avenues of trade
and travel. Only a few miles of canal would provide an all-water route
between the Chesapeake and Delaware bays, thus shortening the long,
hazardous journey down Chesapeake Bay, around Cape Charles, and
up the coast to Delaware Bay by several hundred miles. The distance
of a voyage between Philadelphia and Baltimore would be reduced by
more than 300 miles. At various times during the seventeenth and early
eighteenth centuries the possibility of such a canal, to be formed by
uniting the headwaters of the peninsular streams by a short and shallow artificial channel, was contemplated, but not until the 1760's did
a man seriously devote himself to the project. This person was Thomas

Gilpin of Pennsylvania, and it is he who deserves the title of, if not father, at least grandfather of the Chesapeake and Delaware Canal.

Gilpin's predecessors in recognizing the utility of a Chesapeake and Delaware canal include the first European settlers in the Delaware Valley. In 1638 a group of Swedish colonists chose the valley as their home in the New World. Spreading both northward and southward from their original landing site near present-day Wilmington, the Swedes proved to be a vigorous and industrious people. Although their rule in the Delaware Valley was destined to be brief, these Scandinavian settlers made lasting contributions, including introduction of the log house, to the culture of the area and nation. In 1654, Governor Johan Rising, the last governor of New Sweden, wrote of the need and potential usefulness of a cross-peninsular canal. Reporting to his superiors in Sweden, Rising expressed his belief in the desirability of settling the upper Christina Valley, to the southwest of the original Swedish settlement, for the dual purposes of safety and trade. Populating the valley would make their colony "the more secure against Virginia"; moreover, it would make it possible "to carry on trade with them, making a passage from their river [the Elk, a headwater of the Chesapeake Bay] into the said kill [the Christina], by which we could bring the Virginian goods here and store them, and load our ships with them for a return cargo." [1]

Another early prediction of the canal was made in 1661 by Augustine Herman, Lord Baltimore's surveyor and the proprietor of Bohemia Manor. Herman wrote to an official of the Dutch settlements on the Delaware, Vice-Director Beekman: "The Minquaskil and the aforesaid Bohemia River run there within a league from each other, from where we shall in time have communication with each other by water, which may serve as encouragement to the inhabitants of New-Netherland." [2] Again in 1680 Herman expressed himself as favoring a canal between the two bays, but he had to be content with a cart road which already had been opened between Bohemia Manor and the Delaware.

The need for a canal as a commercial artery continued to grow, and was mentioned by Jasper Danckaerts, a Labadist missionary who toured the American colonies in the late seventeenth century. Danckaerts noted that a Chesapeake and Delaware canal had been "talked

---

[1] Albert Cook Myers, ed., *Narratives of Early Pennsylvania, West New Jersey, and Delaware* (New York, 1912), pp. 139–140.
[2] Federal Writers' Project, *Delaware: A Guide to the First State* (rev. ed., New York, 1955), pp. 335–336.

of" when the Dutch "governed the country," because it "would have afforded great convenience for trade" on the Delaware River. With a transpeninsular canal, the missionary pointed out, the people of Maryland could ship their goods "sooner and more readily, as well as more conveniently" from the Delaware River than from their "Great Bay" — the Chesapeake — and therefore would use the new route frequently. In concluding his remarks on the canal, Danckaerts suggested that "as this is a subject of greater importance than it seems upon the first view, it is well to consider whether it should not be brought to the attention of higher authorities than particular governors. What is now done by land, in carts, might then be done by water, for a distance of more than six hundred miles."[3]

Even more dramatic testimony indicating the commercial need for the canal is found in Dr. Benjamin Bullivant's travel account of the late seventeenth century. He described how goods — and vessels — were transported across the narrow neck of the Delmarva Peninsula in 1697: "about 8 myles below n[ew] Castle is a Creeke, by wch you may come to a neck of Land 12 myles over Crosse wch are drawn goods to & from Mary Land & Sloopes also of 30 tunns are carried over land in this place on certaine sleds drawn by Oxen, & launched again into the water on ye other Side."[4]

Yet the seventeenth-century men who dreamed of a Chesapeake and Delaware canal had to be content with their dreams. Lock navigation was not yet widely known; the intricacies of the problem of constructing a usable canal across the peninsula were dimly seen. Not until the eighteenth century was there a partial understanding of the complexity of the problems; not until the nineteenth was the canal project accomplished. Even then the difficulties proved almost insurmountable. Twenty-five years passed between the time the first spadeful of earth was turned and the long-awaited day in 1829 when the first barge transited the canal.

As indicated above, the first efforts to survey and construct a Chesapeake and Delaware canal were made in the 1760's. Thomas Gilpin, the prosperous Quaker miller and merchant of Philadelphia who initiated the movement, was a man of broad intellectual and scientific interests. Involved in various economic activities in eastern

---

[3] Bartlett Burleigh James and J. Franklin Jameson, eds., *Journal of Jasper Danckaerts, 1679–1680* (New York, 1913), p. 128.

[4] Wayne Andrews, ed., "A Glance at New York in 1697: The Travel Diary of Dr. Benjamin Bullivant," *The New-York Historical Society Quarterly*, XL (January, 1956), 71.

Pennsylvania and the Delmarva Peninsula, he was well aware of the utility of canal communications across the peninsula.

Gilpin was born in Pennsylvania in 1728. He received little formal education but by his own study learned higher mathematics and developed a lasting interest in science. A member of the American Philosophical Society, he prepared papers on such varied subjects as the wheat fly, the seventeen-year locust, a hydraulic wind pump, and the migration of herrings. In 1764 he married the daughter of Joshua Fisher, a prominent Philadelphia merchant, and had three children. His eldest son, Joshua, became perhaps the leading and certainly the most knowledgeable member of the Chesapeake and Delaware Canal Company during the arduous first twenty years of its existence. Thomas Gilpin died in 1778, in Winchester, Virginia, having been sent there in exile by his state during the American Revolution, when he and others refused to sign a declaration of loyalty.[5]

The Gilpin family owned land in three colonies in the period prior to the Revolution. In addition to an estate and a flour mill on the Brandywine Creek in northern Delaware, Thomas Gilpin inherited property located along the Susquehanna River in Pennsylvania. Later he acquired a 1,000-acre tract of land at the head of the Chester River on Maryland's Eastern Shore. Moving to Philadelphia in 1764, he soon began to awaken in other city merchants a realization of their need for improved inland transportation, particularly a Chesapeake and Delaware canal.

Much of central Pennsylvania's produce was being transported to market via the Susquehanna River, which empties into Chesapeake Bay. Since Baltimore enjoyed easier communications than Philadelphia with the head of Chesapeake Bay, the Maryland city was reaping profits from a trade Philadelphia considered rightfully her own. This trade was contributing in large measure to Baltimore's remarkable growth during the 1750's and 1760's. A mere village of less than 200 people in 1750, Baltimore could boast of a population nearing 6,000 by 1770; such growth represented a serious challenge to Philadelphia's western trade. Gilpin proposed a Chesapeake and Delaware canal as one way to recapture and maintain for Philadelphia the expanding and lucrative trade of the Susquehanna. Articles by Gilpin urging construction of the canal began to appear in the Philadelphia

[5] See [Thomas Gilpin], *Exiles in Virginia: With Observations on the Conduct of the Society of Friends during the Revolutionary War* (Philadelphia, 1848); "Memoir of Thomas Gilpin," *Pennsylvania Magazine of History and Biography*, XLIX (1925), 289–328; Carl and Jessica Bridenbaugh, *Rebels and Gentlemen: Philadelphia in the Age of Franklin* (New York, 1942), pp. 345–349.

newspapers and, in order to test the complete practicability of the waterway, Gilpin personally made a careful survey of a canal route from the "Head of Chester," where he owned land, to Duck Creek on the Delaware. Subsequently, with the assistance of residents in the area, Gilpin explored the entire Delaware Peninsula in search of other practicable routes. As many as five canal lines were surveyed, with plans and estimates drawn up for each.[6]

Gilpin was convinced by his explorations that a transpeninsular waterway could be made easily and inexpensively. A line but from 6 to 13 miles long, through a country of easy digging and plentiful water, was all that was required. Gilpin, of course, was primarily interested in having the canal run from his Chester River property to Duck Creek, but he made thorough calculations for other possible routes so that a general comparison of their advantages could be made. He also traveled to England in 1768, evidently to inspect personally the Duke of Bridgewater's canal, completed in 1761. By February, 1769, Gilpin was ready to present his findings to a meeting of Philadelphia merchants interested in the "improvement of the trade of the province," this interest having been stimulated by Gilpin's continued and effective newspaper campaign.

Gilpin's report and proposals to the meeting, much more than mere academic exercises, were detailed and precise. The merchants were favorably impressed and, desiring to learn more, enlisted the aid of the American Philosophical Society. Already a member of the society, Gilpin laid his plans and estimates before that group on February 17, 1769. These plans were referred to the committees for "American Improvements" and "Trade and Commerce," which were asked "to digest the Papers now lying before the Society, for opening a Canal to join the Waters of the Delaware and Chesapeake Bays," and to "prepare a scheme of Application to the Merchants &c of this City, for defraying the Expence" of additional examinations. The society's fund-raising efforts were immediately successful, with more than £200 being obtained. With the American Philosophical Society supplying the personnel, equipment, and skills, and the merchants furnishing the funds, an eight-man Committee of Survey roamed

[6] Brooke Hindle, *The Pursuit of Science in Revolutionary America, 1735–1789* (Chapel Hill, 1956), pp. 210–212. The original papers of the Chester River–Duck Creek surveys are in the Gilpin Papers, Historical Society of Pennsylvania (Philadelphia). See also Joshua Gilpin, *A Memoir on the Rise, Progress, and Present State of the Chesapeake and Delaware Canal, Accompanied with Original Documents and Maps* (Wilmington, 1821), Appendix, pp. 1–16.

the Lower Counties (Delaware) in 1769 and 1770, braving ill weather and enduring physical hardships in order to conduct the surveys.[7]

Charged with the task of determining how water communications could best be opened between Maryland and Pennsylvania, "particularly by what means the large and increasing number of frontier-settlers, especially those on the Sasquehannah [sic] and its branches, might be enabled to bring their produce to market at the cheapest rate, whether by land or water," the committee set out in May, 1769. The first route examined was for a canal running between the Bohemia, on the Chesapeake side, and the Appoquinimink rivers. After having taken the necessary levels and collected other data, the committee made a preliminary report of its findings to the society, which considered it in conjunction with Gilpin's earlier report on the Chester River–Duck Creek route. The two routes were judged practicable, and their construction expenses were estimated, but there were objections to both of them. It was decided that the Bohemia-Appoquinimink route, which would require £40,000 to construct, was too costly, and that Gilpin's more southern route, although much less costly, was too distant from Philadelphia. "It would carry," the committee reported, "all the navigation of the river Susquehanna (which is the great object in view,) too far down into Chesopeak-Bay, for an advantageous communication with Philadelphia."[8]

During the winter months of 1769–70, other routes were examined, including a road which led from Peach Bottom Ferry on the Susquehanna to Christiana Bridge in New Castle County, Delaware. The most extensive survey, however, was made of a northern canal route, also terminating at Christiana Bridge. In all, four canals and three roads were laid out, with the committee recommending construction of both the canal and the road leading to Christiana Bridge, from where communications with Philadelphia were "known to be safe and easy." Both projects were thought to be well calculated to capture the trade of the Susquehanna River, "the natural channel

[7] Minutes of the American Philosophical Society, held at Philadelphia for Promoting Useful Knowledge (United Society), American Philosophical Society Library (Philadelphia), April 7, 21, May 3, 1769. See also "An Abstract of sundry Papers and Proposals for improving the Inland Navigation of Pennsylvania and Maryland, by opening a Communication between the Tide-Waters of Delaware and Susquehannah, or Chesopeak-Bay; with a Scheme for an easy and short Land-Communication between the waters of Susquehannah and Christiana-Creek, a Branch of Delaware; to which are annexed some Estimates of Expence, &c.," Transactions, American Philosophical Society, I (1771), 293–300.
[8] "An Abstract of sundry Papers," pp. 293, 295.

through which the produce of three-fourths of this Province must in time be conveyed to market for exportation."[9]

It has been stated that the canal survey "stirred enthusiasm comparable to that stirred by the prospect of observing a transit of Venus which was about to occur,"[10] but this enthusiasm, if it existed, was soon stifled by the approaching conflict with Great Britain. Moreover, there was doubt as to the ability of Pennsylvania to accomplish so ambitious a project. "Elucidatus" in 1770 praised the "noble inclination of Improvement" within the province, admitting that a Chesapeake and Delaware canal "undoubtedly would be a thing of the first consequence, and the most beneficial undertaking of any yet proposed," but he believed the magnitude of the project required its delay until "a future day." In the meantime, since most of Pennsylvania "lies more convenient to other markets than Philadelphia," "Elucidatus," writing in a style which belied his pseudonym, favored the construction of the road from Peach Bottom Ferry to Christina Creek.[11] Neither this suggestion nor the American Philosophical Society report was acted upon, and after this brief flurry of activity in 1769 and 1770, nothing more appears to have been done to promote a Chesapeake and Delaware canal for more than a decade.

Pennsylvania, in the meantime, turned to alternative methods to improve her communications between Philadelphia and the interior. Overland routes reaching westward from Philadelphia into the Susquehanna Valley were planned, the state at the same time refusing to clear, or permit to be cleared, the natural obstructions to navigation in the Susquehanna River below Wright's Ferry, now Columbia. A canal entirely within the boundaries of Pennsylvania, between the Susquehanna and Schuylkill rivers, was again suggested at this time. But all schemes of this nature were soon halted. Samuel Rhoads's prediction in 1771 that "we expect shortly to be canal-mad" had overlooked political exigencies. Thoroughgoing improvements in inland transportation awaited more settled times after the Revolution, when Pennsylvania once again led the way in reviving the Chesapeake and Delaware canal project.[12]

[9] *Ibid.*, p. 298. See the map which accompanied the society's final report.
[10] Dugald C. Jackson, "Engineering in Our Early History: The American Philosophical Society and Engineering from 1768 to 1870," *Proceedings*, American Philosophical Society, LXXXVI (1942), 49.
[11] *Pennsylvania Gazette* (Philadelphia), January 4, 1770.
[12] Caroline E. MacGill *et al.*, *History of Transportation in the United States Before 1860* (Washington, 1917), p. 213; Bridenbaugh, *Rebels and Gentlemen*, p. 349; broadside addressed "To the Public," Philadelphia, January 15,

In 1785, at the suggestion of the Pennsylvania legislature, commissioners were appointed by each of the three states most closely concerned to confer about the canal and the improvement of navigation on the lower Susquehanna. The states of Delaware and Maryland were reluctant to participate in the conference, Delaware fearing "that such a navigable communication if carried into effect at this time would tend to injure the carrying Trade of this State," but all three states were represented when the conference convened on schedule in November, 1786, at Wilmington, Delaware. The country's leading men, Washington and Madison, Franklin and Rittenhouse, were aware of this event and applauded and encouraged it, but no positive course of action was agreed to at the meeting.[13] Delawareans admittedly were more interested in improving the "Roads of Carriage in this State" than in building a canal; and Washington's prediction that Maryland would refuse to grant Pennsylvania permission "to open a Communication between the Chesapeak [sic] and Delaware by way of the rivers Elk and Christeen . . . if the Baltimore interest can give it effectual opposition" was correct at this time. As yet there were no privileges withheld by Pennsylvania which Maryland desired strongly enough to permit the canal, widely recognized as a potential threat to Baltimore's Susquehanna trade.[14]

Interest in improving inland waterway communications at this time was by no means confined to the Middle Atlantic states. During this period plans for other canals in Virginia and the Carolinas, in Connecticut and Massachusetts, were being discussed. As Joseph S. Davis has pointed out in his study of early American corporations, a total of 74 inland navigation corporations were chartered between 1783 and 1800. George Washington in 1786 was particularly pleased to find the "spirit for inland navigation prevailing so generally," but

1772. A copy of this broadside is in the possession of the Library Company of Philadelphia.

[13] General Reference File, Folder 28, Delaware State Archives (Dover). Hereafter this repository will be cited as DSA. The Delaware commissioners named to represent the state, appointed at the same time that delegates to the Annapolis convention were named, were William Killen, Gunning Bedford, John Jones, Robert Armstrong, and Eleazer McComb. *Minutes of the Council of the Delaware State from 1776 to 1792* (Dover, 1886), p. 971. According to the compilers of *Delaware: A Guide*, p. 336, Benjamin Franklin, Benjamin Rush, and James Madison were among those who attended the Wilmington canal meeting from other states.

[14] General Reference File, Folder 28, DSA; George Washington to James Madison, Mount Vernon, November 30, 1785, John C. Fitzpatrick, ed., *The Writings of George Washington from the Original Manuscript Sources, 1745–1799* (Washington, 1938), XXVIII, 337.

he realized the value of a successful pioneering work. "To begin well . . . is all in all: error in the commencement will not only be productive of unnecessary expence, but, what is still worse, of discouragements." Washington suggested that the services of a professional engineer from Europe be obtained by several canal companies jointly, observing sagely, "one man may plan for twenty to execute." In particular, he suggested that cooperation between the canal promoters in North Carolina and Delaware was possible, as "the distance from Delaware . . . to the Cowper river is not so great but that one person of activity might design for all between them, and visit the whole three or four times a year." [15]

Although Washington's idea was sound and recognized the need for professional engineering advice, it was not carried out. The Chesapeake and Delaware promoters could not have participated in the plan in any case, because the interstate negotiations of 1786 had come to nothing. Pennsylvania was forced to concentrate for yet a few more years on improvements which could be made within her own boundaries. The Susquehanna-Schuylkill canal plan and the movement for improved roads were revived. The canal scheme failed, but the Lancaster Turnpike, begun in 1792, was completed four years later. This was at best a partial solution to Pennsylvania's transportation problem, and the need for improved inland communications continued. Agitation for a Chesapeake and Delaware canal grew stronger.

[15] Joseph Stancliffe Davis, *Essays in the Earlier History of American Corporations* (Cambridge, Massachusetts, 1917), II, 116–118; Washington to William Moultrie, Mount Vernon, May 25, 1786, Fitzpatrick, ed., *The Writings of George Washington*, XXVIII, 439–440.

Formation of the
Canal Company

2

The last decade of the eighteenth century witnessed the promotion of countless internal improvements — roads, bridges, turnpikes, and canals. Since primary reliance at that time was placed on waterway transportation, it is understandable that "Canal and Lock Navigation" schemes were particularly popular. Plans were in the air, according to John Bach McMaster, "for three or four artificial water-ways in every State." The Chesapeake and Delaware Canal project was one of many revived or originally undertaken at this time. According to one contemporary report, it was the most promising of all the important public works of the United States.[1]

An unusual feature of this project, however, was the source of its major support. The canal was to be located in Maryland and Delaware, but neither of these states vigorously supported it; in fact, they were either hostile or indifferent to it. Pennsylvania's great interest in the affair had aroused their suspicions; they feared the canal would favor their northern neighbor exclusively or at least disproportionately. Maryland was concerned about a precipitous decline in Baltimore's Susquehanna trade if the canal were built; Delaware was worried about the loss of its lucrative carrying trade across the peninsula.

[1] John Bach McMaster, *A History of the People of the United States, from the Revolution to the Civil War* (New York, 1890), II, 74; *New York Magazine*, IV (September, 1793), 575, quoted in Davis, *American Corporations*, II, 137.

An articulate statement and able summary of Maryland's opposition to the proposed canal was printed in 1797. The anonymous
author, apparently a citizen of Baltimore, suggested that Maryland's
"sound policy" would be to

adopt some wholesome provisions to retain the exportation of these important articles (wheat and flour) from her own seaports, [rather] than assist
in forming a highway for their safe passage into Delaware. From the great
superiority of situation and expense of portage across the isthmus between
the Chesapeake and Delaware Bays, Baltimore, though much inferior to
Philadelphia in wealth and population, hath of late commenced a degree
of rivalship with that city. Remove the barrier, all competition is immediately terminated. She at once sinks into the station of an inferior or secondary market. . . .[2]

An earlier publication had attempted to answer Delaware's principal objection to the canal — loss of the carrying trade — by pointing to the numerous advantages it would bring to the state. In the
first place, a closer unity among the middle states would result. The
Chesapeake and Delaware Canal, as well as the Potomac and the Susquehanna canals, would bind the states together with a strong cement — mutual interest. Trade would become easy, cheap, expeditious.
Manufacturing and commerce would increase, land would be improved, population would grow, and the respective resources of the
different areas could be exchanged to mutual benefit. A special appeal
was made to the Brandywine flour millers, whose mills were capable
of producing 300,000 to 500,000 barrels of flour annually, to support
the canal project. Much of the wheat processed in Delaware, it was
pointed out, came from Maryland, and the improved transportation
would lower present overland carrying charges by one sixth. The
millers and draymen of Delaware were warned that if their state continued to block the canal, "they may probably be eased in the future
of the burden of being carriers [and processors], as well as the advantages they now enjoy arising therefrom." [3]

This combined appeal and threat did little to change opinion
about the canal in Delaware. The state's implacable stand, in fact,
prompted one Delawarean, admittedly "actuated by the twofold motives of public good and private advantage," to propose to Governor

[2] *Reflections on the Proposition to communicate by a Navigable Canal the
waters of Chesapeake with those of Delaware Bay, addressed to the Citizens of
Maryland* (Annapolis, 1797), quoted in James Weston Livingood, *The Philadelphia-Baltimore Trade Rivalry, 1780–1860* (Harrisburg, 1947), pp. 84–85.
[3] "Observations on the advantages of the proposed canal from the Chesapeake to the Delaware," *American Museum*, XI (January, 1792), 30–33.

sylvania — George Logan, John Hunn, and Presley Carr Lane.[6] These men had been appointed by the Pennsylvania legislature to negotiate with the Delaware legislators in the attempt to arrange terms which would be acceptable to both sides. It was finally agreed that, in return for passage of the act of incorporation, Pennsylvania would either give to Delaware or permit her to transcribe all records and papers in the Pennsylvania land office relating to the three Lower Counties. The larger state, moreover, was to rescind certain portions of its quarantine laws objectionable to Delawareans.

Having thus secured the incorporation of a canal company in Maryland and Delaware, Pennsylvania quickly adopted its own act of incorporation, one which also provided for carrying out the conditions established by the other two states. Delaware was not completely satisfied, however, by the changes made in Pennsylvania's quarantine laws. Not until February 27, 1802, did Governor David Hall of Delaware, convinced at last that Pennsylvania had fulfilled the conditions in Delaware's canal bill, proclaim the canal company's act of incorporation in full force and effect. Two days later, the subscription books of the Chesapeake and Delaware Canal Company were opened.

According to the laws of the incorporating states, a capitalization of $500,000 — 2,500 shares at $200 each — was authorized; when half of that amount was subscribed, the canal company could be organized. Each state appointed men to whom the pledges could be made, and one year was allowed for the campaign. Optimistically, provisions were made in case excessive pledges were obtained, but it proved necessary to extend briefly the period for receiving subscriptions. The stockholders' first meeting, however, set for May 1, 1803, in Wilmington, was not delayed. This meeting, which occurred "at the house of Mrs. Huggins, the sign of the Ship," with seven subscribers present, was only an informal gathering because it was Sunday. At the much larger "general meeting" held the following day in the Wilmington Town Hall, with persons "personally or by Proxy" holding more than 1,400 shares in attendance, the Chesapeake and Delaware Canal Company was organized and officers were elected.[7] Joseph Tat-

---

[6] John A. Munroe, *Federalist Delaware, 1775–1815* (New Brunswick, New Jersey, 1954), p. 244; *Laws of the State of Delaware*, III (Wilmington, 1816), 170–188. See also *A Collection of the Laws Relative to the Chesapeake and Delaware Canal; Passed by the Legislatures of the States of Maryland, Delaware, and Pennsylvania, subsequent to the year 1798* (Philadelphia, 1823).

[7] More than 1,700 shares of stock were subscribed to by 1806. Pennsylvania subscribers, mostly from Philadelphia, pledged to purchase 824 shares; Delaware subscribers, largely from Wilmington, agreed to purchase 712

nall, a Wilmington miller, was named president of the board; of the remaining nine members of the board, four were from Pennsylvania, three from Maryland, and two from Delaware. These men, representatives of the business and professional groups in their communities, were merchants, millers, or lawyers. Two in the last category, Johns of Delaware and Tilghman of Pennsylvania, later became the chief justices of their respective states.

TABLE 1. SUBSCRIPTIONS IN THE CHESAPEAKE AND DELAWARE
CANAL COMPANY, 1803–06 [a]

State	Shares	Subscribers	Amount Paid[b]	Amount Due
Pennsylvania	824	429	$ 73,400.00	$ 9,000.00
Delaware	712	247	11,300.00	59,900.00
Maryland	256	54	18,300.00	7,300.00
Total	1,792	730	$103,000.00	$76,200.00

[a]Source: Joshua Gilpin, *Memoir on the Chesapeake and Delaware Canal* (Wilmington, 1821), pp. 44–45.
[b]Only $100 per share had been called for by the time of the suspension of work.

At the first meeting of the board of directors, held May 3, 1803, a call was issued for the payment of $5.00 on each share of stock by September 1, and plans were drawn up to begin initial surveying operations at once. In June the board appointed a six-man Committee of Survey, which was charged with the task of examining and surveying the several places most suitable for the canal route. The committee, composed of President Joseph Tatnall and directors William Tilghman, Kensey Johns, George Gale, John Adlum, and Joshua Gilpin, was authorized to employ four engineers or surveyors and such other assistants as needed. One thousand dollars was set aside for the committee's use, and it was authorized to borrow $5,000 more if necessary.

Benjamin H. Latrobe, an architect and engineer of growing reputation, was put in charge of the surveying. He later became the chief engineer of the canal company and directed its abortive construction efforts in 1804–06. Cornelius Howard, a Baltimore engineer and surveyor, assisted Latrobe in his early explorations; later John Thompson and Daniel Blaney, of Pennsylvania and Delaware respectively, aided in the engineering duties.

Several points had to be kept in mind by the surveying commit-

shares; Maryland citizens, none of whom were from Baltimore, subscribed to 256 shares. See Table I.

tee and its engineers as they examined the peninsula in search of the best possible location for the canal. The shortest line over apparently firm, level ground was not necessarily the best, or even a possible, route. The nature of the soil, the elevation of the ground, the available water supply, and the location of established trade routes had to be considered. The entrance to the canal at both ends had to be spacious, protected, and readily accessible to a deep channel. Other factors considered in planning the canal's location and dimensions were the amount of capital available, the anticipated traffic, and the nature of the vessels which would use the waterway.

Almost a year was spent in diligent examination of the area. No possibility was overlooked in the search for the best route for the canal. Consideration was given to building a "thorough cut," or lock-free, sea-level canal, but upon examination such a project was deemed financially impossible. According to Latrobe, such a canal at its most feasible location would require a "deep cut" through the dividing ridge of the peninsula, which alone "would more than exhaust the whole Capital of the Company."[8] The minutes of the survey committee and the informative, detailed reports of its engineer, Latrobe, reveal the thoroughness of the company in its initial explorations as well as the widespread attention the surveys commanded. Not the least of the company's troubles during the first year was the arousal of local interests, for as each route was staked a clamor for its adoption was raised by the persons whose land was crossed.

The selfish interests of the local inhabitants — even some of the board members — irritated Latrobe. He confided to Joshua Gilpin that he was so "disgusted with quarrels among the Board of Directors each wanting the canal to be run according to his prejudices or property holdings," that he was almost ready to resign. On another occasion Latrobe commented angrily on what he considered the unnecessary thoroughness of the surveys which required him to frequent "as inhospitable, and wild a country as the peninsula can boast, for no other purpose than to explore it in order to satisfy the public that *no canal* can be carried over it." The reasons for this additional labor were given: "so much are our courageous Stockholders swayed by

[8] "Copy of Reports of the Engineer," October 21, 1803, Chesapeake and Delaware Canal Company Papers, Historical Society of Delaware (Wilmington). Subsequently this collection and repository will be cited as C & D Papers, HSD. To obtain a 70-foot depth through the ridge, Latrobe calculated that it would be necessary to make a cut 200 feet wide at the top. The mile-long section would require the removal of 1,700,000 cubic yards of earth, at an average cost of 50 cents a cubic yard, or $850,000.

public opinion, and local interests, that it is not sufficient that I have laid down a line of navigation where it is evidently most cheaply, most advantageously, and by the shortest course to be effected, but I must also go over every range of ground proposed by every pro-jector who has impudence or interest enough to make himself heard." [9]

Two general routes, which may conveniently be designated the "upper" and "lower" routes, were given primary consideration. The upper route was to run from the Elk River towards Christiana, Dela-ware, debouching either at New Castle directly into the Delaware River, or into the Christina River and thence to the Delaware. This route was roughly parallel to that examined and recommended by the American Philosophical Society in 1769–70. The lower route was to be a shorter, more direct cut in the vicinity of Back Creek on the west and St. Georges Creek on the east. Both routes had ardent supporters, and a debate over the relative merits of each broke out in the newspa-pers in Delaware and Philadelphia.

Interest in the canal location was keen, and the delay in its final determination occasioned by the numerous and meticulous sur-veys — Latrobe in 1806 said a total of 32 surveys had been made — gave rise to much discussion of the subject. William Duane, editor of the Philadelphia *Aurora*, personally investigated the situation in January, 1804. He found it almost impossible to find a Delawarean "totally impartial" on the matter, although Latrobe had "adroitly avoided giving any preference" publicly as to location. But Duane found that the more favorable lower route had few advocates and was not likely to be selected. Moreover, there seemed to be general agreement on the location for the western half of an upper route, from Welsh Point to the village of Bear, although there was con-siderable difference of opinion as to its eastern termination — New Castle, Red Hook, or Wilmington (via Christiana Bridge). Duane summarized the arguments for and against each terminal, and con-cluded by making well-reasoned guesses as to how each of the direc-tors would vote on the question. "It is difficult," he admitted, "to surmise how [they] will act," but Duane decided the scale was tipped in favor of the Christiana route. This analysis was remarkably accu-rate in all its details.[10] In November, 1803, the board had tentatively

[9] Latrobe to John Lenthall, New Castle, November 1, 1803, Benjamin H. Latrobe Papers, HSD (typescript copies of the originals in the Library of Con-gress, Washington, D.C.).

[10] *Aurora*, reprinted in the *Delaware Gazette* (Wilmington), February 1, 1804. See the *Delaware Gazette* of February 8 and 15 for replies to Duane's analysis. His opinions, however, foreshadowed the facts, as Joshua Gilpin

selected the western point at which an upper route canal would begin; locating the eastern terminus was temporarily postponed, and attention was turned towards finding ways of supplying the summit level of the canal with water.

The canal was to begin at Welsh Point on the Elk River below Elkton, and the upper Elk River was to be used as the major source of water. The upper Elk had a sufficient quantity of water at the necessary height, which could be carried by a feeder canal to the summit level of the main canal. While the final surveys were being completed, a new Committee of Purchases began its work of acquiring the necessary land and water rights. Conditional bonds were made with the landowners, but as it was virtually certain that the Elk River was to be the supply channel for the canal, efforts were made to purchase the water rights.

On April 7, 1804, at a meeting of the board in Philadelphia, Joshua Gilpin was able to announce that the purchase of the required water rights had been completed, and that a considerable part of the land for the feeder canal had been acquired. Latrobe reported that he had completed his surveys of the main and feeder canal lines and his examination of the nature of the ground to be cut. Work could begin immediately, he said, particularly the quarrying and preparation of stone for an aqueduct over the Elk River. The board authorized Latrobe to hire "six steady persons," on the "most moderate terms" possible, to open a quarry in the vicinity of Elk Forge, where the feeder canal was to begin. To assist in these operations, Latrobe was authorized to procure "3 Wheel Barrows, 3 Crow Bars, 1 long bar, 6 picks, 3 sledge hammers a set of blowing tools Stone hammers & wedges & 300 feet of 2 in[ch] plank." A temporary agreement with the blacksmith at the forge for repairing the company's tools was to be made; later the company employed Peter Bath as its smith. In addition, the board authorized Gilpin and Latrobe to hire "one or more gangs or bodies of diggers to commence digging immediately upon the feeders."[11]

It was decided first to construct the branch canal from Elk Forge to a point near Aikentown (Glasgow) in Delaware, where it would

verified many years later. The board was agreed as to the western half of the canal, but had come to no final determination regarding its eastern terminus by the time construction of the feeder was halted in 1805. Gilpin to Paul Beck, Jr., Kentmere, Delaware, September 10, 1821, Correspondence on Internal Improvements, Carey Collection, Library Company of Philadelphia, hereafter cited as Carey Collection, LCP.

[11] Committee of Survey Minutes, April 7, 1804, C & D Papers, HSD.

connect with the main canal. There were many reasons for this decision. No water could be supplied the main canal over most of its length until the feeder was built. If the main canal were constructed first, it would deteriorate while the feeder was being completed. Moreover, the smaller canal could serve as a valuable means of transportation during construction of the larger. Finally, the feeder canal, striking "directly into the heart of Pennsylvania," would serve as the basis for a future canal into Pennsylvania.[12]

Advertisements were published in the Philadelphia, Wilmington, Baltimore, and Easton, Maryland, newspapers for digging contracts, boards, tools, and building materials. The contractors, according to the terms established by the canal company, were to furnish the laborers and construct the sections for which they contracted in conformity with the instructions of the company's engineer and his assistants. The company, on the other hand, agreed to furnish the necessary tools and equipment and to provide housing for the laborers.

Much care was taken in the selection of the contractors by Latrobe, now the chief engineer of the canal company, who was put in charge of this task. At least nine separate contracts were made, of which at least three were taken by men known to Latrobe from their previous work in Philadelphia, either on turnpikes in the area or on the well-known waterworks there, which Latrobe had designed and built. In October, 1804, when Latrobe reported to the board on the progress of the work, he described the men who were immediately responsible for building the canal. William Watson was characterized as "attentive and able, sober and civil"; Joseph Pollock was a man of "excellent disposition and a stout workman"; Clegg and Binnerman were men of "unexceptionable character"; and Randle and Coxey were Englishmen of "great respectability" and "most able canal undertakers." Some of the contractors employed later, however, were inexperienced.

The first contractors brought with them about 30 men each, "most known to me," said Latrobe, "as having behaved well in my employ for the last 6 years." Robert Brooke, another Philadelphian who was an engineer and surveyor, was employed as "clerk of the works and deputy engineer." His papers, survey books, and contractor books give additional information concerning the construction of the feeder. It was among his duties to measure and verify the work done by the various contractors.[13]

[12] Gilpin, *Memoir on Canal*, pp. 30–31.
[13] "Copy of Reports of the Engineer," October 1, 1804, C & D Papers,

James Cochran, described by Latrobe as "without exception the most respectable as well as the wealthiest person engaged in the business of canals & roads in America," did much of the work in building the feeder. Of a total of $90,977.03 expended for actual construction, Cochran was paid $18,741.15. His first contract set forth the following terms:

Digging not exceeding 1½ Yds. Earth deep	12½ Cents p Yd Cube
Below that one yard	15 cts
Below that one yard	20 cts
Puddling, the puddle being first measured as Banks	
In Bank per yd.	12½ . . .
Puddling at bottom of the canal	20¢

& if the Clay or Earth be wheeled more than 30 yards an additional 5 Cents for every stage of 30 yards, and so also of Puddling in the Bank.[14]

Construction on the Chesapeake and Delaware Canal began in May, 1804, on the anniversary of the company's organization. Work progressed satisfactorily, although there were a number of problems to be overcome. A lack of suitable accommodations for workers reduced the number of men who could be employed; efforts by the company to build temporary shelters were slow in being realized. It had proven difficult from the beginning to find accommodations for the workmen among the local inhabitants, and it was almost impossible after a serious riot occurred in October, 1804, between the canal workers and the townspeople of Elkton.[15] Other problems resulted from the fact that all the land for the feeder had not yet been acquired, which meant that there were gaps in the branch line, and that the terrain through which the feeder was cut proved unexpectedly difficult. The greatest hardship, however, was inadequate finances. Not all of the shares of stock had been taken up, and many who pledged to purchase shares failed to make even the first $5.00 payment. Although the company announced in June, 1805, that almost 2,100 shares had been subscribed, figures compiled after the company was forced to suspend operations revealed that payments had been made on only 1,792 shares. The increased time and expense needed to complete

HSD. The Robert Brooke Papers are in the New York Public Library. See especially the Contractor's Book, 1804–05.

[14] Heads of Contract with James Cochran, n.d., C & D Papers, HSD.

[15] See George Johnston, *History of Cecil County, Maryland* (Elkton, 1881), pp. 387–388. Latrobe's account of the riot was omitted by the copyist who transcribed his reports for the company records. See Talbot Hamlin, *Benjamin Henry Latrobe* (New York, 1955), p. 207, for a brief account of the riot based on Latrobe's writings.

the feeder canal, moreover, forced a revision upward in the estimated total cost of the canal. It was clear that even if all the shares were subscribed and paid for in full, there would be insufficient money.

After a year of surveying and a year of actual construction work, expenditures totaled $85,915.08. Less than $20,000 remained on hand in June, 1805, and no more money was received from the stockholders during the third year. Work on the feeder could be con-

TABLE 2. CHESAPEAKE AND DELAWARE CANAL COMPANY FINANCES, 1803-06[a]

Year Ends June 1	Amount Paid on Subscriptions	Expenditures	Balance
1803–04	$ 24,265.00	$ 9,510.23	$14,754.77
1804–05	81,548.00	76,404.85	19,897.92
1805–06	—	36,254.19	16,356.27 (deficit)
Total	$103,156.30[b]	$122,169.27	$19,012.97 (deficit)

Analysis of Expenditures

Year Ends June 1	Surveys	Land and Water Purchases	Secretarial[c]	Construction
1803–04	$4,097.47	$ 3,556.56	$1,128.70	$ 727.50
1804–05	569.57	14,520.91	2,854.47	58,461.90
1805–06	.18	2,251.99	2,212.39	31,787.63
Total	$4,667.22	$20,329.46	$6,195.56	$90,977.03

[a]Source: The first three *General Reports of the President and Directors of the Chesapeake and Delaware Canal Company* (Philadelphia, 1804–06).
[b]This is the corrected total, counting interest less unredeemable notes.
[c]Besides customary items, this includes court and lobbying expenses.

tinued only on a reduced scale. Although $100 upon each share had been called for, only $103,000, or 59 per cent of the amount requested, was obtained.

The lack of response to the repeated appeals of the company for payment was due partly to discouragement over the apparent slowness of the work: two years after the company was organized not a shovelful of earth had been removed from the main canal line. In part, however, this represented the absorption of American capital in the neutral carrying trade after war broke out in Europe again in 1805. As Latrobe later commented, "The turnpike roads which have been opened near Philadelphia, as well as the Ch[esapeake] & Del-[aware] Canal were children of the peace of Amiens." [16]

[16] Quoted in Hamlin, *Latrobe*, p. 212.

The dire need for financial assistance had prompted the board of directors to apply to the Delaware and Pennsylvania legislatures for aid in January and February, 1805, but it was not forthcoming. A desperate attempt was made to complete the feeder before the funds were exhausted, in hopes that the prospect of beginning on the main canal in the spring would inspire the stockholders and the state legislatures to contribute, but this could not be done. As Latrobe wrote to a friend in November, the "canal is aground, and all that are embarked with them [*sic*] must go overboard, except the officers." On December 1, 1805, all employees of the company were released and construction was halted while additional funds were solicited.[17]

The canal company officers were most anxious to prevent the interruption from being a prolonged one. Work already done on the feeder would have to be repeated if it were exposed to the weather for any period of time; moreover, tools, materials, and valuable experience had been acquired. It was confidently believed that all of these factors, in addition to more favorable terrain, would permit much more rapid progress on the main canal. Consequently, the company officers zealously made appeals to the state legislatures in Lancaster, Dover, and Annapolis for aid. Despite the eloquence, forcefulness, and soundness of the arguments supporting their pleas, the officers were disappointed in these attempts. As Joshua Gilpin, son of the man who first promoted the canal almost four decades earlier, explained to Secretary of the Treasury Albert Gallatin in 1808, the project was beyond the capabilities of any one state or community. He elaborated on this point:

The city of Philadelphia has zealously supported, and still remains highly interested in its progress, but the representatives of Pennsylvania have so many local objects of the kind in the interior counties, that these are constantly brought into competition with it, so as to prevent its obtaining any aid from thence. The State of Delaware is too feeble in its resources to grant supplies for any work of the kind; and in the State of Maryland, although the interest of the counties contiguous to the Chesapeake are partial to the canal, the city of Baltimore and other parts of the State view it with no little jealousy.[18]

Congress was the only hope of the company.

On the ground that the canal was of national importance, the company presumed to memorialize Congress for aid in December,

[17] *Ibid.*, p. 211n.
[18] *American State Papers: Documents, Legislative and Executive*, ed. Walter Lowrie and Walter S. Franklin (Washington, 1834), Class X, Miscellaneous, I, 754.

1805. The complete petition was a model of the instrument: not only was the petition itself candid and explanatory, but it was accompanied by statements, estimates, maps, and, not the least important, a lobbyist, Kensey Johns. In its application the board pointed to the numerous advantages of the waterway, which would free the coasting trade from the dangers of the sea, shorten water communications between Philadelphia and Baltimore by 319 miles, promote interstate commerce, decrease freight and insurance rates, and facilitate the military defense of the country.[19]

The Senate, which counted among its members the distinguished James A. Bayard of Delaware, a former member of the board of the Chesapeake and Delaware Canal Company, was receptive to the petition and recommended that aid be given the company, either in the form of a subscription to the stock of the company or with a grant of land. It was known that some congressmen doubted the constitutionality of a government subscription to the stock of a private corporation, but that anyone should object to giving land seemed unlikely. As McMaster has pointed out, "Great blocks of it had often been given for church purposes, for schools; to the refugees from Canada; to the French at Gallipolis; to the Marquis Lafayette; to Lewis and Clarke; to the Revolutionary soldiers; nay, to Ebenezer and Isaac Zane for building a road in Ohio. Why not, then, for building a canal in Delaware?"[20] In the House of Representatives, however, although a committee considered "the project as an opening wedge for an extensive inland navigation, which would at all times be of an immense advantage to the commercial as well as to the agricultural and manufacturing part of the community," and that in war "its advantages would be incalculable," it was considered beyond the financial capabilities of the country at the moment to render aid.[21]

This original petition to Congress, discussed in March, 1806, was the first of many from the canal company before federal aid was finally granted the revived company in 1825. With no other person or group to turn to, all hope for completing the canal in the near future vanished. The tools and equipment which had been assembled were sold at a loss, and some of the land purchased by the company was also disposed of in order to pay the company's $19,000 debt. Latrobe took his official departure from the company's employ in June, 1806.

[19] "Facts and Observations Respecting the Chesapeak and Delaware Canal," December 1, 1805, *ibid.*, II, 287–288.
[20] McMaster, *History of the United States*, III, 472–473.
[21] *American State Papers*, Miscellaneous, I, 452.

The company officers continued to meet, general stockholders' meetings continued to be held, but the intervals between meetings became longer and longer. In 1806, the new board was elected to a three-year term, and in 1809 the same directors, with one exception, were named to a five-year term. Failure to raise a quorum prevented a new election at the appointed time in 1814, but at a special meeting in November, 1814, a new board was elected to another five-year term. At this time, Kensey Johns became president, succeeding Joseph Tatnall who had died the previous year. Practically the only action taken by the board of directors during the company's fifteen-year period of somnolence was to make repeated but fruitless appeals to Congress. On three occasions bills providing financial assistance to the canal company passed the United States Senate only to be killed in the House of Representatives.

Even the notorious inadequacy of transportation facilities across the peninsula in the War of 1812 failed to inspire Congress to action, although the war occasioned well-meaning but futile acts on the part of the Maryland and Pennsylvania legislatures. In the winter session of 1812–13, the legislatures of both states authorized a subscription to the Chesapeake and Delaware Canal Company if the United States government and Delaware would similarly subscribe a proportional amount. Congressional consideration of the proposal was delayed until 1816, when the Chesapeake and Delaware Canal project was linked with the chartering of the Second Bank of the United States, but hopes for federal aid to internal improvements were shattered by President Madison's veto of the Bonus Bill. Joshua Gilpin, who had assumed the leading role in keeping alive the legal existence and the hopes of the company, now privately despaired of ever getting assistance from Congress. The basis for Gilpin's foreboding will be seen as the company efforts to obtain federal aid are examined. The initiative leading to the revival of the canal project came not from Washington but from Philadelphia.

Delay and Debate

3

During the time between the cessation of construction activities on the Chesapeake and Delaware Canal in 1805 and their resumption nearly twenty years later, the question of federal aid to internal improvements was one of the most persistent problems facing Congress. The Chesapeake and Delaware Canal played a significant role in the extended congressional debate on this issue, one involving a delicate constitutional question. The canal's prominence in the discussion of this issue stemmed in part from its proximity to Washington, but more directly from its unquestioned national importance and its peculiarity of location which made it more valuable to states other than the two through which it was projected. If any canal had a claim upon the government, this one did, and as such it served as the test case for the principle involved. The desire for a full and objective report on the Chesapeake and Delaware project led to the authorization for a comprehensive report on the transportation facilities and needs of the young nation — Secretary of the Treasury Albert Gallatin's famed "Report on Roads and Canals" in 1808. Although the government program as outlined in this report was not undertaken, the Chesapeake and Delaware Canal was the first project of those recommended by Gallatin to receive, in 1825, federal aid. Subscriptions to the stock of other canal companies, the Chesapeake and Ohio, the Dismal Swamp, and the Louisville and Portland, as well as land grants in support of other canal projects, quickly followed.

As related above, the company's first request to Congress was made December 1, 1805, the release date for all employees involved in constructing the feeder canal. The memorial was discussed in 1806, and a bill granting assistance to the company was drawn up, but consideration of it was postponed until the following year, when it received prolonged discussion. Young Henry Clay, who introduced a similar bill for granting land to construct a canal at the falls of the Ohio, joined Delaware senators James A. Bayard and Samuel White in arguing for a general policy of internal improvements for commercial and military reasons. Even President Jefferson, in his annual message to Congress in 1806, had suggested that the tariff might be maintained and the surplus revenue applied to public improvements. Bayard, White, Clay, and others pointed out that common economic interests would more firmly bind the several states together. They suggested that the basis for a vast internal communication system could be laid by exchanging for stock a few of the millions of uncharted acres in Louisiana, land that, according to Bayard, "cannot be sold in a century."[1]

Vehemently opposed to such a parceling out of public lands were Uriah Tracey and James Hillhouse of Connecticut and John Quincy Adams of Massachusetts. Adams was described as being "violent in his opposition" to the measure because he suspected that logrolling between Mid-Atlantic and Western senators was involved. He attempted to block consideration of the Chesapeake and Delaware bill altogether when he proposed its postponement in favor "of considering a resolution directing the Secretary of the Treasury to report a general plan for internal improvements of this kind."[2] Principally opposed by Bayard, Adams' plan was defeated, but when the canal bill was discussed the following day, Adams renewed his attack and succeeded in getting it postponed indefinitely. This greatly irritated New Hampshire Senator William Plumer, who believed a majority of the Senate supported the bill. "There is really something insidious in this business of postponing," he complained. "The minds of some men shirk from responsibility — They are averse to business."[3]

---

[1] *Debates and Proceedings in the Congress of the United States, 1789–1824* (Washington, 1834–56), 9th Congress, 2nd Session, p. 59. Hereafter this publication will be cited as *Annals of Congress.*

[2] Everett Somerville Brown, ed., *William Plumer's Memorandum of Proceedings in the United States Senate, 1803–1807* (New York, 1923), p. 628; Charles Francis Adams, ed., *Memoirs of John Quincy Adams, Comprising Portions of his Diary from 1795 to 1848* (Philadelphia, 1874), I, 460.

[3] Brown, ed., *Plumer's Memorandum*, p. 629.

Plumer himself had been inclined to oppose the bill at first, but he was converted as the debate proceeded:

. . . when I considered its great importance, the use & value of it to the nation especially in case of an invasion — The great facility it would give in conveying the productions of the country to the markett — The immense importance of inland navigation — with what care & expence all well informed nations have attended to the making and improving of canals — The immense tracts of unlocated lands the United States possess not yet disposed off, not less than 300,000,000 acres on this side [of] the Mississippi — & the wilderness world in Louisiana — That our treasury is overflowing, & our national debt rapidly wasting away — as fast as the terms of payment will permit — the bill met with my hearty approbation, as well calculated to aid a great & important & highly useful national object.[4]

Senator Thomas Worthington of Ohio was convinced by the debate that more reliable information concerning the canal was needed. On the day after the unhappy fate of the Chesapeake and Delaware bill was decided he submitted a resolution directing the Secretary of the Treasury to report the best information he could get as to "the usefulness, the practicability, and probable expense" of the Chesapeake and Delaware Canal, "with his own opinion and reasons thereon." This resolution in effect resulted in the Gallatin "Report on Roads and Canals," for a few days later Worthington withdrew his first proposal, substituting one similar to that suggested earlier by Adams which called for a thorough report on internal improvements in general. This motion was adopted by the Senate on March 2, 1807, by a 22–3 margin.[5]

By the time Secretary Gallatin began collecting the data and preparing his report on roads and canals in America, there was an ever growing concern with the problem of transportation. From feeble beginnings in the late eighteenth century, when short canals improved river navigation and when steps were taken to conquer overland distances with improved roads and bridges, there was developing a widespread interest in projects of this nature. Plans were being made for better and longer canals and for a more complete network of roads. But the planning and sporadic activity connected with these programs lacked coordination. Not until Gallatin's justly renowned report in 1808 were the various local schemes combined into a national system. McMaster believed "there was little in it that was new,"

[4] *Ibid.*, p. 628.
[5] *Annals of Congress*, 9th Congress, 2nd Session, pp. 88–89, 95, 97.

but the broad concept of the Gallatin program, which was to be financed by the government, was original.[6]

Among the many schemes for roads and canals embraced by Gallatin were waterways which would permit uninterrupted navigation along the Atlantic coast. New England could be united with the South by means of sheltered, inland waterways if only four narrow necks of land in the states of Massachusetts, New Jersey, Delaware, and Virginia were traversed by canal. Slightly over $3,000,000 would be needed to construct the four canals; $20,000,000 was the estimated expense of the entire project proposed by Gallatin. He suggested that $2,000,000 per year for ten years be set aside from the annual surplus, then in excess of $5,000,000, for internal improvements. Gallatin believed the federal government should finance the works since they were of national importance. Because they were interrelated and part of a pattern, with the full benefits of one improvement dependent upon the completion of others, all should be completed.[7]

It seemed as if an era of internal improvements was upon the country, but this was prevented by the events leading to the War of 1812. Admirable in its conception, Gallatin's plan was doomed to failure, partly because of the European war which soon engulfed the United States but ultimately because of the question of the government's constitutional authority to engage in such activity.

This was demonstrated when, following the war, plans for a federal internal improvements program were revived in the form of the "Bonus Bill." This bill provided for applying the bonus received from the second Bank of the United States, as well as the dividends paid on its stock held by the federal government, to internal improvement projects of national importance, including, undoubtedly, the Chesapeake and Delaware Canal. Introduced by John C. Calhoun in December, 1816, and ably defended by him in the ensuing debate on economic as well as on military grounds, the bill was quickly passed by Congress, only to be vetoed by President Madison on constitutional grounds.[8] With the failure of this bill, one Delaware editor

[6] McMaster, *History of the United States*, III, 473.

[7] The Gallatin "Report on Roads and Canals," dated April 6, 1808, is in *American State Papers*, Miscellaneous, I, 724–921. The first 18 pages make up the report proper; the remainder is appendix. For a thorough analysis of the report, its recommendations, and subsequent construction on the same or similar routes, see Carter Goodrich, *Government Promotion of American Canals and Railroads, 1800–1890* (New York, 1960), chapter 2, especially the map and tables on pp. 34–35.

[8] For a discussion of the Bonus Bill debate and an analysis of the voting on this question, see Charles M. Wiltse, *John C. Calhoun: Nationalist, 1789–1828*

called upon the people of his state to do the work themselves. "Has the state of Delaware become so sunken and lost, for its political sins," he asked, "that all public enterprize becomes paralized the moment it comes within its pestiferous influence? Or what is the cause, if this is not, that the *Chesapeake and Delaware Canal* rests in its present torpor?" Chiding the Delawareans for their backwardness while the people of New York and New Jersey were distinguishing themselves in the field of internal improvements, the editor recognized that the alleged "Constitutional impediment . . . throws the weight of responsibility back upon the people, and the respective states. If *Uncle Sam* cannot help us, we must help ourselves." He suggested that "ambitious men" could easily distinguish themselves in this field and win "more civic wreaths in one season, than the whole hunting ground of office seekers would bear in a century."[9]

The article on inland navigation in the Philadelphia edition of the *Edinburgh Encyclopedia*, written during this period, also deplored the noncompletion of the Chesapeake and Delaware Canal, "perhaps, to its extent, the most necessary canal which could be formed in the United States. . . . That this very obvious work should have remained to this date unfinished, must be considered as a public reproach."[10]

The moribund Chesapeake and Delaware Canal Company was equally chagrined at its own inability to complete its project, but Joshua Gilpin expressed the opinion of the majority of the board when he doubted that the canal could be revived without outside assistance. The company continued to direct its efforts towards Congress, in the belief, as expressed by Secretary of War Calhoun in 1819 in his report on roads and canals, that the Atlantic chain of waterways "must be perfected by the general government or not perfected at all. No one or two States have sufficient interest."[11] Subsequently bills providing for federal aid to the Chesapeake and Delaware Canal, supported by new petitions from the company, were introduced in Congress by

(Indianapolis, 1944), pp. 134–136. Madison's veto message is in *A Compilation of the Messages and Papers of the Presidents, 1789–1897*, ed. James D. Richardson (Washington, 1907), II, 569–570.

[9] *American Watchman, and Delaware Republican* (Wilmington), April 5, 1817. It is worthy of note that the people of New York undertook to build the state-financed Erie Canal the month after Madison vetoed the Bonus Bill. See Julius Rubin, "An Innovating Public Improvement: The Erie Canal," in Goodrich, ed., *Canals and American Economic Development*, pp. 60–62.

[10] *Edinburgh Encyclopedia*, XIV, 380.

[11] Quoted in *Bulletin*, Atlantic Deeper Waterways Association (June–July, 1919), p. 4. Hereafter the association will be cited ADWA.

Delaware Representative Louis McLane on two occasions, but they failed of adoption. As James Buchanan suggested later, Congress hesitated to invest in the canal until it became known that the enterprise had substantial private support.[12] It was in Philadelphia rather than Washington that the impetus for a revived Chesapeake and Delaware project finally appeared.

Insofar as credit for reviving the canal project can be given to an individual, it belongs to Mathew Carey. He is well known as an author, economist, and publisher, but his ceaseless advocacy of internal improvement projects is less widely known. The chief beneficiaries of his labors in this field were the Union and "Main Line" canals in Pennsylvania, and the Chesapeake and Delaware Canal. Carey was born in Ireland in 1760, but came to Philadelphia at the age of 25 and soon took his place among the leaders of the city. As time went on, the fiery Irishman became increasingly aware of Philadelphia's need for improved communications with the Pennsylvania hinterland. Alarmed at the growing loss of its trade to Baltimore, and realizing that more trade would be siphoned off to the north with the completion of the Erie Canal, Carey sprang into action. He initiated the program which led to the reorganization and revitalization of the canal company in 1821–22, and, a year later, when failure was again imminent from lack of public support, it was Carey who sparked a great subscription drive which rescued the faltering company.[13]

A remarkably full account of the revival of the canal company in Philadelphia can be obtained from Carey's many writings, from the newspapers of the day, and from a body of letters relating to internal improvements which Carey collected and later presented to the Library Company of Philadelphia. Carey described his initial efforts in 1821 and 1822: "I repeatedly urged gentlemen of great standing and influcnce to exert themselves, & resuscitate a project promising such extensive benefit to the city" — the Chesapeake and Delaware

[12] Richard I. Shelling, "Philadelphia and the Agitation in 1825 for the Pennsylvania Canal," *Pennsylvania Magazine of History and Biography*, LXII (April, 1938), 196.

[13] *Dictionary of American Biography*, III, 489–491; Kenneth Wyer Rowe, *Mathew Carey: A Study in American Economic Development* (Baltimore, 1933). For an admirable account of Carey's role in urging Pennsylvania to act in meeting the threat posed to the state's western trade by New York's Erie Canal, which led to the construction of Pennsylvania's "mongrel" canal-railroad main line from Philadelphia to Pittsburgh, see Julius Rubin, *Canal or Railroad? Imitation and Innovation in the Response to the Erie Canal in Philadelphia, Baltimore, and Boston* (Philadelphia, 1961).

Canal.[14] But these early attempts to persuade others to lead the campaign were futile. Much as Carey preferred to remain inconspicuous in the movement, at length he was forced to act. His first step was to issue invitations to 100 or more of Philadelphia's leading citizens, requesting them to attend a meeting at Judd's Hotel on September 11, 1821.[15]

In the meantime, on the eve of the appointed day, there was a special meeting of the American Philosophical Society, at which a committee was appointed to make another Chesapeake and Delaware Canal survey. Significantly, this committee was "authorized to confer, or to act in concert with, any committee that may be appointed by the meeting of the citizens, which it is understood is about to be called for the same objects." [16] When Joshua Gilpin learned of the society's plan for a new survey, he lamented it as a "premature measure," one that would arouse all the old antagonism regarding the canal location. A bitter, lengthy debate over the best route had occurred during the surveying in 1803 and 1804, and Gilpin wished to avoid a repetition of this at all costs. He was much more pleased with the procedure outlined at Carey's meeting on September 11.[17]

John K. Kane, a young, civic-minded lawyer who happened to be in Mathew Carey's printing office the day of the meeting, described the events of that day in his charming and candid autobiography:

Mr. Carey had imagined a scheme for recalling the [Chesapeake and Delaware] project to favour, and called a meeting at one of the hotels to begin his operations. But though he could write and print with a rapidity that before the days of locomotives and electric telegraphs defied all parallel, he could never speak six words without boggling. . . . Mr. Carey, who never had room in his mind for two ideas at once, broached his Canal meeting, and insisted that I should take charge of it. It was in vain that I protested ignorance, total and hopeless: it was afternoon, and the meeting was to be in three hours after. But there was no getting off without a quarrel: Indeed our whole colloquy might have been well mis-

[14] *Autobiography of Mathew Carey* (New York, 1942), p. 117

[15] This information is contained on p. 2 of an untitled publication written and printed by Carey for private distribution, hereafter cited as *Letter to a Few Friends* (2nd ed., Philadelphia, 1825).

[16] *Early Proceedings of the American Philosophical Society for the Promotion of Useful Knowledge, Compiled by One of the Secretaries, from the Manuscript Minutes of Its Meetings from 1744 to 1838* (Philadelphia, 1844), p. 504. The survey committee members were William Strickland, J. G. Biddle, R. Haines, Dr. R. M. Patterson, and Dr. James Mease of Pennsylvania; E. I. du Pont of Delaware; John Adlum and Dr. DeButts of Maryland. Joshua Gilpin's name was added to the list on September 21.

[17] Joshua Gilpin to Paul Beck, Jr., Kentmere, September 24, 1821, Carey Collection, LCP.

taken for one. Carey crammed me with documents: I made the speech; electrified an assemblage of mercantile grannies with my overflowing knowledge of Engineering, topography, and statistics, was placed on the Committee of Five, and became the leading member of the new board of Directors, and what was more important to my finances, its lawyer.[18]

Carey himself gave a less florid account of the well-attended meeting, at which the resolutions he had prepared were adopted. A committee of 25 leading citizens was appointed to add prestige to the undertaking, but the working committee was composed of only 5 members. This group, instead of starting anew as the American Philosophical Society planned, set about gathering all the information possible on the original canal company, its finances, stockholders, officers, and the reasons for the failure of the first construction attempt. Carey and his committee wanted to benefit from every experience of the old canal board. Everyone sensed, even if it was not often expressed, that another failure would be disastrous.

Joshua Gilpin was delighted to learn of Philadelphia's renewed interest in the project so close to his heart. He wrote to Paul Beck, Jr., a Philadelphia merchant and a strong advocate of internal improvements, on the day before Carey's meeting was held: "The board of directors of whom I am one, have long had nothing but adverse circumstances to contend with. . . . It is not indeed until the present moment that they have felt sufficient encouragement to bring the business before the public." He offered to give Beck and his colleagues "full information" about the canal, and revealed to them that he had prepared a brief history of it which he intended to publish now that attention was once again focused on the waterway. "It is so long since there have been any publications on the subject," Gilpin explained, "that matters which were once well impressed on the public, have been forgotten, & many crude and ignorant opinions have gained ground, which have done inconceivable injury."[19] In December, 1821, Gilpin's *A Memoir on the Rise, Progress, and Present State of the Chesapeake and Delaware Canal, Accompanied with Original Documents and Maps* was published in Wilmington.

Gilpin blamed false rumors about the canal for destroying all hope of financial assistance from Congress. "Our city"—Philadel-

[18] *Autobiography of the Honorable John K. Kane, 1795–1858* (Philadelphia, 1949), pp. 21–22. According to contemporary correspondence, Kane is mistaken about his membership on the original Committee of Five. Besides Carey, who served as chairman, the committee consisted of Paul Beck, Jr., Simon Gratz, William Lehman, and William Meredith.
[19] September 10, 1821, Carey Collection, LCP.

phia — must now undertake the work alone, "without waiting for other aid, as all other is utterly hopeless." He cautioned, however, against offending those across whose states the canal must run. "Here," he wrote from Delaware, "the powers of the state lie in a little compass and are easily acted upon — and it is worse in Maryland." If any attempts are made "to disturb the acts of incorporation," he warned, "or [if there are] any violent deviations in the outset, it will be attended with great danger to the basis of the undertaking." Gilpin reminded the Philadelphians of the great difficulty encountered in securing Delaware's act of incorporation, "even when the enthusiasm in favor of the canal was at its height," adding that "conciliation therefore is absolutely essential." He further warned that Delaware and Maryland must continue to have representation on the canal board. There were already five Philadelphians on the inactive board, "which perhaps is as great a number, or at least if we could obtain one more, as we can ever expect to have with any satisfaction to Maryland and this state." [20]

As would be expected, Gilpin urged the committee in Philadelphia to work through the present board of directors. Kensey Johns, chief justice of Delaware and Tatnall's successor as president of the canal company, joined Gilpin in urging

that respect should be paid to the board which is the constitutional organ of the company, whose interests they are sworn to protect, and merit attention by the services of nearly twenty years. There is indeed, sir, one plain mode of proceeding by which this work may be almost instantaneously revived, and that is, instead of wasting the time and patience of the public in desultory experiments, which will only increase the spirit of party, till perhaps every thing be lost — to bestow a generous confidence upon the present board and on what they have done, and enable them to recommence the work where they left it off.[21]

Gilpin and Johns believed that if action were taken at once, preparations could be made during the winter and active operations could begin in the spring. They naturally assumed that the location would be the same, at least that the western half, on which the board had unanimously agreed in 1804, would not be changed, and they strongly recommended that work begin there as soon as possible. The eastern termination, either New Castle or Wilmington, on which the board had divided, could be determined later.

The Philadelphia newspapers in the latter part of 1821 reflected

[20] Gilpin to Beck, September 19, 24, 1821, *ibid.*
[21] *Ibid.*, September 24, 1821.

the renewed interest in the canal. Editors kept their readers informed about meetings relating to it, and correspondents began writing internal improvement letters, all endorsing the project.[22] Precisely what Gilpin wanted to avoid, however, was brought up by "A Subscriber," who called for still another examination of the routes. He hoped that a "thorough cut," or sea-level canal, would be proposed. "Money invested under the present charter, the original plan being pursued, would not yield 1 per cent. to the stockholders." [23] Whether this writer's voice had effect or not, the actions of the citizens' committee ultimately corresponded to his advice more than to Gilpin's.

In October, 1821, Carey's Committee of Five wrote to the board of directors, not offering their assistance and cooperation, but rather asking the present board members to give up their seats in favor of Philadelphians. "The canal," they reasoned, "if completed at all, must, it is evident, be completed by Philadelphia funds"; why should it not also be directed by Philadelphia men? [24] Gilpin, previous to a board meeting, made an unofficial reply to the committee's rather unusual inquiry, stating that as far as he knew no board member was disposed to resign his seat. He repeated his views on the proper makeup of a new board, and again urged cooperation between the committee and the board.[25]

A meeting between representatives of the two groups was arranged. In December, 1821, Gilpin and Johns met the Philadelphia committee and made a tentative agreement about membership on a new board of directors. Carey, "in order to prevent those Mistakes & misconceptions to which verbal communications are liable," requested that Gilpin put the terms agreed upon in writing: "That you & your friends in Wilmington would support a ticket for Directors of the Chesapeake & Delaware Canal, containing the names of five Citizens residing in Philadelphia." [26] Gilpin immediately complied, and it was decided to hold a general stockholders' meeting as soon as possible. Since the charter required at least a month's notice, January 28, 1822, was the day set for the meeting to be held at the company office in Wilmington.

[22] See, for example, *United States Gazette* (Philadelphia), September 18, 1821; *Aurora & General Advertiser* (Philadelphia), September 20, 1821.

[23] *United States Gazette*, September 26, 1821.

[24] Carey, Beck, Gratz, Lehman, and Meredith to the President and Directors of the Chesapeake and Delaware Canal Company, Philadelphia, October 9, 1821, Carey Collection, LCP.

[25] Gilpin to Mathew Carey, Kentmere, October 25, 1821, *ibid.*

[26] Carey to Gilpin, Philadelphia, December 7, 1821, *ibid.*

Mathew Carey, however, became increasingly upset at the forced delays. Since September 11, 1821, the date of his citizens' meeting, Philadelphia's interest in the canal had been aroused. The time was right — action was demanded now. He particularly deplored delaying the general meeting until late January, and sought immediate action. Gilpin replied to Carey's impatience, suggesting that if the committee wanted to act at once, it could begin to receive subscriptions with the understanding that they would be held in safekeeping until the regular company subscription books could be opened, probably around March 1.[27]

For some reason, Carey did not follow Gilpin's suggestion, but neither did he remain inactive while waiting for the stockholders' meeting. His committee obtained a list of the Pennsylvania stockholders in the company — 429 persons in the state had subscribed to 824 shares — and proceeded to collect proxies from them. The Philadelphia contingent arrived at the Wilmington meeting armed with proxies on 511 shares of stock.[28] Of course, they controlled the meeting. Whether merely chafed by the delays experienced since September, or angered by some intervening event, the Philadelphia committee reneged on its agreement with the board of directors, naming a Philadelphia-dominated "board of managers" to direct the affairs of the company until the terms of the regularly elected board members expired in June, 1823. Except for Joshua Gilpin, who still considered himself a Philadelphian despite his residence since 1815 in Delaware, Kensey Johns was the only outsider named to the interim board of managers. It was also voted to move the company office and books to Philadelphia.

Following this coup by the Philadelphia committee, "a numerous and very respectable meeting of the citizens of Philadelphia" was held on February 8, 1822, to hear the committee's report, which was adopted and ordered published.[29] In addition to recounting the events at the stockholders' meeting in Wilmington, the committee reported that it had collected all the laws relating to the canal passed by the three states involved. None of these laws needed revision prior to recommencement of the work. Accurate information about company affairs, its previous construction attempt, and the causes for its failure had been assembled. The committee announced that much factual information had been gained from Joshua Gilpin's book, *Memoir*

[27] Gilpin to Carey, Kentmere, December 21, 1821, *ibid.*
[28] Subscription Book, 1822, C & D Papers, HSD.
[29] *Delaware Gazette*, February 12, 1822.

on . . . the Chesapeake and Delaware Canal, although it felt that the author's opinions as to the best route should be tested by additional surveys. The report concluded with the recommendation that the entire citizenry of Philadelphia support this project, for their very prosperity was dependent upon it.[30]

The following week, on February 15, 1822, at a large meeting of the Chesapeake and Delaware Canal Company stockholders, the new board was authorized to receive subscriptions to the amount of $600,000. Interest in the project was high. The September meetings, the newspaper campaign, the circulation of the proxy list, and the two meetings in February, as well as the publication of Gilpin's history of the canal, which had been dedicated to the "Citizens of Philadelphia, and particularly the Committees of the Philosophical Society and of the City," had attracted wide public attention. Receipt of the necessary subscriptions seemed assured. Two of the canal company directors predicted that the entire $600,000 would be obtained within two weeks. Carey returned to his printing establishment secure in the belief that the Chesapeake and Delaware Canal would soon be a reality.

But delay and disappointment still plagued the project. No time was lost in arranging for new surveys to be handled by William Strickland, but not until May 22, 1822, did the new board begin its campaign for new subscriptions. The results were negligible. Less than $20,000 of the authorized $600,000 was received.[31] What had started out so hopefully and full of promise again seemed doomed to failure.

Mathew Carey reluctantly assumed the reins of leadership once more. By now, he had come to believe that state aid, often promised but never bestowed, was necessary to induce sufficient private subscriptions. He decided to memorialize the state legislature on the subject. On November 13, 1822, Carey recorded in his diary: "This day issued about 50 or 55 circular notices for a meeting to be held at Judd's Hotel, for the purpose of taking into consideration a memorial to the legislature praying aid in the completion of the Canal from the Delaware to the Chesapeake. The memorial was enclosed. The persons addressed were requested to bring a respectable friend or two. . . . Important as were the subjects, only five persons besides myself attended."[32]

Despite this slight response, Carey continued his work. Two

[30] *Ibid.*

[31] *United States Gazette,* April 21, 1823.

[32] Diary of Mathew Carey, 1822–26, University of Pennsylvania Library (Philadelphia), hereafter cited as UPL.

memorials to the legislature eventually were sent, one, according to Carey, signed by 3,500 people and the other signed by 4,400, but nothing occurred in 1822 to relieve the gloom of the canal supporters. By December, even Carey sensed the futility of his labors: "Why should I waste my time, my money, debar myself of enjoyments, and even my rest at night, as well as make myself scores of deadly enemies, laboring to serve a community in which there is not the shadow of public spirit [but rather] sluggish apathy [and] sordid meanness." [33] But, characteristically, Carey's optimism returned. He vowed to make one more effort.

He was heartened by the fact that the canal company petitions and the supplementary memorials to the three state legislatures were finally being acted upon. In February and March, both Delaware and Pennsylvania subscribed to the stock of the canal company on condition that at least $200,000 in subscriptions be obtained elsewhere. Delaware subscribed to 125 shares, the $25,000 to be paid in five annual installments of $5,000 each. Pennsylvania's subscription, obtained after much quibbling in the legislature and after a special report had been received from the board of directors of the canal company, was for $100,000.[34] Maryland, too, in a series of acts passed between December, 1822, and February, 1824, subscribed for $50,000. Some trouble was experienced with the Maryland grant, since it was contingent upon Delaware's prior subscription. Although reluctant to meet its pledge until the last installment on the Delaware subscription was paid, Maryland nevertheless made its grant in February, 1824.[35]

In view of these developments, Carey issued a call on April 10, 1823, for a general meeting to consider ways to promote the canal undertaking. The states had all stipulated that private sources must supply $200,000 if their subscriptions were to be valid, and Carey was determined to comply. His call met with a good response, although, strangely enough, no canal board member attended the meeting. Carey believed the board was offended at his usurpation of their prerogative.[36] At the meeting, Carey read the long *Address to the*

[33] *Ibid.,* December 15, 1822.
[34] The special report was the *Communication from the Chesapeake and Delaware Canal Company; and a Report and Estimate of William Strickland, to the President and Directors* (Philadelphia, 1823).
[35] See *Correspondence of the Treasurer of the Western Shore and H. D. Gilpin, Relative to the Chesapeake and Delaware Canal* (Annapolis, n.d.); Subscription Book, 1824, C & D Papers, HSD.
[36] *Letter to a Few Friends,* p. 4.

Citizens of Philadelphia, couched in energetic terms and giving a realistic picture of the situation, that he had prepared and printed. His detailed study of the company's finances led Carey to conclude that an additional $412,500 was needed to construct the canal. According to Strickland's recent report, a total of $700,000 was required. Added to the state subscriptions and the few private subscriptions obtained in 1822, approximately $100,000 could be relied on from old subscriptions, making a total of $287,500 on hand. Just over 2,000 more shares would have to be sold, but with 120,000 inhabitants in Philadelphia, Carey thought this could easily be done. He discounted the aid which reasonably could be expected from Delaware and Maryland citizens, expressing his faith that the "object can easily be accomplished by Philadelphia alone." He reiterated a plea for a halt to the arguments over the route, stating that any of those being considered would serve Philadelphia equally well, and concluded with statistics which demonstrated that the city's economic decline, both relative and absolute, in the past decade was most serious. Immediate action was necessary.[37]

Once again, Carey's report was unanimously adopted at the meeting and 2,000 copies were ordered distributed. Another committee of 25 citizens was appointed to circulate the *Address*, prepare subscription books, and make the necessary arrangements with the company's board of directors. The group further agreed to recommend the project to their fellow citizens, and to encourage them to support its completion in proportion to their "wishes to promote, and interest in, the prosperity of Philadelphia."[38] The appointment of committees in several wards of the city and the surrounding liberties to procure subscriptions was also authorized.

A feeling of excitement once again pervaded the city. The day after the meeting, four men pledged to subscribe $20,000, more than was obtained during the whole of 1822.[39] Newspapers devoted much space to the new subscription drive, and even printed the names of the larger subscribers. In spite of the auspicious start, success was not instantaneous. Carey was distressed by the slow response throughout the remainder of the first week. On April 16, he despaired to his diary:

[37] Mathew Carey, *Address to the Citizens of Philadelphia* (Philadelphia, 1823), pp. 4–6.
    [38] *Ibid.*, p. 1.
    [39] The four benefactors were James C. Fisher, then president of the "board of managers" and later president of the canal company, Edward Burd, William Short, and Samuel Richards. *United States Gazette*, April 12, 1823.

This day produced a most remarkable instance of the apathy, torpor, and destitution of public spirit, which are so characteristic of Philada. Subscription Books for the Chesapeake and Delaware canal were sent to the U.S. Philada. Farmers Commercial, N.A. and Schuylkill Banks — & to five insurance companies, with a request that the presidents would exert themselves to procure subscriptions. But not one of them procured a single subscription — nor does it appear that they made the least exertion. — And though a genteel man was out all day with 48 Books, he procured but $1000 of subscriptions, being five shares, from three persons. Yesterday, there were $9000 worth of subscriptions recd.

"From the manner in which the affair was explained to the public, & its great importance," Carey went on, "I had flattered myself into the opinion that I should be able to procure 50 or 60,000 Dollars worth of subscriptions Yesterday & today." [40]

Carey's ambitious dreams were finally realized. Ward committees, as authorized, were formed to solicit subscriptions within prescribed areas, and a continuous press campaign was waged. "Every property holder, nay, every individual permanently resident here," stated one newspaper report, "is deeply interested in promoting this useful undertaking; and all, that have two hundred dollars to spare, ought cheerfully to give it their positive aid and support." [41] Carey described his own tireless activity during the campaign: "I abandoned everything for this great object — devoted my whole mind to it from an early hour in the morning till late at night — wrote paragraphs and essays from day to day for such of the newsprinters as were disposed to admit them — and for some time published the names of the subscribers, with the amount . . . as is done in London, in order to excite emulation." The results were both "surprising and pleasing" — within five weeks pledges for $360,000 were obtained.[42]

In an attempt to induce subscriptions from all classes of people, Carey had included a calculation in his *Address to the Citizens* designed to show that laborers earning $6.00 to $8.00 a week could afford to subscribe for single shares. Assuming three years for the construction of the canal, only $67 a year, or approximately $1.25 a week, need be paid on the $200 pledge. This calculation, Carey believed, "procured a very considerable addition to subscriptions of one or two shares." Two hundred and seventy people purchased single shares, and 172 took double shares, thus contributing $122,800.[43]

[40] Diary of Mathew Carey, UPL.
[41] *United States Gazette*, April 12, 1823.
[42] *Letter to a Few Friends*, p. 4.
[43] This calculation was repeated in the Philadelphia newspapers. See the

Moreover, special terms on all subscriptions were announced at the beginning of the campaign. Shares were priced at $200 each, on which $20 was to be paid whenever a total of $300,000 was pledged. The remainder was to be paid in twelve quarterly installments of $15 each. In case the minimum $300,000 was not obtained within five months, the pledges were not to be binding.[44]

Under these terms, Carey's subscription drive gradually picked up speed. In the first nine days, $80,000 was obtained, and the momentum was increasing. Three days later, Carey proudly announced that "the subscriptions amount to $230,000, of which 200,000 have been subscribed within one week." The names of the more prominent subscribers were then given, the double-column list running half the length of the page. In the days that followed other large subscriptions were received.[45] As the campaign neared its goal of $300,000, the pressure of public opinion became evident. Prominent persons and institutions that had not yet subscribed were made to realize that a pledge was expected. One writer thought it necessary to explain why the Bank of Philadelphia, with a capital of $2,500,000, had not subscribed to the canal stock while four other banks with less resources had each contributed $10,000. He pointed out that the bank's charter forbade subscriptions to any stock other than its own; "otherwise there cannot be a doubt that this bank would have displayed an equal degree of liberality."[46]

Five weeks after Carey launched his subscription campaign, one entirely separate from the canal board's meager efforts, a total of $360,000 in subscription pledges had been obtained. As the terms on which the pledges were made had been met, the first installment on the shares was requested. On July 15, 1823, the money was turned over to the canal company and the names of the subscribers were entered on the company ledgers.[47]

News of the canal activity in Philadelphia spread quickly. The Washington *Daily National Intelligencer*, on April 30, 1823, reprinted an article from the *Baltimore American* on the "spirited exertions which are making by our neighbours of Philadelphia" for the Chesapeake and Delaware Canal. The Baltimore author stated that Phila-

Aurora & General Advertiser, April 19, 1823, and the *United States Gazette*, April 21, 1823. The laborers' reward, besides eventual dividends, was to be an increase in and certainty of employment.

[44] *Aurora & General Advertiser*, April 21, 1823.
[45] *United States Gazette*, April 21, 24, 25, 26, 1823.
[46] *Ibid.*, April 28, 1823.
[47] Subscription Book, 1824, C & D Papers, HSD.

delphians saw the Chesapeake and Delaware Canal as an object of vital importance to their prosperity, and their perseverance assured him the canal would be completed. "And precisely in the same degree," he declared, "that this canal will be important and advantageous to Philadelphia, so must it take from the trade of Baltimore." The writer's purpose was not to oppose the Chesapeake and Delaware Canal, but to spur on the efforts of Baltimoreans in the field of internal improvements.[48]

Other cities, in fact, joined with Philadelphia in subscribing to the canal stock. In the vicinity of West Chester, Pennsylvania, David Townsend obtained pledges for $4,000 in one day. "This is a sample of what might be done in the Country," he noted, "if suitable persons would undertake to procure subscriptions. The above amount has principally been subscribed since 5 o'clock this afternoon, without using any extraordinary exertions; and the whole procured since 10 o'clock this morning."[49] Wilmington, Delaware, held its own subscription drive in late April, which brought in "upwards of $30,000."[50] It must be said, however, that these subscriptions were given mainly in the belief that the canal was to pass through the vicinity of Wilmington, as recommended in 1769, as attempted in 1804–05, and as contemplated until 1821. Indeed, it was hoped that Wilmington's generosity would be an added inducement to the Philadelphia directors not to change the location of the canal. The Philadelphia board, however, was determined to review the entire question of the route. Whether from sound engineering advice or from "mean jealousy" toward the people of Wilmington, as some Delawareans later claimed, in January, 1824, a route well to the south of Wilmington was selected.[51]

After Carey's successful subscription drive, the eventual completion of the canal was assured. The July 15, 1823, meeting of the stockholders was looked forward to with keen anticipation. The regular election of a new board was to be held, and construction of the long-awaited canal was to be vigorously undertaken. It seemed likely that Carey, both as a reward for his subscription drive efforts and

[48] *Daily National Intelligencer* (Washington), April 30, 1823.

[49] Townsend to Benjamin Tilghman, West Chester, May 2, 1823, Carey Collection, LCP.

[50] *Daily National Intelligencer*, May 3, 1823.

[51] On the entire question of rivalry between Wilmington and Philadelphia over the Chesapeake and Delaware Canal route, see the *Delaware Gazette*, January 30, 1824, and subsequent issues; and Livingood, *Philadelphia-Baltimore Trade Rivalry*, pp. 81–97.

because of his interest in and knowledge of internal improvements, would be one of the new directors. In fact, a caucus held early in July, with representatives from Philadelphia and Wilmington present, adopted a ticket naming Carey. "But by some juggle," grumbled Carey later, "the mystery of which has never been developed, on the morning of the day of election, another ticket was clandestinely substituted, in which my name was omitted." According to Carey, James C. Fisher, who held 760 proxies, including 20 of Carey's own, "allowed himself to be prevailed on" to nominate not Carey but another man who had not yet subscribed to the canal stock.[52] Carey's wounded pride was assuaged the following year, when, at the annual meeting of the stockholders, this resolution was adopted: "RESOLVED UNANIMOUSLY, That the thanks of the Stockholders be presented to MATHEW CAREY, Esquire, for the zeal and ability with which he promoted a new subscription to this work in the year 1823." [53]

As the stockholders had recognized, it was Carey above all who had revived the canal project. He had restored public confidence in the work, and the company was thus enabled to resume its construction work after a nineteen-year interval. Proof of that confidence is seen in the fact that Congress authorized a subscription of $300,000 to the work in 1825, twenty years after receiving its first petition for assistance from the canal company. In 1829, a second government purchase, one of $150,000, was made of Chesapeake and Delaware stock.

[52] *Letter to a Few Friends*, pp. 5–6.
[53] *Ibid.*, p. 8.

Relocating and Constructing the Canal, 1822-29

4

Even before the government subscription was received, work on a relocated and enlarged canal had begun. Construction began in April, 1824, after approximately two years were spent in making a thorough reexamination of possible routes and plans. William Strickland was engaged in March, 1822, to make the new surveys and to review the evidence upon which the upper route had been selected in 1804. Major developments since that time seemed to warrant such reconsideration. In the first place, the navigation of the Christina River, a proposed eastern debouchment of the canal, had been materially impeded by the construction in 1807 of the Wilmington drawbridge; in addition, a prime objection to routes lower in the peninsula had been removed by the erection of Fort Delaware, which made defense of the lower Delaware River more secure. There was, moreover, as Delawareans hotly accused, no little jealousy of Wilmington on the part of some Philadelphians. If an equally suitable canal line bypassing Wilmington could be laid, it had the support of many Quaker City residents. Finally, landholders south of New Castle and the Christina River who were interested in having the canal come through their property had objected to the upper route. These were the men, believed Joshua Gilpin, who had "ruined the business in Congress." All of them "made a noise about the canal to suit their own interests, tho none of them would give it any aid."[1]

[1] Joshua Gilpin to Mathew Carey, Kentmere, November 3, 1821, Carey Collection, LCP.

Despite these factors, Gilpin remained convinced as to the superiority of the original route and repeatedly warned against reviving local interests by reviewing the choice of routes. He favored immediate resumption of work on the incomplete feeder and the western half of the main line, during which time the eastern termination of the canal could be selected quietly and calmly, but such was not to be. Final determination of a new canal line was eventually announced in January, 1824, but not until after a bitter, acrimonious debate, similar to the one in 1803 and 1804, was carried on in the newspapers.

In the meantime, during the summer of 1822, William Strickland conducted his examinations of "the ground between the waters of the Delaware and Chesapeake." In reporting to the Committee of Survey on May 13, 1822, Strickland announced that he had surveyed and approved the original route, although he recommended a lower summit level than previously planned. Two months later he submitted his report on a lower route for the canal, one whose location had been dictated by the wish to find the "shortest distance between the navigable waters of the two bays." He stated that a 14-mile canal between Newbold's Landing on the Delaware and Back Creek was practicable, although it would require 8 locks of 8-foot lift each at both ends. Because of the expense, Strickland advised against a through cut or tidewater canal. The cost of the 16-lock canal was estimated, exclusive of purchasing land and water rights, at $702,000.[2]

Nothing further could be done in 1822 for lack of funds, but Carey's successful fund-raising campaign permitted the hiring of additional engineers to assist in making further surveys in 1823. Benjamin Wright, a graduate of the Erie Canal engineering school, and John Randel, Jr., also of New York, were hired by the Chesapeake and Delaware Canal Company during the winter of 1822–23. Wright, soon to be recognized as one of the leading canal engineers in the country, had supervised construction of the central section of the Erie Canal. Coming to work for the Chesapeake and Delaware Canal Company in May, 1823, he became its chief engineer in January, 1824, after final location of the canal route. Wright subsequently became the chief or consulting engineer on many other important improvement projects, including the Chesapeake and Ohio Canal, the

[2] Committee of Survey Minutes, May 13, 1822, C & D Papers, HSD; Report of William Strickland to the Board of Directors of the Chesapeake and Delaware Canal Company, July 22, 1822, Carey Collection, LCP.

Delaware and Hudson Canal, the Farmington Canal, the Blackstone Canal, and various railroads in New York, Virginia, and elsewhere.[3]

Randel had been a New York surveyor before being employed by the Chesapeake and Delaware Canal Company, and subsequently was associated with the Pennsylvania canal system, Delaware's New Castle and Frenchtown Railroad project, and the Central Railroad of Georgia. Little information concerning Randel's life apart from his professional career, however, has been found. As early as 1805 he made various turnpike surveys near Albany, New York, and he was particularly active as a surveyor and engineer after 1812. More than 40 volumes of material in the New-York Historical Society relate to Randel's surveys in Manhattan and other parts of the state made between 1812 and 1822. In addition, he laid out a sloop and ship canal across New Jersey in 1816, and three years later drew up plans for an 18-mile ship canal leading from Albany. Randel declined, for "personal reasons," an engineering position on the Erie Canal, but as an agent of certain Albany interests he became involved in a dispute with Benjamin Wright over the route of the canal in the Albany area.[4]

In later life Randel became the proprietor of Randalia, a tract of land in Bohemia Manor, Maryland, where he gained a considerable reputation for eccentricity. In part this was due to the foresighted nature of his ideas, but also to the constant litigation in which he became involved. George Johnston, the historian of Cecil County, Maryland, who wrote of Randel's fondness for litigation, described the man as "strange and eccentric, and full of Utopian schemes and projects." In his last known letter, Randel wrote to John M. Clayton, then Secretary of State, full of enthusiasm for his elevated railway project and for a new city, Morrisania, a spacious and elegant northern extension of New York City he had designed. The plan called for

[3] Noble E. Whitford, *History of the Canal System of the State of New York together with Brief Histories of the Canals of the United States and Canada* (Albany, 1906), II, 1171–72; Hugh G. J. Aitken, *The Welland Canal Company: A Study in Canadian Enterprise* (Cambridge, Massachusetts, 1954), p. 100. Aitken called Wright "without doubt the most experienced canal engineer on the North American continent."

[4] *United States Gazette*, May 1, 1823; James J. Heslin, assistant director and librarian, The New-York Historical Society, to the author, January 1, 1958; Henry TenHagen, deputy chief engineer, New York Department of Public Works, to the author, September 25, 1957. For a full description of the conflict between Wright and Randel in both New York and Delaware, see Daniel Hovey Calhoun, *The American Civil Engineer: Origins and Conflict* (Cambridge, Massachusetts, 1960), pp. 109–113.

"avenues . . . *200 feet* wide, with *Parks* for trees and tasteful shrub-
bery, 80 feet in width in the middle. . . ." He recommended the same
for Pennsylvania Avenue in Washington, claiming that Morrisania,
when built, would be "the most beautiful and comfortable suburban
City you could desire to see." In the same letter, however, Randel
stated that he was currently "out of professional employment," and
asked to be remembered if any vacancies or new positions needing
someone with his professional training occurred.[5]

Although Randel was to become infamous in the history of the
canal company as a result of his successful quarter-million-dollar lawsuit against the company for breach of contract, it was Randel's plan
for the canal that was finally adopted. He arrived from New York to
begin surveying in January, 1823. Already partially acquainted with
the widely known canal, he came to Delaware "full of the thorough-
cut," as company secretary Henry D. Gilpin expressed it. Aware of
the potential commercial and military value of the canal, Randel was
of the opinion that a sea-level canal would be much more practical in
the long run, and he discounted the obstacles other engineers, such
as Latrobe and Strickland, had deemed insurmountable. Latrobe in
1803 had stated that the cost of a tidewater canal, necessitating a cut
through the 80-foot dividing ridge, was far beyond the financial capabilities of the company; Strickland in 1822 agreed, adding that the
infirm texture of the soil in the marshlands near the Delaware River
made a canal there impossible. But Randel was not persuaded by these
reports, although he studied them closely before making complete
resurveys of the lower route, which confirmed his belief that a tidewater canal was indicated. In his report submitted March 30, 1823,
Randel entered "very minutely into the thorough cut plan" and estimated the total cost at $1,200,000, a figure he believed no higher
than for other possible routes when feeder, harbor, and other expenses
were included. This estimate, however, as Gilpin significantly remarked, was founded "on the idea that the soil is a gravelly loam
throughout."[6] The marshy, spongelike soil actually encountered was
the chief factor in adding $1,000,000 to the estimated cost of
construction.

When Benjamin Wright, "on whom principal reliance [was] placed

[5] Johnston, *History of Cecil County*, pp. 391–392; Randel to Clayton,
June 22, 1849, Clayton Papers, Manuscripts Division, Library of Congress. The
time and place of Randel's death are not known.

[6] To Joshua Gilpin, Philadelphia, January 20, March 20, 1823, Henry
Dilworth Gilpin Papers, HSD.

for fixing the route of the canal," arrived in Philadelphia late in May to assume his duties with the canal company, the debate concerning the canal's proper location was in full swing. Henry D. Gilpin, after pointing out to him "the difficulties of opinion & prejudice" he would have to face, supplied him with all of the engineering reports available. Wright studied these diligently; he "seems disposed," wrote young Gilpin to his father, "to give full credit to Latrobe for his skill and accuracy. . . . Far from having any bias against the upper route, he is evidently inclined to it, if he can get water which he looks upon as the great impediment." [7] Later, accompanied by both Strickland and Randel, Wright made a personal examination of the canal ground.

Because of the intense feelings on the subject, however, the board of directors was reluctant to name the location of the canal without additional information. Randel was ordered to make a resurvey of his lower route, and Strickland was ordered to reexamine the upper route as unobtrusively as possible. Their findings were to be submitted to the judgment of an independent authority, the company having already applied to the War Department for the help of the army engineers in making a final decision. The company explained to Secretary of War Calhoun in their request that such assistance "would be greatly serviceable on this occasion not only in leading the Board to a right conclusion but in attracting to it public confidence and unanimity." [8]

Calhoun readily agreed to send the army's Board of Engineers to consult with the company. Brigadier General Simon Bernard and Lieutenant Colonel Joseph G. Totten were instructed to "proceed without delay" and to provide the company full assistance. Additional instructions provided by the Engineer Department may have proved decisive in the eventual location of the canal. "Your services," stated the department communiqué, "will be particularly valuable in determining the nature, extent, and value of the military capabilities of the several routes that will attract attention, and may lead to the selection of that most advantageous to the government." [9] Louis McLane told the House of Representatives in 1825 that it was "owing, in a great degree, to the decision of these United States' Engineers," who recommended the more costly but strategically located lower

[7] *Ibid.*, May 28, 29, 1823.

[8] William Meredith to John C. Calhoun, Philadelphia, May 19, 1823, as quoted in Forest G. Hill, *Roads, Rails, & Waterways: The Army Engineers and Early Transportation* (Norman, Oklahoma, 1957), p. 30n.

[9] J. L. Smith to Bernard and Totten, Washington, June 3, 1823, Letters to Officers of Engineers, Engineer Department, War Records Division, National Archives (Washington, D.C.).

route, "that the cost of the work has exceeded the means of the individual subscription." [10]

Bernard and Totten conducted their personal examination of projected Chesapeake and Delaware canal routes in July, 1823, but were unable, for lack of certain vital information yet to be supplied by the company engineers, to give an authoritative opinion at once. It was arranged for the engineers to return when sufficient new data had been collected to make possible a determination of the route. More precise information was needed on the nature of the soil along the various routes, the volume of water in the different peninsular streams, and the cost of the land, mill seats, and water rights. A meaningful comparison of routes was impossible until all of this information was assembled. [11]

The army engineers returned in November as scheduled, and examined the plans, estimates, and engineering data drawn up by Strickland for an upper route canal, but "a severe and protracted indisposition" having prevented Randel from completing a similar report for the lower route, final selection of the canal line was again postponed until the following January. [12] The repeated delays were exasperating to all, and the tenseness of the situation was reflected in the press. Angry words were hurled at one another by the citizens of Philadelphia and Wilmington, each suspecting the other of gross selfishness and unworthy motives in their location preferences. The people of Wilmington, fearful of injury to the trade of their growing industrial city if any alternate route were adopted, wanted the canal to terminate in their city, whereas the Philadelphians seemed to favor any route other than one passing through the Delaware metropolis. The situation also lent itself to land speculation, although the company attempted to minimize such activity by making the crucial location decision in close confidence.

On January 13, 1824, the desired information having been assembled, a four-man board of engineers, consisting of army engineers Bernard and Totten and civil engineers Wright and Canvass White, then chief engineer on the Pennsylvania State Works, met to recommend a route. After a full week of study, the engineers made their

[10] *Delaware Gazette*, January 28, 1825.

[11] Brigadier General Simon Bernard and Lieutenant Colonel Joseph G. Totten to the President and Directors of the Chesapeake and Delaware Canal Company, July 25, 1823, [Totten's] Official Reports, Engineer Department, War Records Division, National Archives.

[12] Lieutenant Colonel Joseph G. Totten to General Macomb, Philadelphia, December 6, 1823, *ibid*.

unanimous report to the canal company officers on January 20. Six days later this report was unanimously adopted by the board, at which time Benjamin Wright was appointed chief engineer. Announcement of the selection of Randel's lower route was made by publishing the brief report of the examining engineers:

To the President and Directors of the Chesapeake and Delaware Canal Company.

Gentlemen — after a careful examination of all the circumstances, connected with the important question of the most eligible route for a canal across the Delaware Peninsula, we unanimously recommend the following project — viz. Beginning on the Delaware river near New-bold's landing, where an artificial harbour and a tide lock must be provided, the Canal should be cut through St. George's Meadow to St. George's mill dam; there to be lifted by a lock of eight feet; — thence through St. George's mill dam; through the dividing ridge of the peninsula, and through Turner's mill pond, to a lock of six feet at Turner's mill dam; and thence along Broad and Back Creeks to a tide lock near the mouth of Long Creek.

Benjamin Wright, Canvass White,
Joseph G. Totten, Bernard, Brig'r Gen'l.[13]

News of the selection stunned many Delawareans, especially those in Wilmington. Every precedent had pointed to the selection of the upper route, but precedent was not followed. The reaction was immediate; as Mathew Carey expressed it, "a very violent clamour was excited against [the selection], partly by persons interested in the upper route — partly, however, by disinterested persons, who believed . . . that the lower route was impracticable." The editor of the *Delaware Gazette*, Samuel Harker, was particularly vocal in condemning the board's action. "The lower route was fixed upon," he cried, "not because it would be more beneficial to Philadelphia than the upper one, but because it would prevent Wilmington profiting so much by the improvement." He demanded to know other reasons, if there were any, which prompted the selection. Harker, despite his Wilmington bias, sincerely believed that a canal over the lower route was an impossibility, and he continually prophesied its ultimate failure.[14]

Other Delawareans wrote to the editor expressing their great displeasure with the choice. Some questioned the motives of the engineers and the company officers, and others questioned even the legality

[13] *Delaware Gazette*, January 31, 1824.
[14] *Letter to a Few Friends*, p. 6; *Delaware Gazette*, January 30, March 16, 1824. See also subsequent issues.

of the alteration in route after money had been collected and expended on building the upper route canal. Another indication of disapproval is found in the refusal of many Delawareans, even the Bank of Delaware, to honor their subscriptions to the stock of the canal company. In other parts of the country too, there was a decided lack of enthusiasm over the choice. Even in Philadelphia, where opinion was more favorable towards the company's decision, at a stock auction in March, 1824, "there could not be obtained a bid of a single dollar" for Chesapeake and Delaware Canal stock on which $60 to $100 had been paid.[15]

Both technical and commercial arguments were used to denounce the selection of the lower route. In a vitriolic pamphlet written by "a Citizen of Philadelphia," the author doubted that the canal as planned would serve the "great objects which the Philadelphia subscribers to it had in view," for he felt that the difficulties of navigation between Newbold's Landing and Philadelphia would prevent the Susquehanna River trade from reaching the Quaker City. His major objection, however, related to the anticipated size and expense of the canal. Philadelphia should be practical rather than patriotic in applying her capital to improvement schemes, and should devote her attention to construction of a smaller, less expensive barge canal along the upper route. A great canal to form a link in a chain of inland navigation along the Atlantic coast, he contended, "is very properly an object for the attention of the general government, and not of a single city."[16] Another Philadelphia writer, J. C. Sullivan, advanced similar ideas when he stated that a commercial, not a "national accommodation" canal was called for by trade exigencies. Sullivan, a civil engineer, recommended that a small, inexpensive barge canal, "adequate to mercantile accommodations," be constructed.[17]

Such arguments against the canal location went unanswered by the company for many months. Not until June, 1824, in their annual report, did the directors announce their reasons, mostly of a technical nature, for choosing the lower route. Its advantages were given as "entrance into deep water on the Delaware, instead of debouching into a narrow, winding creek, and encountering the delays incident to opposing tides; the entire absence of aqueducts and

[15] *Delaware Gazette*, April 2, 1824.
[16] *Views Respecting the Chesapeak and Delaware Canal. By a Citizen of Philadelphia* (Philadelphia, 1824), pp. 2–3, 17, *et passim*.
[17] J. C. Sullivan, *Suggestions on the Canal Policy of Pennsylvania . . .* (Philadelphia, 1824), pp. 11–12.

tunnels; the shortness; the inconsiderable destruction of mill property — the small number of locks; the rapid despatch of passing craft; the facility with which it may, at any time, be converted into a ship navigation . . . and above all, the consoling certainty of a never-failing supply of water."[18] By this time, work on the new and enlarged canal was already underway.

Preparations for a resumption of construction activity were in progress throughout the latter part of 1823 and into 1824. Calls were made in September, 1823, for installments to be paid on the stock, and five permanent committees of the board were established in October: Works, Accounts, Finance, Old Claims, and Correspondence. The subscription call met with a good response in Philadelphia, but an insufficient number of shares had been subscribed to in order to cover the estimated expense, more than $1,200,000, of the lower route.[19] It was decided, nevertheless, to begin construction at once, for further delay was deemed disastrous. An appropriation from Congress was expected before the present funds were exhausted. Actual construction work began on April 15, 1824, almost nineteen years after work on the original feeder canal was stopped.

Most of the difficulties predicted by the opponents of the lower route, and many others, were encountered during the next five and a half years. The final cost of the canal, $2,201,864, was 82 per cent more than originally estimated by John Randel, Jr.[20] The most difficult and troublesome problems of construction came in the spongy marshlands near the Delaware River, and in the "deep cut," where the dividing ridge of the peninsula was cut through. This excavation, 80 feet deep in places, was regarded at the time as "one of the greatest works of human skill and ingenuity in the world."[21]

Subscriptions totaled only $750,000 when the work began, but contracts, with the pay scale based on Randel's esimate of just over $1,200,000 rather than the slightly higher estimate made by the board of examining engineers, were made for the entire line of canal soon

[18] *Fifth General Report of the President and Directors of the Chesapeake and Delaware Canal Company* (Philadelphia, 1824), p. 12. Hereafter these annual reports will be cited as *General Report*, with number and date.

[19] It was hoped to put all shares on an equal footing. Notice was given in September that shares of old stock on which $50 had not been paid by December 12, 1823, would be sold at public auction or otherwise forfeited. In December, it was announced that $65 was to be paid on all shares by April 1, 1824. *Delaware Gazette*, September 23, December 30, 1823.

[20] Randel's original estimate placed the cost at $1,211,834.74. According to the consulting board of engineers, the cost would amount to $1,354,364.64.

[21] Quoted in Livingood, *Philadelphia-Baltimore Trade Rivalry*, p. 92.

after the route was selected. Randel himself contracted to construct the eastern half; "several of the principal contractors on the Erie Canal" agreed to construct the remainder of the canal. Its total length was to be 13.6 miles, with two tide and two lift locks; the summit level was only 17.6 feet above mean low water in the Delaware River. The eastern entrance to the canal was at Newbold's Landing, soon renamed Delaware City, some 46 miles below Philadelphia. Its western termination was Back Creek, a tributary of the Elk River which was an arm of Chesapeake Bay. The dimensions of the canal prism were set, but during the process of construction it was decided to enlarge them. As finally established, the canal was to be 66 feet wide at the top, 36 feet wide at the bottom, and 10 feet deep. Passing places were planned at half-mile intervals, except in the deep cut area, where they would be one mile apart. A large semicircular harbor was to be constructed in the Delaware River. The inside dimensions of the four canal locks were to be 100 feet by 22 feet.[22]

Satisfactory progress in the work was made during the first year. By June, 1824, a work force of 850 men and 150 horses was actively employed; even during the winter of 1824–25, as many as 600 men remained on the job, and by the summer of 1826, more than 2,600 men were at work. The wages of the canal workers were low, but it is difficult to determine the exact pay because the men were employed by the contractor rather than the canal company. According to Hezekiah Niles, the common laborer in America in 1823 received 62½ to 75 cents a day, although $1.25 had been average in 1795.[23] Coupled with the low wages were shabby living accommodations for the workers. According to a contemporary observer, "The workmen live in companies of fifteen or twenty in *Shanties* — frame buildings along

[22] This description is based upon an article by John Randel, Jr., which appeared in the *Albany Daily Advertiser* (New York), and was reprinted in the *Delaware Gazette*, March 23, 1824. At this time, Randel was estimating the total cost of the canal at $2,000,000, remarkably near the actual figure. His article accompanied an advertisement in the Albany newspaper for contractors and laborers.

[23] Quoted in William A. Sullivan, *The Industrial Worker in Pennsylvania, 1800–1840* (Harrisburg, 1955), p. 73. See also Mathew Carey, *Appeal to the Wealthy of the Land . . . on the Character, Conduct, Situation, and Prospects of Those Whose Sole Dependence for Subsistence is on the Labour of their Hands* (2nd ed., Philadelphia, 1833), which included a letter from Joseph McIlvaine, former secretary of the Pennsylvania Board of Canal Commissioners. McIlvaine, writing in 1831, stated that the average wage of canal laborers was approximately $10 to $12 a month, plus board; "Contractors, in making their calculations, set down 70 to 75 cents a day for each man employed, including wages and food." *Ibid.*, p. 9.

the canal, provided with a cook, or board in more private houses erected for the purpose." [24] Many of the workers were Irish immigrants, and some Negroes were employed. The work force was segregated at first, but later all of the men labored side by side. The Negroes, however, continued to be fed and lodged in separate buildings.

With no unusual difficulties being experienced during the first year, considerable construction progress could be reported to the stockholders in June, 1825. The Delaware tidelock had been completed, and it was expected that the Chesapeake tidelock would be finished before winter. Some disappointment was expressed that the excavations through the marshes had been less vigorously prosecuted than the other work, but recently Randel had been instructed to attend to those sections. In addition, the workers had "suffered by the usual autumnal fevers of the country," the board admitted, "but at no time has the work been suspended, or even materially interrupted." [25]

Others described the Chesapeake and Delaware Canal as "a scene of great activity and diligence." Besides work at each end of the canal, excavation had already begun in the deep cut area, where earth was to be obtained for making the towpath and banks through the marshes. "The work proceeds regularly and constantly," it was reported. "Empty teams continually take the place of those which go off with their loads, and by means of copper tokens given to each driver as he takes away a load, the precise number is ascertained by the overseer. . . . It is difficult to understand the magnitude of the undertaking without personal inspection. The huge chasm at the Buck astonishes the spectator, although not one third of the intended depth has been dug." [26]

The year 1825 had proven productive in other ways, for the federal government had recently become a sizable stockholder in the company, climaxing a twenty-year battle in Congress for federal aid to the project. The company had not slackened in its attempts to get financial assistance from the federal government after the three states, private institutions, and various individuals had subscribed. Indeed, these subscriptions served to renew the efforts and to buttress the arguments of the canal supporters. Two petitions to Congress in 1822, after it became known that a revival was underway, proved fruitless, but a petition in December, 1823, to which a progress report was added in March, 1824, led to the introduction of a bill granting aid

[24] *American Watchman*, May 17, 1825.
[25] *Sixth General Report* (1825), p. 7.
[26] *American Watchman*, May 17, 1825.

to the company. Reported April 1, 1824, but tabled indefinitely in May, the bill was called up during the following session and became the subject of lengthy debate. Representative Joseph Hemphill of Pennsylvania spoke at length upon the history of the canal, the previous attempts to obtain congressional aid, and the progress of the work to date, in urging its adoption. Despite the forcefulness of his appeal, the bill barely passed to a third reading, 86 to 83.[27]

The major debate occurred on the final consideration of the bill. James Hamilton of South Carolina opposed the appropriation on the grounds that the military importance of the canal was overrated, and that private enterprise would eventually complete the work anyway.[28] He was effectively answered by Louis McLane of Delaware, who made a powerful argument for the canal. McLane's speech was reprinted in the *Delaware Gazette* because, said the editor, it contained all the arguments for the bill and was the best statement he had seen upon the subject. McLane opposed further delay while new surveys were being made, as proposed by some, because more than enough information was already available to justify the appropriation. He believed that the work would not be completed by individual enterprise alone, because the canal was "more a national than an individual work." Neither could the three states most intimately concerned build the canal alone. In Delaware and Maryland support of the project was confined to a small area, and Pennsylvania had committed itself to a large program of improvements within the state. Because of the peculiar conditions prevailing, and the conflicting interests, McLane believed the government should aid individual spirit and complete a work which would otherwise be abandoned. Only $700,000 of the estimated $1,200,000 had been subscribed; an immediate need for the government subscription existed.[29]

Samuel Breck of Pennsylvania supported McLane's position. He believed the project would fail without government aid. Citizens of Philadelphia currently held a total of $4,000,000 in unproductive internal improvements stock, including Chesapeake and Delaware Canal stock; Breck was sure no more aid could be obtained from that quarter.[30]

Arguments based on the military advantages of the canal, its na-

[27] *Register of Debates in Congress, 1824–1837* (Washington, 1825–37), 18th Congress, 2nd Session, pp. 216–224.
[28] *Ibid.*, pp. 285–290.
[29] *Ibid.*, pp. 290–297. See also the *Delaware Gazette*, January 28, 1825.
[30] *Register of Debates*, 18th Congress, 2nd Session, p. 302.

tional character, and the enterprise and zeal of individuals to date were enlisted to combat opponents who held constitutional objections or maintained the Chesapeake and Delaware Canal was a local project. Representatives from New York, New Jersey, and South Carolina spoke against the bill, but opposition in those states was not unanimous. The bill in the House passed by a comfortable margin, 113 to 74. In the Senate, after a brief discussion in which Senator Tazewell of Virginia vainly attempted to add a rider to the bill calling for a subscription to the Dismal Swamp Canal Company, the Chesapeake and Delaware Canal bill, authorizing a subscription for 1,500 shares, or $300,000, was passed. Signed by President Monroe on his last day in office, the bill became law March 3, 1825.[31] News of the appropriation, not altogether unexpected, was received with great joy among the canal enthusiasts.

This year of triumph in Congress was also the year in which a prolonged dispute between the company and its chief contractor began. The difficulties stemmed from the company's abrupt and unjustified dismissal of John Randel, Jr., in the fall of 1825. New contracts with others were readily made and work was quickly resumed, but a controversy which was to continue for more than ten years followed. The dismissal and the resulting lawsuits not only alienated many friends of the canal but also brought severe financial loss to the company. Randel's permanent legacy to the company was an indebtedness from which it never freed itself.

The facts in the case can be briefly summarized. After selection of the canal line early in 1824, and in spite of his deep disappointment at being overlooked when the position of chief engineer was filled, Randel had agreed in March, 1824, to build the difficult eastern half of the canal according to the specifications and estimates he himself had drawn up. In cases of dispute over the amount of work done by the contractor, however, Benjamin Wright, as the chief engineer, was to be the sole "umpire and judge." The section of the contract which later was to cause so much trouble stated that "if, in the opinion of the Engineer," the contractor "refuses or unreasonably neglects to prosecute this contract," and the engineer certifies the same to the company, the company had the power to declare the contract abandoned and thereby exonerate itself from its obligations. Finally, ac-

[31] *Ibid.*, pp. 285–302, 322–333, 672–678, 686; Carter Goodrich, "National Planning of Internal Improvements," *Political Science Quarterly*, LXIII (March, 1948), 35.

cording to the contract, the work was to be completed within four years.[32]

These terms were similar to ones accepted by the other contractors; the subsequent problem originated not in the contract but in the characters of Randel and Wright. The two men were unable to work together peacefully. The board of directors, in effect, was forced to make a choice between the two; it was decided to retain the services of Wright but to dismiss Randel. The charges against Randel, however, were not well founded, either morally or legally.

That hostility existed between the company's chief engineer and its principal contractor soon became apparent. Indeed, Randel's employment proved to be a disruptive influence within the company from the start. Quarrelsome by nature, the volatile contractor-engineer incurred the wrath of Delawareans at the outset by seeking his laborers in New York rather than in the area of the canal itself. The editor of the *Delaware Gazette* charged Randel with selfishness for himself and his state. "It seems to be the determination of the managers of the business of the canal," the local editor commented angrily, "that the people of Delaware shall have nothing to do with it but to pay their money, for the purpose of giving employment to the citizens of other states, to make a great frog pond to perpetuate the remembrance of their ill nature, and the *astonishing genius* of Mr. Randel."[33]

After the excavating work began, Randel again became involved in disputes concerning his manner of executing his contract and the certification of the amount of work done. In addition, Wright used the authority granted him as chief engineer to lower the schedule of prices to be paid Randel for his work. This action, taken after Randel had made his subcontracts, substantially if not completely reduced his margin of profit and seemed so patently unfair that it caused one board member to resign in protest. Paul Beck, Jr., who had been very influential in reviving the canal project in the early 1820's, dissociated himself from the company's direction in September, 1824. As he explained in his letter of resignation, he had "unfortunately differed from a majority of the Board as to the merit, ability, and correctness of Mr. Randel, who from the description of the last report of your committee is going fast to ruin . . . not in my opinion from any fault of his, but from the error of others. . . ." Beck observed that Randel had been allowed only $636 for a month's work, during

[32] "Articles of Agreement between John Randel, Jr., and the Chesapeake and Delaware Canal Company," March 26, 1824, C & D Papers, HSD.
[33] *Delaware Gazette*, March 30, 1824.

which time upwards of 100 men were daily employed by him, at an expense of approximately $2,500, and declared that he could not, "under these circumstances, conscientiously sit longer at the Board." [34]

Randel continued on the job, however, despite the payment controversy and a serious physical illness. He realized his professional reputation was at stake. He had often been commended by outsiders for the manner in which he conducted the work, and was anxious to prove his ability and inventiveness. During a canal-railroad debate in Pennsylvania in 1825, for example, Randel, referred to as "that excellent engineer," was mentioned in an influential pro-railroad pamphlet as a builder of one of the few tramways in the country. Described as "a wooden railtrack, which has proved very efficacious," the device was used to carry earth from the excavation near the deep cut eastward to the marshy sections. (Later in life Randel became an early advocate of elevated railroads.)

Bimonthly reports to the board submitted by Randel indicated his progress in constructing the canal, and revealed that he had a work force of 514 men and 154 teams of horses in the field in June, 1825, although the company was soon to charge him with not pushing the excavation "with that vigour which would have comported with the wishes and orders of the board." On July 30, 1825, Wright certified unreasonable neglect by Randel, and two months later, notwithstanding a report by board members Gillespie and Jones that 700 men were at work under Randel on September 27, the board discharged the contractor and declared his contract canceled. A brief hearing had been granted Randel, but his "explanation and excuses [were] unsatisfactory" to the board, and a suit was instituted against Randel to recover money loaned to him by the company. In retaliation, Randel filed suits against Wright personally and against the company for breach of contract. In a case fraught with technicalities, ambiguities, and complexities, Randel was eventually awarded judgment in the amount of $226,885.84 against the company. His suit against Wright was dropped. [35]

But these developments were of the future. At the time, as Henry D. Gilpin admitted, the dismissal of Randel "of course puts us

[34] Paul Beck, Jr., to the President and Directors of the Chesapeake and Delaware Canal Company, Philadelphia, September 6, 1824, Carey Collection, LCP.

[35] Calhoun, *American Civil Engineer*, pp. 110–111; *Reports of Cases Argued and Adjudged in the Superior Court and Court of Errors and Appeals of the State of Delaware*, ed. Samuel M. Harrington (Wilmington, 1901), I, 42–43, 322.

in a good deal of bustle." In the words of a Delaware newspaper editor, the episode caused a "perfect explosion among our Canal folk. . . . Randel has been dismissed from service, George Gillespey [*sic*] is in a perfect fret . . . Isaac C. Jones is far from being in a good humour, Turner Camac is like him, and Matthew Carey has nibbled his pen afresh, and written and published an Appeal to the Public in condemnation of the conduct of the Directors, and for the purpose of righting the wrongs of Randel." [36]

Indeed, Carey did become the chief defender of Randel. Interesting himself once again in the affairs of the company, Carey rushed into print a lengthy pamphlet in which he attacked Wright and the majority of the board of directors. His indignant essay, entitled *Exhibit of the Shocking Oppression and Injustice Suffered for Sixteen Months by John Randel, Jun. Esq. Contractor for the Eastern Section of the Chesapeake and Delaware Canal, from Judge Wright, Engineer in Chief, and the Majority of the Board of Directors*, appeared within two weeks of Randel's discharge. The young engineer, asserted Carey, had spent $13,639 of his own money on the canal, had worked nine months without pay, and had several hundred men on the job — as certified by board members Isaac C. Jones and George Gillespie — when he was charged with failure to fulfill his contract. Moreover, Randel had completed 43 per cent of the work in thirteen months, although he had received a four-year contract. Carey charged that Wright had acted from personal animosity towards Randel in certifying neglect. Three years earlier Randel had "proved that Judge Wright had unnecessarily extended the Erie Canal 19½ miles, and wasted $630,000," by choosing a circuitous rather than a direct route for the canal between Schenectady and Albany. Carey repeated the charge that Wright had informed the board he would no longer cooperate with Randel and forced them to choose one or the other. There is no doubt that much personal antagonism between the two New Yorkers existed; in June, 1824, Wright had privately described Randel as a "complete *hypocritical, lying nincompoop* (and I might say scoundrel if it was a Gentlemanly word)." He admitted that Randel was going into debt to prosecute his contract and was in danger of failing.[37]

[36] Calhoun, *American Civil Engineer*, p. 110; Henry D. Gilpin to Joshua Gilpin, October 1, 1825, C & D Papers, HSD; *Delaware Gazette*, October 14, 1825.
[37] Carey, *Exhibit of the Shocking Oppression . . . Suffered . . . by John Randel, Jun.* (2nd ed., Philadelphia, 1825), p. 8; Calhoun, *American Civil Engineer*, pp. 110–111. Randel's accusations against Wright were contained in his

Carey believed this was caused by deliberate action on Wright's part in arbitrarily reducing Randel's compensation from the company. On one portion of the canal, the original contract allowed Randel 16.7 cents per cubic yard of excavation, on the basis of which he made subcontracts at 14 cents. Providing buildings and boarding for the men, however, added more than 2 cents per cubic yard to Randel's expenses. But Wright, upon learning the terms of the subcontracts, reduced Randel's allowance to 14.5 cents, which was "$15,000 less than the contracts already made by Mr. Randel [and] brought him in debt that amount of money." It was also charged that Wright delayed certifying work, thereby depriving the contractor of working capital, and that he had induced the board to order Randel to conduct work on wet ground in unfavorable winter conditions. Philip Ricketts, one of Randel's assistants who supplied Carey with much information concerning Randel's work, averred he had seen instructions from the board to increase the number of men employed on the meadows during the winter season when they were "repeatedly inundated" and "labourers could not be procured to work in cold water & ice." Randel had no alternative but to disobey the orders given or to incur heavy additional expenses by obtaining the machinery which would permit underwater work. "So anxious was he to comply with every wish of the Directors," said Ricketts, "that he adopted the latter alternative," spending upwards of $1,900 to meet "these most unreasonable orders."[38]

Carey's efforts on behalf of the deposed contractor were unavailing. His plan to call a stockholders' meeting to register their disapproval of Randel's treatment failed of support, the board steadfastly refused to answer the accusations against it (an action Carey interpreted as "a plain acknowledgement of their flagrant injustice; for if their conduct were correct, they would be indifferent who knew all the particulars"), and the pamphlet and other writings defending Randel, published and distributed at Carey's personal expense, did not arouse much interest. "It is melancholy," mused Carey, "to think that such a villainous course of conduct . . . should be viewed with so much apathy, notwithstanding, as far as I can learn, the public

pamphlet, *Description of a Direct Route for the Erie Canal, at Its Eastern Termination, with Estimates of Its Expense, and Comparative Advantages* (Albany, 1822). The author has seen the revised edition of this work published in Albany in 1836.

[38] Philip Ricketts to Mathew Carey, Philadelphia, October 6, 1825, Carey Collection, LCP; Carey, *Exhibit of the Shocking Oppression . . . Suffered . . . by John Randel, Jun., passim*; Calhoun, *American Civil Engineer*, p. 111.

sentiment is most decidedly against the board. But what avails feeling, however strong, without effort!" Carey later noted that he had spent $150 in seeking justice for Randel and that it had made enemies for him and was all "to no purpose," but he had no regrets. He considered his part in the affair "one of the best acts of my life."[39]

Randel himself was ultimately more successful than Carey in seeking retribution, but the wheels of justice moved slowly. While his lawsuits were pending, Randel remained active as an engineer, although a taint upon his character remained. In 1827–28, he was in charge of the 170-mile survey made of the North Branch of the Susquehanna River in Pennsylvania. Among the members of his 40-man crew was young Charles Ellet, Jr., on his first job. Ellet praised the man who first introduced him to the engineering profession, one in which Ellet was to distinguish himself before his untimely death in the Civil War. He described his mentor as "shrewd" and "calculating" but also as "a sociable, pleasant, agreeable companion," and defended Randel's accomplishments on the North Branch survey. Young Ellet wrote his sister "that our party, has done more work than (forgive the boast) ⅔rd of the Engineers' in the State of Pennsylvania, have done this year, and that too with a raw and inexperienced party. . . . Still in the face of every disadvantage has the principal part of the work been accomplished, by the skill, industry, experience, and perseverance of Mr. Randel. And after all the privations and hardships' which he has undergone for the people of Wilkes Barre, his only thanks' have been hard thoughts; and his only reward ingratitude; so difficult it is for a man *once persecuted*, to ever find peace again; our reception here may appear otherwise in the papers', but they do not relate the facts."[40]

Following his service in Pennsylvania, Randel was named the

[39] Diary of Mathew Carey, November 2, 4, 22, 1825, UPL.

[40] Charles Ellet, Jr., to his parents, Wilkes-Barre, June 15, 1827; Ellet to his sister, Wilkes-Barre, November 4, 1827, Ellet Papers, Transportation Library, University of Michigan (microfilm copy in the University of Illinois Library). For an evaluation of Ellet's career as an engineer, see Gene Dale Lewis, Charles Ellet, Jr., Early American Engineer, 1810–1862 (unpub. diss., University of Illinois, 1957).

Hubertis M. Cummings, historian of the Pennsylvania canal system, has called Randel a "disreputable" person, but this characterization seems to have been prompted by a misreading of the Pennsylvania canal records. See "James D. Harris and William B. Foster, Jr., Canal Engineers," *Pennsylvania History*, XXIV (July, 1957), 197. Cf. Instructions to Engineers, &c., 1826–29, and Surveys and Correspondence, 1825–29, Pennsylvania Canal and Public Works Papers, I, Pennsylvania Division of Internal Affairs, Bureau of Land Records, Harrisburg, and Canal Papers, North Branch Division, 1827, PHMC.

principal engineer of the New Castle and Frenchtown Railroad Company and built one of the first general-purpose railroads in the United States. He must have taken particular delight in constructing what was destined, for a time, to be the foremost competitor of the canal company. The 16-mile rail line completed in 1831 roughly paralleled the waterway. Later Randel surveyed and reported on the route for the Delaware Railroad Company, chartered in 1836, but its line was not constructed until the 1850's. In the meantime, Randel was employed as the chief engineer of the Central Railroad and Banking Company of Georgia, and assisted in the location of its line between Savannah and Macon before he resigned in May, 1837, again over a route controversy.

As the Randel case was before the courts until 1834, the most serious repercussions from Randel's dismissal felt by the company occurred after that date. At the time he was dismissed there was but a temporary interruption in the work. The board awarded contracts for finishing Randel's portion of the canal to several individuals, rather than again relying on one man. Within a month, these new contractors were advertising for 1,000 laborers, 300 carts, and 600 to 900 horses. Indeed, at the time the new contracts were made with Randel's successors, the date for completion of the canal was advanced a full year, to March, 1827. Otherwise, the contracts were unchanged from the one originally made with Randel. By no outward sign did the board acknowledge awareness of the criticisms hurled at it, and no public statement such as demanded by Carey to justify its actions was issued. A letter sent in reply to the anxious inquiry of the governor of Pennsylvania stated that there was no foundation for the alarmist reports circulating to the prejudice of the company, and expressed again the board's confidence in an early completion of the canal.[41]

The sanguine hopes for an early completion were not realized. Unexpected difficulties in construction, a misunderstanding with another contractor, and financial problems contributed to the delay. A particularly vexing construction problem faced the canal builders in the eastern marshes, where it was necessary to bring in firm upland soil to form the canal banks and to build the towpath. The marshes had to be filled, sometimes to a depth of 40 or 60 feet, before suitable banks were formed. At one spot, while the attempt was being

[41] *American Watchman*, October 25, 1825; *Delaware Gazette*, October 14, 1825; James C. Fisher to Governor John Shulze, Philadelphia, November 16, 1825, Chesapeake and Delaware Canal Papers, PHMC.

made to build an embankment across a bog, "for 17 successive mornings, no trace of the labours of the preceding day was visible; everything had been swallowed up." [42]

While the engineers were battling the forces of nature in the marsh areas, elsewhere parts of the canal were being completed, and "cities" were laid out at both ends of the canal line in anticipation of future greatness as commercial centers. During the first week in October, 1826, Summit Bridge, a 247-foot span across the partially excavated deep cut of the canal, was completed. By June, 1827, four of the seven sections of the canal, the Delaware harbor, the eastern tidelock, and both western locks had been completed. Work on the middle sections, comprising the marsh and deep cut areas, had been delayed for almost four months by an injunction arising out of a dispute with contractor J. F. Clement, but work was resumed there on April 1, 1827, and progressed satisfactorily thereafter. A year later the eastern section of the canal was opened to traffic, with canal boats passing from the Delaware River inland to Summit Bridge: "Sloops, heavily laden, are continually flying between these two points; and the Lady Clinton packet boat runs daily on the same route." [43]

Philadelphia steamboats began making regular calls to the company's harbor at Delaware City, and excursion trips to the canal to view the work in progress were customary events in the summers of 1828 and 1829. Delawareans frequently journeyed to the canal line to admire the magnitude of the project, and one of the attractions of spending a recuperative week at Brandywine Springs in New Castle County was a ride to the canal area. The most impressive sight was at the summit level, where a wedge of earth 230 feet wide at the top, 36 feet wide at the bottom, and some 80 feet deep had been sliced from the ridge. The gaping hole was spanned by a wooden covered bridge in a single arch. A vista worthy of true admiration in the 1820's had been created.

During the course of construction, it had become increasingly clear that the subscriptions to the company stock would not build

[42] *The Register of Pennsylvania* (ed. Samuel Hazard, Philadelphia), I (June 28, 1828), 415.

[43] *Eighth General Report* (1827), no page; *Ninth General Report* (1828), p. 9. See also the manuscript book in the C & D Papers, HSD, containing the measurements of the "excavation done by Messrs. Clement, Blackstock & Van Slyke." These measurements were made by Henry Heald and Daniel Livermore in March, 1827, "by order of the Referees in the Suit of J. F. Clement vs. the Chesapeake & Delaware Canal Company."

the canal. Unfortunately for the stockholders who had hoped for dividends within a reasonable number of years, the company was forced to borrow money in 1826 and again in 1827. The company obtained a loan of $350,000 from the Bank of the United States in July, 1826, and the following January an additional $200,000 was borrowed. In August, 1827, the company borrowed another $150,000, but considered that at least an additional $300,000 was necessary to complete the canal. In January, 1828, a fourth loan was made tc obtain this sum. In a letter to the governor of Maryland, Presidenı Fisher explained the necessity for having borrowed $1,000,000, but he expressed his conviction that the amount would be sufficient to complete the project, and that "before the close of the year, an active trade will be seen on the surface of the Canal." [44]

Similar optimism was displayed by the board at the annual stockholders' meeting in 1828, but construction problems in the difficult marshland and deep cut areas continued to be unusually time-consuming and expensive. Strict economy measures were instituted by the board in September when they ordered the release of as many "superintending subordinate Engineers" as possible, and of all of the "Supernumeraries." Even Benjamin Wright, the chief engineer, was freed from his contract after December 1, 1828, so that he could make "permanent arrangements" with the Chesapeake and Ohio Canal authorities. Already the payment of interest on the loans was proving burdensome, and additional work "in dressing and finishing" the canal was necessary before tolls could be collected. At the same time, December 29, 1828, that the board appropriated $28,991.13 to pay the semiannual interest due on its loans, the draft of a memorial to Congress seeking an additional subscription from the government for 750 shares of stock was approved. This memorial was presented in the House of Representatives by Levin Gale, a resident of Maryland's Eastern Shore who later became a director of the canal company. A bill providing for a second government appropriation, this one of $150,000, to the Chesapeake and Delaware Canal Company was drawn up and quickly adopted, despite attempts by Senator Tazewell again, as in 1825, to amend the bill to include a subscription to the Dismal Swamp Canal Company. Tazewell announced that he opposed subscriptions to either company and would vote against the bill in any event, but he felt it was his duty to his constituents to offer

[44] James C. Fisher to Governor Kent, Philadelphia, January 31, 1828, Letter Book, 1822–32, C & D Papers, HSD.

the amendment. The Chesapeake and Delaware bill was signed into law by President Adams on March 2, 1829.[45]

As a result of the indebtedness and other financial difficulties encountered by the company after its canal was completed, it was impossible to declare dividends on the stock until 1854, thirty-one or in some cases fifty-one years after the stockholders had pledged their money. With the company sinking deeper and deeper into debt during the final years of construction, one Delaware editor caustically asked the management if they had not reached the bottom of their treasury before the bottom of their canal was reached. The company's financial difficulties were reflected in the market value of its stock. In June, 1826, the month preceding the first company loan, stock on which $185 a share had been paid brought $115, but four months later stock with a par value of $200 per share was quoted at $60 to $65.[46]

Despite these embarrassments, the last remaining obstruction in the canal near Summit Bridge was removed on July 4, 1829, when water was admitted to the entire length of the canal. The occasion was one of great moment for the canal directors and their supporters, but the small celebration planned was ill-favored by the weather. Nevertheless, an official party of company officials, the mayor of Philadelphia, and other citizens of Pennsylvania, Delaware, and Maryland passed through the canal in a rain-soaked barge to mark the festive, though dampened, occasion.[47]

Work on the canal was not completely finished by July 4. While certain finishing touches were being made, plans were taking shape for formal canal dedication ceremonies. Various people formerly connected with the canal company in an official capacity, such as directors or engineers, as well as dignitaries in the United States, were invited to attend the opening celebration, set for October 17, 1829. Benjamin Wright, busily engaged as chief engineer of the Chesapeake and Ohio Canal Company since 1828, was unable to accept, but Joshua Gilpin, who had served as a director of the company for twenty-one years prior to his retirement from the board in 1824, accepted the invitation to join in celebrating the long-awaited event.

[45] Board Minute Book, September 15, December 29, 1828, March 12, 1829, C & D Papers, HSD, hereafter cited as Board Minute Book; Henry D. Gilpin to Levin Gale, Philadelphia, January 3, 1829, Letter Book, 1822–32, C & D Papers, HSD; *Register of Debates*, 20th Congress, 2nd Session, pp. 60–63.

[46] *Delaware Gazette*, June 9, October 31, 1826.

[47] *Delaware Register* (Wilmington), July 11, 1829; *Niles' Weekly Register* (ed. Hezekiah Niles, Baltimore), XXXVI (July, 1829), 317.

Gilpin more than anyone else had kept alive the hopes of the company during the prolonged interruption of the work after 1805; his invitation recognized him "as one of the earliest, most efficient, and most constant friends of this great work." Among those to send regrets were such varied personages as President Andrew Jackson and the Consul-General of Sardinia, M. Cararadofsky de Thaet.[48]

Preparations for the event at the canal line were left in charge of Caleb Newbold, Jr., superintendent of the work. A large slide occurred in the deep cut area a few days before the opening, but the canal was clear for the opening-day procession through the canal. Large vessels were prudently barred, for "a small mistake [would] ground one & do much harm." Arrangements were made with the garrison of Fort Delaware for the firing of three full salutes of 24 guns each, and countless other details were looked to by Newbold in preparing to receive the crowd. "If the day proves fine you will see people enough," he assured director William Platt, "& I wish with all my heart it was over." [49]

The day proved fine indeed, and hundreds of distinguished visitors, company officials, and other excursionists, citizens of Philadelphia, Wilmington, and the surrounding country, including two Philadelphia military companies, were present. Three steamboats were necessary to carry the Philadelphia party alone. The Fort Delaware salutes were answered by vessels lying near St. Georges and Summit Bridge. The group assembled at Summit Bridge, where Robert M. Lewis, chairman of the Committee of Works, announced the completion of the work to the president of the company, James C. Fisher. Lewis gave a brief résumé of the history of the canal, and spoke of the immense difficulties encountered in construction. Fisher made a brief reply before the official party returned to their steamboat, the new *William Penn*, where a dinner was served. Following the meal, an address on internal improvements was given by banker Nicholas Biddle.[50]

As a permanent memorial of the event, at the next annual meeting of the stockholders, it was decided to erect "a suitable tablet, as

[48] John K. Kane to Joshua Gilpin, Philadelphia, October 7, 1829, Gilpin Letter Book, Alderman Library, University of Virginia, Charlottesville; C & D Papers, HSD.

[49] Caleb Newbold, Jr., to William Platt, Delaware City, October 15, 16, 1829, C & D Papers, HSD.

[50] *Register of Pennsylvania*, IV (October 24, 1829), 268–272; Thomas Payne Govan, *Nicholas Biddle: Nationalist and Public Banker, 1786–1844* (Chicago, 1959), p. 102.

a memorial of the date of the commencement of the work, and of its completion," at the canal line. According to the monument duly erected at Summit Bridge, the total cost of the canal was $2,250,000. The average cost per mile was approximately $165,000, an extraordinarily high figure in comparison with the per-mile costs of other canals and attributable to the greater size of the canal prism and the depth of the deep cut. The cost per mile of the Erie Canal was $19,000; of the Pennsylvania canals, $22,000; of all New England canals, $13,000.[51]

It was with great pride that the company directors announced the completion of the canal to the stockholders the following June. The project "which by many was considered a desperate and hopeless enterprise" then exhibited "a bright prospect of usefulness to the community and revenue to its proprietors." The directors were encouraged by the amount of trade already given to the canal, and saw signs that the trade would soon be materially increased, particularly by traffic from other internal improvements currently underway, such as the Delaware and Raritan, the Dismal Swamp, and the Chesapeake and Ohio canals.[52]

[51] *Eleventh General Report* (1830), p. 17; Alvin F. Harlow, *Old Towpaths: The Story of the American Canal Era* (New York, 1926), p. 83.
[52] *Eleventh General Report* (1830), p. 7.

The Canal in 1830

5

CHESAPEAKE AND DELAWARE CANAL.

Notice is hereby given, that this CANAL is *NOW OPEN FOR NAVIGATION*. The Locks are 100 feet in length, by 22 feet in width, and the Canal can be navigated by Vessels within those dimensions, and drawing 7 feet of water.

The rates of Toll have been fixed so low, as to make this the CHEAPEST as well as the most EXPEDITIOUS and *Safe* channel of communication, between the waters of the Chesapeake and Delaware.

Horses for towing vessels may be hired at reasonable prices at each end of the Canal.[1]

With the publication of this announcement, the Chesapeake and Delaware Canal Company began its eventful ninety-year career as canal owner and operator. Its 13.6-mile waterway had been constructed during the height of the "canal era" in the eastern United States, but the year in which the canal enjoyed its first full season of operation was marked also by the introduction of the railroad into America. Other factors which might well have caused some misgivings on the part of the company's supporters were the extremely heavy debt incurred by the company during construction and the Randel lawsuit still pending, but there is little evidence to indicate that anything other than a spirit of supreme confidence pervaded the company at the time of the canal's completion.

[1] Broadside, 1829, C & D Papers, HSD.

"This stupendous public work," as it was designated by Hezekiah Niles in 1829, consisted of a canal just under 14 miles long, running between an arm of Chesapeake Bay and Delaware River and interrupted by only four locks. The locks, 100 feet long by 22 feet wide, limited the size of vessels which could navigate the canal, but their dimensions were ample to accommodate vessels ordinarily used in the bay and coasting trade. Owing to insufficient water at the outset, the canal could pass only vessels drawing less than 7 feet of water, but soon the full projected depth of 10 feet was obtained.[2]

Because of the low summit level of the canal, only 17.6 feet above sea level, a breathtaking view presented itself to the observer at Summit Bridge, where a huge wedge of earth had been removed from the dividing ridge of the peninsula. The water glistened some 60 feet beneath the floor of the single-span, 247-foot bridge. According to Niles, "the passage through the deep cut and under the summit bridge . . . is awfully grand and beautiful." Excursions from Baltimore and Philadelphia to the canal, described as "a noble monument to the skill of the engineers and the perseverance of our citizens," were regular features during the summer of 1830. In addition to the high-level bridge at the summit, there were three other bridges across the canal in 1829, and another was constructed in 1830. Villages optimistically named Delaware City and Chesapeake City appeared at either end of the canal during the construction period, although in 1829 Chesapeake City was described as having no buildings other than a lock house and tavern.[3]

The Chesapeake City tavern soon gained a reputation for being an "excellent house," where "Good cheer and plenty of Ducks, Canvass backs and red heads, for the amusement of sportsmen, may be met with." At the Delaware City end of the canal, a harbor of "substantial wharf-work" extended 500 feet along the shore, from which piers at either end projected 250 feet into the river. Access to the canal was provided by the Delaware tidelock, situated at the edge of the river. The lockpit, dug through peat and soft mud, proved difficult and expensive to build, and afterwards to maintain. In order to obtain a suitable foundation for the lock walls, over 800 piles were driven deep into the earth to support two heavy platforms designed

[2] *Niles' Weekly Register*, XXXVII (September 26, 1829), 70.
[3] *Ibid.*; "Geology of the Route of the Chesapeake & Delaware Canal: Being the Report of a Committee of the American Philosophical Society, appointed to examine certain documents & geological specimens illustrative of that work," 1829, American Philosophical Society Archives, American Philosophical Society Library.

to hold the lock, but extensive repairs shortly after the canal opened were needed to repair the lock and strengthen its foundation. Immediately adjacent to the lock, the canal was enlarged to 90 feet in width to form a large basin, a mooring area for ships awaiting passage through the lock and a sheltered, landlocked harbor for vessels during severe storms.[4]

In order properly to control and facilitate the movement of vessels through the canal, detailed regulations were adopted by the company in 1829. These concerned the types of vessels to be admitted, the procedure to be followed in transiting the waterway (rules on passing, priority at locks, and speed limits were established), and the authority of the company agents in dealing with violations of the rules.[5] Such rules and regulations, customary ones for the period, were drawn up at the same time that a schedule of tolls was prescribed. Since the original charters granted the company back in 1799 (by Maryland) and 1801 (by Delaware and Pennsylvania) had listed maximum tolls, it was necessary for the company to get legislative permission to alter the tolls to suit present conditions and to establish, if possible, rates for all commodities which would be transported through the canal. An itemized list of "tolls to be paid by vessels navigating the Chesapeake and Delaware Canal," compiled in 1829, mentioned 206 products, ranging from alum, bacon, and bark to wool, wood, and wine. The toll on all commodities varied from 1 cent per bushel on grain to $12.00 per boatload for fresh fish. Undecked boats similarly laden were charged $6.00, but all the other toll rates on cargo were under $2.00, with most set at less than 50 cents per unit. Empty vessels paid $4.00 per transit, although vessels on which full tolls were paid on passing through the canal were permitted to repass toll-free within the next 30 days. Strangely, passengers were not included on the toll sheet, an omission that was to prove extremely costly later.[6]

Tolls were first collected late in August, 1829, although receipts amounted to less than $10.00 for the month. In September, following the appointment of two toll collectors, each bonded at $5,000, toll receipts mounted rapidly. By mid-October, just under $300 a

[4] A thorough description of the entire canal, with each of its seven sections and the construction difficulties therein discussed at length, may be found in the *Eleventh General Report* (1830). See also *Register of Pennsylvania*, V (January 23, 1830), 53–55.

[5] "Regulations To be observed by Vessels navigating the Chesapeake and Delaware Canal," July 13, 1829, C & D Papers, HSD.

[6] Toll Sheet, 1829, *ibid.* The board approved the original schedule of tolls on July 7, 1829.

week was being collected. James B. Stevenson became the collector at Delaware City; John Clement served as the first collector at Chesapeake City. These men were each to receive $750 annually for their services. In 1830, however, in consideration of the additional expense incurred by the Chesapeake City collector in attending two locks, his salary was raised to $1,000. Besides the collectors, there were four "keepers of Locks and Bridges" who were paid $20 per month. The bridge tender at St. Georges, who also looked after the lift lock there, received an extra $5.00 monthly.[7]

Regularly scheduled passenger barges, as well as ordinary freight vessels involved in the bay trade, began passing through the canal at once. Barges owned by the Pennsylvania, Delaware and Maryland Steam Navigation Company, better known as the Citizen's Line, which also operated steamboats on the Chesapeake and Delaware bays, were the first to make regular use of the canal. The vessels of this line, described as being "beautiful specimens of the naval architecture of Baltimore," were specially designed to fit the canal locks. These barges, with outside dimensions of 21 by 90 feet and comfortably appointed inside, presented a striking contrast to the customary canal boat of the day. Pulled by five or six horses hooked in tandem and moving at a rapid trot, they could traverse the canal in approximately two hours, thereby completing an all-water communication between Philadelphia and Baltimore. The time required for the three-stage journey was from eight to ten hours. A Southern traveler, B. L. C. Wailes, passed through the canal two months after it opened, entering it at Chesapeake City on December 24, 1829:

Passed through it (distance 16 miles) in 2¼ hours. There are four locks & several Bridges made to turn out of the way of the Canal Barge. The weather became clear & extremely mild . . . & enabled us to have a fine view of its whole extent. At the Sumit [sic] level there is a fine bridge 70 feet above the water, spanning the whole extent of the Cut, which must be at least 150 feet (of frame, covered & neatly painted). It springs from Rock abutments & has no arch. Near the Sumit level there have been large slides or slips of the Bank of the Canal owing to the springs & marshy nature of the ground. These have been overcome by thatching the Banks with Coarse Straw or Grass.[8]

[7] Board Minute Book, September 28, 1829, August 23, 1830. John Toppin was the keeper at St. Georges, James Nolan at Newbold's Bridge, Isaac Clement at Summit Bridge, and John Ash at Turner's Bridge. *Ibid.*, July 7, 1830. Samuel W. Trenchard succeeded John Clement as Chesapeake City collector in September, 1830.

[8] *National Gazette*, as quoted in the *Delaware Register*, July 11, 1829; John Hebron Moore, ed., "A View of Philadelphia in 1829: Selections from the

The following year a second line of passenger barges, in conjunction with steamboats operating on the Delaware between Philadelphia and Delaware City and on the Chesapeake between Baltimore and Chesapeake City, began operations, and an intense rivalry between the two lines developed. This second line, the old Union Line which previously had crossed the peninsula via turnpike, boasted in 1830 of two new steamboats, the *George Washington* and the *Robert Morris*, and of several "superior canal barges." Each navigation company made arrangements with the canal company for special rates of toll. The first year each passenger line paid the canal company $20 per day for the passage of a single barge each way, plus 25 cents for every passenger aboard, with "no charge to be made for using a part of the Canal while any obstruction prevents the passage of boats through the whole of it." The following season new arrangements were tried. For one line of barges running each way once a day, the rate was $8,000 a year; for a second daily line operated by the same company the rate would be $5,000, with these charges to be reduced proportionately if the canal were obstructed from causes other than ice. In return, the passenger barges were given preferential treatment during transit. These vessels were permitted to travel at rates more than twice as fast as those authorized for the general trade, always were to be given the inside lane when meeting or overtaking slower moving freight vessels, and were granted priority in passing the locks and bridges.[9]

In addition to the two passenger lines, freight-carrying packet boats began operating between Philadelphia and Baltimore, Alexandria, Fredericksburg, Petersburg, Richmond, and Norfolk at frequent intervals; and a new packet line from Philadelphia to Port Deposit, on the Susquehanna River, was established in 1830. Moreover, "a variety of transient vessels" trading with the Eastern Shore of Maryland utilized the canal.[10]

Traffic through the canal was heavy from the beginning. It was reported by Hezekiah Niles that late in September a heavily laden schooner, "being the *first*, we believe, of her class," had passed through the canal; the following week he noted the establishment of a new packet line for the transportation of heavy goods. One traveler

Journal of B. L. C. Wailes of Natchez," *Pennsylvania Magazine of History and Biography*, LXXVIII (July, 1954), 354.

[9] *Poulson's American Daily Advertiser* (Philadelphia), March 25, 1830; Henry D. Gilpin to William Meeteer, Philadelphia, August 3, 1829, March 11, 1830, Letter Book, 1822–32, C & D Papers, HSD.

[10] *Register of Pennsylvania*, V (January 23, 1830), 53–55.

in November counted 10 vessels through the Chesapeake City locks between 2 o'clock in the afternoon and dusk, and the following morning 9 more vessels entered the canal before 8 o'clock. Later in the month Niles reported that 20 "sloops and schooners" passed through the canal in a single day; by then tolls were averaging $100 a day, and they remained high until the canal was closed by ice on January 29, 1830. By that time a total of 798 vessels, paying $8,552.59, had passed through the canal. It was reopened on February 23, and from that date until June 1, the end of the first fiscal year, 1,634 passages brought in $18,613.20. Niles noted that more than 18,000 barrels of flour, in addition to large amounts of whiskey, wheat, and iron, passed through the locks during the first three weeks following the reopening. In one week, 102 vessels, counting the two daily lines of passenger boats, proceeded through the canal. "Products from Lancaster have reached Philadelphia, by water," announced Niles, "and it is thought that flour may be transported from one city to the other for 25 cents per barrel. . . ." In April, 1830, the Chesapeake City toll collector received $600 in 24 hours; by September, the weekly tolls were averaging from $1,300 to $1,500.[11]

The economic impact of the canal on the surrounding area was immediate. Niles pointed out in October, 1829, that wood was commanding a "rather higher" price than usual at Baltimore, which was "said to be caused by the new market opened by the Chesapeake and Delaware canal, through which large quantities will pass from the upper parts of the bay to Philadelphia." Baltimore merchants generally noticed a sudden decrease in their trade from the Susquehanna Valley. One Baltimore firm expressed fear that the diverting influence of the canal on the Susquehanna trade would, in fact, "be disastrous to the interests of the city." Another Baltimore company reported that the canal had ruined the city's wheat trade with the Brandywine flour mills. The Brandywine millers, passing their sloops through the canal, began collecting wheat for themselves rather than continuing to trade with Baltimore by the sea route. Besides altering established trade routes, the canal also served to reduce freight rates, insurance rates, and the hazards of navigation between Chesapeake and Delaware bays. In addition to these economic factors, the strategic importance of the canal and its central role in providing sheltered Atlantic coastal navigation were recognized. Ac-

[11] *Niles' Weekly Register*, XXXVII (October 10, 1829), 98; (October 17, 1829), 116; XXXVIII (April 17, 1830), 140; *Poulson's American Daily Advertiser*, April 9, 1830; Board Minute Book, September 13, 1830.

cording to a committee of the House of Representatives in 1831, "the value of this noble improvement to the nation, as a link of the Atlantic canal along the sea coast, cannot be too highly appreciated." [12]

During the calendar year 1830, the first full year of operation, the total revenue of the canal company from tolls equaled $50,663.76, and the following year it increased to $68,102.62. Most of the canal tonnage was eastbound. Freight arrived in Philadelphia from all parts of central Pennsylvania by way of the Susquehanna River, Chesapeake Bay, the Chesapeake and Delaware Canal, and the Delaware River. It has been estimated that during its first thirty years of operation, between one quarter and one half of the revenue of the canal company came from the Susquehanna traffic. Interruptions in the navigability of this river, caused by flood, drought, and ice, had a marked effect on the income of the canal company.

Despite the auspicious beginning of the canal in terms of tonnage and revenue figures, there were a number of problems to be solved. Although water was admitted to the whole length of the canal in July, and its official opening was celebrated in October, 1829, the canal was still in an unfinished state in many respects, and there were continuing large-scale improvement and maintenance expenses. John Cowper, an official of the Dismal Swamp Canal Company who transited and inspected the Chesapeake and Delaware Canal a few days before its formal dedication on October 17, 1829, wrote the board of directors that he, in common with his fellow citizens of Virginia, was most interested in "your Canal," and that he was "much pleased and gratified with the work, *as far as it is finished*, but I much fear, that you will experience much inconvenience and damage to the Canal from the passage of the Barges, unless the Banks are lined. . . ." [13] The board's experience had already proved Cowper's observation to be correct. Accordingly, the stoning of the banks in sections outside the deep cut, where this precaution previously had been taken, was authorized. As another means of protecting the banks, it was decided that no steamboats, rafts, floats, tows, or arks would be permitted to use the canal. In 1830 this prohibition was lifted on all types of craft except steamboats, it having been demonstrated to the satisfaction of the board that such vessels, properly operated, would not en-

[12] *Niles' Weekly Register*, XXXVII (October 31, 1829), 153; Livingood, *Philadelphia-Baltimore Trade Rivalry*, p. 94; "Report on Internal Improvement," February, 1831, *Register of Debates*, 21st Congress, 2nd Session, Appendix, p. xxxvii.

[13] John Cowper to John K. Kane, William Platt, and Robert M. Lewis, Norfolk, October 14, 1829, C & D Papers, HSD. The italics are supplied.

danger the embankments. Indeed, rafts and arks accounted for a large proportion of the canal trade after 1830. Further steps taken to improve the canal included the purchase, for $2,250, of a dredge for channel maintenance, and the erection of lamps and mileposts along the towpath.

A special committee's report to the board of directors in 1832 spelled out the difficulties of the company with its property in 1829. It was well known, stated the report,

that the canal was in very few respects, a complete work, when it was opened for navigation in the fall of 1829. The banks were not consolidated, and were in fact but partially formed. The chamber of the canal was of unequal depth, bars were yet to be removed in many places, before an uninterrupted navigation could be had by vessels drawing more than seven feet of water. The walling of the sides had been confined to the deep-cut and even there it scarcely extended above the water line; elsewhere the banks of the canal were unprotected. The bridges were imperfect also, and one of the locks was soon afterwards exposed to very serious injury. The provision for the maintenance of a proper supply of water was incomplete, the masonry of the western locks on the summit was not sufficiently elevated, there was no effective waste weir, to secure the work from the dangerous consequences of a sudden flood. The culvert beneath the canal and the north drain intended to discharge the waters of the low grounds on the North West of the line was altogether inadequate to that object. The culvert indeed was after a little while closed as useless or dangerous. . . . The slips, which from the first have marked the peculiar character of the summit banks . . . have required the services of many laborers and skillful supervision. All these and many other particulars of less moment have called for the appropriation of large sums of money. . . .

The committee estimated that upwards of $154,000 had been expended during the first three years to combat, if not eliminate, the defects listed above; there remained only $300 worth of repairs yet to be made, it was believed. An increase in trade, however, accompanied by permission for "the most rapid passage of barges," both of which were anticipated, would require additional protection for the banks and the installation of a steam-powered pump to maintain the summit level water supply, the cost of which was estimated at $15,000.[14]

Another serious problem, and one less simple in its solution since it involved improvements outside the jurisdiction of the company, concerned the navigability of Back Creek, the channel connecting the western end of the canal at Chesapeake City with Elk River. In

[14] Committee [on Board Reorganization] Report, Board Minute Book, December 5, 1832.

January, 1830, the canal company forwarded memorials to Washington requesting the Congress to appropriate funds to improve Back Creek. Senator Isaac D. Barnard and Representative Joseph Hemphill, both of Pennsylvania, were asked to present the petitions. In the accompanying letters, President Robert M. Lewis remarked that the canal itself was in "good shape," and that the prospects were good for having "a very large trade next season," but, he added, "the difficulties in the navigation of Back Creek are so apparent that it is presumed most of the members of Congress (and there are many) who have passed through it must be fully aware of the necessity of its improvement." The following month "the owners & agents of the different packets & steam boat lines that ply between this city & the [Chesapeake] ports" also memorialized Congress on this subject and described the difficulties and delays encountered by their vessels in navigating the approach channel. It was estimated in February that the cost of the improvement would be approximately $50,000, although as yet no detailed survey by an engineer had been completed. The canal company considered that it had neither the right nor the means to undertake the project itself.[15]

A subsequent letter to Joseph Hemphill outlined the navigation problem more specifically and described the current operations and economic importance of the canal:

The canal is doing well. Last week 169 vessels passed thro: and during that time $2,289 were received for tolls — four passage [sic] Barges attached to the steam Boat Lines pass daily, and carry nearly all the travellers between the North and South, from some of whom we hear complaints in consequence of their occasional detention as the Steam Boats cannot pass each other in the upper part of Back Creek at low water. The Canal is but just begining to develope the good effects that will result from it: But it has already afforded data, on which to form some estimate, of the immense trade which will now be facilitated, and promoted by this new avenue. The community now feel, and appreciate, the benefits received by the completion of this arduous, and difficult work. Which but for the good feelings of our friends, and the fostering of the government, might at this time perhaps have been pointed at, as a Monument of the folly of its projectors and supporters. But it is now viewed with very different feelings, its success is no longer doubtful and it is considered only as a great public benefit.[16]

Consequently, at the request of the House Committee on Roads and Canals, Colonel Stephen H. Long of the army's Topographical Engi-

---

[15] Robert M. Lewis to Isaac D. Barnard, Philadelphia, January 22, February 2, 1830, Letter Book, 1822–32, C & D Papers, HSD.
[16] Robert M. Lewis to Joseph Hemphill, Philadelphia, April 15, 1830, *ibid.*

neers made a report and estimate of the Back Creek improvement project early in April. Long, who stated he was "very politely accompanied" to Back Creek by President Lewis, was afforded "every facility" to become acquainted with the channel and the obstructions to its navigation. After remarking that the importance of the canal nationally, the facilities it provides "for personal transportation" to and from Washington, and the relation it bears to a system of inland navigation parallel to the coast, "in which the nation is most deeply interested," were all explained in a variety of statements already presented to Congress, Long proceeded with his report. He agreed that there were serious impediments to safe and rapid navigation in the creek. In addition to shallowness, which rendered the canal inaccessible in times of low water to deep-draft vessels otherwise able to transit the canal, the "sinuosities" of the channel, numerous and abrupt, made its navigation much more difficult than appeared from the charts of the waterway. Long pointed out that vessels often ran aground, especially when the wind was unfavorable, and frequently were forced to wait a change of wind and tide before resuming their journeys. Finally, the channel terminated at Chesapeake City "in a space so contracted as to preclude all conveniences" for mooring vessels or turning steamboats. The engineer therefore recommended, in order to make Back Creek "adequate to the commerce" of the Chesapeake and Delaware Canal, that the channel be widened, deepened, straightened in several places, and that a turning and mooring basin at least 600 by 250 feet be constructed. He estimated the total cost to be $40,000.[17]

The canal company was much encouraged by Colonel Long's report, and by the inclusion of an appropriation for the project in a general appropriations bill which passed both houses of Congress late in the session. Robert M. Lewis and John K. Kane twice appeared before congressional committees in Washington to assist in getting the bill adopted, but all to no avail. President Andrew Jackson "pocket vetoed" the bill for reasons explained in his annual message to Congress on December 6, 1830. The Jacksonian policy of limiting, on

[17] "Harbor of Delaware City, and the Navigation of Back Creek," *House Executive Documents*, No. 199, 25th Congress, 3rd Session (Washington, 1839), pp. 1–4. Long's report to General Charles Gratiot, chief of engineers, was dated April 3, 1830, but it was not printed until 1839, when it accompanied an engineering report on the Delaware City harbor submitted by H. Belin, dated December 21, 1838. For a discussion of other instances of government engineering aid to private waterway groups, by Long and others, see Hill, *Roads, Rails & Waterways*, especially chapter 6.

occasions at least, the role of the national government in the financing
and constructing of internal improvements was followed in this case.

Only shortly before the failure of the Back Creek appropriation
Jackson had issued his famous Maysville Road Bill veto, and his next
annual message to Congress devoted much space to an explanation
and defense of his internal improvement policy. The president opposed
federal aid to projects of a "local character" or to "private associations" engaged in making improvements on the general grounds that
this would lead to a dangerous aggrandizement of government power as
well as "prevent an equitable distribution of the funds amongst the
several States." He objected, moreover, to any appropriations for
internal improvements until the national debt was extinguished, after
which time he suggested there could be a distribution of the federal
surplus to the states according to the number of their representatives
in Congress. Although the House committee, headed by Joseph Hemphill, which considered and reported on this portion of the President's
message, took issue with his statements and presented an able summary and justification of previous federal aid to internal improvements,
in which the Chesapeake and Delaware Canal had figured prominently,
it was not able to have its views generally accepted. The canal company was forced for many years to contend with the limitations imposed by the inadequacies of its western approach channel.[18]

In addition to complaints about Back Creek accommodations,
the company was mildly criticized for unnecessary delays in passing
the locks — on the one hand because the Delaware City collector was
unusually slow in calculating the tolls, and on the other hand, in a
more serious matter, because the Chesapeake City collector had
undertaken the business of towing and discriminated against those
who did not use his services. The first collector was requested to speed
up his calculations, but the second, after an investigation of the complaints, was dismissed from his post.

Finally, the financial condition of the company was a cause for
concern. Despite the gratifying revenue from tolls during the first
months, the company was unable to meet either of the semiannual
payments of interest, each of $30,000, on its loans in 1830, or to
repay certain temporary loans which fell due during the same year

[18] Board Minute Book, March 8, May 3, 1830; "Second Annual Message
[of President Andrew Jackson]," December 6, 1830, *Messages and Papers of the
Presidents*, III, 1063–92. See especially pp. 1071 ff., and the Maysville Road Bill
veto in *ibid.*, pp. 1046–56, and the House committee's reply in "Report on Internal Improvement," February, 1831, *Register of Debates*, 21st Congress, 2nd
Session, Appendix, pp. xxxv–xlii.

without resort to additional borrowing. Only a little more than $1,200,000 had been received by the company from the sale of stock, and this figure includes the federal and state subscriptions which amounted to a total of $625,000. The remainder of the $2,200,000 cost of construction was supplied by a series of loans obtained in 1826, 1827, and 1828 amounting to $1,000,000. The incompleteness of the canal in 1829 and the consequent extremely high "maintenance" charges throughout the 1830's, coupled with the service charges on the large sum of money previously borrowed, constituted a tremendous burden. The annual interest on loans, exclusive of various temporary loans made from time to time, was $60,000, an amount slightly in excess of the average revenue of the company during the initial decade of business. In addition, there were extensive claims instituted by various landholders on the peninsula for damages resulting from flooding caused by the canal's blocking the normal drainage channels — and from time to time old claims dating from temporary occupancy of land during construction were successfully pressed.

Strict economy measures, instituted by the company as early as 1828, were continued, with personnel being reduced to a minimum and such extras as a subscription to the *Daily National Intelligencer* newspaper being eliminated. Benjamin Wright had left the company's employ on December 1, 1828, with the understanding that he would be available for consultation if necessary on a per diem basis. According to a committee report in 1832, ordinary expenses incident to the company's operation were approximately .5 per cent of the total expense of the canal, an extremely low figure. This included annual salaries for the president and the superintendent of $2,000 each; the secretary-treasurer received $600, and a messenger and porter received $100. Two toll collectors, four lockkeepers and their assistants, and three bridge tenders received a total of $2,870 from the company annually. With miscellaneous items such as oil for lighting bridges and locks, and office expenditures, the total "regular or ordinary annual expenditures," excluding repairs or other "extraordinary expenses," amounted to about $8,000. A total of $4,000 was allotted for contingent expenses and for normal maintenance work, thus making the annual charge for "keeping the works in good order, collecting the tolls, superintendance of the line of canal, and attending to the business of the corporation generally, about $12,000. . . ." The company felt that there was "no similar work in the United States on which the annual charges can be so small." The outlook for the company was bright once the property was put in order and the revenue of the company increased sufficiently to service and reduce its permanent debt. Unfortunately, the former proved alarmingly expensive and delayed by several years the accomplishment of the latter.[19]

A reorganization of the board of directors also had followed the completion of the canal. In part this too was an economy measure, but it also represented an effort to improve the administrative efficiency of the company. The resignation of James C. Fisher as president in 1829, following more than twenty-six years of service to the company as board member and (since 1823) as president, offered an opportunity for broad changes to be made along lines suggested by Fisher in his letter of resignation.

Robert M. Lewis, a member of the board since 1823 and chairman of the Committee of Works at the time the canal was completed, was elected the fourth president. As Fisher recommended, the new president was called upon "to perform more in detail the practical duties of the work," for which the compensation was suitably increased. Lewis was a merchant in Philadelphia who, by reason of the experience gained in directing the construction of the canal during the latter stages, was well qualified for these additional duties, and he proved indefatigable in performing all the tasks of his office. He regularly visited the canal every two weeks, or more frequently if required, and gave full reports to the board concerning the property periodically. Shortly after Lewis took office, it was found possible to eliminate the position of assistant superintendent, then occupied by Daniel Livermore, leaving only Caleb Newbold, Jr., superintendent of the works, in charge of company affairs at the line of the canal. In addition to the president's reports, Newbold, who later became president of the company, delivered weekly reports to the board concerning traffic, toll receipts, and maintenance. The board itself was organized into five standing committees: Accounts, Claims, Correspondence, Finance, and Stock. Later a permanent Committee on Tolls was established.[20]

The third major company officer in 1830, in addition to Lewis and Newbold, was Henry D. Gilpin, a young lawyer in Philadelphia and the son and grandson of two of the leaders of the movement in the eighteenth and early nineteenth centuries for construction of the

[19] Committee [on Board Reorganization] Report, Board Minute Book, December 5, 1832.

[20] First Minute Book, Stockholders' Meetings, 1803–1909, October 26, 1829, C & D Papers, HSD, hereafter cited as Stockholders' Minutes; Board Minute Book, June 14, 1830.

canal. Gilpin, who later served with distinction as board member and counsel for the company and sat briefly on President Martin Van Buren's cabinet as Attorney General, had become the first secretary of the company at the time of its reorganization in 1822, and he served in that capacity for ten years. His personal correspondence, especially with his father, Joshua Gilpin, during the decade of his service, reveals much concerning company affairs. After enduring the tribulations of canal planning and construction, the Gilpin family looked forward to the successful operation of the waterway.

Landslides and Lawsuits:
The First Decade of Operation

6

The operation of the canal during the first five years was plagued by a number of minor problems which prevented it from bringing in the revenue expected, but these difficulties, it was hoped, would soon be ended. Beginning late in 1833, however, a series of major misfortunes struck the company. It never fully recovered from the financial disasters experienced during the first decade. Until the company property and franchises were purchased by the federal government in 1919, the canal company was continually in debt. In only 11 of the 116 years of the company's existence was it able to make small dividend payments, in cash or in stock, to its stockholders.

At first it appeared that the canal would fulfill the expectations of its most hopeful supporters. Commercial activity was stimulated by the population growth and westward expansion of the 1820's, and traffic across the Delaware Peninsula reflected this. Within a few years it supported not only the canal and a previously constructed turnpike, but also a railroad, one of the earliest in the United States, the New Castle and Frenchtown. Canal income from tolls rose from $51,000 in calendar 1830 to $68,000 in 1831, and the company confidently predicted a revenue of $90,000 for the following year. Pointing out that other internal improvement projects, such as the Delaware and Raritan Canal and the Camden and Amboy Railroad across New Jersey, and the Chesapeake and Ohio Canal and the

Baltimore and Ohio Railroad reaching westward from Chesapeake Bay were underway, the board remarked that the Chesapeake and Delaware Canal, "being so situated, that *it* is necessarily the great thoroughfare between the internal improvements of the North and South — must prosper with their prosperity, independent of its own increasing sources of success. . . ."[1]

But instead of increasing in calendar 1832, toll receipts declined and continued to do so in each of the four succeeding years. The causes were many: temporary interruption in canal navigation resulting from slips, breaches, or low water; poor navigability on the Susquehanna River; competition from the New Castle and Frenchtown Railroad, completed in 1831, which paralleled the canal and immediately captured a portion of the transpeninsular trade. The major cause of financial distress in the 1830's, however, stemmed from the impediments to free navigation of the canal imposed by John Randel, Jr., in his eventually successful efforts to compel the company to honor his quarter-million-dollar judgment awarded by the Delaware courts in 1834. Not until 1837, following the settlement of Randel's claim, did company hopes and revenues begin to rise.

As previously indicated, because of the incomplete state of the canal in 1830, much time and expense went into improvements during the first few years. It soon became apparent that a waste weir, or vent, at the summit level was needed in order to prevent flooding within the canal prism itself during the spring, but steps also had to be taken to assure the canal of an adequate supply of water during the long, dry summers. A full lock of water was lost from the summit each time a boat passed through the lift locks. This, coupled with losses by evaporation or occasional breaches in the canal banks, made it necessary to devise a way to lift water from the lower level of the canal into the upper. In 1837, a steam-operated pump was purchased and installed at Chesapeake City to raise water from Back Creek. The major supply of water for the 9-mile summit level, in addition to normal rainfall, remained St. Georges Creek. This had been supplemented in 1829 by the purchase of two millseats which included their dams and reservoirs above the summit level, but on several occasions the reduced depth of water available at the summit restricted the size of vessels permitted to enter the canal.

It was also necessary from the outset to continue taking additional steps to "secure the banks" from injury caused by fast-moving

[1] David Budlong Tyler, *The Bay & River Delaware: A Pictorial History* (Cambridge, Maryland, 1955), p. 63; *Twelfth General Report* (1831), pp. 11–12.

TABLE 3. TOLLS AND TONNAGES, 1830–50[a]

Year Ends June 1	Tolls Received	Passages	Total Tonnage
1830	$24,658	2,379	61,500
1831	61,223	5,280	153,400
1832	63,073	5,633	154,000
1833	61,160	6,790	160,490
1834	54,092	5,438	105,470
1835	47,511	4,889	91,600
1836	35,572	2,467	114,680
1837	56,482	5,433	100,000
1838	67,495	6,568	131,700
1839	67,518	6,034	120,260
1840	54,113	4,363	112,430
1841	69,415	6,384	125,980
1842	78,008	7,528	139,520
1843	66,018	5,973	127,200
1844	98,014	8,413	188,410
1845	97,559	8,778	195,040
1846	101,208	9,684	291,380
1847	167,510	12,054	341,580
1848	186,286	12,810	338,800
1849	173,030	11,802	351,550
1850	198,364	12,912	361,640

[a] Source: "Comparative Statement showing Receipts, Expenses, percentages and Tonnage of Mdze.," 1830–1919, C & D Papers, HSD.

barges or bad weather. Other repairs required from time to time were alterations in the wicket gates on the locks and repair or renewal of the several pivot bridges across the canal. In 1830, moreover, a culvert placed under the eastern end of the canal for drainage purposes proved defective, and had to be closed. With the usual water courses blocked by the canal and only a single drainage channel remaining, the marshes adjacent to the canal became flooded. This subjected the company to numerous, sometimes exorbitant claims for damages. In 1831–32, a new and larger culvert was built underneath the canal without interrupting navigation, although the prevailing depth of water was lowered to only 6 feet. The board could announce in 1833 that the flooded marshes had been satisfactorily drained by the new culvert and that the claims arising from the flooding had been "adjusted and liquidated."[2]

At the same time that the flooding claims were being settled, a

[2] *Thirteenth General Report* (1832), pp. 7, 9; *Fourteenth General Report* (1833), p. 8.

special committee of the board was diligently seeking to settle all obligations of the company to those involved in building the canal. During 1832 final settlements were made with all of the contractors (excepting, of course, John Randel, Jr.) "employed in constructing the canal, locks, bridges, and walls," with the final balances due them paid.[3]

Later in the decade considerable trouble was experienced with the lock and harbor at Delaware City. As reported to the stockholders in 1836, a leak in the lock there delayed opening the canal in the spring for several weeks. Moreover, the piers stretching out into the Delaware River from Delaware City to form the harbor were badly in need of repairs, and the harbor channel was filling up. Application once again was made to Congress seeking government assistance in repairing the eastern entrance to the canal, and once again a report was made by an army engineer, H. Belin. He described the importance of the harbor and canal to the country, the nature of the obstruction, and the best method to be followed in making the necessary improvements, estimated to cost $20,000, but nothing further was done by the government.[4] The company made certain piecemeal repairs itself, and used its dredger to keep the channel between the canal entrance and deep water in the Delaware River at the minimum depth required.

A few attempts to defraud the company were discovered during the first years of operation. Ship masters resorted to false declarations of cargo to avoid the full toll, safe in the realization that the company was legally powerless to punish any offenders caught. The company first attempted to stop this by "strict supervision," and by application to the Secretary of the Treasury, who appointed one of the company's toll collectors a customs inspector for the United States, but not until action was taken by the state legislatures were the frauds effectively ended. According to laws passed in Maryland, Delaware, and Pennsylvania in 1832, captains and agents using false manifests in an effort to defraud the canal company were liable to fines, up to double the amount of the tolls involved in two states, up to $20 in one, plus court expenses.[5]

As a means to increase the revenues of the company and to

[3] *Thirteenth General Report* (1832), p. 8.

[4] "Harbor of Delaware City, and the Navigation of Back Creek," pp. 4–6. Belin's report was dated December 21, 1838.

[5] *Twelfth General Report* (1831), p. 9; *Thirteenth General Report* (1832), pp. 11–12; *A Collection of the Laws Relative to the Chesapeake and Delaware Canal* (rev. ed., Philadelphia, 1840), pp. 58, 60, 61.

improve the accommodations offered to the public, special attention was given to the subject of permitting steam-powered craft to use the canal. The question was first raised in June, 1831, when application was made to the board for permission to use steam-propelled passenger barges in the canal, so that canal barges "might rival in speed, as they would in comfort and conveniences, any other way of crossing the Delaware peninsula." Perhaps the plan was prompted by the imminent completion of a railroad across the peninsula, although locomotives were not used on the line until the following year. Perhaps it was occasioned by similar experiments in canal navigation by steam power recently made in Great Britain, which had attracted considerable attention and were described in William Fairburn's book, *Remarks on Canal Navigation, Illustrative of the Advantages of the Use of Steam as a Moving Power on Canals,* published in London in 1830. The results of the trials abroad were a subject of great interest to canal enthusiasts in the United States, especially "at a period when the battle has waxed warm between the advocates of rail-roads and of canals." Fairburn's contention that boats moving at 10 to 12 miles per hour caused less agitation in the water than boats traveling from 4 to 6 miles per hour, if proved, would strengthen the case of the friends to canals considerably. Fairburn had concluded that the substitution of steam for animal power "would dispense with the annual repairs and maintenance of the horse paths; the complaints and delays arising from drivers, horses, &c. would be avoided, and many contingent expenses saved by the introduction of this never failing and very effective agent, as a moving power for the towage of boats on canals." [6]

The Chesapeake and Delaware Canal Company directors decided to investigate for themselves the possibilities of steam navigation on their canal. After a favorable preliminary examination and report, the purchase of the necessary boats, engines, and equipment to determine the "probable benefits" of steamboats on the canal was authorized on February 4, 1833. A canal boat with a reputation for "quickness" was acquired in May, and the firm of Rush & Muhlenburg agreed to supply the steam engine and accessories for $1,200. Under the direction of President Lewis, certain alterations in the vessel itself were also made.

Another Lewis, W. D. Lewis of Philadelphia, a commission merchant and an official of the Union Line, which was then transporting

[6] *Thirteenth General Report* (1832), p. 11; "On the Rapid Movement of Boats on Canals," *Journal of the Franklin Institute,* XII (August, 1831), 92–96.

freight and passengers between Philadelphia and Baltimore, using the New Castle and Frenchtown Railroad for the passage across the peninsula, observed this activity somewhat unhappily. He described the converted canal boat in this way: "She is an old Del & Hudson Canal boat to which they have put a false Bow . . . is 88 ft long & 20 ft wide over her guards — her wheels are at the side as usual — her Engine said to be of 8 horse power — She is an experiment merely & I think will fail." The original dimensions of the boat had been 80 feet by 10 feet, but the two paddle wheels, each 4½ feet wide and placed on either side of the vessel, nearly doubled its width. After preliminary trials in September on the Schuylkill River, during which the speed of the boat proved satisfactory despite its small engine and the "slight apparent swell produced . . . at the highest speed of which the engine was capable," were noted with gratification, the company officials consented to further trials on the canal. The great need for improving motive power on canals was recognized by all. Not only would this increase the speed and economy of canal transportation, but also it would relieve the hard-pressed animals employed in high-speed towing. As Professor A. D. Bache pointed out in his report on the trials, "To any one who has witnessed the labour with which the rapid travelling upon this canal in barges towed by horses is accomplished, and the violent effects upon the banks, produced by the great swell raised, a desire to substitute some less painful and less destructive method of navigation can hardly fail to occur."[7]

Three conditions were tested during the brief September trials on the Chesapeake and Delaware Canal: use of the steamboat alone, use of the steamboat in towing light passenger barges, and use of the steamboat in towing heavily laden freight vessels. Care was taken to obtain accurate figures concerning the speed and engine capabilities of the boat, but the greatest interest was in observing the effects of the high-speed travel on the canal banks. Rather complete data compiled during the trials can be found in Bache's published report in the *Journal of the Franklin Institute*. Bache observed that the wake from passenger barges being towed by horses was at least three times as great as that produced by the steamboat. In using the steamboat alone, the wave created by the bow was disposed of by the paddle wheels; in towing barges, the barges themselves effectively

[7] Diary of W. D. Lewis, August 1, 1833, Society Collection, HSD; A. D. Bache, "Experiments made on the Navigation of the Chesapeake and Delaware Canal by Steam," *Journal of the Franklin Institute*, XVI (December, 1833), 362, 363–364.

disposed of the remaining swell created by the towboat. Some difficulty was experienced through "sheering" because the helmsmen of
both the steamboat and the barges or sloops being towed were un-
accustomed to the "new circumstances." Moreover, the appearance
of several passenger barges, at which times the towed vessels were cast
loose from the steamboat, interrupted the trials repeatedly, but the
results were nonetheless considered conclusive. Speeds of up to 7
and 8 miles per hour were "attained by even this imperfect model"
steamboat which used an engine too small and weak for the vessel
on which it was mounted; these speeds "compare with those which the
labour of eight horses is capable of producing. . . ." Bache concluded that the experiments "go far to remove, entirely," any doubts
concerning the advantageous application of steam on "the larger
class of canals," and that steam power may be substituted for horse
towing with great savings to the canal, particularly at high velocity.[8]

The trials were reported to the board in October as having produced the "most satisfactory evidence" concerning the applicability
of steam to canal navigation, and company counsel was asked to
investigate the right of the company under its charter to place steam
towboats on the canal. Curiously, however, the steamboat was then
sold, although the committee in charge was requested to procure
and retain a model of the vessel for "future purposes" of the company. Undoubtedly the troubled financial condition of the company
prevented any immediate action to acquire a fleet of steam tows and
the necessary legislative sanction to operate them.[9]

An independent "Canal Steam Transportation Company" was
projected in Philadelphia in 1835, which would carry freight "much
cheaper than it ever has been carried" as well as tow rafts and barges
through the canal, but it was several years before steam navigation
was introduced on the waterway permanently. In the meantime, rapid
transit of the canal continued to be accomplished by passenger barges
rushed through by straining, sweating horses. With as many as ten
or eleven animals laboring in tandem, it was possible to complete the
journey in slightly less than two hours. A temporary cessation of
regular passenger travel through the canal came in 1832, when the
old Baltimore transportation company, the Citizen's Line, which had
joined with the Union Line, began using the newly completed railroad as its route across the Delaware Peninsula. A dispute over rates

[8] Bache, "Experiments made on the Navigation of the Chesapeake and
Delaware Canal by Steam," pp. 361–373.
[9] Board Minute Book, October 7, 1833.

had induced the combined companies to refuse to renew their contracts with the canal company. The rates had been increased in 1831 to $10,000 annually for one daily line of passenger barges, and the board voted to maintain these rates during 1832.[10]

Passenger travel resumed in 1833, however, with the establishment of a new line between Philadelphia and Baltimore. The People's Steam Navigation Company began operations in May, 1833, running its new steamer, the *Ohio*, from Philadelphia to Delaware City. Following the canal passage in "elegant and commodious" barges, passengers boarded the *Kentucky* at Chesapeake City for the run down the bay to Baltimore. With the Union Line operating its steamers (the *William Penn* and the *Robert Morris* on the Delaware, the *George Washington* and the *Charles Carroll* on the Chesapeake) in opposition, a lively rivalry developed between the two lines. Although the Chesapeake and Delaware Canal Company felt that the inducements of safety and comfort on the canal would counterbalance the more rapid speed possible by railroad, and disinterested observers noted that the new People's Line offered "cheaper and better" service, and that it was "far superior" to the other in size, speed, and "elegance" of the boats, Union Line officials were hopeful that the shorter overall time by the steamboat-railroad route would give their line superiority.[11]

On May 2, 1833, two days before the People's Line commenced regular operations, a trial of the new *Ohio*'s speed against the *William Penn* was made. Announcing an excursion to Delaware City, the owners of the *Ohio* planned its departure to coincide with that of the *William Penn* on its regular run. As W. D. Lewis of the Union Line noted, "The Penn took no goods and was fairly prepared for the contest; no doubt the case was the same with the Ohio." The results were inconclusive, for a slight accident to the *Ohio* required it to run 20 minutes using only one engine, but the almost simultaneous arrival off New Castle of the two steamboats proved that the difference between them was slight, to the relief of Lewis and the evident disappointment of the *Ohio* proprietors. Later, following damages to the *William Penn*, the faster *Robert Morris* was put on the line opposite the *Ohio*, and the "question of speed" was settled on the

[10] *Delaware Gazette*, August 21, 1835; Board Minute Book, February 6, 1832.
[11] Carl D. Lane, *American Paddle Steamboats* (New York, 1943), p. 29; Henry Ridgely to Ann Ridgely, Baltimore, July 10, 1833, *A Calendar of Ridgely Family Letters 1742–1899 in the Delaware State Archives*, ed. Leon deValinger, Jr., and Virginia E. Shaw (Dover, 1951), II, 291; Diary of W. D. Lewis, May 27, 1833, HSD.

Delaware in favor of Lewis' company. On the Chesapeake end of the route, Lewis conceded that the *Kentucky* "may be considered as having the advantage of our boat. . . ."[12] The intense rivalry between the two lines was evidenced by the early races, but the Philadelphia and Wilmington newspapers quite properly condemned this reckless and dangerous practice. By mid-May, the steamboats began running at different hours.

The appearance of the new line was welcomed by the people of Delaware. In the previous month, a cow grazing near the railroad tracks had wandered into the path of a speeding locomotive. "To those who would escape the sparks and cows on the railroad," the editor of the *Delaware Gazette* wrote, "and withal would travel without quite annihilating space, this [new] line will afford an easy and pleasant communication between Baltimore and Philadelphia." A more basic reason for its warm reception was the widespread opposition to the railroad-steamboat line. Earlier in the year the company had obtained from the Delaware legislature a law granting it the exclusive right of transporting passengers and freight by "railway, or road to be used or travelled by locomotive engines, or engines propelled by steam," in central New Castle County. Monopolies, especially during the Jacksonian era, were extremely unpopular. Moreover, the existence of a second line would force rates down and improve service.[13]

When the new line began operating via the canal, it announced through rates of $3.00 per passage; the same day, the Union Line reduced its fare from $3.00 to $2.00. After one week the People's Line similarly reduced its fare. Rates to competitive way points also were lowered, generally by half, by the rivalry, but both lines fared well during the year, somewhat to the surprise of Lewis. The opposition, he wrote, "put a bold face on their business, say they are doing well; [and] talk much of the number of passengers they are carrying &c. but I incline to the belief from all the information that I can get that they do not average more than 30 through passengers each way daily which I confess is more than I believed they would be able to get nor can I now think it will last." He admitted that the People's

[12] Diary of W. D. Lewis, May 2, 27, 1833.
[13] *Delaware Gazette*, May 7, 1833, quoted in William F. Holmes, "The New Castle and Frenchtown Turnpike and Railroad Company, 1809–1838; Part III: From Horses to Locomotives," *Delaware History*, X (April, 1963), 256; *Acts of Incorporation of the New Castle and Frenchtown Turnpike Company. Passed by the Legislatures of Maryland and Delaware* (Philadelphia, 1837), p. 39.

Line would carry the "peninsular passengers . . . of course & during the pleasant season a good many excursion passengers. But when September comes & the days begin to shorten I think the faces of the People's Line folk will begin to lengthen — we shall see." [14]

Despite the agent's pessimism, the freighting business as well as the passenger trade of both lines increased during 1833. Lewis observed late in August that his company's vessel had carried "370 packages of Goods ($102.)" on one trip, making it "the greatest day we have had for Goods." The People's Line was also enjoying a heavy freight business for the month. The Union Line suffered a marked loss of traffic early in September following an accident on the New Castle and Frenchtown Railroad caused, according to Lewis, by "the stupidity of Raybow," the engineer, in "checking" the company's new locomotive, the *Virginia*, "too suddenly." Twice in one day the inexperienced engineer derailed parts of his train — two cars the first time, five the second. In the latter case, two of the cars "were crushed in & had to be left on the road — no body was much hurt, but the alarm was excessive, and our boats from Baltimore in the morning line both yesterday and today have been unusually small. . . ." Lewis was even more exasperated when he learned that "the opposition" was doing all it could to magnify this "most mortifying & disgraceful incident" by publishing accounts of it in the Baltimore newspapers. Passenger travel from Philadelphia remained near normal for the Union Line, but in Baltimore, where "the greatest effect can be produced by our opponents," the decline was sizable. The company's passenger trade was affected again in November, following an accident on the Camden and Amboy Railroad in New Jersey.[15]

After one year of serious competition, however, officials of both the railroad and the canal were anxious to curb the rivalry and increase the rates. A shrewd agreement worked out between the two companies accomplished these aims, although it served to destroy the People's Line, which, despite its successful start, was still a financially insecure corporation. The railroad-steamboat company agreed with the canal company to pay $1,000 per month for running a single line of barges through the canal, with the minimum payment for the year being $6,000. As long as no other company conveyed passengers through the canal, the railroad would pay an additional $15,000 to the canal company annually. The railroad directors, as a recent historian of the company has stated, "had no intention of actually sending pas-

---

[14] Diary of W. D. Lewis, June 15, 1833.
[15] *Ibid.*, August 31, September 10, November 5, 1833.

sengers through the canal, but were simply insuring their company against competition." In effect, the companies had agreed that the railroad should enjoy a monopoly of passenger travel between Philadelphia and Baltimore, and that the canal should continue to carry most of the freight which passed along the same route.[16]

This arrangement continued for two years, during which time the People's Line ceased to exist. It tried to survive by carrying passengers across the peninsula in stages, but this outmoded system was ineffective in competition with both canal and railroad. In 1837, with no further steamboat competition in sight, the railroad ceased to run even occasional passenger barges through the canal and considered its agreement with the canal company abrogated. When suit was threatened, the railroad agreed to make a settlement of $15,000, but the canal company's concern for the immediate gain in 1834 was a costly error in the long run. Not until 1842 did regular passenger service through the canal resume.

In the meantime, after four years of moderately successful operations, the canal company's fortunes suddenly took a turn for the worse. Late in 1833 a storm severely damaged the canal embankments, interrupting navigation for ten days. The following spring, a large mass of earth in the deep cut, over 1,000 feet long and reaching back from the canal 200 feet, began slipping into the channel. The immediate employment of a large group of men to remove the sliding earth prevented a complete cessation of navigation, but the weight of the slip forced up the bottom of the canal three or four feet above its regular level. Similar though smaller slips occurred at other places along the canal line. While the company's dredger was clearing the bottom of the canal, a more serious mishap occurred.

A huge breach in the canal embankment at the point where the canal crossed the former bed of Broad Creek caused the trouble. The break was 150 feet wide, through which the water in the upper level of the canal rapidly escaped. Three and one half feet of water along 7 miles of the upper level, as well as all 10 feet in the remaining 2 miles of it, were lost before a dam could be thrown across the canal above the break. Working rapidly to repair the breach, the company had the canal open within 30 days for vessels drawing 6 feet of water or less, but the ramifications of the disaster remained throughout the year.

The most serious consequence of the troubles during the spring

[16] Holmes, "New Castle and Frenchtown Railroad," p. 260; Board Minute Book, February 18, March 19, 1834, December 6, 1836, January 17, 1837.

of 1834 was the loss of water from the summit level, although, besides the embankment, a bridge abutment and the towpath required extensive repairs. In order to replenish the water in the canal, it was necessary to drain the reservoirs, leaving no source of supply during the dry summer months which followed. Only limited accommodations could be offered by the canal for the remainder of the season. In reporting the bad news to the stockholders in June, 1834, company officials attempted to be philosophic about their troubles, recognizing that the fortunes of all internal improvement projects fluctuated. "The past year," they said, "may emphatically be called the gloomy period of this company." As it happened, however, that judgment was decidedly premature.[17]

In January, 1834, John Randel, Jr., was awarded damages in his suit against the company to the amount of $226,885.84. The long-pending case had at last been concluded and, as the company admitted in its report to the stockholders, "the questions that arose in the course of the trial, in relation to the construction of the contract between Mr. Randel and the Company, were very generally, in all material points, decided against the Company." The embarrassed financial condition of the company, however, made it impossible for the judgment to be paid at once. Indeed, after an appeal to higher courts failed, the company foolishly made no effort at all to arrange a settlement with Randel or to honor his claim in any way. Controversy over the claim was to continue for another two years, which caused the revenues of the company to suffer enormously. Admittedly, the company had difficulty throughout the 1830's in paying the high costs of maintenance and improvement, and in servicing its debts, and in July, 1833, it was forced to suspend interest payments on its permanent loans. Previously, various temporary loans had been obtained to meet interest payments, but even this was now impossible, although the company did manage to borrow the funds in 1834 to make the extensive repairs required following the disastrous breach in the canal line. The Randel claim, however, seemed completely beyond the capabilities of the company.[18]

This case is notable in Delaware legal history as well as in the canal company's history. Described as "one of the most famous lawsuits" in the state's history, it featured eminent counsel for both parties. Chief company counsel was James A. Bayard; John M. Clayton,

[17] *Fifteenth General Report* (1834), p. 13.
[18] *Ibid.*, p. 11.

later to become Zachary Taylor's Secretary of State, represented Randel. An early biographer of Clayton described the pleadings in this case as "an imperishable monument of the industry and science of Clayton — for no other man had anything to do with their preparation." He also pointed out that never before had a "finding of such magnitude for merely unliquidated damages" been rendered in the United States.[19]

The company was disillusioned by the adverse verdict of the court, but as the decision was not totally unexpected, several courses of action had been planned. Appeals to the higher courts were instituted and, following Bayard's appearance before the board to explain his view of the legal status of the company's property and the effect of the judgment against the company, the board resolved to collect no tolls in Delaware. All tolls except those on way vessels were to be received at the western end of the canal, in Maryland, or at the company office in Philadelphia. This was an obvious stratagem to prevent Randel from attaching the tolls in Delaware, where he had been awarded the judgment.

With all its property and tolls already mortgaged, the company felt it was improper to give Randel's claim priority over its other obligations. Without the loans which made completion of the canal possible, Randel's claim would have had no basis at all. Nevertheless, the company's ostrich-like attitude toward the claim led to a vicious legal battle from which Randel, backed by the state of Delaware, eventually emerged victorious. At one point in the struggle, President Lewis was prevented by the board from visiting the canal line and supervising the repair of a new land slip because of the likelihood of his arrest if he ventured into Delaware.[20]

In response to the company's policy of collecting no tolls in Delaware, Randel took matters into his own hands by attempting to collect tolls himself. The engineer would have had no chance of success had he not received the support of the authorities in Delaware, especially those in New Castle County. Literally hundreds of captains, who had already paid tolls on their vessels and cargoes, were arrested in Delaware upon their refusal to pay them again and held as garnishees of the canal company. Randel's purpose and methods were vividly described by Nathan Bunker, a Philadelphian, in a letter to the governor of Pennsylvania:

[19] Joseph P. Comegys, *Memoir of John M. Clayton* (Wilmington, 1882), p. 26; *Reports of Cases [in] Delaware*, I, 34–35, 42, 151–181, 322.
[20] Board Minute Book, February 12, 1834.

By a perversion of the attachment laws of the state of Del: a certain John Randell . . . has been for some 6 to 8 months past inflicting most grievous injuries upon the citizens of this commonwealth. . . . The locks of the co[mpany] are in [Maryland, and] as in all such cases tolls are cash: they are paid & must be paid before the vessels can enter the canal, [but] so soon as they reach the limits of Del: State Randall arrests them & garnishees them as debtors to the canal co. & they are compelled to give a Bail bond in double the amount of toll (paid only a few hours previous) with sufficient surety to the sheriff &c in default of obtaining it are dragged 17 miles to New Castle prison & then incarecrated [*sic*], untill some humane friend, hearing their situation bails them out. . . .

Many of these persons are strangers in Del: (tho Known in this city & Baltimore) & cannot find bail: & must go to prison for a debt they never owed. to obtain this process, Randall swears they are indebted to the canal co. and when I asked him how he freed himself from perjury, he replied, "it appeared at first alarming, but his counsel" (Senator Jno. M. Clayton) had appeased his conscience by telling "him that if they were not in debt to the co. they ought to be because the co. ought not to have collected the toll of them untill his debt was paid" — and on the same occasion he declared that "believing the co. to be insolvent he saw no other way to get his debt of 226,000 $, but by thus trammelling the public trade he expected and hoped to compel the citizens of Philada, and Baltimore to raise by general contribution this large Sum of money to enable him to pay his lawyers fees, & other debts that he owed & leave him something to live on" — these and many other facts will be sustained by legal testimony, if required.[21]

Robert Polk was hired by the board to post the bail for any captain arrested in the attachment process while the company appealed to the Delaware legislature for relief. The company took the position that the canal, created by the states of Maryland, Delaware, and Pennsylvania as a "public highway" free upon the payment of tolls, was being "virtually obstructed" by Randel's actions "in violation of the charter of the Canal company." According to it, if a vessel passed through the canal without paying the toll, the company was empowered to seize and sell it. Only if the proceeds from the sale did not pay the toll was its captain liable. Yet "persons have been arrested and imprisoned in a place where they are strangers and without friends, in doing what the charters of Pennsylvania, Delaware, and Maryland declare they have a perfect right to do, viz., use the Canal as a 'public highway,' after payment of the tolls."[22]

[21] Bunker to Governor George Wolfe, Philadelphia, March 6, 1835, Chesapeake and Delaware Canal Papers, PHMC.
[22] *Sixteenth General Report* (1835), p. 12. Randel was acting pursuant to a Delaware law passed February 10, 1829, for "expediting suits against cor-

The Delaware Court of Errors and Appeals, however, in a decision rendered in November, 1835, decided in favor of Randel and upheld the legality of the attachment process. After some deliberation, the company decided to appeal this case on a writ of error to the Supreme Court of the United States. John Sergeant of Philadelphia was asked to appear for the company. The case was heard during the January, 1836, term of the court. In a lengthy decision read by Associate Justice Joseph Story, designed to review the Supreme Court's consistently narrow interpretation of Section 25 of the Judiciary Act of 1789, providing for appeals, the case was dismissed for want of jurisdiction. The judgment of the Delaware court, Story remarked, had no reference to any constitutional question, but proceeded on the "general principles" of laws applicable to garnishment. If indeed, he concluded, taking a not-so-gentle slap at the company, we were compelled to draw any conclusion, it would be that the payment of the tolls in Philadelphia "was a meditated fraud upon the garnishee laws of Delaware, and a violation of the charters and by-laws of the company. . . ."[23]

While this "ship captains' case" was proceeding through the Delaware courts and up to the Supreme Court, Randel sought recourse also in the Delaware legislature and later in the Maryland courts. His efforts to have a law passed in Delaware enabling him, as a judgment creditor, to sell the corporate rights and franchises of the company narrowly failed of adoption. But Randel declared he was not giving up. "I am a ruined man," he wrote in a Delaware newspaper, "but however crushed and powerless I may be, I have yet a right to appeal . . . to the justice of the public." He asked his creditors, especially the "poor men who worked under me while a contractor," to be patient yet a while longer. In the meantime, as the editor of the *Delaware Gazette* announced, "The attachment of tolls at Delaware City is not nor will not be discontinued," and he cautioned men not to follow the unlawful practice of paying tolls to the company in Philadelphia. As for the Maryland end of the canal, it was announced that measures were underway to stop the company "from inflicting wrongs on canal users" there, and to "vindicate the

porations." *Laws of Delaware*, VII, 338–343. The Chesapeake and Delaware Canal Company is mentioned specifically, in that if judgments obtained against the company are not satisfied within 60 days, "the plaintiff may attach the tolls due, or to become due, of the said company." *Ibid.*, p. 340.

[23] *Reports of Decisions in the Supreme Court of the United States*, ed. Benjamin R. Curtis (Boston, 1855), XII, 172.

laws that they have insulted in their endeavors to evade the payment of their just debts by such unjustifiable means." [24]

These measures consisted of a suit filed in the Maryland Court of Chancery designed to attach the tolls collected at Chesapeake City and have them applied to the payment of Randel's claim. Despite the eminence of the company's counsel in Maryland, Reverdy Johnson and Roger B. Taney, Randel's suit was successful and John Clement was appointed by the court to receive all tolls in Maryland. Pending the outcome of an appeal to the High Court of Appeals in Maryland, however, the company was permitted to continue collecting the tolls itself on condition that it set them aside awaiting the decision. Randel thereupon temporarily ceased the arrests of the captains in Delaware, and the trade of the canal picked up slightly.

The company's defeat in the Maryland courts, coupled with the Supreme Court's refusal to accept jurisdiction in the ship captains' case, convinced the board that further litigation would be futile. Randel, upon learning that the Delaware ruling had been upheld, again announced his determination to collect tolls in Delaware until his judgment, plus interest, an amount in excess of $250,000, was satisfied. He triumphantly claimed vindication for the course he had followed to secure his judgment and protect his reputation. In ten years of litigation, every decision in Delaware, in Maryland, and in the Supreme Court had been in Randel's favor. "The Company," he cried, "now stands . . . convicted of the charge of compelling Captains of Vessels to pay *double toll*; — the very charge which they endeavored to make against me, when they themselves were the extortioners!" [25]

As the board explained to its stockholders, it had resisted Randel's claim by every possible legal means, as long as its counsel felt there was a chance, but the recent decisions forced the adoption of a new policy. Early in 1836, after a series of special meetings of the board and lengthy consultation with representatives of the loan-holders of the company, it was decided to end the controversy with Randel by making arrangements to pay his claim in full. An agreement between Randel, represented by John M. Clayton and John Scott, and the company and its creditors, represented by Robert M. Lewis, Charles Chauncey, and Henry D. Gilpin, was made in Washington on March 26, 1836, but Randel refused its terms. The following month, however, new "Articles of Agreement between John Randel,

[24] *Delaware State Journal*, February 14, 1835, quoted in *Niles' Weekly Register*, XLVII (February 28, 1835), 453; *Delaware Gazette*, April 10, 1835.
[25] *Delaware Gazette*, February 5, 1836.

Jr., and the Chesapeake and Delaware Canal Company" were worked out after repeated conferences, the terms of which the board's "Randel Committee" considered as favorable as before. President Lewis was requested to take the necessary steps to carry out its provisions, signed on April 19, 1836. This required not only its acceptance by the loanholders of the company, which was granted on April 23, and the stockholders, done May 23, but also new legislation in Maryland and Delaware. As Randel insisted upon immediate action, petitions were sent to the governors of the two states requesting special sessions. The Maryland General Assembly met in May and quickly enacted into law the bill prepared by the company. One additional clause, prohibiting the company from exercising banking privileges or from making the canal navigable for ships, was inserted.[26]

A special session of the Delaware legislature was convened in June, having been delayed by the death of Governor Caleb P. Bennett. A full explanation of the controversy, and his reasons for summoning the legislature, were given by the new governor, Charles Polk. Polk considered that speedy settlement of the controversy was necessary to protect the interests of the citizens of Delaware and to uphold the honor of the state:

I consider that the faith of the State is pledged, that this great national highway, so important to the whole country as furnishing the best means of transportation both in peace and war, shall be maintained and preserved according to the modes prescribed in the charter under which it was constructed; and it is evident that unless some relief can be given to those interested in it by legislative provision, this noble work, which now presents one of the proudest monuments of human industry, may speedily go to decay or utterly fail to answer the beneficent purposes which it was designed to accomplish. In the trade of this canal, a large portion of the people of the State are deeply interested, and they feel that they have the right to look to you, Gentlemen, for the redemption of the trade from its present embarrassments. . . .

He further pointed out that the loans of the company exceeded $1,250,000 dollars, which served to a great extent to transfer the beneficial interests in the canal from the stockholders to the creditors. It was only proper, Polk believed, that corresponding changes in the charter be made, giving the creditors a voice in the election of officers and the right to participate in other ways in the government of the enterprise. He concluded by praising the company for its action since the Supreme Court decision in observing the laws of the state, and

[26] Board Minute Book, April 19, May 30, 1836.

recommending that a law similar to the one passed by Maryland be adopted. The desired law was quickly passed by both houses; it was signed by the governor on June 15, 1836.[27]

As a result of the new legislation, the agreement between Randel and the company was implemented. This provided for the funding of all outstanding debts of the company, including Randel's judgment. New twenty-year certificates of indebtedness, drawing interest at 6 per cent, payable semiannually, were to be issued, but Randel's preferred debt was to be paid first, within five years — his certificates were to bear the words "entitled to priority of payment and transferable." At a special stockholders' meeting on September 1, 1836, followed within the hour by a meeting of the loanholders, the charter alterations of the previous summer were formally accepted, and new elections were held. At this time the number of board members was increased from 9 to 14. With the Randel controversy officially ended, Robert M. Lewis again reminded the board of his long-standing desire to resign from his arduous duties as president. At the new elections, Davis B. Stacey was named as Lewis' successor. Thus the Randel case became the Randel Loan, or the Loan of 1836, amounting in all to $1,593,184.46, but it proved hardly less of a problem. Randel's portion of the debt was paid, but not until 1847 was it possible for the company to pay even the interest on the rest of the loan.[28]

The real loss to the company during the controversy with Randel resulted from the decline in trade and the consequent inability of the company to make certain necessary repairs to the canal. Major slips occurred in 1834, 1837, and 1839; the locks at either end of the canal fell into disrepair; a three-week interruption to navigation came in 1837 when the Chesapeake City lockgate gave way; and long periods of insufficient water in the canal during the summer months obstructed traffic. As Hezekiah Niles had pointed out during the height of the troubles, shippers were "much vexed" by the double claim for tolls. If something was not done, he predicted that the canal, "that vast work," would rapidly decay, "as the tolls will be diminished, and neither party will feel willing to expend its receipts in keeping the canal in a state of repair."[29]

[27] *Journal of the Senate of the State of Delaware, at an Extra Session* (Dover, 1836), pp. 6–8. The law may be found in *Laws of Delaware*, IX, 26–32.
[28] *Seventeenth General Report* (1836), p. 8; Board Minute Book, April 19, July 5, 1836.
[29] *Niles' Weekly Register*, XLVII (February 21, 1835), 428.

Many ship captains, rather than subject themselves to possible embarrassment and delay, avoided the canal altogether. The Pennsylvania General Assembly undertook an inquiry early in 1835 into the causes of the "obstructions" to the "free and unembarrassed use of the Chesapeake and Delaware Canal," and requested the governor to seek to remove them, "so that the citizens of the Commonwealth may have the full benefit and advantages from this great public highway" contemplated by its charter and supporters. Delaware Attorney General James Rogers explained Delaware's laws governing attachment in a reply to Governor Wolfe's request for information, and stated that "the right of passage . . . has not been impaired." He admitted, however, that "much inconvenience may have been produced to many individuals" whose vessels were attached. But it was just these "inconveniences" which had caused the canal trade to drop off. The revenue of the company steadily declined from an early high of $63,073 in 1831–32 to $35,572 in 1835–36. Following the Randel settlement, however, company income jumped to more than $67,000 in both the 1837–38 and 1838–39 revenue years.[30]

The increased revenue was applied to making certain long-needed repairs to bridges, locks, banks, towpath, and drains. In addition, as previously mentioned, a steam-operated pump was installed at Chesapeake City. The higher, more constant water level thus achieved not only facilitated navigation throughout the year but also helped prevent slips and other injuries to the banks. A diving bell to be used in underwater lock repairs and two ice boats, designed to keep the canal open to navigation as long as the Delaware River itself remained open, were acquired in 1838. Furthermore, in order to keep abreast of new developments in canal navigation abroad, the company requested Professor A. D. Bache of Philadelphia, who had assisted in the steamboat trials on the canal in 1833, to make certain investigations for it during his visit to Europe in 1836. He was given "a letter of credit on London for Fifty Pounds Sterling . . . to be applied to the purchase of such drafts, plans, books &c as in his opinion may seem best calculated to effect the object intended."[31]

The increased income of the company was not sufficient, however, for all purposes. The financial embarrassments of the early 1830's, aggravated in the extreme by the Randel affair, were not easily

[30] Extract from the House of Representatives Journal, February 26, April 13, 1835, Chesapeake and Delaware Canal Papers, PHMC; James Rogers to Governor Wolfe, Wilmington, March 9, 1835, *ibid.*

[31] Board Minute Book, September 19, 1836.

overcome. It had been necessary from the beginning to borrow to meet the interest payments on the company's construction debt, and by 1834 it was necessary to suspend payments completely. During the "Biddle panic," when the Bank of the United States, one of the chief creditors of the canal company, tightened its credit provisions, additional security for a $240,000 loan previously secured by the company's common stock was required. An added indignity was suffered when the bank sued the company for back interest. Confessing judgment, the company's dredger and other chattel property were sold at a marshall's sale in the fall.[32]

The first decade of operation had been a trying one. As they entered the second decade, the board members faced their task with a new realism. Considerable attention towards the end of the 1830's had been given to improving the administrative organization of the company, to utilizing the capabilities of the company officers to the fullest, and to avoiding false economies in maintenance and repair. When Caleb Newbold, Jr., of Delaware, became president of the company in 1838, after serving many years as superintendent, he continued to exercise many of his former duties. The functions of his successor as superintendent, John R. Price, of Delaware City, were redefined, and a new form for making weekly reports to the board was drawn up. The new reports were to give the board complete knowledge, section by section, of the state of the works and the progress of repairs, if any, as well as reports on personnel and equipment. With such an approach, the canal company faced the future with a cautious optimism.[33]

[32] *Ibid.*, November 18, December 23, 1833, January 17, 1837.
[33] *Ibid.*, February 6, July 10, 1838.

May the Company Charge
a Passenger Toll?

7

Considering the reverses suffered during the late 1830's, the canal was in remarkably good physical shape at the beginning of its second decade of operation. According to a report to the stock- and loanholders in December, 1840, the canal was "in excellent Condition with a good prospect of a large increase of trade . . . since the annual meeting in June last the depth of water of the Canal has been much improved by the use of the Company's dredger; it has not at any time during the Season been less than Six feet & half, although the Steam pump has been run but forty-one days."[1] Various improvements made during the 1840's served to keep the canal operating at a high level of efficiency. A large, 217-acre reservoir capable of maintaining a head of water 23 feet above the summit level was constructed in 1840 and 1841, which thereafter helped furnish an adequate supply of water at all times of the year. Water at the summit remained a limiting factor, however, as increasing traffic required that larger and larger amounts be available. Later in the decade a new bridge at St. Georges was built, the wood in all the lockgates and wickets was replaced, new wharves were constructed at both Delaware City and Chesapeake City, and lamps were installed at Delaware Harbor and at all the locks to facilitate night travel.

The canal continued to be a point of interest for tourists in the

[1] Stockholders' Minutes, December 1, 1840.

[101]

1840's, as it had been in the previous decade. It was described at length in guidebooks to the area as well as in the personal accounts written and sometimes published by travelers. None who passed through the canal failed to be impressed by the magnitude of the work ("it is said to present the greatest excavation hitherto attempted in this country, the drains constructed for the passage of the waste water being nearly equal in magnitude to the largest canal in New York") and the magnificence of the Summit Bridge ("The floor of the bridge is 90 feet above the bottom of the canal; extreme length 280 feet. Independently of the interest excited by the bridge, the view of the canal from its commanding height is grand beyond description"). Even the clearness of the water in the canal impressed one commentator: "This canal is fed by the waters of the Delaware, which presents an appearance as transparent and beautiful as spring-water, which is increased in beauty when viewed at one of the tide-locks, which when filled with these delightful transparent waters rising to a great height, and bearing up a sloop or steamboat, presents a scene worthy of admiration." [2]

The improved facilities, nonetheless, were insufficient to meet all the requirements of a steadily increasing traffic. Before the decade ended, the company was planning its first major expansion. In June, 1845, a special board committee strongly urged that the locks be enlarged so as to accommodate the larger class of vessels then engaged in bay navigation. Because the financial status of the company, although improving, was poor, the committee recommended in May, 1846, just after the Mexican War commenced, that application be made to the federal government for aid in constructing the new locks. The resolution appointing Henry D. Gilpin, Robert M. Lewis, and George Cadwalader as the committee to make the application stressed the importance of the waterway militarily:

[2] J. S. Buckingham, *America, Historical, Statistic, and Descriptive* (New York, 1841), I, 433; [Gideon Miner Davison], *The Fashionable Tour: A Guide to Travellers Visiting the Middle and Northern States, and the Provinces of Canada* (4th ed., Saratoga Springs, 1830), pp. 54–55; J. C. Myers, *Sketches on a Tour Through the Northern and Eastern States, the Canadas & Nova Scotia* (Harrisonburg, Virginia, 1849), pp. 40–41. Another particularly interesting and thorough account appears in Richard H. Randall, ed., "Travel Extracts from the Journal of Alexander Randall, 1830–1831," *Maryland Historical Magazine*, XLIX (1954), 251–256; and a lively book with an early description of Delaware City is E. T. Coke, *A Subaltern's Furlough: Descriptive of Scenes in Various Parts of the United States, Upper and Lower Canada, New-Brunswick, and Nova Scotia, During the Summer and Autumn of 1832* (New York, 1833), pp. 22–23.

Whereas, in the present unsettled and precarious State of the foreign relations of the United States, it is of great importance to have capacious inland water communications, between the Northern and Southern Sections of the Country, And, as it is believed that highly desirable advantages would be Secured both to the Community and to the General Government, by increasing the Capacity of the Locks of the Chesapeake and Delaware Canal . . . therefore

Resolved, that, for the purpose of obtaining funds for the construction of Locks . . . of greatly increased size, that this Board, will take means to grant to the Government of the United States the privilege of passing through the Delaware and Chesapeake Canal the Steamers, Revenue Cutters and other Vessels of the U. States, and any of its military or naval forces, munitions of War and Stores, free of Toll — provided, a transfer be made to the Canal Company of the Stock held in it by the United States, and such other aid be granted, as will enable the Company, greatly to enlarge and facilitate the Communication . . . by way of this Canal. . . .

It was considered by the board that if its capital stock were reduced by $450,000, the amount of the government's two subscriptions, the company could more easily obtain a loan to finance the construction.[3]

The committee proceeded to Washington, where they had conferences with President Polk and various cabinet members, all of whom were receptive to the general plan proposed. Secretary of the Treasury Robert J. Walker, the man in charge of the government-owned stock, "not only approved the proposed arrangement . . . but very readily [agreed] to state his opinion on the matter, in writing. . . ." In his letter to the committee, Walker stated his belief that it would be proper for the government, in all cases, to sever its connections with private corporations, and particularly the Chesapeake and Delaware Canal Company, for as yet no revenue from the stock had been produced. He suggested, however, that the large amount contributed to the canal company by the government was sufficient to justify a toll remission on all public vessels, in peace as well as war.[4]

Following these preliminary conferences, the committee drafted its memorial to Congress, appending the correspondence with Secretary Walker. The memorial was referred to the House Committee on Commerce, where a bill was drawn up "after a full conference"

[3] Board Minute Book, May 19, 1846.

[4] Ibid., June 9, 1846; "Documents Relative to the Chesapeake and Delaware Canal, and the Conditional Transfer of the Stock Held Therein by the United States," Senate Documents, No. 370, 29th Congress, 1st Session (Washington, 1846), p. 4. The company's memorial, dated June 3, 1846, appears on pp. 1–2 of the document.

with the company committee. In reporting its actions to the board upon returning to Philadelphia, the committee stated its confidence that the bill would pass at the present session, "if efficient measures be pursued to obtain the requisite action upon it; but they also suppose that unless strenuous efforts be made this measure like many others, in consequence of the press of business will be suffered to remain on the files of the House and not acted on until so late in the Session that it may not pass." Evidently the "efficient measures" called for by the committee were not adopted; the bill was not acted upon by Congress in 1846, and efforts three years later to revive it failed, nor was a suggestion by a correspondent of the *New York Tribune*, that the government buy up the residue of the stock, enlarge the canal, "and throw it open to the commerce of the world free of toll," followed at that time. When the new locks were built and a new method for increasing the water supply of the summit level was adopted in the early 1850's, both were financed through private loans obtained without recourse to federal aid.[5]

Much of the increased trade which necessitated expansion plans came as a result of improved towing services on upper Chesapeake Bay. The completion of canals penetrating the Susquehanna Valley, particularly the Susquehanna and Tidewater, added to the business of the Chesapeake and Delaware Canal, but it also created a need for cheap, reliable transportation through Chesapeake Bay to the canal. Philadelphians were anxious, following the opening of the Susquehanna and Tidewater Canal in 1840, to make the communication from Havre de Grace, at the mouth of the canal, to Philadelphia as cheap and expeditious as from Havre de Grace to Baltimore. A steam towboat company was proposed in 1840 by Caleb Newbold, Jr., president of the Chesapeake and Delaware Canal Company, when he experienced difficulty in hiring or purchasing steamboats suitable for towing canal boats between Havre de Grace and Chesapeake City and between Delaware City and Philadelphia. Newbold believed that the Philadelphia merchants were deeply enough interested in the trade of the Susquehanna to be willing to take decisive action. He appointed a Committee of Three to confer with the merchants "and devise measures for the Establishment of a line of Steam-Tow Boats. . . ." Chartered in Pennsylvania early in 1841 and composed largely of members of the Philadelphia Board of Trade, the Philadelphia and Havre de Grace Steam Tow Boat Company was successful from the beginning.

[5] Board Minute Book, June 9, 1846; quoted in *Eureka* (New York), I (July, 1847), 163–164.

Only 961 vessels were assisted during the initial year of operation, but more than 4,800 were being towed annually by 1847.[6]

To assist the new company in getting started, the canal directors agreed to subsidize it to the extent of $2,000 annually. At the same time, a reduction in tolls on goods carried by the towing company was granted, and Gideon Scull, the first president of the steam towboat company, joined the canal board in June, 1841. After the transportation company became established, the cash subsidies stopped; instead, in 1843, the canal company invested $1,000 in the capital stock of the new corporation, but the practice of granting special rates, in the form of "drawbacks" or rebates, to commodities shipped from the Susquehanna Valley continued. The canal company had been pleased to note in 1842 that the toll reductions had resulted in higher total receipts. Thereafter, working in conjunction with the officials of the Susquehanna and Tidewater Canal and the Steam Tow Boat companies, it usually granted specific requests for drawbacks on through freight. In May, 1843, for example, following an application from the Philadelphia firm of Hart, Andrews, and McKeever, "a Drawback of one cent per barrel [is to] be allowed on all flour . . . proved to the satisfaction of this Company to have come direct from Pittsburg through the Tide-Water Canal; provided, the Tide-Water Canal Company shall reduce in the same manner two cents per barrel on the Same Flour." A more sweeping agreement was made in 1848 regarding the Lancaster and Susquehanna Slackwater Navigation Company. Both canal companies agreed to cut their rates by 30 per cent on all commodities carried by the line, provided that the towing companies do likewise, that the transportation company keep "a sufficient line of boats to accommodate all the trade which may apply to them," and that full toll be paid by the line on freight originating outside the Susquehanna Valley. As a result of the growing trade of the Susquehanna and the special arrangements made concerning it, at least half of the canal boats towed from Havre de Grace headed for wharves in Philadelphia rather than Baltimore. The revenue from this trade alone accounted for more than 25 per cent of the total income of the Chesapeake and Delaware Canal Company.[7]

In addition to steam tows to and from the canal, in 1842 a "steam packet line" through the canal was established by James B.

[6] Board Minute Book, June 2, July 7, December 1, 1840; Livingood, *Philadelphia-Baltimore Trade Rivalry*, pp. 75, 95–96.
[7] Board Minute Book, March 2, 9, 1841, May 2, 1843, March 7, 1848; Livingood, *Philadelphia-Baltimore Trade Rivalry*, p. 75.

Peck and William Lore, but it proved short-lived. A special meeting was held in November, 1842, in regard to the lack of "care or judgment" on the part of the "Captain or engineer of the Steamboat Errickson, by which the property and works of the canal company have been placed in jeopardy." The owners of the vessel were notified of their liability in case of injury to the canal, and copies of the company's regulations governing navigation through the canal and the board's resolution were enclosed. When complaints against the packet line continued the following year, the company lost its privilege of using steamers in the canal.[8]

While steamboats were temporarily excluded from the canal, passenger travel upon it resumed. Between 1836 and 1842 no regular passenger service by way of the canal existed, but in August, 1842, a newly established transportation line operating between Philadelphia and Baltimore restored passenger barges to the canal. The following year a second line of passenger barges was established. A revolutionary development came the next year, in 1844, when continuous waterway service between Philadelphia and Baltimore was inaugurated by the Baltimore and Philadelphia Steamboat Company. This company used narrow, shallow-draft steamboats, which were propelled by the Ericsson screw rather than by the customary paddlewheels. Billing itself as the "Ericsson Line" and thereby emphasizing its use of the screw propeller, only recently introduced in the country by its Swedish inventor, John Ericsson, this company carried passengers and light freight through the canal until the 1930's.[9]

From time to time, other steam packet lines designed to operate through the canal were established. Each sought special privileges in rates, speed, or priority at locks, but the company policy in these regards was firm. As the Merchants' and People's Transportation Company was informed in 1847, "no distinction is or is intended to be made" regarding any of the lines "transporting goods commodities and produce on the Canal." The existing rates of toll and the regulations respecting the speed and conduct of steamboats in the canal were to be "strictly adhered to"; violations of either could result in modification or withdrawal of the privilege of using the waterway.[10]

The increasing trade of the canal brightened the financial outlook of the company. In the early part of the decade, that portion

[8] Board Minute Book, May 30, August 2, October 8, 1842, March 21, April 4, 1843.
[9] *Ibid.*, August 16, 1847; Tyler, *Bay & River Delaware*, p. 64.
[10] Board Minute Book, May 4, 1847.

of the Loan of 1836 known as the Randel Debt, which originally amounted to $229,820, was a matter of grave concern. The 1836 agreement under which the loan was permitted stated that Randel's debt was to be given priority and paid within five years or that a holder of any portion of it could sell the canal and any other property of the company. As the end of the five-year period approached with very little reduction in the Randel Debt having been made ($224,107.10 remained outstanding in July, 1841), it became necessary to make a new loan. But subscriptions to the new loan, given at the same terms as before and payable in 1851, were easily obtained because of the bright prospects of the company. The certificates issued to make up the Extended Randel Debt were gradually redeemed, and the entire Randel Debt was extinguished on time in July, 1851.

The company was able to turn its attention next to the holders of the regular Loan of 1836, to whom as yet not even one payment of interest had been made. In 1846, the year in which toll receipts first exceeded $100,000, a special Committee on Assets recommended that a 2½ per cent dividend on the interest due the loanholders be paid. This suggestion was rejected in June, but the continued good fortunes of the company caused the committee to propose in December an even larger dividend on interest: "the comm: find that the active and prosperous trade of the Canal for the past six months has been such as greatly to increase the revenue of the company above that of any of the preceding similar periods, and will fairly warrant an increase of the amount in the payment of Interest." Recognizing, however, that "a very large payment of Interest *at this time*" would unduly raise the expectations of the loanholders and affect the market price of the loan, and that only a small payment would be possible in July, the committee recommended a 4 per cent dividend. This was duly paid early in 1847.[11]

Later in the year, because of the "increased and progressively increasing revenue" of the company, steps were taken to arrange for the payment of all back interest, amounting by that time to almost $900,000. As the Committee on Finance stated in its report of June 8, 1847, current income was then "more than sufficient" to meet current interest charges, but it would be a long time before the arrearages could be paid from the excess of earnings over current interest and expenses. It was recommended instead that permission be obtained from separate meetings of the stock- and loanholders to borrow the

[11] *Ibid.*, June 23, December 15, 1846.

amount of money necessary to meet the unpaid interest. By making a regular payment of 6 per cent in July, 1847, the company reduced the remaining unpaid interest to exactly half the original debt. Then, the requisite permission having been obtained, the company created the Funded Debt of 1847, by which all arrearages were converted into interest-bearing certificates payable in twenty years. The bonded indebtedness of the company in 1847 thus totaled $2,389,777.48, $1,593,184.99 under the Loan of 1836, $796,592.49 under the Funded Debt of 1847.[12]

The interest on this debt exceeded $143,000 annually, but hereafter the company regularly met its interest payments, and began to salvage its reputation. In 1843, at a celebration marking the centennial of the American Philosophical Society, one of the speakers reviewed the society's role in sponsoring early surveys for the Chesapeake and Delaware Canal. He noted the original attempt to build a canal along the upper route, the one recommended by the society's committee, and deplored its eventual abandonment. Constructing the canal on the lower route, an undertaking the committee had judged "beyond the abilities of the country" in 1769, was completed only "at an enormous cost" and "proved ruinous to the company that undertook it." A year later, under greatly different circumstances, the canal company was similarly described by a rival railroad company as being "notoriously insolvent," a valid characterization at the time. Its common stock in the early 1840's was practically worthless and had been for many years. When the canal company acquired 500 shares of its own stock for its sinking fund in 1843 from the state of Pennsylvania, the shares, with a par value of $200, were purchased

[12] *Ibid.*, June 8, 1847; Thomas P. Cope, I. Pemberton Hutchinson, and Henry D. Gilpin to Robert J. Walker, Secretary of the Treasury, Philadelphia, June 26, 1847, C & D Papers, HSD. These three board members had been appointed by Walker to represent the shares of the United States at the stockholders' meeting scheduled for July 12. They explained in great detail the financial history of the canal company, and gave their opinion on the course that would be "most for the interest of the United States as stockholder to take." In recommending support for the funding measure, these men pointed out that as soon as a surplus beyond the interest occurred, it would be used to pay a dividend to the stockholders, "who have so long waited, without any return for their investment; and who could not, in any other way, receive one for many years to come."
Secretary Walker agreed to go along with the proposal on condition that the stockholders representing a majority of all shares of the company excluding those held by the United States first give their consent, and that the United States would not become responsible for any of the company's debts. Walker to Cope, Hutchinson, and Gilpin, Washington, July 2, 1847, *ibid.*

for less than $5.00 each. By 1848 the company valued these shares at $60 each, but it is true that the market price of the common stock of the canal company remained well below par. Yet financial success is not to be equated with commercial success. In 1868 Henry V. Poor, an eminent transportation authority, grouped the Chesapeake and Delaware Canal with the Erie Canal and the Delaware and Raritan Canal, calling the three the only commercially successful canals in the United States.[13]

The more secure financial status of the canal company in the late 1840's reflected, of course, a sizable increase in toll receipts. Receipts for the decade averaged $123,541, more than double that received during the initial decade of operations. The average annual income, moreover, exceeded $180,000 during the last four years, 1847–50. As operating expenses for the period 1841–50 averaged $35,801, the profits before interest payments amounted to $87,740. In order to keep toll receipts at their peak, revisions in the rate schedules were constantly being made. The philosophy, then as now, was to charge "what the traffic will bear," that is, to set the rates at a point to maximize receipts without driving the freight to alternative routes or agencies of transportation.

It was necessary to get toll revisions approved by the stockholders until December, 1840, when the authority to "alter & modify the Tolls . . . as it may to them appear necessary to promote the interests of the Stockholders and Loanholders" was granted to the board. Early the following year, the toll on various items ranging from buffalo robes to oyster shells, including such important commodities as flour, pig iron, and hardware, was reduced by amounts ranging from 20 to 40 per cent. The board was pleased to point out to the stockholders in June, 1842, that while the toll rates went down, the total receipts went up.[14]

Toll rates were also forced down sharply on some items by railroad competition, a factor which had long influenced the canal company. Within less than three years after the canal was completed, a railroad paralleled it across the peninsula, thereby inducing it to ex-

[13] Address of Dr. Robert M. Patterson, at the "Celebration of the Hundredth Anniversary, May 25, 1843," *Proceedings*, American Philosophical Society, III (1843), 27; *Delaware Gazette*, February 11, 1845; Henry V. Poor, "Sketch of the Rise, Progress, Cost, Earnings, Etc., of the Railroads of the United States," *Manual of the Railroads of the United States, for 1868–1869* (New York, 1868), p. 13.

[14] *Twenty-third General Report* (1842), p. 8; Stockholders' Minutes, December 1, 1840.

periment with new modes of propelling canal boats. As the canal
company stated in 1833, "In the transportation of passengers, and
of the light articles of merchandise, the competition is now so great
between canals and railroads, that in each mode, every means of
improvement is becoming requisite, to keep pace with the other in
the facilities offered to the public."[15] Financial difficulties prevented
the adoption of steamboats by the canal in the 1830's, but competition with the New Castle and Frenchtown Railroad Company was
partially controlled through "arrangements" concerning rates and
types of goods to be carried. Both of these companies were threatened
within a few years by the construction of a continuous railroad between Philadelphia and Baltimore, completed in 1838. The Philadelphia, Wilmington, and Baltimore Railroad Company, which within
five years acquired control of the New Castle–Frenchtown line, immediately captured much of the passenger business between its terminal cities. Not until continuous waterway service was provided
through the canal by means of the Ericsson Line did a sizable passenger trade return to the canal.

In the meantime, competition from the intercity railroad began
to be felt in freight traffic too. Upon learning early in 1843 that "The
Rates of Freight on Merchze. by the Baltimore Rail Road [had] been
recently very much reduced," a canal committee charged with recommending measures to "prevent the loss of that trade to the Canal"
proposed reductions in toll rates by as much as 50 per cent. Again,
however, arrangements were made with the railroad "by which toll
on passengers, through the canal, and the freight on merchandise, was
adjusted. . . ." Recognizing the canal's dominant role as a freight
carrier and the railroad's as a passenger carrier, company officials
agreed that the railroads would charge not less than the high figure of
50 cents per hundred pounds on all merchandise except livestock
moving from Baltimore to Philadelphia; conversely, the canal company's passenger tolls, while not prohibitive, were placed high enough
to give the railroad an advantage. The canal tolls were to be based on
the fare demanded by the subsidiary New Castle and Frenchtown
Railroad for crossing the peninsula, and could be as much as 50 per
cent of the railroad fare from Philadelphia to Baltimore, exclusive of
steamboat fare. As in its earlier negotiations with railroads, the canal
company soon had cause to regret having made the arrangement.
Within less than two weeks, the charge was made that the railroad

[15] *Fourteenth General Report* (1833), p. 11.

company had acquired an interest in one of the new steamboat lines trading through the canal, and immediately adopted "inconvenient & injudicious hours of departure," thereby turning passengers away from the canal. As canal official Henry Cope explained in his letter:

> If the railroad should countenance measures which lessen the Tolls which properly fall to the Canal under the agreement . . . it is obvious that the benefit of the arrangement to the Canal will be . . . defeated. And what is now done to discourage passengers from going through the Canal may by increasing the rates & by delays &c. after a time not only turn away passengers, but freight also.
>
> The obviously proper course for the rail road to pursue is to allow . . . the natural course of trade through the Canal under the agreement without interference on their part [either directly or indirectly]. . . . It is unquestionably true as we have frequently mutually said in the course of our conversations, that an agreement to be permanent must be to mutual advantage & be rigidly adhered to according to its true intent.

M. Brooke Buckley, president of the Philadelphia, Wilmington, and Baltimore Railroad Company, replied to Cope's letter and denied the charges in it, but within a year the agreement was rescinded by the canal company and a bitter struggle between the railroad and canal forces followed.[16]

In 1846 and again in 1849, it was possible for the canal company to raise its tolls. The higher rates applied to all except sailing vessels and boats engaged in the trade of the Susquehanna and Tidewater Canal. The disparity was designed to give the sailboats, at a disadvantage in terms of speed, a slight advantage in costs. In the latter year, the steamboat rates on certain items were restored to the charter rate; "on all other articles, the same rates of tolls as now charged when carried in sail vessels, with the addition thereon of fifty per cent."[17]

Traffic through the canal in the 1840's consisted mainly of timber, lumber, grain, and flour, as well as various items classified as groceries and dry goods and certain other miscellaneous products. Tonnage exceeded 200,000 for the first time in 1846, and it remained above 300,000 for the rest of the decade. The bulk of the raw materials, and therefore total freight, moved west to east. Trade between

[16] Board Minute Book, February 7, March 14, 1843; *Address of the Board of President and Directors of the Chesapeake and Delaware Canal Company, to the Stock and Loanholders of that Company* (Philadelphia, 1845), p. 4; Henry Cope to Abraham J. Lewis, Philadelphia, July 29, 1843, Board Minute Book, September 5, 1843.

[17] Board Minute Book, March 31, 1846, January 2, 1849.

Philadelphia and Havre de Grace, Port Deposit, and Baltimore continued to constitute a majority of the whole. Among the bulky items westward were bacon, fish, groceries, sugar, molasses, and gunpowder. E. I. du Pont de Nemours & Company, a leading manufacturer of the last product, shipped via the canal, however, only as the last resort. The powder company considered the toll rates excessive, but the canal company refused to lower them below 10 cents per hundredweight. If possible, Du Pont engaged freight for the Chesapeake region around by sea, or arranged to have wagons transport the kegs of the explosive to the Elk River, where Chesapeake Bay craft received them.[18]

In 1844 the right of the canal company to charge a toll on passengers was challenged. The question arose when a group of Baltimore citizens desired to establish a passenger line through the canal and sent an inquiry to the company. President Newbold assured them that the canal company was "not compelled by any engagement to exclude travelling from the canal but, on the contrary [was] anxious to increase it. The Toll is not prohibitory we having had a large business in Passengers during the past season, nor is it too high considering the cost of our canal." The group, still not convinced that the passenger toll was at the proper level, applied to the Maryland legislature for a charter and asked that a lower toll be fixed by law. When it was discovered that the company had never been granted the right to charge such a toll at all, the Maryland legislators corrected what they considered to be an oversight and fixed the fare at not more than 25 cents per person. In order for the new law to become operative, it was necessary for the Delaware legislature to pass similar legislation and for the stockholders of the company to accept the charter alterations within 60 days, but neither of these steps followed. Governor William B. Cooper declined to convene the legislature, and the stockholders, at a meeting on May 1, 1844, refused to accept the Maryland law. Not only did they consider the toll rate inadequate, but they believed that acceptance of the law without Delaware's approval might jeopardize the company's charter.[19]

The significance of the Maryland law is that it awakened the railroads in Delaware to the possibility that passengers might be excluded from the canal. John M. Clayton, who became the lawyer for

[18] MacGill, *History of Transportation*, p. 220; *Twenty-sixth General Report* (1845), pp. 12–13; Letter Book, E. I. du Pont de Nemours & Company, 1840–44, *passim*; Francis G. Smith Correspondence, Old Stone Office Records — Gunpowder, Eleutherian Mills Historical Library (Wilmington).
[19] Caleb Newbold, Jr., to Hutchinson and Weart, Philadelphia, January 2, 1844, Board Minute Book; Stockholders' Minutes, May 1, 1844.

the railroad companies in their subsequent battle with the canal company, had urged Governor Cooper to call the special session, and even offered to write the message issuing the call, because he considered the Maryland act a blow intended to cripple the Philadelphia, Wilmington, and Baltimore Railroad, from which Delaware annually received approximately $10,000 in direct payments, and much more indirectly. "Maryland is largely interested in the Baltimore and Ohio Railroad as Delaware is in the Wilmington Rail road," Clayton observed, and because the Wilmington line refuses to carry passengers from Baltimore to Philadelphia at $2.50 each, to oblige the Baltimore and Ohio which had engaged to transport passengers from Wheeling to Philadelphia for $13, "the State of Maryland now *punishes* the Rail road by granting a new power to the Canal company (never granted before) to carry passengers. . . ." He also referred to the monopoly of steam transportation given to the New Castle and Frenchtown Railroad in 1833, at which time the railroad was required to accept $25,000 of unproductive stock in the Chesapeake and Delaware Canal Company, the total amount of the state's subscription in 1824. The object of the 1833 law was to protect the railroad, and admittedly referred to rival railroad lines, but now to grant passenger transportation powers to the canal "would be to 'Keep the word of promise to the ear, But break it to the hope!' " Clayton therefore recommended that the legislature be called immediately to give the state and the railroad the opportunity "to have without delay some counter action . . . to protect us from the oppression . . . of Maryland. . . . By my advise the Rail Road has not moved in the matter. We let the canal ask the call. When called we will be heard."[20]

When the governor refused to act, the railroad took matters into its own hands and made formal complaint to the Attorney General of Delaware, Edward W. Gilpin, that the canal company had usurped powers not granted it. Gilpin notified the company on May 21, 1844, that if it continued to transport passengers, he would move under a writ of *quo warranto* to seek a forfeiture of its charter. Gilpin stated that according to his interpretation of the law, only persons "necessarily or properly engaged" in the navigation of vessels or the transportation of commodities, "paying the toll imposed by the charter, have a right to pass the Canal without charge for their passage."[21]

[20] Clayton to Governor William B. Cooper, New Castle, March 27, April 5, 1844, John M. Clayton Papers, DSA.

[21] Edward W. Gilpin to Caleb Newbold, Jr., Wilmington, May 21, 1844, in *Address of the Board*, pp. 10–11.

Observing that one state had granted the company the right to charge passenger tolls while the other had challenged even its right to transport through the canal persons not necessary to the navigation of a vessel, Newbold informed Attorney General Gilpin that the company desired "to obtain a judicial decision on the questions involved." In the meantime, having been assured by counsel of its right to do so, he declared that the company would continue to permit persons to pass through the canal free of charge. Thus voluntarily the company ceased to demand payment from passengers until its charter could be altered so as to make specific the right of the company to exact such a charge.[22]

At the next regular session of the Delaware legislature, which convened in January, 1845, the company applied for the necessary amendment to its charter. In its original memorial to the legislature, the company stressed the historical importance of the canal, the subscriptions to it by three states and the federal government, and pointed out that it had always been assumed the canal would carry passengers. Indeed, the common preamble to laws passed in Maryland and Pennsylvania during the War of 1812 making conditional subscriptions to the canal company contained these words indicating passenger travel expectations: ". . . during the time of war against the United States of America, by forming the great link of an inland navigation of six or seven hundred miles, and thereby establish a perfectly safe, easy, and rapid transportation of our armies, and munitions of war, through the interior of the country." [23]

The canal petition was strongly opposed by the railroads in Delaware, and the result was one of the stormiest sessions of the legislature ever held. By contemporary standards, two giant corporations were met in deadly battle, with few holds barred. On the one hand it was contended that it was important to the public that various communications between all parts of the country should be encouraged, "under such regulations as will prevent monopoly, and at the same time give a fair remuneration to such as expend their capital in opening and maintaining the same . . ." and therefore that it was "both just to the said company and expedient to the State of Delaware" that specified tolls on passengers be allowed to the company. This had always been the case, from the time the canal opened until 1844, and certain agreements with the very railroads then objecting to the new law had recognized this. On the other hand, the railroads took the point of

[22] Newbold to Gilpin, Philadelphia, May 29, 1844, *ibid.*, p. 11.
[23] Quoted *ibid.*, pp. 12–13.

view that such a grant would be injurious to their companies and deplete the income of the state. They pointed out that the "object of making the Canal was not to carry passengers, but goods, wares and merchandise; while the great intent for which Rail-roads were constructed, was to carry passengers." To grant the canal its request and permit navigation of the waterway with "steamboats propelled upon a principle not then discovered" would violate the monopoly rights granted to the railroad in 1833.[24]

The Philadelphia, Wilmington, and Baltimore Railroad Company admitted to being deeply in debt, having contracted loans of over $2,800,000, including $80,000 from the state of Delaware, while earning an income barely large enough to cover the interest on the debt. Despite this indebtedness, however, the railroad spent over $100,000 annually within the state, most of which went to mechanics and laborers on its lines. In addition, a tax of $4,000 and interest of more than $4,800 were paid directly to the state, whereas the canal company, exempted from taxation at the time of its incorporation, had "never paid the State one dollar, either by way of tax or bonus, in return for all the important privileges which have been granted to it." The railroad was not seeking relief from taxation; all it asked was that things be left as they were: "No such right as that of charging for passengers was ever conferred upon the Chesapeake and Delaware Canal Company. The object of constructing the Canal was to carry freight. . . . Our business, that of transporting passengers, has hitherto been unfortunate for us . . . [but] it is inequitable and unfair to defeat the just expectations held out to us by our Charter, by now transferring a portion of our business to others."[25]

For more than three weeks this subject agitated the people of Delaware and its legislature. Details of the proceedings at Dover were widely reported, and numerous petitions were presented to the legislature from all over the state. As the Dover correspondent for the *Delaware Gazette* stated early in January, the canal company bill "still attracts a great deal of attention. . . . Our town is full of visitors, and our landlords are doing a good business. . . . Mr. Buckley, President of the railroad, is here, with Wm. H. Rogers, John M. Clayton, M. W. Bates, and Robert Frame, and one or two others. Mr. Newbold, on the part of the Canal, has Caleb S. Layton, Ed. Wootten, Andrew C. Gray, John W. Houston, and others."[26]

[24] *Ibid.*, pp. 26–27; *Journal of the House of Representatives of the State of Delaware* (Dover, 1845), p. 141.
[25] Quoted in *Address of the Board*, pp. 20–22.
[26] *Delaware Gazette*, January 17, 1845.

On the day this report was published, a petition signed by 275 citizens of New Castle County asking that the canal bill be adopted was received in the legislature. Sussex County residents, however, opposed the bill in their petition. Many inhabitants of the southern county regularly traded through the canal, and they feared that passengers aboard their craft — wives or friends — would be charged. Some looked upon the controversy as a party measure, and tried to identify the Democratic party with the canal and free enterprise, and the Whig party with the railroad and monopoly rights. Several canal supporters spoke often of "public convenience and accommodation," and gave voice to the cry, "Down with monopoly!" but the bill did not develop into a party question. "A chartered monopoly is against both Democratic and Whig principles," stated "A Citizen" in giving his reasons for supporting the canal bill.[27]

At length, on January 22, the House committee considering the memorials announced that it was unable to agree upon a bill and, "presuming that the members of the House generally, like the members of the committee, have diversified views upon this important and interesting subject," it reported "formally and without prejudice" the bill submitted by the canal company. This bill, in addition to granting the right to charge passenger tolls and changing the date of the annual meetings from June to January, included a section designed to obviate the railroad's financial argument, by which the canal company would agree to guarantee the railroad loan from the state. The committee reporting the bill then recommended that a debate before the bar of the House by counsel for both corporations be held that evening.[28]

By 7 o'clock, the scheduled time for the debate to begin, the floor and gallery in the hall of the House of Representatives were filled. Andrew C. Gray, later to become president of the canal company and to serve in that capacity for more than thirty years, led off with what was described as "a very good speech." He was followed by two speakers for the railroad, William H. Rogers and John M. Clayton. These three speakers occupied the whole of the evening and the succeeding day. Caleb S. Layton, a canal attorney, spent most of the third day in presenting the final statement for the canal. The Dover correspondent did not like Layton's remarks, because of his "exceedingly bad taste . . . in all his speeches, whether before the court or the people. His common slang and vulgar anecdotes are very dis-

[27] *Ibid.*, January 14, 17, 21, 1845.
[28] *Journal of the House*, pp. 140–142.

gusting to every man of any refinement of taste," although he admitted it was a "stronger speech" than expected.[29]

Five days after the close of the extraordinary debate of counsel, during which time the representatives continued the debate, the canal bill was effectively defeated. The crucial section of the bill was stricken before the remaining sections were adopted. Instead of granting the canal company the right to charge a passenger toll, the legislature enacted a law "for the protection of the investment of this State in the loan of the Philadelphia, Wilmington, and Baltimore Railroad Company," designed to prevent a canal passenger toll until the year 1856, the year in which the railroad loan fell due. The brief law stated that "the faith of the State of Delaware shall be, and is hereby pledged, until the first day of April, A.D. 1856, that no power shall, during the said period, be granted to the said Chesapeake and Delaware Canal Company to charge a toll on passengers transported on the waters of their said Canal, or to carry passengers thereon." In a pamphlet published by the company explaining the unusual course of events in 1844 and 1845, the board felt it was unnecessary "either to descant on the propriety or policy of one or more corporations attempting to buy the privilege of injuring another, — or to make any remarks as to the value of 'the considerations' for which the *faith of a State* may be pledged." [30]

The company was deeply chagrined at losing a lucrative source of revenue, especially because of the illogic of the railroad's position. A passenger line of steamers, paying no toll on the canal, could afford to carry passengers at a lower rate than if a toll charge had to be included in its fare. The board resolved to continue permitting passengers to use the canal free of direct charge, as a means of encouraging the passenger lines and bringing more freight business to the canal. To do otherwise would force passenger business to the railroad and reduce the ability of the steamboat lines to carry freight at unusually low rates. It noted, with a certain gleefulness, in June, 1845, that the Philadelphia, Wilmington, and Baltimore Railroad had cut its freight rates from 50 to 5 cents per hundred pounds because the canal continued its passenger service. "But the result shows an advantage gained by the Canal Company . . . as [the railroad rate reduction] has compelled the steam and other vessels to reduce their charge to ten cents per 100 pounds, which has caused a considerable increase in the

[29] *Delaware Gazette*, January 31, 1845.
[30] *Address of the Board*, pp. 6, 43.

amount carried through the Canal, without any reduction in the rate of toll, and thus adding to the revenue."[31]

The question of the company's rights regarding passengers did not end with the failure to get a passenger toll authorized by the state of Delaware. There was still the unresolved matter concerning the rights of the public to use the waterway, described as a "public highway" in the laws authorizing its construction. This was the main issue in the case of *Perrine* v. *the Chesapeake and Delaware Canal Company*, heard by the Supreme Court of the United States during its December, 1849, term. Chief Justice Roger B. Taney remained consistent to the philosophy he had previously best expressed in the Charles River Bridge case when he ruled that, although unable to collect a toll for its services, the canal company could not prohibit passengers from using the canal.

The case originated following an application in 1847 by John A. Perrine of Princeton, New Jersey, for permission to operate a passenger and freight line through the canal between Camden and Baltimore. Quite possibly, as certain canal board members suggested many years later, Perrine was acting at the behest of the Ericsson Line.[32] No other evidence of a "Perrine Line" of steamboats has been discovered. Selection of a man from a state other than one in which the canal company was chartered insured that any dispute which arose would go to the federal rather than the state courts. Ericsson Line officials apparently hoped to eliminate the necessity of making special arrangements for having their vessels admitted into the canal.

Whatever the circumstances surrounding the initiation of Perrine's request, the canal company accepted the challenge. The board replied that it claimed the right to exclude passengers unless "special permission" for their transit was granted, such permission being conditional upon receiving a "fair rate of toll for each passenger."[33] This new policy had been adopted late the previous year. Evidently a satisfactory arrangement was made with the Ericsson Line, although its terms were not recorded in the company minutes and other records of it have not been found, for this line continued to run its freight and passenger vessels on the canal. Perrine, however, objected to the necessity of a special arrangement and claimed the right of navigating

[31] *Twenty-sixth General Report*, p. 8.

[32] Hood Gilpin, Charles Chauncey, and Richard Vaux Buckley, *In re Application of the Chesapeake and Delaware Canal Company to have its charter amended by the State of Maryland* (Philadelphia, 1906), pp. 4–6, 16–17, *et passim.*

[33] Board Minute Book, March 30, 1847.

the canal with his boats, paying only a toll on the freight aboard, or the $4.00 charge for empty vessels if only passengers were being carried.

Anxious to get a ruling on its rights, the company decided to stand firm and instructed the keeper of the Delaware lock to deny Perrine's passenger boats admission to the canal unless he paid a toll of $1.00 for each passenger carried. Perrine thereupon filed a "bill in equity" in the Circuit Court of the United States, Delaware District, seeking an injunction to prevent the recent instructions of the board from being carried out and "to test the right of the Company to prevent or charge a toll for the transportation of passengers through the Canal." The case was heard during the May, 1847, term of the court, with James A. Bayard and Henry D. Gilpin representing the company. The court found against the company, but the fact that one judge had dissented, claiming that "There is no use granted to the public of this navigation for transportation of passengers, more than there is right granted to the company to take toll on passengers," encouraged the company to appeal the decision to the Supreme Court.[34]

Nearly three years passed before the high court rendered its decision, a powerful statement drafted by Chief Justice Taney. In it Taney rejected each of the major contentions of the canal company and supplied added information concerning his views on the rights of corporations as opposed to the rights of the public. A corporation, he said, is "a mere creature of the law," and it can exercise no powers except those conferred upon it. In cases where ambiguities concerning those powers exist, they must always operate against the corporation and in favor of the public. "The rights of the public are never presumed to be surrendered to a corporation, unless the intention to surrender clearly appears in the law." The philosophy of this decision was strikingly similar to that in the first decision that Taney wrote as Chief Justice. In the *Charles River Bridge* v. *Warren Bridge* case in 1837, he had rejected the "doctrine of implied contracts" in ruling that corporate charters could not confer implied powers beyond the specific terms of the grant. His faith as a Jacksonian in a free, competitive economy was expressed in both decisions.[35]

[34] *Ibid.*, March 30, April 24, 1847; *Supreme Court of the United States, No. 141. The Chesapeake and Delaware Canal Company, Defendant, vs. John A. Perrine, Complainant. Opinion of Hall, District Judge, May Term, 1847* (Philadelphia, n.d.), p. 3.
[35] *Reports of Decisions in the Supreme Court*, XVIII, 86, 94; *Charles River Bridge* v. *Warren Bridge*, quoted in *Liberty and Justice: A Historical Record of American Constitutional Development*, ed. James Morton Smith and Paul L. Murphy (New York, 1958), p. 176.

Two specific questions were involved in the canal company case: (1) may the company charge a toll on passengers in Perrine's boats? (2) may Perrine navigate the canal to transport passengers, paying toll upon the boats as empty? In delivering his opinion, Taney reviewed the history of the canal company and emphasized the conditional nature of its charter which made it a compact among the three incorporating states. In authorizing the canal company, Pennsylvania agreed that the Susquehanna River was to be a public highway, but the canal "was intended to be equally free and open." To insure this, Pennsylvania had inserted the clause that neither Maryland nor Pennsylvania could alter the charter of the company without the consent of the other. The river and the canal, Taney reasoned, were "portions of the same line of navigation, and there could be no reason of justice or policy for stopping at the canal the passengers who came down the Susquehanna on their way to Philadelphia." In other words, it could not be assumed that either Maryland or Pennsylvania had intended to give the canal corporation the power to interrupt that line of communication. Both waterways were to be public highways.[36]

With that as general introduction, Taney then proceeded to examine the powers of the company in regard to tolls. The articles on which tolls could be levied were enumerated in the charter, with the amount specified; "Passengers are not mentioned. . . ." As corporations may exercise only those powers specifically conferred upon them, he concluded that no passenger toll could be "lawfully taken."[37]

In regard to the second question, Taney recognized that the company based its prohibition of Perrine's passenger boats on section 11 of the Maryland charter: "The said canal . . . when completed, shall forever thereafter be esteemed and taken to be navigable as a public highway, free for the transportation of all goods, commodities, or produce whatsoever, on payment of the toll imposed by this act." But to interpret the section to mean that only "goods, commodities, or produce," not passengers, could be transported was inconsistent with other parts of the charter and "any just rule for the interpretation of statutes. . . . The error consists in treating words, which were intended as a limitation of the powers of the corporation, as a restriction upon the rights of the public."[38]

The Chief Justice admitted that water travel was "inconsiderable and unimportant" when the charters were granted, compared with its

[36] *Reports of Decisions in the Supreme Court*, XVIII, 85–86.
[37] *Ibid.*, p. 86.
[38] *Ibid.*, pp. 88–89.

importance at the present time, and that "nobody anticipated the immense increase which the invention of steam navigation has produced." But vessels in trade had always carried passengers, and water travel was especially widespread in Maryland, with its broad bay and many navigable tidewater streams. It could not be inferred that the Maryland legislature meant to authorize the company to "deprive the public of the cheapest and most convenient mode of passing from the Chesapeake Bay to the city of Philadelphia" in adopting its charter. The legislature might well have granted the company the right to take a toll from passengers, but it was the duty of the court to expound the law as it was, not to enlarge the powers of corporations. He concluded that the company was without authority to refuse passage to passenger vessels.[39]

Exception was taken to Taney's ruling on the second question by three members of the court. Justice McLean, who wrote the dissent for the three, felt that both questions should have been answered negatively. The company was not required to accommodate the public as a duty, except as the charter imposed this, and the existing charter imposed no obligation on the company to transport passengers, to do that for which it received no compensation. The majority opinion, however, stood, and as a result of the decision of Taney's court, the Chesapeake and Delaware Canal continued to provide free passenger service for thousands annually. The canal thus became toll-free for passengers some seventy years before it became, in 1919, toll-free to vessels, following its purchase by the government.

[39] *Ibid.*, pp. 90–92.

Prewar Problems: The 1850's

8

The canal weathered its second decade of operations without experiencing any major maintenance problems, although the increasing trade in the 1840's indicated that its accommodations would soon have to be improved. The water supply available at the summit proved to be inadequate, and the limited capacity of the locks prevented many vessels customarily employed in the bay and coastal trade from using the canal. Other facilities, such as bridges and lockgates, were steadily deteriorating. A considerable amount of the company's income during the early part of the 1850's was appropriated to the repair or replacement of canal property.

Enlargement of the canal locks and provisions for increasing the water supply had been contemplated as early as 1846, but repeated applications to the government for assistance had failed. The company thereupon undertook to remedy the most pressing problem, that of water supply, itself. While considering possible ways of financing the improvement, the company decided to sponsor a contest "for the best design of a steam pump" suitable for use at Chesapeake City. The pump was to be capable of lifting at least 200,000 cubic feet of water per hour a distance of 16 feet. Announcement of the competition was made in August, 1848: $300 was offered as first prize, $200 for second prize, and $100 was to be given "for any other design the company chooses to retain."[1]

[1] *Blue Hen's Chicken* (Wilmington), August 18, 1848.

[122]

The number of entries in the contest exceeded all expectations; some 50 plans were submitted, and slightly over half of them retained for further study. Not until the winter of 1850 did the company make its final decision, for the task of evaluating the different designs proved exceedingly difficult. A suggestion by two outstanding Philadelphia engineers, Samuel V. Merrick and John H. Towne, that a steam-operated lifting or scoop wheel rather than a pump be used particularly intrigued the board, and it requested further details. The two men submitted a model of their device, together with estimates of the construction and operating costs, in February, 1849, and in March, all the designs, models, and estimates were referred to engineers John C. Cresson and M. W. Baldwin for expert evaluations.[2]

After considerable study, Cresson and Baldwin declined making a specific recommendation, but they did expound upon the general principles which should guide the company in making its selection. "Of all the known methods of raising water for economical purposes," they pointed out, "the three varieties represented in your drawings and models, to wit — the force pump, lifting pump and scoop wheel, are believed to approach most nearly to excellence, and to relative equality as respects practicability and theoretical economy." Theoretically, any of the three would be suitable, and should yield "economical results." The selection therefore should be governed by relative first cost and durability, which criteria prompted the engineers to eliminate the force pump from consideration. The choice lay between a simple lifting pump and a scoop wheel, and they suggested that since the two were so nearly equal in all respects, the one be selected which could be constructed at the lower cost.[3]

Enlightened by the report but not relieved of its responsibility to make the final determination, the committee making the selection at length was able to reduce the choice to three by selecting the best of each of the three possible types. In reporting this much progress to the board in December, 1849, the committee recommended that the persons submitting the three plans should be paid $100 each, according to the company offer. Following adoption of one of the plans, the remainder of the awards would be paid. After "numerous meetings," including interviews with "several of the proposers of Plans and Explanations," the committee held a special meeting on April 8, 1850, to make its final decision. When a vote was taken, two members of

[2] Board Minute Book, October 3, November 4, 1848.
[3] John C. Cresson and M. W. Baldwin to Thomas Gilpin, Philadelphia, May 22, 1849, entered *ibid.*, May 29, 1849.

the committee, including its chairman, Thomas Gilpin, favored the lifting pump; three favored the scoop wheel according to the plan of Merrick and Towne. President Newbold, when he was consulted, also expressed himself in favor of the wheel.[4]

The committee members delayed making their final report to the board, however, until they had inspected a steam pump used at the United States Dry Dock in Brooklyn. The committee journeyed to New York in December to observe the pump in action, but it was deemed "so expensive in its construction and movement, as to render it entirely unsuitable for us." Instead, they returned to their original choice and recommended the "Scoop wheel, and the kind of Engine as suggested by Messrs. Merrick & Son under such guarantees as to both the performance of the Engine and Wheel as the Board may deem entirely satisfactory." Four members of the committee now signed the report, but Gilpin still disagreed with the majority and asked to be excused when the same committee was requested to carry out the recommendations in the report.[5]

A contract for the scoop wheel and engine with the firm of Merrick & Son was made early in the following year, with the amount set at $22,000. The machinery was to fit the specifications previously drawn up by the board and be capable of raising a minimum of 200,000 cubic feet of water an hour at reasonable cost. The contractors guaranteed that less than 560 pounds of coal would be consumed each hour in raising the water. Considerable progress in building and erecting the wheel and engine was made by November, but a short delay came when a cracked bedplate under the engine had to be replaced. It was possible to make a brief trial of the wheel in April, 1852, but more extensive tests were made in July when it was left in continuous operation for 78½ hours. During this time, the average quantity of water raised per hour was 227,160 cubic feet, at an average coal consumption rate of 613 pounds an hour, or about 540 pounds for every 200,000 cubic feet lifted.

A close check was maintained on the performance of the water wheel during its first months of operation. A tiny notebook among the company archives contains data for the period from June 9 to July 14, 1852, listing the speed of the engine and wheel, the volume of water raised, the amount of coal consumed, and the total running time. A typical entry reads as follows: "24 June. Engine and Wheel ran 12 hours to day. The dip of wheel was 1 foot 8 inches Revolutions of

[4] *Ibid.*, May 7, 1850.
[5] *Ibid.*, December 24, 27, 1850.

Engine 21 to the Minute Of Wheel 2 in 55 seconds, Measurement taken by Hedrick & Poole. Average depth in Schute 7.111 inches, time in passing 30 feet, 4 seconds, Amt. thrown 201,330 C Feet 4 tons 300 pounds of Coal consumed in 12 hours."

The machinery performed close to the standards required, but there remained some question about the durability of both the wheel and engine. In November, 1853, the president stated that he believed the wheel itself could be braced and reinforced to make it adequate for the job, but a more powerful steam engine, or a second engine "of like power with the present one and working at right angles to it at the opposite end of the shaft is absolutely required." He favored building the second engine, "for reasons entirely familiar and well known to all who have knowledge or experience in the working of Steam Engines," although that would require a large addition to the building then housing the equipment. A committee appointed to study the problem agreed with the recommendations, and the same firm of Merrick & Son was authorized to do the work.[6]

Within a short time after the scoop wheel and single engine were installed, an illustrated article in the *Journal of the Franklin Institute* described their technical features. The wheel, 39 feet in diameter and 10 feet wide, was made of wood and iron, and consisted of 12 "buckets." As the wheel revolved, water scooped into the buckets flowed out lateral discharge openings located near the center of the wheel. "Toothed segments, forming spur wheels 39 feet diameter at pitch line and 11 inches face, 3¼ inches pitch, are bolted, one on each rim, and gear into two pinions four feet diameter, keyed to the fly wheel shaft of a condensing beam engine, the cylinder of which is 36 inches diameter and 7 feet stroke." With the engine running at normal speed, 24 revolutions per minute, the wheel made 2.46 revolutions and delivered the contents of 29.5 buckets. A "dip" of 20 inches was maintained by gates located between Back Creek and the feeder sluice and regulated by floats.[7]

After the second engine was added in 1854, the wheel performed still more satisfactorily. The board was informed in March, 1855, that the "Lifting Wheel with the new and old engine attached has been set to work; the result thus far is most satisfactory." By use of the addi-

[6] *Ibid.*, November 22, 1853.
[7] "Chesapeake and Delaware Canal Wheel for Raising Water," *Journal of the Franklin Institute*, LV (February, 1853), 93–95. Possibly this account was written by Samuel V. Merrick, who helped design the wheel and whose company installed it. Merrick was a founder of the Franklin Institute and served as its president between 1842 and 1854.

tional steam engine, the revolutions of the engines were reduced to 18 per minute, the wheel to 2, but its dip was increased to 28 inches. "The Engines work with entire ease to themselves, and to the Wheel, the consumption of fuel will be diminished and the quantity of water increased." In 1856, as feared, it was necessary to replace the water wheel with a sturdier model, at a cost of $6,000, but thereafter no major troubles were experienced.[8]

The huge water wheel and steam engines remained in continuous use for the duration of the waterway's existence as a lock canal, or from 1852 until 1927, and their fame increased as the years passed. In 1873, in an article on "The Big Canal Wheel at Chesapeake City" in a Delaware newspaper, it was stated that the "immense wheel . . . is one of the curiosities of the country. There is none like it in the United States." After pointing out that the wheel, powered by two 150-horsepower engines with two immense boilers which consumed 8 tons of Cumberland coal daily, could lift 170 tons of water a minute and usually ran 18 to 24 hours a day, the article mentioned a recent performance of the wheel. A breach in the canal wall in 1873 let much of the water escape from the summit level. After the break was repaired, the wheel refilled the 9-mile level of the canal in just ten days, "one of the greatest feats in hydraulic ever recorded."[9]

President Newbold did not live to see the water wheel completed or the other improvements made later in the 1850's. He died January 10, 1852, at the age of 70, having served the company as director, superintendent, or president during the twenty-nine years since its revival. Robert M. Lewis, who had previously served as president, was elected to complete Newbold's term of office, although he was relieved of the necessity of regularly visiting the canal. Because of the added responsibility which fell upon the secretary, Peter Lesley, and the superintendent, John R. Price, the salaries of both were increased. In 1853, Andrew C. Gray of New Castle, Delaware, whose only previous connection with the canal company had been his occasional employment by the company as its legal counsel in Delaware, became the sixth president of the company and served until his death in 1885. Gray was a highly respected lawyer in Delaware who gave up his practice of

[8] Board Minute Book, March 15, 1855.

[9] *Every Evening* (Wilmington), August 1, 1873. See also Greville Bathe, "The Lift Wheel Pumping Plant of the Chesapeake and Delaware Canal," chapter IX of *An Engineer's Miscellany* (Philadelphia, 1938), pp. 101–116. The canal enlargement project of the 1960's has encroached upon the original location of the wheel, but provisions have been made for moving and preserving this unique feature of the old lock canal.

twenty-seven years in order to accept the presidency of the canal company.[10]

One of Gray's first tasks upon becoming president was to supervise the construction of new, enlarged locks for the canal. In January, 1853, the board was told by President Lewis that "an increase of the facilities in passing the Locks is necessary, and that a further increase of the means of Lockage will probably be soon required to accommodate the increasing trade of the canal, in coal and other bulky articles." The frequency of lockages in the past year had increased from one every 29 minutes before June 1 to one every 22 minutes since then, Sundays excepted, and the trade showed no signs of diminishing. Accordingly, a committee was appointed to hire a competent engineer "to look into the expediency and expense of doubling or enlarging the present locks, so as to accommodate the anticipated increase of trade on the canal." When Gray succeeded Lewis in April, 1853, he was requested to proceed without delay with the plan for new locks.[11]

A prominent civil engineer of Philadelphia, Ashbel Welsh, who later became president of the American Society of Civil Engineers, was employed in July, 1853, to plan and supervise the new construction. Reporting in September, Welsh expressed his belief that, in order to provide the best service, the locks should be 220 feet long, 24 feet wide, and 10 feet deep. He suggested that only three locks be constructed, with one of double lift replacing the two then in use at Chesapeake City. To reduce by half the amount of water lost in locking vessels in and out of the canal, he recommended that a "saving basin" be constructed adjacent to the large single lock. The sides of each lock were to be of rubble masonry, and faced with timber; two of the lockgates were to be of the swinging, horizontal type, one was to be a dropgate. Welsh's recommendations were accepted by the board, and his specifications for constructing the locks were printed.[12]

Sealed bids for doing the work were received from four contractors, with the prices ranging from $171,000 to $280,000. The high bid was immediately eliminated, but the two middle bids exceeded the engineer's estimate of $210,000 by only $5,000 and $6,000. As the low bid from the firm of Candee, Dodge, and Reed was from "parties who have hitherto been strangers in this section of the country," and although they were highly recommended by previous em-

---

[10] *Every Evening*, January 14, 1885.
[11] Board Minute Book, January 4, April 26, 1853.
[12] Specification of the Additional Locks on the Chesapeake and Delaware Canal, September, 1853, C & D Papers, HSD.

ployers, Gray favored accepting the bid of $216,000 from Rice, Stone, Vandever, Quigly, and McClanahan: "Four out of five of these gentlemen reside in the neighborhood of the Canal in Delaware and Maryland. They are well known in that part of the country, are men of means, experienced and energetic contractors." He believed it would be in the best interests of the company "to contract with them even at their higher bid on account of their business connections with the people of Delaw. & Maryd. and of the possible injury that may accrue to the Company in consequence of not employing them . . . & giving it to strangers at a price which there is ground to fear is lower than it can be done for, especially as the amount of the bid of the former exceeds the estimate of the Engineer only $6,000." The board rejected this reasoning, although its correctness was soon proved, and voted to accept the bid from Candee, Dodge, and Reed. The locks were to be completed by June, 1854, and a security was requested to assure faithful performance.[13]

It then was necessary to arrange for the financing of the new locks. Once again the company looked to the federal government, holder of more than one third of its common stock, on which $13,500 had recently been paid in dividends. A petition seeking either an appropriation or a loan from the government was submitted to Congress in February, 1854, and referred to the Committee on Roads and Canals. This committee declined to recommend either the appropriation or the loan, and instead considered a bill authorizing the Secretary of the Treasury to dispose of the company stock held by the government at public auction. Only $13,500 had been returned on an investment of $450,000 in almost thirty years, the cost of the waterway as a result of the new lock construction and resulting necessary enlargement of the approaches to the canal would swell to nearly $4,000,000, and part of the company's funded debt was to fall due in 1856, thus making it almost certain that no more dividends would be paid for several years. "This," the committee informed Secretary of the Treasury James Guthrie, "as well as the general objection to the Government holding stock in private corporations, both with a loss to itself and injury to individual stockholders, has induced the committee to pursue the course above indicated." Unfortunately for a subsequent generation of company officials, Guthrie disagreed and the government retained its stock in the company.[14]

[13] Board Minute Book, September 13, 1853.
[14] A Member of the Committee on Roads and Canals to James Guthrie, Secretary of the Treasury, Washington, March 20, 1854, copy in C & D Papers, HSD.

Disappointed again at not having received further aid from the government, the company resumed its efforts to raise the necessary amount through new loans. In July, 1853, the stockholders and loan-holders had approved a loan application of up to $500,000 to finance necessary new construction. On the basis of the engineering report and the bids received, the Finance Committee considered that a loan of $250,000 would be sufficient and took steps to market the necessary bonds. But it proved difficult to find purchasers for the new bonds. The secretary-treasurer of the company reported in May, 1854, that he had received "no sealed proposals for the loan of $250,000 or any part thereof." Eventually subscribers to most of the loan were obtained, but they paid only $87 for every $100 certificate issued, and were given equal privileges with the holders of the loan due in 1856.[15]

While the financing was being arranged, construction of the new locks proceeded rapidly and without interruption to the trade of the canal. The contractors, however, were forced in June, 1854, to seek a modification in their contract price, having encountered "unforeseen difficulties in the prosecution of the work" and an "increase in the price of labour and materials." The total amount paid to the contractors on an original bid of $171,000 was $249,738.36; the total cost of the enlargement, including real estate costs, engineering fees, and additional dredging, was more than $350,000. The excess was paid from current income, profits in 1854 exceeding $46,000. The new locks, although more expensive than anticipated, were extremely well built and remained in use until 1927. Following completion of the new locks, the Ericsson Line steamboats grew in size until eventually there were only inches to spare when these oddly proportioned, awkward-looking vessels squeezed into the locks.[16]

In addition to the improvements achieved by enlarged locks nearly double the size of the originals and by the scoop wheel which made it possible to maintain a 10-foot rather than an 8-foot depth of water at most times in the year, various other steps were taken. Steam towboats for use on the canal, in addition to the teams of mules commonly used, were admitted in 1852, and in 1860 a telegraph line erected between Delaware City and Chesapeake City improved the service of the canal. Earlier a telegraph office had been opened in Delaware City, as a condition of the canal company's subscription to the Ocean, Delaware, and Philadelphia Telegraph Company, but

[15] Board Minute Book, May 2, June 20, 1854.
[16] *Thirty-sixth General Report* (1855), p. 7.

not until 1860 was a line strung between the two villages at either end of the canal.

The maintenance problem continued to be one of great magnitude on this as on most other canals; indeed, most predictions concerning the canal's future and its potential earning capacity failed to allot enough money to the repair and upkeep of the property. The company officials, in listing only those items which had received attention during the past year, reported in June, 1852, that Delaware Harbor, greatly obstructed with mud because of recent heavy storms, had been cleared by the company's dredgers; that the pivot bridge at St. Georges had been replaced, the old one too decayed to repair; and that major repairs had been made to Summit Bridge. "The Skewbacks on each of the sides of this bridge, which received the thrust, and sustained the weight of the two center ribs or arches, were found to be so much decayed, as to place this costly bridge in great jeopardy; requiring the defective timber to be removed, and its place supplied by sound wood of larger dimensions." In addition, "large quantities of earth" had been removed from the sides and bottom of the canal in the deep cut, a small harbor for vessels at Chesapeake City had been built, and houses had been erected for the superintendent and both lockkeepers at Chesapeake City. The board explained that these ordinary and extraordinary expenses, as well as the service on the debt, had absorbed the year's revenue. "These circumstances are to be regretted. But it may not perhaps be too sanguine to infer from the preceding statements, that the net income of the Company may hereafter realize the hopes and long cherished expectations of its Proprietors." [17]

Traffic passing through the canal in the 1850's did, indeed, reach new highs. Tonnage exceeded 400,000 in 1852, 500,000 in 1854, and 600,000 in 1857, and averaged just under 500,000 tons annually. Toll receipts failed to keep pace with the increases in tonnage, but income for the decade averaged $220,440, while expenses averaged $55,514. The chief items of trade were grain and lumber as usual, but coal now joined the list of leading items. In the 1840's, less than 20,000 tons of coal passed through the canal annually, whereas in the following decade more than six times that amount, over 127,000 tons a year, was carried through. Bituminous coal from the Cumberland fields was shipped north, anthracite coal from Pennsylvania was shipped south through the canal. Trade from the Susquehanna Valley

[17] *Thirty-third General Report* (1852), pp. 8–12.

continued to dominate the overall traffic statistics, and the steam towboat service on upper Chesapeake Bay remained important to both
the fortunes of Philadelphia merchants and the canal company. Between the opening of the Susquehanna and Tidewater Canal in 1840
and June 1, 1860, more than 50,000 vessels from that canal had been
towed to Chesapeake City for passage through the Chesapeake and
Delaware Canal. In 1857, statistics published in *Hunt's Merchants'
Magazine* giving the number of canal boats towed to Philadelphia
as compared to Baltimore demonstrated that Philadelphia continued
to receive slightly more than 50 per cent of the Susquehanna trade.[18]

TABLE 4. NUMBER OF CANAL BOATS TOWED TO PHILADELPHIA AND
BALTIMORE, 1849–57[a]

Year	To Philadelphia	To Baltimore
1849	2,262	1,560
1850	2,576	1,640
1851	2,933	2,047
1852	2,899	2,412
1853	2,842	2,521
1854	2,317	2,556
1855	3,137	2,642
1856	3,024	2,648
1857	2,292	2,317

[a]Source: *Hunt's Merchants' Magazine*, XXXVIII (1857), 383.

Several factors prevented a more rapid growth in the trade of
the canal. Railroad competition increased following the completion
of inter-sectional or trunk line railroads in the early 1850's, particularly the Pennsylvania Railroad. This line was completed through
to Pittsburgh in 1852, and it succeeded in attracting "a considerable
portion of the light and valuable merchandise" which formerly had
been carried by way of the Chesapeake and Delaware Canal and the
Baltimore and Ohio Railroad "to and from the West and South Western States." Another factor was an increased use of the outside route
from Philadelphia to Norfolk and Richmond. For the most part, the
vessels employed in this trade were steamboats, many of which were
too large for the original canal locks. This was one important consideration which induced the board to go even further into debt to

[18] MacGill, *History of Transportation*, p. 221; *Thirty-fifth General Report*
(1854), p. 8n; *Hunt's Merchants' Magazine*, XXXVIII (1857), 382–383. See
Table 4.

provide better and enlarged accommodations on the canal in 1853 and 1854.[19]

The increasing competition with railroads and other forms of transportation also forced the company to make constant revisions in its toll schedules. Competition with the Pennsylvania Railroad for the western trade led the company to reduce rates on traffic destined for Wheeling, Virginia, or beyond to only 20 per cent of the regular rates. The Committee on Tolls believed the drastic cut necessary "to secure any portion of the trade to the West." Later, in 1859, the company resolved to set a maximum payment of $50 on sail vessels, "owing in part to the anticipated opening of the Atlantic and Chesapeake Canal [from Albemarle Sound to Norfolk, Virginia] and that vessels now going by the outside passage (by sea) to and from southern ports, may be induced to pass through the canal, via the Chesapeake Bay."[20]

Other problems were encountered in regard to the collection of tolls. The schedule of tolls adopted early in 1850 and printed for distribution listed in detail the sail-vessel rates on all commodities. A separate brief list at the bottom of the printed sheet listed the steamboat and steam-towed boat rates, except for those engaged in the trade of the Susquehanna and Tidewater Canal. On a few articles, the full rates authorized by the charter were to be charged; on all other articles, the same rates as applied to the sail vessels, with the addition of 50 per cent, were levied. Special regulations printed on the toll sheet revealed many of the problems the canal company faced in its day-to-day operations. A system of charging vessels that did not pass all the way through the canal, based upon the number of locks passed, was set forth; the policy of the company when tolls were to be charged by weight was clarified — all such packages were to have the weight of the package and its contents "marked legibly thereon: and in the absence of such marks, the package or parcel shall . . . be taken as 'NOT ENUMERATED OR UNKNOWN,' and assessed or charged accordingly"; and steamboats, rafts, floats or arks would be admitted to the canal only under special permission. Rafts of deep-floating oak were barred altogether, and all rafts or floats of lumber or timber were charged higher rates than vessels carrying the same items.[21]

[19] *Thirty-third General Report* (1852), pp. 6–7.
[20] Board Minute Book, March 8, 1853, March 1, 1859.
[21] Toll Sheet, March 5, 1850, C & D Papers, HSD. Oak rafts were barred because they floated very low in the water and constituted traffic hazards. Ac-

There was reason to suspect some of the freight manifests offered by the shippers, particularly those of some of the transportation lines trading through the canal which paid their tolls monthly in the Philadelphia office, and those offered by persons rafting lumber and timber through. On one occasion the company paid a bonus of $200 to a man in Chesapeake City for "the valuable information given by him" in regard to frauds in the measurement of timber passing through the canal. Earlier, in March, 1846, David F. Karsner had been appointed as the company's "Examining Agent" in order to prevent "Frauds in the payment of Tolls," but despite his diligent work the problem continued. A special committee on the "returns of manifests" was appointed in 1849 to study the matter, particularly the method used by the Ericsson Line in reporting its freight trade. Although the committee saw no necessity for changing the manner of keeping accounts, it suggested the appointment of another "agent whose duty it should be frequently and diligently to examine the original manifests and the returns of all the lines passing through the Canal, as also those of transient vessels. In the large business of the . . . canal, it is thought that this duty faithfully performed would save much to this company by detecting or preventing omissions whether the result of design accident or carelessness." Joseph S. Hinchman was duly appointed, having been hired jointly with the Susquehanna and Tidewater Canal Company; although Hinchman was soon removed from the position for reasons not given, a successor was found to do the job.[22]

To tighten its control over the shippers of timber through the canal, the company appointed its own measurer of the amount of timber in the rafts and floats seeking passage. Because of the unwieldy nature of the rafts, the company also adopted a new regulation concerning them:

No float of Timber, Boards, or other Lumber, shall be allowed to be so disposed of, or placed in such a position, as to obstruct the channel of BACK CREEK, or the approach to or departure from the lock, of any boat or vessel, or of another float, having permission from the Collector

cording to R. Dudley Tonkin, son of one of the prominent Susquehanna lumbermen, most shippers added enough white pine to such rafts "to carry the oak above the water level." *My Partner, the River: The White Pine Story on the Susquehanna* (New York, 1958), p. 28. See also Joseph Dudley Tonkin, *The Last Raft* (Harrisburg, Pennsylvania, 1940), especially pp. 88–97, for a discussion of the Susquehanna Valley's ship-spar industry and the movement of the spars through the Atlantic coastal canals en route to shipyards in Philadelphia and various New England ports.

[22] Board Minute Book, April 1, 1857, March 24, 1846, March 6, 1849.

of tolls to enter the Canal. And it is hereby made the duty of the proper officers or agents of the Company to enforce this resolution, by bringing suit against the party violating it, as often as the same may be violated. And in order, as far as possible, to prevent a recurrence of such difficulties as are complained of, it shall not be lawful for any float to be brought within two miles of the Maryland lock, until the same shall be fully prepared to enter the Canal.

It was necessary to have strict regulations over this type of craft, for the company was responsible for keeping the canal in a good and safe condition. In March, 1854, the owners of the canal boat *Adriatic* received damages from the canal company caused by a "collision with floating logs in [the] canal."[23]

The new regulation and the appointment of the company measurer proved irksome to the shippers of timber, even the legitimate ones, but the company was convinced of the necessity of both. George Churchman, a lumberman of Kensington, Pennsylvania, represented the viewpoint of the shippers to the Philadelphia market in a letter to an official of the Du Pont Company in 1853:

I write rather hastily — yet will State Some of our grievances we have Suffered at the hands of the Del. & Ches. Canal Coy. for years gone by — & having time to got Cool perhaps will skip Some of the hard words we have often repeated — *First*. Our River bill (of Purchase) are not allowed as Sufficient to pass through the Canal — *Second*. The Company puts their own Measurer on our timber & his acct. *only* will admit us in and out, for his work we pay & find a man or men to assist, the Company paying nothing, for the year of 1852 I think we paid the Measurer about 480 or 500 $ exclusive of help — and worse than all the detention in getting into the Canal & through has been the worst feature in the Case — I believe we can prove of a Month or more delay of a gang of men (8 to 12) & not getting a locking of timber through — I now speak of one mans party & perhaps three or four parties nearly all in the Same bad fix not allowed to Lock even when nothing else was doing — Keep a gang of men up all night perhaps get three or four lockings in, perhaps none "answer no water" no boats or vessels Coming down, you Cannot go up — *Thirdly* the monopoly in towing from which we have Suffered much delay & insolence — we have had *permission* to move our utentials — bed & bedding provisions &c. from a Shanty in the Creek to another in the Canal — on a raft or locking of timber — exposed — shourery & wet april day — hauled into the lock — a vessel coming in Sight ordered by the Same Worthy to haul out — vessel in — we kept back — well Soaked & all hands slept in wet beds & buffaloes that night which would have been moored between the Showers, in Short we Could not lock in when vessels was present & Scarcely when

[23] Regulations to be Observed by Vessels Navigating the Chesapeake and Delaware Canal, and Back Creek, March 5, 1850, C & D Papers, HSD; Board Minute Book, March 7, 1854.

not expected. We pay one Cent pr Cub Foot on timber and I think 83 cents
pr Cu ft on Sawd lumber when on timber, Sawd lumber in vessels did (&
perhaps yet) pay 62½ cts—*Fourthly*, the timber men on their Stock alone
pay generally about one eight or tenth of the whole amount of Tolls received annually — last year we must at the same ratio of receipts in Canal
or aggregate, have paid about one fourth or fifth of whole amount in a
round Sum Say from 50 to 55000 $ Toll

Our Moneys have been paid without trouble or cost — to them & I
think we should have had better treatment — or at least worthy of some
consideration —

It is but justice to Say that we have had last year better treatment &
less delay — had we been Subject to the Same attention as formerly — the
Season would have been too short for us.[24]

Churchman, though perhaps somewhat overstating his case, correctly emphasized the considerable amount of timber and lumber
which moved through the canal. In the 1850's, tolls were paid on
approximately 50,000,000 square feet of lumber and 2,800,000 cubic
feet of timber annually.

Canal transportation in the country as a whole remained important throughout the decade of the 1850's, and indeed some of
the better located waterways enjoyed their peak tonnages long after
the Civil War. In 1853, in a report submitted to Congress by Israel D.
Andrews on the trade and commerce of the United States and Canada,
the Chesapeake and Delaware Canal was described as the "only improvement of any considerable importance in Delaware. . . . The
work bears a similar relation to the commerce of the country with
the Raritan canal, and makes up a part of the same system of internal
water-navigation. It is also the channel of a large trade between Chesapeake bay and Philadelphia and New York." The New Castle and
Frenchtown Railroad, "once of considerable importance," was a work
of only "local importance" by that time; and the Philadelphia, Wilmington, and Baltimore Railroad, located on one of the best routes
in the country for lucrative traffic, still derived its income "chiefly . . .
from its passenger traffic." In an appendix to the work, Andrews
submitted his careful estimates on the total commerce of the country
for 1851. The coasting trade remained the most important but canals
played a significant role: "The canal commerce of the United States
is prosecuted upon about 3,000 miles of canal, which, excluding the
coal trade, cleared and landed an average of about 6,000 tons per

[24] George W. Churchman to E. I. du Pont de Nemours & Company,
Kensington, Pennsylvania, January 25, 1853, Old Stone Office Records —
Woolen, Eleutherian Mills Historical Library.

mile. . . . At 6,000 tons per mile 3,000 miles gives 18,000,000 tons, valued at $66 the ton, and forming a gross sum of $1,188,000,-000." The railroads, on the other hand, with more than three times the mileage, did a gross business of 10,815,000 tons, "which, from the general character of railway freight, as being of a lighter and more costly character than water freight, may be valued at $100 the ton; this would give an aggregate of gross railway commerce amounting to $1,081,500,000."[25]

Financially, the 1850's seemed to be the time when the company fortunes were on the upswing. Randel's debt was eliminated in 1851, and in 1853 it was possible for the first time in the fifty years since the organization of the company to declare a dividend on stock. In that year the net profits from a total revenue of $246,283 amounted to $39,483, and the board declared a 3 per cent dividend on the capital stock which amounted to $38,188.90. Construction of the new locks and other improvements prevented similar dividend payments during the remainder of the decade, but it was hoped that the resulting increased accommodations of the canal would permit regular dividends thereafter. In 1856 all debts of the company were consolidated in a new issue of bonds amounting to $2,800,000. The canal property and franchises were mortgaged as security for the loan, payable in thirty years, with interest at 6 per cent payable semiannually. Authorization of the loan had been granted by the Delaware and Maryland legislatures in February, 1855, and January, 1856, respectively.

Although the amount of the loan was only slightly less than the cost of the canal to date, which indicated the greatly reduced value of the common stock, the canal in 1856 was in good shape and the revenue of the company was increasing. It was recognized that the annual interest on the loan, $168,000, would absorb most of the revenue, but provisions were made in 1856 for the regular retirement of a portion of the loan. A Dividend Fund set up in that year required that $25,000 a year, if that amount of surplus was available, should be used to purchase the company bonds, such bonds to be canceled and converted into stock for distribution among the stockholders. It is possible that the company had hopes of eventually retiring the entire debt, or at least reducing it to manageable proportions, and

[25] "Report of Israel D. Andrews on the Trade and Commerce of the British North American Colonies, and upon the Trade of the Great Lakes and Rivers," *Executive Documents*, No. 112, 32nd Congress, 1st Session (Washington, 1853), pp. 315–316, 904–905.

considerable progress was made during the following three decades, but a final blow to those hopes came with the discovery that there had been a fraudulent overissue of bonds by two employees of the company amounting to more than $600,000. A mortgage loan of $2,600,000, instead of one below $2,000,000, had to be refinanced in 1886. But these unhappy revelations were for the future. At the time the prospects of the company looked good. Despite the critical nature of the political situation at the end of the 1850's, the canal company was relatively secure financially, the possessor of a modernized and valuable property, and it was heading into the most prosperous period of its history.

The Canal in the Civil War

9

The intrinsic value of the Chesapeake and Delaware Canal was vividly seen during the Civil War. The judgment of those who in the 1820's had called for government participation in financing the waterway because of its strategic national and military importance was amply vindicated. Through the canal were carried troops and equipment, guns and ammunition, food and clothing, and other supplies of every description; Confederate prisoners were transported via the canal to Fort Delaware, an island fortress a mile offshore from Delaware City which doubled as a prison; "hospital boats carried back to the North wounded men who could have been moved in no other way."[1] New highs were reached in total tonnage transiting the canal, with an average annual traffic in excess of 790,000 tons between 1862 and 1865. Although these tonnage figures were often exceeded in the postwar years, never again did the company income surpass $424,313 in a single year, the amount of the toll receipts in 1864–65.

Early in the war, moreover, the canal demonstrated its military usefulness and significance in a dramatic way. Shortly after the inauguration of President Lincoln, the national capital was threatened with the possibility of being captured or absorbed into the Confederacy. Loyalties were divided in Washington as well as in the surrounding states of Virginia and Maryland when Lincoln took office, and an uneasy

[1] Robert Rossiter Raymond, "The Chesapeake and Delaware Canal in the Civil War," *Professional Memoirs*, Corps of Engineers, United States Army, and Engineer Department at Large, III (1911), 269.

calm prevailed for more than a month. Seven states had seceded and more were considering the step when the firing on Fort Sumter and the subsequent call for 75,000 volunteers by Lincoln in mid-April forced a decision. Virginia seceded on April 17, 1861, and only the refusal of Governor Thomas H. Hicks, the Unionist governor of Maryland, to convene the legislature at once prevented the possibility of Maryland quickly following suit. The sentiment in Baltimore was clearly pro-Southern, and the few available militia companies from the North which were being rushed to the defense of Washington by way of Baltimore antagonized certain elements within the Maryland city.

On April 18, only three days after Lincoln's call for volunteers, a small number of "unarmed and ununiformed Pennsylvanians" arrived in Baltimore on their way to Washington. They had traveled from Harrisburg on the Northern Central Railroad. Because continuous railway service through the city did not exist, the troops marched from the Bolton Station to the Camden Street Station, where the trains for Washington were boarded. A "howling mob" displaying secession flags and cheering for Jefferson Davis escorted the Pennsylvania militia as it marched through the city, but no blows were struck or shots fired. On the same day, troops from Massachusetts' Sixth Regiment, also en route to Washington, passed through New York amid the cheers of a crowd, making "a triumphal march through the city." [2]

The following day, when the Massachusetts troops reached Baltimore, a riotous attack was made upon them as they proceeded through the streets to the Camden Station. The hourly progress of the soldiers as they made their way south from New York had been reported in Baltimore by telegraph, and tension within the city mounted. Colonel Edward F. Jones, in command of the regiment, had learned during the morning of April 19 that the movement of his troops through Baltimore might be resisted. Accordingly, he ordered ammunition distributed but gave strict orders for a quick march through the city and for no retaliation unless the group was fired upon. When the train arrived, it was first attempted to have the railway cars towed through the streets with the troops inside. After 9 cars in the 35-car train had safely reached the Camden Street Station, despite the jeers, stones, and brickbats hurled at them, the surging mob, estimated to consist of 10,000 people, blocked the passage of any more. According to a Confederate

[2] Bradley T. Johnson, "Maryland," in *Confederate Military History: A Library of Confederate States History*, ed. Clement A. Evans (Atlanta, 1899), II, 17; Frank Moore, ed., *The Rebellion Record: A Diary of American Events, with Documents, Narratives, Illustrative Incidents, Poetry, Etc.* (New York, 1862), I, 32.

history of the incident, the passage of the 9 cars "was as much as human nature could bear. The mob of infuriated men increased every minute and the excitement grew. The stones out of the street flew up and staved in the car windows." [3]

It was then decided to march the men to the station. As the troops debarked from the stalled cars and began marching in columns of four towards Camden Street Station, Mayor George W. Brown joined the captain of the leading company and persuaded the crowd to let them pass. This was done, but the unruly crowd closed in again on the troops behind. A northern newspaper account of the Baltimore riot described the scene which followed:

The military behaved admirably, and still abstained from firing upon their assailants. The mob now commenced a perfect shower of missiles, occasionally varied by a random shot from a revolver or one of the muskets taken from the soldiers. The soldiers suffered severely from the immense quantity of stones, brickbats, paving-stones, &c.; the shots fired also wounded several. When two of the soldiers had been killed, and the wounded had been conveyed to the centre of the column, the troops at last, exasperated by the treatment they had received, commenced to return the fire singly, but at no time did a platoon fire in a volley. [4]

Eventually the troops fought their way to the station and quickly departed for Washington while the Baltimore police attempted to quiet the mob and count the toll. Three of the soldiers had been killed outright, and one was to die later of a fractured skull. Thirty-six of their number were wounded. The toll among the rioters was likewise heavy, with eight persons killed and many wounded. Prominent and respectable citizens of Baltimore, as well as its rougher element, had participated in the attack, trying to repel what they considered an invasion of the state of Maryland. [5]

While this group continued to control the city, other troops en route to Washington returned to Philadelphia to await new orders. In the meantime, the Baltimore officials were seeking to prevent more troops from entering their city. After a public meeting was held on the afternoon of the day of the riot, at which $500,000 was voted for the defense of the city, President Lincoln was notified by Mayor Brown and Governor Hicks to "send no more troops here." Lincoln's response

[3] Johnson, "Maryland," p. 20.
[4] *New York Times*, April 20, 21, 1861, quoted in Moore, ed., *Rebellion Record*, I, 34.
[5] Charles B. Clark, "Baltimore and the Attack on the Sixth Massachusetts Regiment, April 19, 1861," *Maryland Historical Magazine*, LVI (March, 1961), 47

was that additional troops should be "prepared to fight their way through, if necessary." Still later in the day, Mayor Brown learned from the president of the Philadelphia, Wilmington, and Baltimore Railroad Company that additional troops from Philadelphia were going to be sent through Baltimore. When this information was received, Brown and Police Marshall Kane agreed that the railroad bridges on both the Philadelphia, Wilmington, and Baltimore and the Northern Central railroads should be destroyed to protect the city. These men later testified that Governor Hicks also approved of the plan, although Hicks denied it. At any rate, two parties were sent out on the night of April 19 and the bridges were burned as far north as the Gunpowder River. The Philadelphia newspapers carried this report of the event:

Last night a mob from Baltimore, lying in wait for the train from Philadelphia, at Canton, fired a pistol at the engineer, who stopped the train. The crowd, compelling the passengers to leave the cars, occupied the train, and forced the engineer to take them back to Gunpowder Bridge. There the train was stopped, and the crowd set fire to the draw of the bridge and waited till that portion was burned; returning to Bush River Bridge, the draw was likewise burned. The mob then returned to Canton Bridge and burned that. The train then conveyed the mob to the President-street station.[6]

According to Kane, who headed one of the two parties, the damages inflicted under Police Board sanction were slight, although unauthorized persons subsequently multiplied their extent. Nevertheless, rail communications with the North were completely disrupted. Even the telegraph lines north of Baltimore were cut. Alarm at the events in Baltimore spread throughout the country. The volunteers retreating through Wilmington by train on their way to Philadelphia reported the details of the riot and its aftermath. Armed soldiers patrolled the streets of Wilmington for days afterwards. Anna Ferris, a resident of the city, described the feelings of the people in northern Delaware:

The excitement & suspense are almost intolerable, & the circumstances transpiring around us seem incredible. Yesterday the Massachusetts & Pennsylvania volunteers were attacked by a mob in Baltimore & a number on both sides killed & wounded — & last night the Bridges on our railroad were burned to prevent any more troops being forwarded for the defense of the National Capital — All at once the flames of Civil War seem raging around us. . . . The telegraph wires have been cut, Rail

[6] *Ibid.*, pp. 54–55; *Philadelphia Press*, April 20, 1861, quoted in Moore, ed., *Rebellion Record*, I, 35.

roads torn up, & mails from the South suspended, and we are all the time agitated by alarming & conflicting rumors.

We seem threatened not only with war but anarchy, as the Capital & the Government are in great danger, & the means for their defense very much obstructed & cut off — Baltimore is in possession of the mob, & under martial law, and we feel the greatest anxiety about our friends there, but can hear nothing from them.[7]

Washington was completely isolated from the North save for a single avenue of communication — waterways. The series of events beginning with the secession of Virginia and followed by the Baltimore riots and the severing of communications between Washington and the North threatened the swift capture of Washington by the Confederates. Benjamin Perley Poore described the despairing mood of the city in those days: "Meanwhile, Washington City had been for several days without hearing from the loyal North. At night the camp-fires of the Confederates, who were assembling in force, could be seen on the southern bank of the Potomac, and it was not uncommon to meet on Pennsylvania Avenue a defiant Southerner openly wearing a large Virginia or South Carolina secession badge. The exodus of clerks from the departments continued, and they would not say good-bye, but *au revoir*, as they confidently expected that they would be back again triumphant within a month." The Reverend Charles B. Boynton, who at one time was the chaplain of the House of Representatives and who later taught at the United States Naval Academy and wrote a history of the United States Navy during the Civil War, stated that the boast that Washington would be captured by the end of May was not an unreasonable one. In view of the Potomac River defenses erected by the Confederates, and the "formidable army" rapidly being organized in Virginia, it was a great "mystery" to him that Washington was not taken.[8]

Part of the solution to Boynton's mystery lay in the existence of the Chesapeake and Delaware Canal. It was imperative to the safety of the capital that reinforcements be dispatched to Washington at once, and a Delaware shipowner came forward with an idea for accomplishing this by utilizing the canal. On April 20 Captain Philip Reybold reminded the federal authorities in Philadelphia that certain propeller-

[7] Ferris Diary, April 20, 1861, quoted in Harold Bell Hancock, "The Political History of Delaware during the Civil War, Part II: The Coming of the War," *Delaware History*, VII (March, 1957), 241–242.

[8] Ben: Perley Poore, *Perley's Reminiscences of Sixty Years in the National Metropolis* (Tecumseh, Michigan, 1886), II, 80; Charles B. Boynton, *The History of the Navy during the Rebellion* (New York, 1867), I, 307.

driven steamboats would fit the locks of the canal, and suggested their use to carry troops to Washington. Acting at once on the suggestion, the government commandeered all such steamboats in and around Philadelphia on the 20th. The troops in the city once more headed south.

Some of the propeller steamers were sent, without passengers, through the canal during the night to Perryville, Maryland, on the north bank of the Susquehanna River, where more men and supplies had been rushed by rail. At daybreak the troops, many of them members of the Massachusetts Eighth Regiment, were loaded aboard the vessels and carried down Chesapeake Bay below Baltimore to Annapolis. Landing there, they traveled the remaining distance to Washington by railroad, arriving late on April 21.[9]

When other troops who had been sent in steamboats too large to fit the Chesapeake and Delaware Canal locks completed the journey around the cape and arrived at Annapolis, it was discovered that Southern sympathizers had partially destroyed the railroad leading to Washington. In addition, all of the locomotives on the line had been taken away except one, which was dismantled. But one of the men in the regiment, commanded by General Benjaminin F. Butler, had helped build that particular locomotive and was able to repair it, and 19 men responded to the call for engineers to operate it. After the track also was repaired, the new route to Washington via Perryville and Annapolis remained open.[10]

The steamboat *W. Whildin* was one of those seized on April 20. According to a deposition made by its captain, Abraham Colmary, in connection with another matter, the vessel was loaded and ready to

[9] Testimony of Philip Reybold before the Agnus Commission, "Report of the Commission appointed by the President to Examine and Report upon a Route for the Construction of a Free and Open Waterway to Connect the Waters of the Chesapeake and Delaware Bays," *Senate Documents*, No. 215, 59th Congress, 2nd Session (Washington, 1907), pp. 44–45. Hereafter this will be cited as *Agnus Report*.

[10] "F. J. O'B." described how his regiment, the New York Seventh, "got from New York to Washington" via the outside route in a letter published in the *New York Times*. At 4:30 P.M. on April 20, after arriving in Philadelphia by rail, they boarded the steamer *Boston* and set sail. The first evening "passed delightfully." Because of the short notice for making the steamer ready, however, the vessel was "imperfectly provisioned," and much too small for the 1,000 men aboard, who were forced to sleep "dovetailed." The above information also came from this account, quoted in Moore, ed., *Rebellion Record*, I, 148–154. See also William J. Roehrenbeck, *The Regiment That Saved the Capital* (New York and London, 1961), for a detailed narrative of the New York Seventh's services in the defense of Washington between April 19 and June 3, 1861.

proceed on its daily run when "it was seized and employed under charter by the Government agents at Philadelphia and loaded with company stores for Perryville in Maryland, having first unloaded the goods intended for her regular route — the said Boat continued in Government employ under this Charter until some day in June. . . ." Afterwards, a new contract was made at a lower rate per day with the owners of the vessel, and it remained in the service of the government. During the entire war, the government seized some 144 propeller steamboats for use on the Atlantic coastal bays, rivers, and canals.[11]

It has often been stated that the existence of the canal in 1861 saved Washington from capture. Alvin F. Harlow, in his study of American canals, wrote that "The C. and D. Canal nullified these [Confederate] offensive arrangements and doubtless saved Washington," and John Maloney, ostensibly quoting an army engineer, remarked that the troops who were rushed through the canal to Annapolis "arrived in Washington when Confederate troops were storming the bridges across the Potomac. Lincoln himself said the canal was the Union's salvation." The origin of these statements seems to have been the testimony of Captain Philip Reybold before the Agnus Commission, a special commission established by President Theodore Roosevelt in 1906 to investigate the possibilities of a ship canal across the Delaware Peninsula and the desirability of federal purchase of the existing Chesapeake and Delaware Canal. Reybold, whose father had originally suggested use of the canal to the federal authorities in 1861, related the story to the commission and stated that if the canal had not existed, the Confederate Congress would have convened in Washington rather than Richmond. Had there been no canal, he said, "You would never have heard the cry of 'All quiet on the Potomac' going up, although you might have heard the cry of 'All quiet on the Delaware,' and the blood that soaked into Virginia soil would have been poured out in Pennsylvania and New Jersey, and reconstruction would have taken place in the North instead of the South." [12]

Although the latter portion of his statement was extreme, the general tenor of Reybold's remarks was accurate. Following the Baltimore

[11] Deposition of Captain Abraham Colmary, n.d., Shipping Folder No. 4, Society Collection, HSD; Philip Reybold, "Land-Locked Navigation Along the Atlantic Coast," *Report of the Proceedings of the Third Annual Convention of the Atlantic Deeper Waterways Association* (Philadelphia, 1911), p. 328. Hereafter these reports will be cited as ADWA, *Proceedings*, followed by the date of the conventions.

[12] Harlow, *Old Towpaths*, p. 228; John Maloney, "Chesapeake Odyssey," *National Geographic Magazine*, LXXVI (September, 1939), 379; Testimony of Philip Reybold, *Agnus Report*, pp. 44–45.

riots, telegraphic communications were disrupted for a week, and it was several weeks before the railroad bridges and tracks between Philadelphia and Baltimore were repaired. By that time, because of the troops rushed to Washington by improvised routes and methods, the quick offensive against Washington which the Confederates had been planning was postponed and General Butler had gained control of Baltimore and surrounding areas sufficiently to assure retention of Maryland within the Union. General Bradley Johnson, a Maryland soldier who joined the Southern cause and later was to write the history of Maryland's part in the Civil War, stated that "Maryland's heart was with the Confederacy, but her body was bound and manacled to the Union." [13]

During the critical period between April and June while overland communications were disrupted, the Chesapeake and Delaware Canal was, to use the words of Reybold again, "the key to the whole Federal situation." Chesapeake Bay as far north as the Potomac River was controlled by the Confederates and the river itself was heavily fortified by a series of batteries below Washington. "The Federal Government had absolutely no means of transportation upon the Chesapeake Bay until the boats were sent through the Chesapeake and Delaware Canal . . . when they afforded the only means of furnishing troops for the defense and for the salvation of the national capital." Throughout this time the canal was repeatedly used to transport troops on their way to the front. In late April the Indianapolis militia traveled 800 miles by railroad without changing cars, but upon reaching Philadelphia it was necessary to go the remaining distance by water. Again, early in May, 14 propeller steamers from Trenton, New Jersey, carried four regiments of soldiers through the canal to war. "The whole brigade, with its four pieces of artillery," stated the *Daily National Intelligencer*, "arrived in Annapolis on Sunday, May 5th, in twenty-eight hours from Trenton, and proceeded directly for Washington. It is stated that the 14 transports, with a strong convoy, Commander F. R. Loper, made a splendid appearance, steaming in two lines down the Chesapeake. They had been greeted by a great Union demonstration as they passed along the Chesapeake and Delaware Canal." [14]

From then on, the canal was an important part of the inland waterway used by the government for the transportation of supplies to the

[13] Johnson, "Maryland," p. 17.
[14] Reybold, "Land-Locked Navigation," p. 330; Fred Albert Shannon, *The Organization and Administration of the Union Army, 1861–1865* (Cleveland, 1928), I, 229; *Daily National Intelligencer*, May 7, 8, 1861, quoted in Moore, ed., *Rebellion Record*, I, 268.

army. For use on the coastwise canals and bays the government seized and chartered, in addition to the 144 propeller steamboats, 89 steam tugs and 842 freight barges, a total of 1,075 vessels. This figure constituted nearly one third of all the vessels chartered by the government during the war. The chief advantage of the inland waterway, of course, was the protection afforded to the vessels using it from the Confederate raiders as well as from the ordinary hazards of outside navigation. Many ships which ventured away, either by choice or necessity, from the intracoastal channels fell prey to various Confederate cruisers.[15]

On the canal line itself, immediately following the attack on the troops in Baltimore, considerable anxiety was felt for the safety of the works. The alarming rumors that secessionists were planning an attack upon the Du Pont gunpowder mills, that Northern troops passing through Wilmington were to be attacked, that Fort Delaware was to be seized, and that the canal walls and locks were to be destroyed circulated throughout the state of Delaware. These reports so disturbed the Secretary of War that he sent 200 men to reinforce the 30-man garrison at Fort Delaware and ordered the Pennsylvania militia to patrol the canal. The value of the canal was recognized by Secretary Cameron even before a military reconnaisance report submitted later in the year emphasized again the need for the canal: "It is of great importance that the communication between the Delaware and Chesapeake should be kept open by means of the canal in case the lower part of the Delaware River should be blockaded by an enemy." [16]

Company officials in Philadelphia, however, showed little signs of alarm initially, refusing to believe that "the political troubles that now exist" might interrupt the trade of the canal. They assured certain lumbermen in Pennsylvania on April 18 that their products would receive "every protection" the company was "capable of giving under the laws," and the following day agreed to guarantee the timber, up to 2,000,000 cubic feet, from risk of confiscation between Port Deposit and Delaware City. Upon application, however, the company donated $500 to the Home Guards in Delaware, formed late in April. They declined a similar request from the Philadelphia Committee on Public

[15] Reybold, "Land-Locked Navigation," pp. 328–329; Emerson D. Fite, "The Canal and the Railroad from 1861–1865," *Yale Review*, XV (August, 1906), 198. According to Fite's figures, 283 American vessels, with cargoes valued at $25,000,000, were taken by some 25 Southern privateers and cruisers.

[16] Hancock, "Political History of Delaware," p. 242; Colonel C. M. Eakin, "Report of the Military Reconnaissance of the Susquehanna River and of the Country Comprised within the River; part of the Chesapeake Shore, the Chesapeake and Delaware Canal, and a line from Harrisburg to Philadelphia. Made in 1861," Society Collection, Historical Society of Pennsylvania.

Safety in 1861 on the grounds that they had already contributed to authorized personnel for the protection of their property, but in 1863, just after the Confederate invasion into Pennsylvania which led to the battle at Gettysburg, a small contribution to aid in forming a volunteer regiment "for the protection of Philadelphia" was made. The company also invested part of the money set aside for emergencies in government bonds, the "five-twenties." In addition, in a precaution never before taken, the company obtained duplicate gates for all the locks, "to be ready in case of damage or loss, to those now in use," and the size of the contingency fund, for use "in case of accident," was increased slightly in June, 1862.[17]

Apart from incidental references, however, and the large increase in trade enjoyed by the company, there is little in the company records to indicate that the war was going on. The company created a "United States Account," so that government vessels could pass the locks without payment or delay, and the accumulated manifests were presented later for payment. In addition, special rates were granted to private vessels employed by the government. F. R. Loper requested in November, 1863, that his steamers, "trading between New York and Chesapeake Bay by the outside route," be permitted to pass through the canal upon payment of a set toll. The company thereupon agreed that Loper's steamers, "as they are in the service of the United States, shall have the privilege of navigating the Chesapeake and Delaware Canal: each steamer to pay the sum of one Hundred Dollars upon each trip through, loaded, and returning, if light, to be passed through *toll free*." Other shippers on government account requested and obtained special rates on particular items, such as the hay, corn, and oats carried between New York or Philadelphia and Baltimore. One final indication of the war was the 2½ per cent tax imposed by the federal government on the gross receipts of corporations.[18]

Repair or replacement of Summit Bridge was the only major maintenance problem faced by the company during the four wartime years. By 1864 the huge covered bridge, built nearly forty years earlier, was in an advanced state of disrepair and had become hazardous to travelers. A special committee viewed the bridge in June, 1864, in order to recommend appropriate action. While in New Castle County, the committee inspected not only the bridge but the entire property, which was found to be in a generally satisfactory condition.[19]

[17] Board Minute Book, April 18, 19, May 7, 1861, July 1, August 5, 1862, August 4, 1863.
[18] *Ibid.*, October 7, 1862, November 3, 1863, October 11, 1864.
[19] See *ibid.*, July 5, 1864.

In regard to the bridge, however, the committee had this to say: "The High Bridge at the deep-cut has become so much dilapidated as to require early attention. Both the President and the superintendent recommend the substitution of a Drawbridge, as at the other crossings. High masted vessels will be spared the trouble of striking their masts while the elevation may be sufficient for steamers and barges to pass under the bridge. The general travel it is thought may be about as well subserved as by the present precarious structure." It was therefore recommended that plans and estimates for both repairing and replacing the bridge be made and submitted to the board. In October, plans for a new drawbridge at the summit were approved. The contract called for the new structure to be completed during 1865, and announcement of its completion was made to the stockholders in 1866. The old bridge, it was reported, "since Sailing vessels of much larger tonnage and capacity than in former years are daily passing through the Canal, had become a great annoyance; its repair would have cost as much as the new one, and the annoyance to the trade would necessarily be continued." It was believed that the new bridge would add "much convenience and facility" in passing masted vessels through the canal, although some schooners which regularly plied the canal had special "drop masts" to permit them to pass under the old Summit Bridge.[20]

As the foregoing indicates, the Civil War period proved to be one of prosperity for the Chesapeake and Delaware Canal Company. Not only did the canal carry its full share of war supplies, but the general freight transported increased markedly. This was true for most canals and railroads during the Civil War. It was remarked in the *American Railway Journal* that the year 1863 was "the most prosperous ever known to American railways." Erie Canal traffic also increased tremendously during the war, with the number of boats in use on the canal doubling between 1860 and 1863. Time was found even during this period to give considerable attention to increasing the transportation facilities available. "Nothing is more characteristic of the period," wrote Emerson D. Fite, "aside from interest in war and politics, than the efforts of rival cities to gain commercial supremacy, to build additional means of transportation both on land and sea, and especially to improve communications with the West." [21]

Throughout the war the Chesapeake and Delaware Canal demonstrated its enormous value as a means of transportation for troops,

[20] *Ibid.*; *Forty-seventh General Report* (1866), p. 9; *Journal–Every Evening* (Wilmington), October 16, 1959.

[21] *American Railway Journal*, January 2, 1864, quoted in Fite, "The Canal and the Railroad," p. 195; *ibid.*, p. 199.

supplies, and other war materials. Both the country and the company profited. Heavy tonnages moved through the canal during the war and, contrary to general expectations, the trade remained at a high level afterwards. The board predicted in 1866, after examining the present sources of canal income and the many that were being developed, and recognizing that "the convenience of the Canal, as well as its capacity for doing a larger business is now better known and appreciated by the public than ever before," that its trade and income would be maintained at approximately its present level. The canal works were in a "state of greater efficiency than at any former period" and, with only ordinary repairs, they would remain so for many years.[22]

[22] *Forty-seventh General Report* (1866), p. 7.

Postwar Prosperity
and Decline

10

The general prosperity enjoyed by the canal company during the Civil War continued for several years after the war, but a series of events in the early 1870's caused a sharp decline in toll receipts. For nine consecutive years beginning in 1871, the canal company's income decreased. In 1870, toll receipts amounted to $414,203; in 1879, they were $150,387. The average for the ten years was just under $280,000 as compared with an average of $378,000 for the previous five years. Traffic through the canal in the late 1870's declined somewhat, although it did not tumble downward as rapidly as toll receipts.

In the immediate postwar period, the canal officials were pleasantly surprised by the continuation of a vigorous trade, for a substantial decrease had been anticipated when the war ended. When this failed to materialize, the board issued a buoyant statement about the steadily improving financial status of the company, pointing out that the Funded Debt within the past ten years had been reduced by $640,000 from its initial level of $2,800,000. This resulted in a savings on interest of $38,400 annually, the equivalent of an annual 3 per cent dividend on the capital stock. Moreover, the amount of the Funded Debt was lower than it had been for twenty years, ever since the unpaid interest on the Funded Debt of 1836 had been added to the principal in 1847. It was "with extreme gratification" that the board recommended a cash dividend of 3 per cent to the stockholders in 1866, and expressed its confidence that thereafter annual dividends of at least 3 per cent could be paid.[1]

For a time it seemed as if the board's statement was a conservative one. After the 3 per cent dividend of 1866, the first one declared since 1853 and only the second in the company's history, semiannual dividends of 3 per cent were declared in the next six years. Reductions in the Funded Debt also continued to be made during this time. In 1872 the face value of the bonds outstanding was only $1,993,750, but it proved impossible for the company to lower its bonded indebtedness further. A serious accident to the canal works in 1873, causing damages of nearly $100,000, interrupted the regular redemption of company bonds as well as dividend payments to the stockholders. After repairs were made, attempts to declare annual dividends again were made, but the depressed income of the company in the late 1870's and thereafter prevented this. Dividends of only 2 per cent were paid in 1875 and 1876, and they were the last.

A total of 17 cash dividends were paid the stockholders in eleven different years. All of the dividends were of 3 per cent, except for the final two 2 per cent declarations. In addition, two stock dividends, one of 25 per cent and one of 30 per cent, were made in 1866 and 1869. This slightly increased the number of shares each stockholder held and consequently increased his subsequent dividends. In 1867 the par value of each share was reduced from $200 to $50, but this had no effect on an individual's total holdings and was done to facilitate the transfer of the shares. At the time the legislatures of Delaware and Maryland granted the alteration in the stock's par value, they also authorized semiannual general meetings, primarily so the stock- and loanholders could authorize the semiannual dividend declarations as recommended by the board.

As the 17 dividend payments totaled 49 per cent of the capital stock, these, together with the two stock dividends, meant that an investor received a little more than $120 for each $200 share originally purchased, plus a 52.5 per cent increase in the number of shares held. Some of the stock had been purchased as early as 1803, but most was obtained in 1823 and afterwards. If the family of an original investor in the company retained the stock after dividend payments on it were halted in 1876, in hopes that there would be future dividends or a division of assets when the company was liquidated, it was to

[1] *Forty-seventh General Report* (1866), p. 8.

be disappointed on both counts. The government purchase price in 1919 equaled the amount of indebtedness of the company with none left for the stockholders. If, however, as Mathew Carey asserted he had done, most people and institutions had invested in the Chesapeake and Delaware Canal Company with no thought of direct remuneration, but rather to foster the "spirit of improvement" abroad in the early nineteenth century and to reap the indirect benefits of improved communications and national defense, then these persons and groups were well served.[2]

One important factor in permitting a brief period during which regular dividend payments were made was the physical condition of the canal. At the end of the war, the canal was in unusually good repair. A new Summit Bridge had been built late in the war, and the old one was dismantled. One of the oldest known photographs of the canal or its properties pictures the razing of the big wooden covered bridge and reveals its iron Howe truss-type replacement in the background. In the meantime the water wheel and its two steam engines were overhauled and restored to good working order. Finally, the work which had been going on almost continually ever since the canal opened in 1829 to lessen the hazard of land slips into the canal prism was begining to produce the long-awaited results. Only one minor interruption to trade occurred in the 1860's, which otherwise was heavy and growing. In June, 1869, a Delaware newspaper reported that business "has been greater, so far, this season, than ever was known up the Canal since it was completed. It has even exceeded the immense business done during the war, the receipts ranging from $16,000 to $17,000 per week." Later in the year, another newspaper revealed that "Five hundred and seventy-one vessels, including steamers, barges, and canal Boats, have passed East and West, through the Chesapeake and Delaware Canal, for the week ending Friday, [November] the nineteenth, (19th). Nearly five million feet of lumber, and over fifteen thousand tons of coal passed eastward. . . ."[3]

Improvements made early in the 1870's added to the confidence of the board. New lockgates were installed in 1871 to replace the old ones in use for the past fifteen years. The same year the water-raising machinery received its "usual and necessary repairs" and was

[2] Carey's remark concerning his motivation for internal improvement investments is quoted by Carter Goodrich in his excellent study of *Government Promotion of American Canals and Railroads*, p. 292. Goodrich also speaks of the early nineteenth century "spirit of improvement" on pp. 3–16.

[3] Board Minute Book, October 6, 1868; *Delaware Gazette*, June 11, 1869; *Wilmington Daily Commercial*, November 23, 1869.

"in the best working order, and the Canal as a whole is capable of passing safely and satisfactorily the large trade which it now enjoys." The following year extensive improvements in Back Creek, at the entrance to the lock at Chesapeake City, provided easier access to the canal for all vessels. In 1873, the canal was described as being "in excellent condition," and even after the extensive flood damages of that year it was quickly restored to "good navigable condition." [4]

Because of the security of the canal, the board had ceased in the mid-1860's to appoint the Acting Committee, which previously had met weekly to advise the president and handle the urgent business affairs of the company between regular board meetings. Thereafter the president and superintendent were given more responsibility in maintaining the canal works. Only monthly reports from the superintendent were required after June, 1860. Increasingly the board concerned itself with purely financial matters, as is revealed by its only two standing committees — Tolls and Finances — as well as by the business discussed at the board meetings.

At this time the company of Brady & Sons of Delaware City was handling most of the towing through the canal. The canal company itself was without transportation powers, but it exercised a certain amount of control over the accommodations to be offered and the towage rates to be charged. In 1863 arrangements were made with the Bradys to increase the rates. For single-team towing, the charge ranged from $2.00 to $3.75, depending upon the size of the vessel; for double-team towing, the charge ranged from $4.50 to $6.00. For each raft of timber towed through the canal, "owing to the increase in cost of forage, harness, and wages of men and drivers," a maximum toll of $6.00 was levied. During the war reduced towing rates (as well as reduced tolls) were given vessels on the "United States Account." [5]

In 1866, because of a revision by the government in the plan of measuring vessels which lowered the registered tonnage of vessels, the Bradys' towage charges were similarly revised and at the same time somewhat increased. This was in keeping with the general policy of the canal company during this time to raise salaries and wages. President Gray's salary was increased to $4,000 in 1868; the salary of the company secretary, Henry V. Lesley, was raised to $3,000;

[4] *Fifty-second General Report* (1871), p. 7; *Fifty-third General Report* (1872), pp. 6–7; *Fifty-fourth General Report* (1873), p. 6; *Fifty-fifth General Report* (1874), p. 7.
[5] Board Minute Book, October 6, 1863, March 7, 1865.

his assistant, J. A. L. Wilson, therafter received $2,000. On the other hand, the rates of toll were gradually being forced downward by the growing competition of both railroads, especially the powerful Pennsylvania Railroad, and steamships which used the outside route for transporting freight between the bays. The average canal toll in the early 1850's was 60 cents per ton; in the early 1870's it was only 27 cents. Moreover, increasingly large rebates to the towing companies were necessary to attract trade to the canal. These rebates were carried on the books as expenses.

Competition for the coal trade of the canal, which averaged well over 500,000 tons a year between 1865 and 1875, was particularly strong. In 1866 the canal company offered a rebate of 5 cents a ton to any party shipping at least 50,000 tons through the canal. The regular toll was then approximately 20 cents a ton, although later in the year this rate was lowered to 17 cents, and to 15 cents on coal from the Wyoming Valley of Pennsylvania. Similar steps had been taken by other canal companies in Pennsylvania "in order that the [Wyoming] coal should go via canal, in place of Rail Road." The company also offered a bonus of $1,500 to the Delaware and Chesapeake Towing Company, the successor to the Philadelphia and Havre de Grace Steam Tow Boat Company, if it towed 100,000 tons of coal from Baltimore to Philadelphia via the canal. If 200,000 tons were towed through, $2,500 would be paid. In 1869 this agreement was changed to a flat bonus of 5 cents a ton, provided that additional facilities for the transportation of coal be added by the towing company. The agreement continued in 1870, although the bonus was lowered to 3 cents. Despite these efforts, the coal trade declined from a high of 742,775 tons in 1872 to 323,363 in 1879. Both the Delaware and Raritan and the Chesapeake and Delaware canals, it was reported in 1873, "have lost a large and valuable trade in Cumberland coal." This loss was reflected in the total income of the canal company, for in the 1870's and 1880's coal dominated the canal's traffic statistics, usually amounting to 40 to 50 per cent of all traffic. By 1883 the toll on coal was down to 9 cents a ton. An agreement with the Pennsylvania Railroad in that year returned the rate to 20 cents, where it remained until 1893, but the coal trade continued to decline.[6]

Traffic on the canal exceeded 1,000,000 tons for the first time

[6] *Ibid.*, May 15, July 3, August 7, 1866, April 7, 1868, March 2, 1869, March 1, 1870; *Every Evening*, September 10, 1873.

in 1869, something that occurred in only ten other years as long as the waterway remained a lock canal. The tonnage continued above the 1,000,000 figure for seven years. After a decline in 1876 through 1879, total tonnage through the canal again exceeded 1,000,000 tons in 1882 through 1884. Coal, lumber, grain, and groceries remained the principal commodities carried. Although the number of passages each way was approximately the same, except for the timber rafts which passed only west to east, more than 80 per cent of the tolls was paid by the eastbound trade.

The most severe damage to the canal works since the great breach of 1834 occurred in 1873. A week-long rainstorm beginning on August 12 damaged the lower level banks and towpath and interrupted trade for several days. A large number of barges and rafts gathered at either end of the canal while the necessary repairs were being made. Then, just at the time when the canal was filled with the temporarily delayed craft, the heaviest rainfall in the memory of local residents occurred, causing new and extensive damage to the canal and to the vessels within it. The rain "destroyed and damaged, more or less, nearly the entire line of towpath, berme, and guard banks, filling the prism of the Canal with at least one hundred thousand yards of earth, sand, gravel, stumps, &c." It caught about 100 vessels in the canal, and tossed them about like leaves in a windstorm. Some were forced out of the canal by as much as 300 yards. It was reported that one barge hit a stable a short distance from the canal and killed two horses; the bowsprit of another vessel damaged a church near the canal line at St. Georges.[7]

Another disaster followed on the heels of the first, for at 2 a.m. on the morning after the deluge the large reservoir of the canal broke, compounding the damage already inflicted and decreasing the ability of the company to make speedy repairs and refill the canal. When the reservoir gave way, an abutment of the bridge used by the Delaware Railroad in crossing the canal was washed away. About 12 miles of railroad track were also damaged in the flood. The calamity caused by the August rains was the more discouraging because it was totally unexpected. The board stated in its report on the disaster that "An immunity from the damages of heavy rainfalls for a period of nearly forty years had led us to believe that, whatever other misfortunes might befall the Chesapeake and Delaware Canal, it was in this respect safe.

[7] *Fifty-fifth General Report* (1874), pp. 4–5; *Every Evening*, August 21, 22, 1873.

TABLE 5. TOLLS AND TONNAGES, 1851–90[a]

Year Ends June 1	Tolls Received	Passages	Total Tonnage
1851	$215,889	13,582	389,440
1852	190,141	12,833	411,340
1853	246,283	15,065	477,630
1854	246,695	14,897	534,080
1855	225,224	14,391	536,970
1856	225,483	13,554	568,580
1857	229,081	14,628	616,170
1858	207,006	12,863	543,510
1859	202,350	12,134	496,100
1860	216,256	12,710	523,150
1861	195,946	11,347	596,294
1862	231,555	11,713	501,389
1863	293,124	14,293	674,305
1864	309,113	15,417	782,670
1865	424,313	12,811	916,973
1866	350,940	11,496	729,918
1867	346,196	12,131	726,666
1868	300,076	10,993	853,874
1869	368,684	14,169	1,180,206
1870	414,203	15,650	1,245,928
1871	406,704	16,394	1,312,816
1872	365,989	14,726	1,318,772
1873	330,222	14,078	1,258,732
1874	278,601	12,444	1,189,729
1875	252,333	11,689	1,132,456
1876	237,616	12,247	991,180
1877	187,918	10,858	792,584
1878	169,650	10,042	842,714
1879	150,387	8,328	714,184
1880	189,805	10,560	929,590
1881	161,531	8,935	675,069
1882	209,840	10,931	1,019,733
1883	196,322	10,420	1,080,472
1884	185,925	9,590	1,002,346
1885	205,263	9,260	877,396
1886	204,174	9,036	769,983
1887	189,304	8,960	755,944
1888	190,090	9,056	795,601
1889	183,550	8,570	736,879
1890	163,797	6,769	686,067

[a]Source: "Comparative Statement showing Receipts, Expenses, percentages and Tonnage of Mdze.," 1830–1919, C & D Papers, HSD.

The judicious construction of the towpaths, guard-banks, and locks and their appurtenances, with the yearly repairs and additions thereto, receiving as they did the constant and vigilant care of the officers in charge of the works, it was believed gave ample security and protection from any possible floods." The unprecedented rainfall demonstrated that no amount of care could insure the canal from loss and damage.[8]

The monumental task of repairing the canal and refloating the landlocked barges and sailing vessels adorning adjacent marshes and cornfields was ably supervised by John R. Price, superintendent of the canal since 1838. Although it was estimated that the damages would amount to from $200,000 to $600,000 and that at least 60 days would be needed to repair the canal, Price had it open for vessels of 8-foot depth on September 27, and by mid-October full depth was restored. A call was issued at once for men and equipment, and some 600 persons responded. The necessary dredges, scows, and tugs were obtained; additional wheelbarrows, picks, and shovels were purchased; and work was continued around the clock. The lower level between Delaware City and St. Georges was repaired first, and the grounded vessels were returned to the canal. After the breaches in the upper level walls were closed, the water wheel at Chesapeake City was set to work refilling the canal. The cost of the repairs was $92,103.70, to which the estimated loss of revenue of about $40,000 during the busiest season of the year should be added.[9]

The losses suffered in 1873, coupled with the business depression which began the same year, prevented a profit from being earned and seriously depleted the small cash reserves of the company. But it was expected that prosperity would soon return. Despite the month's hiatus in traffic, 1,258,732 tons of freight passed through the canal in 1873. This was only 60,000 tons less than the record tonnage carried the previous year. "The canal is now in good navigable condition," the board reported in 1874, "better, in fact, than it was before the break." As it happened, however, the downward trend in total receipts continued unbroken until 1880, by which time they were less than half what they had been even in the disaster year of 1873. In 1877, following a precipitous $50,000 decrease in revenue, all salaried employees of the company suffered a pay cut of from 12½ to 25 per cent. At the same time, steps were taken to improve the

[8] *Fifty-fifth General Report* (1874), p. 4.
[9] *Every Evening*, August 23, 24, 1873; *Fifty-fifth General Report* (1874), pp. 5–6.

administrative efficiency of the company and to reduce expenditures. Business was so poor during the 1870's that a new transportation company, the Chesapeake, Delaware, and Hudson line established for the "purpose of doing a large carrying trade in coal, etc., through the Chesapeake and Delaware Canal," did not survive the decade. The canal company subscribed $10,000 to the stock of the transportation company and granted it equal privileges with the other companies regularly using the canal, but the new company failed in 1879. After transferring its boats and paying all bills and outstanding accounts, its officials distributed the small amount remaining among the stockholders. The Chesapeake and Delaware Canal Company received $1,152.60 from the $10,000 invested nine years earlier.[10]

The growing misfortunes of the company were compounded by a concerted movement, beginning in the 1870's, to construct a ship canal, or lockless, sea-level waterway, between the Chesapeake and Delaware bays. The inadequacy of the existing lock canal for certain types of trade, particularly the transatlantic trade of Baltimore, had become apparent. The National Commercial Convention, held in Baltimore in September, 1871, focused attention on the subject by petitioning Congress to direct a survey to be made for a ship canal between the bays, "and, if found to be practicable, desirable, and valuable to the great interest of the country, [to direct] that the said ship-canal be constructed."[11]

The Chesapeake and Delaware ship canal movement fostered in Baltimore was part of a national movement for improved waterway transportation in the United States which began during the Civil War. In 1863, responding to a call signed by 14 senators and 80 representatives in Congress, 2,000 delegates attended a great waterway convention in Chicago to support improvements in the Illinois and Michigan and the Erie canals. The following year a Louisville convention urged improvements in the Ohio River. During this time, as Emerson D. Fite has stated, "Enthusiasm for canals was very strong and seemed to be worldwide." The Suez Canal was under construction, and talk of either a Nicaraguan or Panama canal was increasing. Local projects

[10] *Fifty-fifth General Report* (1874), p. 7; Board Minute Book, July 3, 1877, October 4, 6, 1870, March 4, 1879.

[11] Quoted in "Survey with a View to Construction of a Ship-Canal to Connect the Waters of the Delaware and Chesapeake," *Senate Executive Documents*, No. 39, 46th Congress, 2nd Session (Washington, 1880), p. 2. Hereafter this document, compiled by Major William P. Craighill of the United States Army engineering office in Baltimore, will be cited as *Craighill Report*.

favored along the Atlantic seaboard, in addition to the ship canal desired by Baltimoreans, were ship canals across New Jersey and Cape Cod.[12]

In March, 1872, the House of Representatives called upon the Secretary of War to supply it with full information on the subject of the proposed Chesapeake and Delaware ship canal, "and to state how much time would be saved by such improvement in the passage of ships from Baltimore to and from Liverpool and other foreign ports, and whether the building of such canal would not materially advance the interests of commerce." Major William P. Craighill of the Corps of Engineers, in charge of the army engineering office at Baltimore, drew up the report submitted by Secretary Belknap in response to the House's request. Craighill pointed out the need for a careful survey and comparison of the possible lines for a ship canal before definite answers to the questions posed by the House could be given, but he predicted the entire feasibility of such a canal because the country through which it would pass was favorable and suggested that $20,000 be appropriated for the surveys. The length of the canal would probably be from 30 to 55 miles, and it would shorten the distance of a journey from Baltimore to Liverpool by about 182 miles. At first little attention was given to the property of the Chesapeake and Delaware Canal Company far to the north of Baltimore, because Baltimoreans were anxious to have as direct an outlet to the Atlantic Ocean as possible. Craighill reminded his superiors that a canal between Chesapeake Bay and the Delaware River existed, "but this has neither depth nor width enough for the accommodation of steamers or sailing-vessels designed to cross the Atlantic. Whether, considering the objects to be accomplished, the location of this canal is admissible, even if deepened and widened, is a question for determination after the completion of a survey and estimates." [13]

Various documents appended to Craighill's report of March, 1872, supplied additional information and revealed the strength behind the ship canal movement. In February, 1872, a joint committee from the Maryland legislature, accompanied by Governor Ponder of Delaware, had visited Brigadier General Andrew A. Humphreys, chief of engineers, to voice its support of the project. James T. Earle's remarks on the occasion of this visit were included in the appended

---

[12] Fite, "The Canal and the Railroad," pp. 201–203.
[13] Craighill to Brigadier General Andrew A. Humphreys, chief of engineers, March 25, 1872, *Craighill Report*, Appendix 3, pp. 28–29.

material. Earle had asserted that "for many years the intelligent portions of the populations of both States," Maryland and Delaware,
have considered a ship canal, "under the developing influence of the
necessities of trade, as a fact which must sooner or later occur." Such
an improvement would not only benefit Baltimore, a great and growing city whose commerce was limited only by poor access to the ocean,
but the entire Atlantic coast and the states of the Mississippi Valley
trading with Baltimore. The Chesapeake Bay port was nearer than
New York to Chicago via existing railroad lines by an average of
152 miles, and was nearer to St. Louis by an average of 210 miles.
This made their proposed ship canal a national work, one which
should be built "without reference to cost, by the shortest line between Baltimore and the ocean." [14]

Shortly after this report was submitted to Congress, the Maryland legislature incorporated the Maryland and Delaware Ship-Canal
Company. The following year the Delaware legislature also granted
a charter to the new company. At the time this bill was being considered in Dover, President Gray warned the board of the old canal company that a ship canal would seriously affect the interests of their
company and suggested that "prompt measures" be taken to "place
the interests of the Company in a proper light before the Legislature. . . ." Gray was authorized to employ counsel to represent the
company during the session of the legislature. At the April meeting
of the board, Gray reported that the ship canal bill had passed after
being amended, but that as amended "there was every reason to
believe that the canal would not be constructed." No details concerning the amendments were given, but perhaps Gray was referring either
to the stipulation that the tolls were not to exceed 10 cents per ton
or to the denial of transportation powers to the canal company. "Certain expenses" amounting to $3,500 were incurred by the company in
this attempt to safeguard its interests.[15]

In the meantime, the Maryland and Delaware Ship-Canal Company was organized and preparations were made to undertake the
necessary surveys to locate its route. In a report submitted by Julius
Stahel, general manager of the ship canal company, to the president
and directors in October, 1872, the "entire feasibility" of the project
was asserted, and the results of a preliminary investigation of five
separate routes were given. Stahel recommended that detailed sur-

[14] *Ibid.*, Appendix 2, pp. 25–28.
[15] Board Minute Book, February 4, April 1, 1873.

veys of all five routes be made. Only one of the routes was situated north of Baltimore. It extended eastward from Chesapeake Bay via the Sassafras River, and was located only 10 miles south of the existing Chesapeake and Delaware Canal. It was this route which General W. C. Brown, the company's chief engineer, recommended early in 1874, after having inspected the deep cut section of the Chesapeake and Delaware Canal in December, 1873.[16]

Benjamin H. Latrobe, a Baltimore descendant of his famous namesake, served as consulting engineer for the ship canal company and confirmed the correctness of Brown's selection. Reporting on July 4, 1874, to President Horace B. Tebbetts of New York City, Latrobe gave his reasons for approving the Sassafras route — primarily the good approaches to it on either side of the peninsula — and then estimated the cost of ship canals of differing dimensions there. A canal 15 feet deep and 80 feet wide at the bottom would cost $8,064,829; a canal 21 feet deep and 90 feet wide would cost $10,454,064; a canal 25 feet deep and 100 feet wide would cost $12,473,643. Options to the land along the proposed route were obtained by the company, and various efforts were made to interest the government in building a ship canal along their Sassafras River route rather than along the route of the original Chesapeake and Delaware Canal or along other possible routes to the south.[17]

In 1878, after several years of agitation by the company, the people of Maryland, and other interested persons, the Rivers and Harbors Act adopted by Congress on June 18 authorized the army engineers to undertake the necessary surveys for a ship canal between the Chesapeake and Delaware bays. Major Craighill was put in charge of conducting the investigation, which began in August, 1878, and continued until December, 1879. The canal was to be 26 feet deep at mean low water, 100 feet wide at the bottom, and 178 feet wide at the top. It was to be lock-free except for two 60-by-600-foot tide locks. A preliminary report was submitted to Congress in February, 1879, on three of the six routes eventually surveyed, giving comparative estimates of costs on the most southern, the most northern, and the most direct intermediate route. The estimated total cost of the southern Ferry Creek route was $16,250,000; of the intermediate Queenstown route, $34,000,000; of the northern Sassafras route, $8,120,000. The estimates for the latter route were based upon

[16] *Craighill Report*, Appendix 4, pp. 30–33, Appendix 5, pp. 33–36.
[17] *Ibid.*, Appendix 5, pp. 34–36.

the earlier surveys of Brown and Latrobe made for the Maryland and Delaware Ship-Canal Company, although revised prices for excavation were used. N. H. Hutton, the engineer of the Baltimore Harbor Board who personally supervised the field work done for the preparation of the report, compiled complete records on the tides, the nature of the soil in the peninsula, the variations in elevation, and the number of days the different routes had been obstructed by ice in the past. For purposes of comparison, he obtained the ice figures for the Chesapeake and Delaware Canal, 1855–78. During those twenty-four years, the canal had remained navigable throughout five winters, and in only three had it been closed more than 50 days (81 days in 1856). The average for the period was 23½ days a year, which figure could be used for the nearby Sassafras River route. The approach channels to the southernmost routes had been obstructed only an average of 10½ days in the past twenty-four years.[18]

In November, 1879, Craighill submitted a much lengthier report on all six routes then under consideration. The length of the routes was based on distances from Baltimore to a common point at sea 12 miles outside the Delaware breakwater near the mouth of Delaware Bay. The distance to this point from Baltimore by the outside route then in use was 325 miles, or 33¼ hours, allowing 10 miles per hour in open, 7 in dredged channels. The speed through the canal portion of the inside routes was computed at 5 miles per hour. The six routes, running from south to north, with distances, costs, and savings, are as follows:

Route	Length (miles)	Canal (miles)	Est. Cost (millions)	Transit Time (hours)	Time Saved (hours)
Choptank River	149.8	37.7	$16.5	19.5	13.8
Wye River	128.4	43.0	26.3	17.8	15.5
Queenstown	107.3	53.8	37.3	17.0	16.3
Centreville	106.4	51.0	41.5	16.5	16.8
Southeast Creek	115.8	38.4	25.0	15.8	17.5
Sassafras River	129.3	16.2	8.0	15.1	18.1

Craighill then made some general observations on the relative advantages and disadvantages of the routes. "A very formidable objection

[18] "Preliminary Report on Surveys with a View to Construction of a Ship Canal to connect the Waters of the Delaware and Chesapeake Bays," *House Executive Documents*, No. 91, 45th Congress, 3rd Session (Washington, 1879), p. 3. Hutton's detailed report on which this document was based is in *Craighill Report*, Appendix 1, pp. 5–25.

to the more northern routes would be the necessity of maintaining a deep channel directly across the natural set of the currents of Chesapeake Bay, where it would be almost certainly filled rapidly by the profuse sedimentary deposit to be expected there." It also "would be next to impossible" to navigate the bay north of Baltimore during periods of running ice, "even with the use of ice-boats." As soon as the icebreakers cleared the way above the channel, the field of ice would move away from the channel, taking the cleared path with it, and leave the job to be done over again. The approaches to the Choptank or southern route, however, were "in the direction of existing navigation and useable at all times." He discounted the rumors of quicksand along the northern routes, basing this both upon the borings recently made by Hutton and the experience of the Chesapeake and Delaware Canal Company. President Gray had informed Craighill earlier in the year that no quicksand had been encountered during the construction of the canal. The slides which had occurred periodically until approximately ten years before were caused by "the percolation of water between the inclined strata of the various clays and mud cut through, causing one layer or stratum to slide over the lower one." Craighill concluded his remarks by pointing out the importance of a ship canal not only to "Baltimore locally" but to "Baltimore the outlet of many States of the great West" and to other eastern and northern ports. "No argument is necessary to show the great value, in time of war with a maritime power, of such an interior line of communication between the great Chesapeake and Delaware Bays and their tributary streams, as this canal would be." [19]

In 1880, Craighill attached a supplement to his previous report, in which he gave the results of the army engineers' survey of the Sassafras route, rather than Brown and Latrobe's. The new estimate placed the cost at $8,500,000, slightly more than the earlier figure. In this report Craighill observed that the Sassafras River route was preferred by many because it was the cheapest of those estimated. But if a northern route was to be seriously considered, Craighill believed it would be "desirable also to determine the cost of enlarging and otherwise modifying the existing Chesapeake and Delaware Canal. . . ." The entrance to it was only a few miles from the Sassafras River, he pointed out, and the United States had already spent about $500,000 on the original canal. [20]

[19] *Craighill Report*, pp. 4–5.
[20] *Ibid.*, p. 47.

These engineering reports were referred to the Committee on Transportation Routes to the Seaboard, which earlier, in the so-called Windom Committee report, had recommended further development of inland waterways as one way of regulating railroad rates and improving the existing transportation system. In 1881, after examining the various proposals for a ship canal, with the maps, charts, and surveys of the several routes, and after considering the memorials of the Maryland legislature and the statements of various commercial organizations in Baltimore as well as of the senators and several of the representatives of Maryland, this committee reported that it was convinced of the need for the canal. It would be important in the event of war, but its immediate importance lay in "the present enormous and rapidly increasing commerce from the port of Baltimore to European countries." The committee, however, emphasized that the benefit would not "inure either wholly or in great part" to Baltimore or Chesapeake Bay ports, but mainly to producers in those sections of the country where products were carried by the railroads with eastern terminals on Chesapeake Bay. Rather than recommend construction along any of the routes proposed, the committee instead suggested, in view of the magnitude of the work in importance and expense, that still another "careful survey" of the routes be made to determine the one most feasible for the canal. In March, 1881, Congress appropriated $10,000 for the survey.[21]

Captain Thomas Turtle supervised the survey of 1881, but before a final report was made the Rivers and Harbors Act of August 2, 1882, appropriated an additional $10,000 for the ship canal surveys. The Secretary of War was requested "to report to Congress which of the various routes surveyed will afford the greatest protection in case of war, and the greatest facilities to commerce by cheapening the cost of transportation from the city of Baltimore to the Atlantic Ocean, together with the cost of said improvement and its approaches, and the annual cost of maintaining and operating said canal when constructed: *Provided*, that nothing herein shall be construed to commit the Government to proceed with the construction of the said improvement." Because of the recently deepened channel in Chesapeake Bay, the new

[21] D. Philip Locklin, *Economics of Transportation* (4th ed., Homewood, Illinois, 1954), pp. 219–220; "Report of the Committee on Transportation Routes to the Seaboard . . . relative to the ship canal between the Chesapeake and Delaware Bays," *Senate Reports*, No. 898, 46th Congress, 3rd Session (Washington, 1881), pp. 1–2.

appropriation was used to provide for additional and deeper borings necessary to complete the cost estimates for a deeper ship canal.

Turtle computed the construction costs of three canals: the Choptank River route, $18,184,766.29; the Sassafras River route, $11,409,909.81; the Back Creek route, $7,605,471.39, exclusive of the cost of purchasing the existing canal along that route. He commented on the military advantages of a Chesapeake and Delaware ship canal, but pointed out that the canal would have to be built before a war started because it would be too late to build it afterwards. He compared the rapidity of transit and the security of the southern Choptank route with the two northern routes, to the advantage of the latter, although the ice obstruction was unquestionably greater there. This was reflected in the estimated maintenance charges on the three routes. The maintenance work included icebreaking, dredging, lighting, and superintending the canal, and was greatest on the short Back Creek route because of the need for three iceboats. Annual maintenance charges there were estimated at $123,580, as compared to $111,080 on the Sassafras and $114,980 on the Choptank route.[22]

The most important and significant portion of this report was its strong recommendation, first made by Craighill and seconded by both the chief of engineers, General Horatio G. Wright, and Secretary of War Robert T. Lincoln, that a special commission be appointed to report on which of the routes surveyed best met the requirements set forth in the Rivers and Harbors Act. The two main objects of the canal, to promote the defense and commerce of the country, were both of national importance. Craighill suggested even the composition of the commission in a letter to Wright on December 5, 1882: one army officer of high rank, not in the Corps of Engineers; one navy officer of high rank; one officer from the Corps of Engineers; one civilian from Baltimore, to represent the interests there; and one civilian from the northern half of the Mississippi Valley, to represent the western interests having Baltimore as their Atlantic port. As he stated in a subsequent letter to Wright, the ship canal subject "is one which requires study on the part of experts. In my judgment it is not altogether a question to be decided from the standpoint of the engineer.

---

[22] "Letter from the Secretary of War [Robert T. Lincoln] transmitting . . . Copies of Reports from Lieut. Col. W. P. Craighill and Capt. Thos. Turtle, Corps of Engineers, upon surveys for a ship canal to connect the Chesapeake and Delaware Bays, &c.," *Senate Executive Documents*, No. 6, 48th Congress, 1st Session (Washington, 1883), pp. 3–24.

For this reason I suggested its consideration by a mixed commission. I feel quite sure the honorable Secretary of War has not the time to study the details of this problem, and I would greatly prefer he should be advised by such a commission as has been recommended, or, perhaps, by some other of a different composition, rather than hear only my opinion. . . ."[23] Craighill's suggestion was not acted upon for over a decade, but it was his plan for the establishment of a special commission that led eventually to the purchase and conversion of the Chesapeake and Delaware Canal by the government.

[23] Craighill to Wright, Baltimore, December 5, December 20, 1882, *ibid.*, pp. 25–27.

The Chesapeake and Delaware bays. (*Corps of Engineers, U.S. Army*)

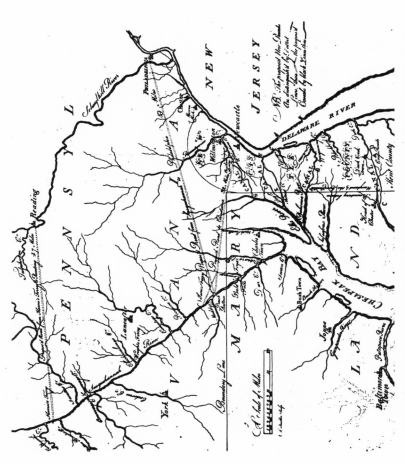

American Philosophical Society Surveys, 1769–70. (*American Philosophical Society*)

Joshua Gilpin (1765–1841), director, 1803–24. (*Historical Society of Delaware*)

Benjamin Henry Latrobe (1764–1820), first chief engineer. (*Maryland Historical Society*)

Joseph Tatnall (1740–1813), first president. (*Historical Society of Delaware*)

Kensey Johns (1758–1848), second president. (*Historical Society of Delaware*)

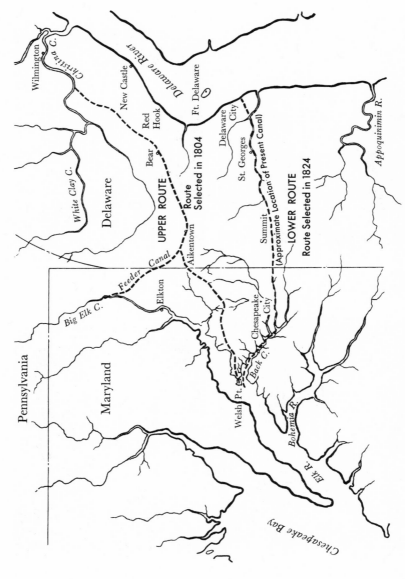

Upper and lower canal routes. (*Redrawn from Corps of Engineers map*)

Mathew Carey (1760–1839), reviver of the canal project, 1820's. (*Free Library of Philadelphia*)

William Strickland (1787–1854), canal company engineer, 1823–24. (*Free Library of Philadelphia*)

Henry D. Gilpin (1801–60), secretary-treasurer and director of canal company. (*Chicago Historical Society*)

Andrew C. Gray (1804–85), canal company president, 1853-85. (*Historical Society of Delaware*)

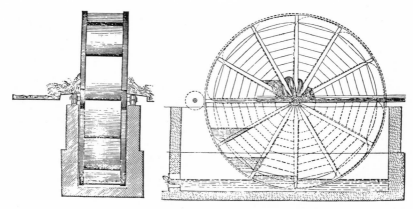

The lifting wheel at Chesapeake City. (*The Franklin Institute, Philadelphia*)

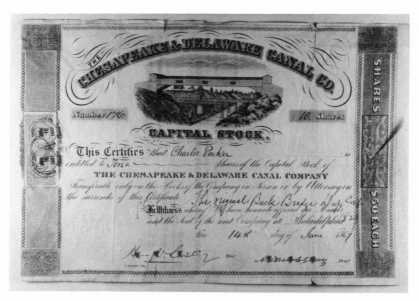

Stock certificate, showing original Summit Bridge and its replacement. (*Historical Society of Delaware*)

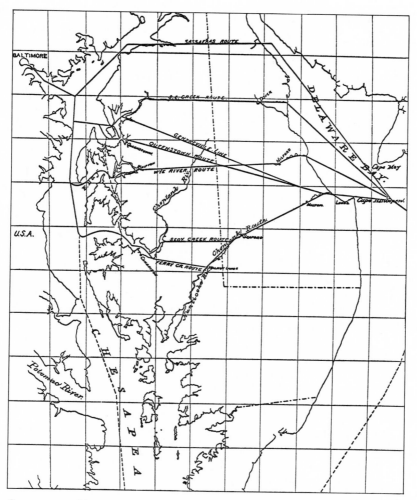

Government ship canal surveys, 1880's. (*From* Casey Report)

An Ericsson Line steamboat in the canal. (*From 1908 Ericsson Line timetable in author's possession*)

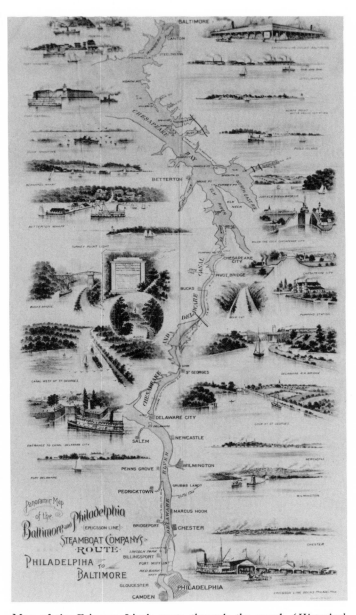

Map of the Ericsson Line's route through the canal. (*Historical Society of Delaware*)

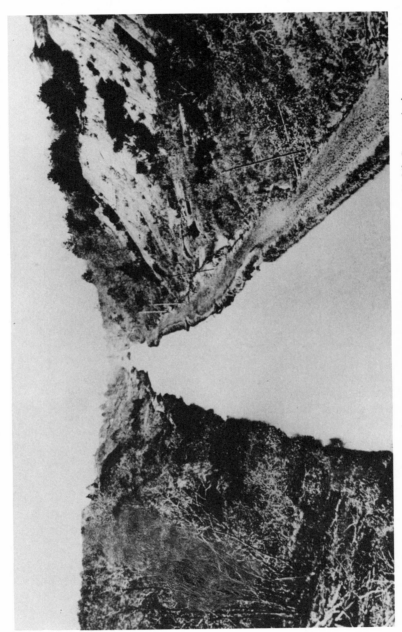

View of the canal prior to its enlargement, showing the bank stabilization problem. (*Gulf Oil Corporation*)

Dissensions and Defalcations: The 1880's

11

While the first faltering steps towards government acquisition of the canal were being taken, the company was faced with a continuing decline in revenues and upsetting internal problems. Business remained at approximately the level reached at the end of the 1870's, the annual tonnage for the period averaging slightly more than 864,000. This figure was boosted by the fact that tonnages exceeded the 1,000,000 mark three times during the decade of the 1880's; revenues, however, amounted to only $191,580 annually. A bitter dispute, moreover, among the company directors over company policy marred the corporate image and prevented effective measures being taken to boost revenues. Finally, the lingering hopes for eventual financial solvency were completely shattered in 1886 by the revelation of a $650,000 loss through embezzlement.

Early in the decade efforts were made to provide the company with additional sources of income by having it exercise certain "transportation powers" which recently had been acquired. The board had requested a charter alteration, which would authorize the company to engage in the business of towing and transportation, from the state legislatures in 1877, after a prolonged controversy over this matter. Some of the board members opposed any actions which would infringe upon the interests of other companies involved in transportation, particularly the Baltimore and Philadelphia Steamboat Company (Ericsson Line) which operated through the canal. When the matter was referred to a special committee in 1877, it was agreed that "the interests" of the canal company might be "greatly served in the future by obtaining at this time the powers of transportation of Merchandize and passengers," but the committee emphasized that there was "no necessity whatever of exercising such powers at this time and so long as the present relations continue with the Baltimore and Philadelphia Steamboat Company." An immediate application, nevertheless, was made to the Delaware General Assembly; the desired law was enacted on February 1, 1877. The canal company was granted "full power and authority to exercise and enjoy transportation powers, and for that purpose to hold, use, possess and own steam and sail vessels, barges and other craft, and, in addition thereto, to hold, occupy, rent or own all such wharves, docks, stores, storehouses and offices as may be necessary for the transaction of a transportation business by the said Company."[1]

Upon failure of the company to use its additional powers, the stock- and loanholders in 1880 adopted a resolution strongly urging the board to consider using its authority to own and operate vessels "to obtain for the canal its natural and fair proportion of the trade and travel of the country." Moncure Robinson, chairman of the committee which recommended the above action, explained the views of his committee to the board: "It will be inferred from the language of the resolution that the committee are satisfied that the canal does not receive its fair proportion of the trade and travel of the country . . . that the income of the Company may be materially increased . . . and that action under it to a greater or less extent is indispensable to the future welfare and prosperity of the Company." Not since 1876 had the company earned a profit on its business, and the company investors were anxious to reverse this trend.[2]

Pursuant to the above resolution, the board requested President Gray in October to investigate the possibilities of entering into the transportation business and the competition which would be encountered. The Bradys' towing business was to be examined too. The following month Gray, after studying the information he had obtained, advised "the immediate construction of not less than two Iron steamboats of as large capacity, as the locks of the Company may permit, and of as high speed and as perfect accommodations, both for freight

[1] Board Minute Book, October 1, November 5, 1872, January 16, 1877; *Laws of Delaware*, XV, 504.
[2] Stockholders' Minutes, June 7, 1880.

and passengers as may be attainable, consistent with due regard to the safety and economy of running the boats, and wear of the canal banks." He suggested that bonds not exceeding $200,000 be issued to finance the construction. These recommendations were tabled by the board in November, and upon their consideration in December, much to the exasperation of some, including board members John R. Baker and Thomas A. Biddle and company secretary Henry V. Lesley, the board decided that it was "inexpedient at the time" to alter the "present policy" of the company. The policy in question was that of fostering the virtual monopoly of the Ericsson Line in carrying water freight between Philadelphia and Baltimore and New York and Baltimore. The Ericsson Line, the principal user of the canal, paid a percentage to the canal company on its total freight business. In 1880 the percentage toll was 10 per cent; in 1884, when a general increase in toll rates was made, it was raised to 15 per cent. Other steam transportation companies using the canal, however, continued to pay the rate established for sail vessels plus 50 per cent, which was the regular so-called steam rate.[3]

The board's decision not to alter its policy prompted several proprietors of the company to seek a place on the board in order to promote the company's welfare. In June, 1882, Baker and Biddle were joined on the board by A. Sydney Biddle, Charles Chauncey, and John Haug, all of whom were anxious for the canal company to enter the transportation business. These men were convinced that persons more interested in the welfare of the Ericsson Line than the canal company were determining policy for both companies. A resolution similar to the one proposed by President Gray in 1880 was introduced in August, 1882. It authorized new board member John Haug, a skilled marine engineer and architect, to draw up the plans and estimates for a steamboat suitable for use in the canal. Haug's drawings were presented to the board at its September meeting and discussed at length, but again the subject was tabled. In October, the group once again presented its plan for the immediate construction of steamboats to be operated by the company and moved that the contracts be let at once. The vote on this motion ended in a 6-6 tie, with President Gray among those voting against the resolution, which thus failed of adoption. The lack of quorums at subsequent meetings prior to the new elections in June, 1883, prevented further action.[4]

[3] Board Minute Book, November 10, December 7, 1880.
[4] Ibid., August 1, September 5, October 3, November 7, 1882.

The failure to obtain a quorum grew out of a stormy meeting of the stock- and loanholders in December, 1882. It was proposed at this meeting to appoint a committee composed of the presidents of the Philadelphia Trust Company, the Pennsylvania Company for Insurance on Lives, and the Insurance Company of North America, each company having large interests in the canal. "Whereas, a difference of opinion exists in the Board of Directors as to the policy to be pursued by the Company in exercising its rights of transportation," this committee was to be asked to examine the question and to advise the company accordingly. When the vote was taken on the resolution, considerable argument resulted over the legality of certain proxies, including those for voting the stock of the United States and the state of Maryland. The persons holding these proxies, one of whom was the president of the Ericsson Line, had only recently attempted to qualify themselves as proprietors in the canal company by obtaining one or two shares of its stock. Although their votes were disallowed, the resolution appointing the committee still failed by a vote of 7,049 to 7,793. Following defeat of this resolution, John Cadwalader, the holder of only $3,000 in canal bonds and two shares of canal stock but the owner of 1,630 shares in the Ericsson Line company, then proposed, in effect, that the men added to the board in June, 1882, be removed. After declaring the seats on the board vacant, the proprietors proceeded to have a new election. A. Sydney Biddle, Thomas A. Biddle, and John Haug were not reelected, but these men refused to relinquish their seats on the grounds that the December election was illegal. Less than 2,000 shares of stock had been represented at the time of the election. An impasse resulted at the January, 1883, meeting of the board, after which those in sympathy with Cadwalader absented themselves from subsequent meetings, making quorums impossible.[5]

A bitter struggle for proxies occurred prior to the important board election of 1883. A pamphlet issued by directors Thomas A. Biddle, John R. Baker, John Haug, Charles Chauncey, and A. Sydney Bidddle in May, 1883, entitled *Questions for the Consideration of the Stock and Loanholders of the Chesapeake and Delaware Canal Company, regarding the decline of its prosperity, the means of arresting it, whether the policy of the Company should be determined by the owners of it, or by the owners of the Ericsson Line*, reviewed

[5] Stockholders' Minutes, December 4, 5, 1882.

their struggle to obtain the exercise of transportation powers by the canal company and enlisted the support of other stock- and loan-holders. They substantiated the charge that "persons largely interested in other corporations with diverse interests from those of the Chesapeake and Delaware Canal Company" were influencing the direction of the canal company and warned that unless the revenues of the company were increased before 1886, the date the Mortgage Loan of $1,993,750 became due, the company would probably be liquidated. Only the exercise of transportation powers, in their opinion, would restore prosperity.

This appeal of Biddle and his associates was unavailing, for in June the five directors involved, in addition to Gustavus S. Benson, were not reelected. The results of the balloting were very close: 9,356 votes were necessary for election, and the five unsuccessful candidates received 8,146 votes. A formal protest of the proceedings was made by Moncure Robinson, who objected to the majority adopting a ticket which eliminated all those who had voted with the minority on the question of transportation powers. Robinson was satisfied that this minority on the board represented most of "those having a real interest in the welfare & prosperity of the Company." Henry V. Lesley, also in sympathy with the Biddle group, was removed in June, 1883, as company secretary, a post he had held for almost thirty years. His assistant, J. A. L. Wilson, succeeded him, and Wilson's former position was filled by B. P. Hutchinson, the son of one of the company directors. Lesley endeavored to carry on the struggle for transportation powers and tried to obtain proxies for the election of 1884. He wrote two pamphlets designed to expose the conflict of interest among various board members. His *Vindication of the Late Secretary of the Company* appeared in November, 1883, and an *Appendix to the Vindication of the Late Secretary of the Company* was published the following March. He charged that "the chronic poverty" of the canal company was "a natural consequence of a particular policy governing its Board of Directors," a policy "dictated by the interests of the Ericsson Line," and observed that the financial ratings of the company since the election of the "Ericsson Line Board" in 1883 had noticeably declined. Using as his barometer the price of the Mortgage Loan of the company, Lesley pointed out that the bonds, formerly selling at 70, had advanced to 92 when it appeared that the company would use its transportation powers. After the June election, however, the price returned to approximately 70, while the price of the Ericsson Line stock, already selling at double its par value, advanced.[6]

As a result of the charges repeatedly made by Biddle, Lesley, and others, the stock- and loanholders approved the appointment in June, 1883, of a committee to investigate the "relations, engagements or Contracts" existing between the canal company and the Ericsson Line, although John Cadwalader blocked a second resolution instructing the board to go ahead with plans to build and operate two steamboats, and the committee originally appointed failed to make a report. The board did request President Gray to state his views on the subject, and he submitted a letter he had written to Thomas A. Biddle on May 3, 1883, in which he denied the existence of any intimate relationship between the two companies: "I know of no contracts, written, verbal, or implied, between the Ericsson companies and the Canal Company, giving the exclusive right to the Ericsson Line of carrying freight through the Canal for any length of time. Such a contract, the Canal Company has, under its charter, no power to make." [7]

Gray explained that the canal was a "free highway" for the transportation of commodities in all vessels not using steam, upon payment of the prescribed tolls. "The use of Steam as a propelling power, is by permission, solely to be granted, refused, revoked when granted, at the discretion of the canal company. Such use is conditioned upon the payment of the same tolls as other vessels are required to pay, with the addition of fifty per cent to the tolls for the privilege of using steam." All steamers were subject to the additional charge. When the percentage system adopted "some years ago" for the Ericsson Line was used, the percentage was fixed so as to cover both the tolls and the steamer surcharge. Gray believed, however, that competing freight lines were not "conducive to the interest of the Canal Company," and that a single line, if fully equipped to provide adequate freight service between Philadelphia and Baltimore and New York and Baltimore, "not liable to be subsidized by competing lines, conducted with enterprise, intelligence, efficiency and willingness, would better subserve the interests of the canal." He admitted that the canal company, "while it could not prevent competing lines in the canal, would

[6] *Ibid.*, June 5, 1883; Henry V. Lesley, *Chesapeake and Delaware Canal Company. Appendix to the Vindication of the Late Secretary of the Company* (Philadelphia, 1884), p. 4; Lesley, *Chesapeake and Delaware Canal Company. Vindication of the Late Secretary of the Company* (Philadelphia, 1883), pp. 9–10.

[7] Stockholders' Minutes, June 5, 1883; Board Minute Book, July 3, 1883.

not encourage such competing lines," but on the contrary "would manifest a policy not friendly" to their establishment.[8]

Gray was not willing for either a third company or the canal company itself to undertake to establish a freighting business competitive with the Ericsson Line, on either of the two routes through the canal it served, and his wishes were followed. As the board stated in a communication to the newly established Interstate Commerce Commission in April, 1887, the canal company "is not a Common Carrier. It is simply the owner of the Chesapeake and Delaware Canal, and as such receives toll from those using the same for the purposes of transportation; but it is not itself engaged in that business; and does not own, or have any interest, in any of the boats or vessels engaged in traffic upon said Canal."[9]

Throughout most of the 1880's, the canal and its works were in good repair, although the limited accommodations of the waterway were increasingly evident. In order to pass the new 450-ton barges in use in 1885, it was necessary to maintain the water in the canal at the maximum possible depth, which required certain repairs to depressed sections of the banks. A new iron summit bridge, the third of five built there between 1826 and 1960, was constructed in 1882–83. On August 1, 1883, the building which housed the water wheel and its two steam engines burned, but the machinery inside sustained little damage and pumping was resumed August 11. Minor difficulties were again experienced in the deep cut when still another slip occurred late in the decade, but prompt action prevented the canal from being blocked.

Traffic through the canal remained relatively stable, and a thorough toll revision in 1884 produced more revenue and let the company once more operate in the black. During the winter of 1883–84, after a seven-year period in which only twice had the company realized a net profit, both of less than $5,000, the toll committee analyzed the returns and discovered that, in some cases, articles were carried "at a rate below the actual cost per ton to the Canal Company," with coal being the worst offender. Tolls therefore were increased in a number of cases. Because of a proposition made by John Wilson, general freight agent of the Pennsylvania Railroad, to join with the canal company "in making a general increase in the rates on all merchandize, both by canal & rail," it was possible to raise the toll on coal

[8] Board Minute Book, July 3, 1883, April 5, 1887.
[9] Ibid., April 5, 1887.

from 7 to 20 cents. The other increases were less radical, but they were such that permitted the board's proud announcement to the proprietors in 1885 concerning the financial results of the toll increase. Business for the calender year 1883 had resulted in a deficit of $20,758; business in calendar 1884 resulted in a profit of $29,799. Most of the difference was accounted for by an increase in the total receipts; expenses were only $14,000 less in the latter year.[10]

According to an analysis of the canal's trade made in March, 1886, by J. A. L. Wilson, the secretary-treasurer of the company who later confessed to embezzlement, the principal revenue came from the Ericsson Line steamers trading between New York, Philadelphia, and Baltimore and carrying assorted cargo. From a total revenue during 1885 of approximately $200,000, more than $69,000 came from this source. The leading bulk items carried through the canal were coal, wood, oysters, wheat, and iron, although in quantities considerably diminished since approximately 1870.

Wilson assigned various causes for the diminution in trade of certain products: "The almost total loss" of the timber trade was caused by "the exhaustion of the Forrests [sic]"; "The Lumber trade from Penna. is lost principally by Railroad competition"; the once-great peach trade disappeared because the peach-growing belt was "removed from the Canal & vicinity by the exhaustion of the Soil [and] We lose some by Railroad competition." There was also a growing tendency for some products to use the outside or sea route rather than the canal in passing from Chesapeake Bay northward. Of nearly 1,000,000 tons of coal shipped from Baltimore to points north, only 121,000 tons passed through the canal. Finally, the trade in wheat and other grains had been seriously affected "by the competition of grain from the West coming directly to the eastern cities by rail." Wilson pointed out that the average canal toll had declined from 48 cents per ton in 1866 to 18 cents in 1885, and he was convinced that causes more fundamental than "a want of attention to our toll sheets" accounted for the overall decline in traffic and revenue since the prosperous days immediately following the Civil War.[11]

In spite of the traffic decline, the net profits during the fiscal years 1885 and 1886 exceeded $58,000. As a result of this achievement, the board was optimistic about the possibility of extending the

[10] Ibid., March 15, 1884, May 28, 1885.
[11] J. A. L. Wilson, "Analysis of the Canal Trade," March 18, 1886, C & D Papers, HSD.

TABLE 6. ANALYSIS OF THE CANAL TRADE, 1850–87 (in thousands)[a]

Year Ends June 1	Coal (tons)	Lumber (sq. ft.)	Timber (cu. ft.)	Grain (bu.)	Flour (bbls.)	Groceries (lbs.)	Dry Goods (lbs.)	Iron (tons)
1850	54	44,795	2,145	1,826	114	32,103	23,645	30
1851	60	46,454	2,231	1,831	134	36,451	22,342	30
1852	60	49,294	1,528	2,044	120	37,940	16,345	23
1853	87	56,968	3,882	2,018	128	40,169	17,682	32
1854	123	56,548	3,414	2,113	110	39,130	15,243	39
1855	178	62,262	2,930	1,470	116	37,847	14,277	36
1856	161	64,534	4,014	1,760	156	37,580	13,108	46
1857	203	65,144	2,900	1,908	201	36,642	14,755	42
1858	178	52,544	2,904	1,896	155	34,193	16,979	27
1859	175	35,648	3,152	1,065	101	34,358	26,812	36
1860	193	58,833	3,143	1,646	148	43,072	31,303	37
1861	195	55,080	3,185	1,277	198	43,801	31,592	27
1862	150	32,211	4,148	2,350	117	69,070	31,655	23
1863	177	59,600	4,024	2,883	180	59,885	20,156	42
1864	218	57,740	5,309	1,341	207	76,471	19,998	38
1865	361	33,597	7,037	866	168	67,419	14,672	26
1866	268	28,665	4,723	706	122	61,058	17,573	35
1867	382	42,925	4,770	1,553	114	53,657	19,744	42
1868	331	42,990	4,114	1,687	221	134,684	19,756	42
1869	577	87,535	3,933	882	215	151,761	20,254	73
1870	581	86,528	4,698	870	368	172,556	18,886	69
1871	689	102,478	5,611	815	255	121,623	13,474	44
1872	743	70,772	2,253	762	248	113,055	15,840	53
1873	741	69,888	3,538	254	147	127,946	20,902	48
1874	568	50,795	3,250	249	151	156,416	22,490	33
1875	510	45,414	2,577	193	137	191,380	16,216	45
1876	403	43,942	1,052	349	198	177,421	16,445	36
1877	353	33,451	834	349	194	123,432	13,596	28
1878	370	33,590	1,287	353	285	158,558	13,098	32
1879	323	21,583	1,530	291	170	134,880	12,829	25
1880	403	33,517	1,737	435	111	128,639	16,702	41
1881	349	26,279	1,057	233	93	108,000	12,658	31
1882	488	30,936	1,765	264	98	127,306	12,031	32
1883	430	28,507	1,183	399	71	119,684	10,450	36
1884	426	25,970	1,164	446	93	127,829	8,264	25
1885	441	23,073	383	263	65	97,771	5,811	18
1886	376	28,234	368	584	57	71,218	6,802	22
1887	326	27,039	640	45	33	38,053	5,034	24

[a]Source: "A General Statement of Leading Items of the Business of the Chesapeake and Delaware Canal from its Commencement," 1830–87, C & D Papers, HSD.

Mortgage Loan due July 1, 1886, for an additional thirty years. A committee was appointed in June, 1885, to consult with counsel and to mature "the best plan for its extension." There was some fear, as expressed in 1883 by the group anxious to acquire transportation powers, that the loanholders would insist upon payment in 1886 and thus force a foreclosure on the mortgage. As the committee explained in December, 1885, however, the loanholders already effectively controlled company affairs and there would be no advantage to a foreclosure which would eliminate the interest of the stockholders in the company and possibly destroy the company's franchise. In the critical election of 1883, the loanholders, with one vote for every $50, cast 11,956 votes; 6,212 votes were cast by the stockholders; in 1884, the loan vote exceeded the stock vote by 9,758 to 6,337 and in 1885 by 7,382 to 5,069. The committee then gave two important reasons for having the loan extended:

The state of Maryland has remained a large Stockholder in the Company, and from this cause that state has not taxed our property & franchises. Legislation in Maryland has frequently been required, & probably may be again; & it seems wise and proper for the Loanholders to sustain the property, & not to sacrifice the stock value, especially during a period of general depression.

The United States too, hold more than ⅜ of the capital stock and if legislation by Congress favoring a ship canal is secured, then the route of the present canal would be selected; or, if another route be preferred, an indemnity for the resulting injury to the present property could be fairly asked.

"A foreclosure and extinguishment of this interest," it concluded, "appears therefore to be unjustifiable." [12]

Arrangements were made early in 1886 with the Home Improvement Company of Philadelphia for the acceptance of any bonds which the present holders decided not to extend. A commission of 2 per cent on the entire amount of the loan was to be paid the investment company for its services. Although $1,993,750 of the original $2,800,000 loan remained outstanding, the company planned to redeem an additional $18,750 and extend only $1,975,000. The interest rate on the new thirty-year loan was to be lowered from 6 to 5 per cent.

A "Summary of Business of the Chesapeake & Delaware Canal for 29 Years, from June 1st, 1856, to May 31st, 1885" was drawn up, printed, and distributed among the loanholders to acquaint them with the financial history of the company and to induce them to renew

[12] Board Minute Book, June 2, December 15, 1885.

their bonds. The document pointed out that the company's total income during this time was $8,034,220.07, and its total expenses exclusive of interest on loans were $2,628,092.45. Deducting the interest payments on the mortgage loan, amounting to $3,919,950.31, from the net income of $5,406,127.62, the profit for the period amounted to $1,486,177.31, most of which had been distributed among the stockholders. "The average annual profit during the twenty-nine years has been $186,418.19, equal to 9⅓ per cent on the present indebtedness." The average tonnage was 872,061 tons, with traffic heaviest during the decade following 1865. Then an average of 1,089,710 tons a year was carried, but an average of 892,549 tons was carried in the decade ending in 1885. It was expected that similar amounts of traffic would be carried in the future. Security for the $1,975,000 loan would be a property which had cost $3,989,365.07 to construct.

A crushing blow to the hopes of the canal company for eventual financial solvency came just one day before the Mortgage Loan of 1856 was to be refinanced. On the morning of June 30, when President Joseph E. Gillingham, who had succeeded the late Andrew C. Gray only the year before, arrived at the company office, he discovered a letter from J. A. L. Wilson announcing a shortage of more than $600,000. Subsequent audits determined the exact figure to be $609,200 lost through the issue of unauthorized bonds, and $52,740.47 through the misappropriation of cash. The fraudulent bond issues had been occurring since 1862, and the cash withdrawals since 1883. Wilson's contrite and rather pathetic written confession informing the company of its misfortune is reproduced in full:

Dear Sir: There is an over issue of the Bonds of this Company amounting to $615,200.50. The balances in the Banks has not for a long time been what I represented them. This rough sheet hastily prepared will show you just what there is on hand, the amount of over issue, [and] the amount as Loan extended which is greater than I have told you. Having hoped against hope still to cover my crime by misrepresenting the amount extended, until they stopped the extension. Then there was no hope for me and I began to prepare for a living death with all the nerve I was master of. The sheet will show the balance of cash on hand, including contingent Fund and everything. When this past weeks receipts are collected for $43,464.19. I have been so driven that I have not been able to count up exactly what it should be, but you can ascertain in a few moments by entering the checks paid since June 1st & footing up. The difference will be the correct balance that should be on hand. All the books as far as I know are correct and will show things exactly as they are. The cash book and ledger are in balance correct, except that the money represented is not all there. The Stock Ledger is all right, in every way and foots up correctly, unless there happen to be clerical errors somewhere. The Loan Ledger balances agree with the amount on the sheets and Interest Book and show the exact amount of Loan outstanding and who holds it. The[y] foot up E. & D. excepted, $2,595,263.72. The Ledger alone showing the additional $10,686.81 of the dividend fund. The bank books are in my desk where I have always kept them hidden. When balanced they will show, I think, just what you will find in this. The Delaware City Bank account is all right. The others are terribly short and have been for a long time. There are also two $1,000 bonds Lehigh Valley R.Rd. gone. Otherwise those securities and all others are intact, in the box at the Fidelity. If I may say a word to advise in your perplexity that I have brought upon you, these Securities can be realized on by sale or loan immediately, so that the Interest may be paid on Thursday. There will be plenty for that, of course the Investment Company will not be bound by their Contract and will not take the bonds. The holders will be obliged to extend or take possession of the Canal. The loss will fall on the Stockholders, unless the Bondholders get frightened and sacrifice their holdings. The income of the Canal will be sufficient to pay all expenses & 5% interest on $2,600,000, only $10,000. more than they have been paying recently and $15,000. less than they paid up to 1863. I don't say this in any excuse of myself, but only God Help me to make it as easy for you as possible. I had intended to spend the day in fixing everything as straight as possible, in order that I might leave behind me no more trouble for others than was necessary, and then have written you a more full account of it. But as you know I have had no chance, now it is too late.

What can I say, my heart and life is broken. Though I care little for myself, but what of my family and friends who have loved me and believed in me and trusted me. I took this great burden on myself *alone* and you don't know what the word means. Three years ago last June because I had been partly responsible for it and had not grace or courage enough to bear the shame as long as I could hide it. God only knows the terror and shame of the burden of it. Yet I have borne it and hidden it and tried to appear happy and cheerful and tried to make those around me happy as far as I could, while the canker has been eating out my own vitals. I am an old man before my time. I cannot take time to talk of this. I only want to say Mr. Lesley and I are alone responsible for all that is wrong in all this. We have deceived our friends and superior officers as you have been deceived. We have made use of innocent friends in the Company and out, to buy and sell and borrow on the Bonds. People who thought us, as they, above suspicion; who trusted us and our word. I want to say for Palmer Hutchinson [Chairman of the Finance Committee], may God forgive me and he for what he will suffer by it. That not only was he unconscious of any wrong as yourself or dear old Mr. Gray, but he has had no opportunity, except by chance, of finding out or by acting as a spy on my actions, which he has been too honorable to do, what has passed careful examinations by examiners who were more experienced than he, might readily escape his notice, who was not called in to examine. Mr. Lesley and

I alone must bear it, as we alone did it. And now I must go far away to distant lands to live a living death, old, poor, and friendless there or to remain
quietly near home till I rest. Oh, God, how I *need rest* — rest and then come
back to submit to the penalty I have deserved. I have not yet decided. My
friends bid me go away. What good is there in staying. Who will think
better of me for it? Not one will think it, though they will say it. But I
must now go, for I am too broken and unnerved to meet you and Mr.
Hutchinson, Mr. Swift and others, of more kind friends who I have so
terribly wronged. The hours are flying and I must go. I have told my friends
yesterday and they have broken me down. How I stood it today I don't
know. How gladly would I help you in all this trouble; were I only innocent.
I must go and hide and bear my burden.[13]

After reading this startling letter, Gillingham immediately called
a special meeting of the board and steps were taken to correct the
disorders. Payment of the interest due on July 1 was postponed until
an expert examination of the financial records could be made and
the actual indebtedness of the company established. While new arrangements for the refinancing of the debt were being made, the stock
and loan transfer ledgers were closed. Accountant Lawrence E. Brown
was employed on July 1 to audit the books. Although Brown's final
report was not submitted until December, plans were announced in
September for the establishment of a new Mortgage Loan. It had been
learned that the overissue of bonds had been going on for so many
years that nearly all the large loanholders had some of the fraudulent
bonds. Having been advised by counsel that the company was liable
for the overissue and that innocent holders of it were "entitled to the
security of the mortgage," the company proposed that new certificates
for the total amount of the loan outstanding, genuine and fraudulent,
be issued, the loan of $2,602,950 to run for thirty years at 5 per cent
interest per year. The interest due on the old loan in July was to be
paid on October 1, 1886.[14]

In making this proposal, the company pledged that all its earnings in excess of the 5 per cent interest charges, after paying current
expenses and maintaining a moderate reserve for contingencies,
would be used to reduce the loan to the amount it would have been
had no overissue occurred. In other words, all earnings were appropriated for the benefit of the loanholders. The stock of the company,

[13] J. A. L. Wilson to Joseph E. Gillingham, Philadelphia, June 29, 1886,
C & D Papers, HSD.
   [14] Board Minute Book, June 30, August 3, September 7, 21, October 5,
November 9, December 7, 1886. Brown's report is entered in the minutes for
December 7, 1886. See also the *Sixty-eighth General Report* (1887).

already practically valueless except for voting purposes, now became completely worthless. The net receipts of the company in the two preceding years had averaged $147,000, and the interest on the new loan would amount to $130,147.50. In 1893, because of a further decline in revenues, the interest rate on the loan was reduced to 4 per cent. This lowered the annual interest payment to $104,118, and it was regularly paid.[15]

Brown's audit revealed that Henry V. Lesley had initiated the fradulent practice of issuing the unauthorized bonds, and accordingly warrants for the arrest of both Wilson and Lesley were obtained. After a year-long search, Wilson was arrested in Canada and Lesley in Pennsylvania. Both men pleaded guilty to the charges preferred against them and were sentenced to prison, Lesley for eight years and Wilson for six. The total loss to the company, exclusive of the annual interest payment on the overissue, of $643,383.95 was charged to profit and loss. This included the amount of the overissue and the embezzlement plus some $15,800 spent in investigating the loss, less $10,000 recovered from Wilson's bondsmen, the Guarantee Company of North America, and the amount realized on the sale of property owned by Wilson, including some mining stock in Colorado. It was also learned in 1911, some thirty-five years after the event, that Lesley and Wilson had appropriated to their own use $51,187.50 in dividends belonging to the United States government.[16]

Care was taken to avoid a repetition of the unfortunate loss caused by the dishonesty of company employees. When Coleman L. Nicholson became secretary-treasurer in August, 1886, he was bonded at $25,000 rather than $10,000 and the practice of having monthly audits of the books by an accountant was instituted. Nicholson remained with the company until his death in 1916, serving for the last eleven years of his life as its president. His integrity and devotion to the company coupled with that of President Gillingham's could not undo the damage that had been done. The future of the Chesapeake and Delaware Canal as a privately owned property grew dimmer as time passed.

Consequently, the growing demand for more modern transportation facilities went unfulfilled, for it was impossible to finance the improvements required. The general decline of waterway transporta-

[15] Board Minute Book, September 21, 1886, April 4, 1893.
[16] *Sixty-eighth General Report* (1887), p. 7; Board Minute Book, January 9, 1912.

tion throughout the nation in the 1880's was the result of many factors, including increasingly severe, sometimes unfair, railroad competition and the obsolescence of waterway accommodations. A vicious circle was apparent, in that waterway traffic declined because of inadequate facilities, but improvements could not be financed because of the declining business. J. T. Rothrock pinpointed a crucial problem when he criticized the accommodations of the canal in 1884: "Who does not dread the Chesapeake and Delaware Canal, if he has any regard for his own vessel? Mine fared probably as well as small craft usually do in making the transit. . . . The helmsman of the canal-boat managed to jam my yacht against the rocks of the towpath, much to the injury of her planking. However, his associates remarked, by way of apology, 'The fellow is only half-witted.' I did not see the explanation made the rent in the plank smaller. It was a relief to be 'locked out' into Delaware Bay."[17] His all-too-typical experience helped develop the widening belief that a lock-free ship canal connecting Chesapeake and Delaware bays was necessary. If the debt-ridden owners were unable to make this improvement in their property, then another company or the federal government should do it.

[17] J. T. Rothrock, *Vacation Cruising in Chesapeake and Delaware Bays* (Philadelphia, 1884), p. 157.

The Revival of Inland Waterway Transportation

12

The demand for an improved Chesapeake and Delaware waterway coincided with a general movement for improved facilities. During the last decade of the nineteenth century the renewed interest in water transportation carried over, and reached large-scale proportions after the turn of the century. The reason was clear. By 1900 most waterways were in a deplorable condition, the combined effect of relentless railroad competition and inadequate facilities. They had been unable to keep pace with current transportation requirements. The peak tonnages and earnings on the better located canals came in the 1870's, after which the unprecedented development in railroads arrested further increases in waterway traffic. According to economist Harold G. Moulton, in the last quarter of the nineteenth century, "In all cases the traffic on the waterways failed to keep pace with that on the railroads, and in nearly every case the tonnage on the water routes declined absolutely."[1]

The Erie Canal carried its highest tonnage of 6,673,370 tons in 1872, the same year that the Chesapeake and Delaware Canal reached its peak of 1,318,772 tons. Similarly, the large traffic of 2,837,532 tons enjoyed by the Delaware and Raritan Canal in 1872 had been exceeded slightly only once (in 1866). But then a general and almost unbroken decline set in, which by 1900 saw traffic drop

[1] Quoted in Bureau of Railway Economics, *An Economic Survey of Inland Waterway Transportation in the United States* (Washington, 1930), p. 33.

to 623,751 tons on the Delaware and Raritan, to 639,543 tons on the Chesapeake and Delaware. The much greater decline on the former canal was largely attributable to railroad ownership. In 1871 the Pennsylvania Railroad acquired control of the canal across New Jersey by means of a 999-year lease, admittedly for the purpose of eliminating competition.

Despite the decline in waterway traffic, many people remained convinced that water transportation was cheaper than any type of land transportation. It was also believed that waterways were effective regulators of railroad freight rates. Consequently various plans for the improvement of rivers and canals were promulgated in the 1890's, although not until after 1900 and considerable agitation by countless local and regional commercial organizations boosting waterway development were some of them enacted.

The Chesapeake and Delaware Canal suffered during the decline of waterways in the 1880's and 1890's. In only four of the ten years between 1890 and 1899 did the company realize a small net profit on its operation. The net loss for the decade was approximately $23,000, which was made up by permanent borrowings from the contingent fund. Economy became the keynote of the company's operations, and steps were taken to reduce expenditures by cutting salaries, obtaining a reduced office rent, and delaying maintenance work at the canal. President Gillingham voluntarily accepted a salary reduction, although a committee studying this problem refused to recommend it, as it was "very important that the Canal Company should have at its head a President whose knowledge of our business and whose standing in the community will insure our receiving proper consideration both from customers and other carrying companies." The salaries of the other company officers were also lowered slightly, and the company decided to sublet its board room to a "responsible tenant," retaining the privilege of meeting there monthly.[2]

As it was necessary on several occasions in the early 1890's to borrow to meet the semiannual interest payments, the company acted in April, 1893, upon the Finance Committee's recommendation to lower the interest rate on the Mortgage Loan from 5 to 4 per cent. A letter sent to each loanholder explained that "notwithstanding the greatest economy consistent with the proper maintenance of the works, this Company did not earn the full interest on its bonded indebtedness of $2,602,950 from June 1889 to June 1892." To meet the deficien-

[2] Board Minute Book, June 3, 1890.

cies, $21,645 was taken from the contingent fund. A further deficiency being expected for 1893, "owing to the recent long and cold winter," the loanholders were asked to accept the smaller interest until the securities in the contingent fund had a market value of $100,000, "when, if the earnings permit, you will again be paid the five per cent." This proposal was accepted by the creditors at the general meeting in June, 1893. Because the emergency fund never reached the required $100,000, the 4 per cent interest rate was paid during the remainder of the company's existence.[3]

Not only lack of funds, a condition aggravated by the business depression, but the expectation that the government would soon purchase the property caused the postponement of normal maintenance work in the 1890's. In 1906 the company's new president, Frank L. Neall, made a confidential report to the board in which he pointed out that the former policy of keeping "the expenses of operation and repair" at the barest minimum had had its "natural result" — "the property has deteriorated until today, in some features, it is unsafe." All the lockgates badly leaked and were in danger of collapsing, most of the banks and bridges needed repairs, and a thorough dredging of the canal was required. Neall estimated that the "absolutely necessary" repairs would cost $60,000: "We call these expenditures extraordinary but they are in reality ordinary expenses which should have been distributed over the past fifteen years and which are now characterized as extraordinary because it is necessary to meet them within a period of three years."[4]

The company's failure, however, to maintain its property adequately in the 1890's is understandable. Congressional actions fostered the belief that a ship canal would soon be constructed across the Delmarva Peninsula, and the company at length determined to do all in its power to have its route accepted. Upon learning in 1892 that Senator Anthony Higgins of Delaware had introduced a bill for a ship canal survey along the route of the existing canal, the board investigated the possibilities of a ship canal more thoroughly and at first considered making the conversion itself. In September Professor Lewis M. Haupt, a member of the engineering department of the University of Pennsylvania, laid before the board a plan for enlarging the canal "to accommodate ocean steamers and other vessels of deep draft." With the aid of maps, drawings, and statistics, he made

[3] *Ibid.*, April 4, 1893.
[4] *Ibid.*, January 6, 1906.

a lucid presentation and concluded by estimating the probable increase in trade and the return upon capital invested in the project. At the same meeting Daniel Baugh from the Trades' League of Philadelphia announced that his organization had endorsed the ship canal project and recommended action upon it.[5]

A Ship Canal Committee was immediately appointed by the board to study the matter. It declared itself in "hearty accord" with Haupt and his associates, stating that a sea-level canal would not only be a financial success but be of great commercial value, especially to Baltimore and the entire state of Maryland. Because of its embarrassed financial condition, however, the company was unable to consider constructing it. Instead the company gave its unqualified assistance and support to the Casey Commission appointed in 1894 by President Cleveland to examine and determine, from the surveys already made, the most feasible route for a ship canal from Chesapeake Bay to Delaware Bay.

The special board was composed of five men with Brigadier General Thomas L. Casey, the chief of engineers, at its head. Captain George Dewey of the navy, Colonel William P. Craighill of the army, E. Porter Alexander of South Carolina, and Mendes Cohen of Maryland were the other members. Casey convened the group in Washington on November 1, 1894, after which a full discussion of the ship canal subject took place. Craighill, who twelve years earlier had suggested that such a commission be appointed and who was thoroughly conversant with the details of the problem at hand, supplied invaluable assistance to his colleagues in the course of their deliberations. All of the relevant government records were examined, especially the engineering reports of Craighill and Turtle made in 1879–83, and other records were obtained and studied. A public hearing was given a group from Baltimore, headed by General Felix Agnus, formed to promote the construction of a Chesapeake and Delaware ship canal. Agnus, who twelve years later was to preside over a similar government commission, informed the Casey Commission that Baltimore opposed three of the seven ship canal routes previously surveyed and consequently under consideration. Objections to the southern Choptank River route and to the northern Sassafras River and Back Creek routes were lodged, based on the belief that shippers would not use them. The Baltimore committee favored any one of the four central, more direct routes between Baltimore and the Atlantic Ocean, pro-

[5] *Ibid.*, September 1, 1892.

vided it be a true ship canal, free of locks. Captain J. Frank Supplee of the Merchants and Manufacturers Association emphasized the latter point: "a free ship canal, wide enough to admit the commerce of the world, no Baltimorean is opposed to."[6]

In opposition to the routes favored by Baltimore, a circular letter, signed by, among others, Joseph E. Gillingham, president of the Chesapeake and Delaware Canal Company, set forth the advantages of the existing canal as the best route for the ship canal. This letter was sent to Casey in November by William T. Malster, president and general manager of the Columbian Iron Works and Dry Dock Company of Baltimore. Malster listed seven specific advantages enjoyed by the northernmost route. Located just to the south of a straight line joining Baltimore and Philadelphia, it offered the most direct and safest connection between Chesapeake Bay ports and large eastern ports. A ship canal there would permit the quickest passage from Baltimore to the sea, because of the shorter distance of canal to be traversed at slow speed. There would be a saving in the original cost of construction and in the annual charges for maintenance and operation. The country possessed, moreover, an accurate knowledge of the engineering problems to be overcome on this route, and it was the best protected in case of war. Finally, in perhaps his weakest point, Malster claimed there would be less liability to ice obstruction, although others too discounted the ice problem.

Frederick Schriver, president of the New York and Baltimore Transportation Line, a subsidiary of the Ericsson Line, stated in a letter to Craighill that "our steamers run regularly every day (or worse, every night), and though the use of a tug is required to assist them during the heavy ice season, still they experience less trouble on account of ice than they have had in the lower bay from the same cause." He asserted that the short northern canal route would be the fastest and safest of all. Schriver stated he was not prejudiced in favor of the present canal, but he thought that his company's experience of operating through the canal for the past fifty years was worth something.[7]

[6] "Letter from the Secretary of War, transmitting the Report of the Board appointed under the River and Harbor Act of August, 1894, to examine and determine, from surveys heretofore made, the most feasible route for the construction of the Chesapeake and Delaware Canal," *House Exececutive Documents*, No. 102, 53rd Congress, 3rd Session (Washington, 1894), Appendix, pp. 93–99. Hereafter this will be cited as *Casey Report*.

[7] *Ibid.*, pp. 104–106.

Additional support for Malster's and Schriver's position in 1894 came from the canal company itself. It joined in "calling attention to the advantages possessed by the line of our canal over any other proposed route," and supplied the commission with full statistical and general information. A copy of the *Seventy-fifth General Report* forwarded to Casey was included in his final report.[8]

After considering the material and statements placed before them, Casey and his colleagues made their report to Congress. According to their instructions, they were to select the route "which in [their] judgment shall give the greatest facility to commerce and will be best adapted for national defense." On both grounds, it was unanimously agreed that the "most feasible route" was the Back Creek route, "which is substantially located upon the line of the existing Chesapeake and Delaware Canal." The board noted that most of the pressure for a ship canal heretofore had come from Baltimore, a port with a sizable foreign commerce seeking direct access to the ocean, but it based its recommendations more upon the advantages to coastwise than to foreign traffic:

The gain in time arising from the use of any of the routes by foreign traffic is so small in comparison with the duration of the entire voyage, that vessels will not for so slight an advantage be prone to risk encountering the delays to which navigation is liable in restricted channels. This board is of the opinion, supported by the information at hand, that a canal constructed on any of the suggested routes would be used largely by domestic or coastwise trade, and probably to but a very limited extent by foreign commerce.

This fact, however, had no bearing upon the size of the canal to be constructed, for in order to be useful in national defense, its dimensions needed to be such as to pass ocean-going vessels.[9]

Although its decision was not based on this, the board also pointed out that the northernmost route would be much cheaper to construct, that there would be fewer bridges and therefore fewer land obstructions, and that ice was not expected to be a problem on any route. "But the selection of the more northern route is especially indicated when its adaptation for national defense is considered." The route had to be defended, and a recently approved project for the defense of Philadelphia would serve to protect both Philadelphia and the eastern entrance to the existing canal: "Any one of the other

[8] *Ibid.*, pp. 106–108; Board Minute Book, November 13, 1894.
[9] *Casey Report*, pp. 4–5, 6.

routes would require special fortifications for the defense of its Delaware Bay end, and the width of this bay and the character of its shoals and westerly shore are unfavorable to a system of complete defense at a cost at all within reason." Finally, since such a canal "must eventually form but a link in a chain of interior navigation passing to the north to and through the waters of New York Harbor," the northern route again was "best adapted, affording as it does the minimum of restricted canal way and the minimum of total length." [10]

For the first time since the government had authorized the original ship canal engineering reports in 1878, the route of the existing Chesapeake and Delaware Canal received favorable mention. A long struggle remained, however, before the government would act upon this and subsequent recommendations, all of which continued to favor conversion of the lock canal. Nevertheless, the selection made by Casey's commission was not a popular one, especially in Baltimore. An editorial in the *Baltimore American*, a newspaper owned by General Agnus, lamented the board's work as wasted effort: "After all the earnest work of the City of Baltimore for a ship canal, the Commission appointed by President Cleveland has killed the enterprise. Its selection of the 'Back-Creek' route . . . is grotesque. . . . In its present shape, the canal is dead, dead as a door nail. No ship canal will be dug along that route. . . . Some day a ship canal will be constructed, but it will be . . . not an inland ditch to the mud flats of the Delaware River." The disaffection of some, coupled with the government's desire for economy following the panic of 1893, prevented positive steps from being taken at once to acquire and convert the Chesapeake and Delaware Canal. Not until 1906 did Congress once again authorize another investigation of the subject. By this time a "water renaissance" was in full swing. [11]

According to William R. Willoughby's recent study of waterway transportation, the activity on behalf of waterway development during the early 1900's was unprecedented. "With the possible exception of the twenty-five years following the close of the War of 1812," he wrote in 1961, "at no time in the history of the American people has interest in rivers and canals been quite so intense as during the first ten or fifteen years of the present century. They wrote about waterways, talked about them, created dozens of associations to promote

[10] *Ibid.*, pp. 5–6.
[11] *Baltimore American*, December, 1894, in the Letters, Pamphlets, Magazines Re Sassafras Canal File, Society Collection, Maryland Historical Society (Baltimore).

their development, and persuaded their congressmen to vote millions of dollars for their improvement." [12]

The reasons for this revival of interest are not hard to discover. In addition to the beliefs, already mentioned, that transportation by water was considerably cheaper than railroad transportation and that waterways would serve as effective regulators of railroad rates, there was the simple factor of need. A "freight congestion and car famine" situation occurred on the railroads, reaching critical proportions in 1906 and 1907. The railroads, once hostile to any competition from waterways, recognized during this time the advantages of having water communications developed. The presidents of both the Pennsylvania and the Baltimore and Ohio railroads in 1904 announced their approval of the project for deepening the Chesapeake and Delaware Canal, and James J. Hill, perhaps the most influential railroad leader of the period, made a more sweeping endorsement of waterway development in a speech delivered to the Lakes-to-the-Gulf Deep Waterway Association in 1908. Hill stated that no intelligent railroad man feared waterways as a competitor, not because they were "either unimportant or powerless, but because the two carriers are supplementary instead of mutually destructive." "The future of the waterway is assured," he declared, "not so much as a competitor, but as a helper of the railroad." Hill previously had remarked that it would require the expenditure of $5,500,000,000 to equip the nation's railroads to handle all of the traffic then offering. [13]

Finally, the conservation movement of the early twentieth century gave additional vigor to the advocates of waterway improvements. Under the leadership of President Theodore Roosevelt, Gifford Pinchot, and others, the country was made to realize that waterway development would assist in preserving the nation's land, forests, wildlife, and mineral resources. As Pinchot said in an address to the first

[12] William R. Willoughby, *The St. Lawrence Waterway: A Study in Politics and Diplomacy* (Madison, 1961), pp. 72–73.

[13] *Ibid.*, pp. 73–74; Anthony Higgins, "The Greater Canal from the Delaware Viewpoint," ADWA, *Proceedings* (1908), p. 141; James J. Hill, *The Future of Rail and Water Transportation* (n.p., n.d.,), pp. 4, 10.

S. A. "Waterways" Thompson, long the secretary of the National Rivers and Harbors Congress, repeated the point about the mutual benefits of railway-waterway development in a colorful way in 1924: "If Noah had prophesied a drought, instead of a flood, and had issued bonds to construct an irrigation system, instead of building an Ark, he would have been a bright and shining example of business sagacity compared to a railway man who opposes the improvement of waterways." "Is Transportation Cheaper by Water than by Rail?" *Congressional Digest*, III (September, 1924), 392.

annual meeting of the Atlantic Deeper Waterways Association, "Forest protection . . . is waterway protection"; he pleaded for concerted action by "forest men," "river men," and "Atlantic Deeper Waterways men" to foster their common aim: "I've gotten very tired of having the different branches of this great movement of ours, for the conservation of natural resources, beaten in detail. There should be concentration and coordination."[14]

Professor Lewis M. Haupt, who became a member of the board of directors of the Chesapeake and Delaware Canal Company in 1906, emphasized many of these points in a series of articles written between 1895 and 1910. He studied the European experience in developing waterways and pointed out that the millions of dollars spent in France, Germany, Belgium, Holland, and elsewhere to improve their navigable waterways, "because of the admittedly great economies of the water-borne traffic," also served to increase railway traffic. He believed the European example "should serve to impress upon the most incredulous the fact that the improvement of the internal waterways of the country is not injurious to the great railroad interests, and that . . . there are advantages which far outweigh the small loss of revenue that may possibly result from the withdrawal of the bulky freights which are too often carried at a loss and serve to congest the terminals."[15]

It was generally agreed that certain waterways should be restored to carry the low-grade bulk freight which was clogging the railroads and delaying the shipment of other commodities which trains were best able to carry. The railway effort in the latter nineteenth century to eliminate water competition had, if anything, been too successful. By 1908, with a network of 225,000 miles of line, the railroads were unable to meet the transportation demands of the country. Some roads discriminated against certain types of freight and accepted only the high-value commodities on which the return was worthwhile. Even the great advantage of speed was lost because of the traffic congestion. Freight movements by rail from Philadelphia to New York in 1907, for example, required a week or more because of terminal delays, whereas the slower but steady waterways carried their much smaller volumes of freight between the two points overnight. "It is the old

[14] Gifford Pinchot, "Forestry and Waterways," ADWA, *Proceedings* (1908), pp. 169–170.
[15] Lewis M. Haupt, "The Urgent Need of Waterway Legislation," *North American Review*, CLXXXI (September, 1905), 423–425. See also Haupt, "Waterways: An Economic Necessity," *Forum*, XXXIV (January, 1903), 453–465.

story of the race between the tortoise and the hare," said Joseph E. Ransdell of Louisiana, a member of the House of Representatives' Committee on Rivers and Harbors and president of the National Rivers and Harbors Congress. "The former won in spite of his slow movements because he kept going. And the boats win for the same reason. They do not slumber on side tracks, as the hare and the railroad, but keep moving like the patient tortoise and win every time." [16]

A series of developments between 1900 and 1910 marked the renewed interest in waterways. During this time a number of local commercial organizations were formed to promote various waterway developments, and regional organizations, composed largely of merchants, manufacturers, and civic organizations, arose to boost more comprehensive schemes. The two most influential were the Lakes-to-the-Gulf Deep Waterway Association, formed in 1906 to promote construction of a channel sufficient for ocean-going vessels from Chicago to the mouth of the Mississippi via the Illinois River, and the Atlantic Deeper Waterways Association, organized the following year to further the construction of an inland waterway stretching from Boston to Key West by uniting the natural bodies of water along the coast via a series of short canals. There was also a powerful national organization, the National Rivers and Harbors Congress, which was formed in 1901 and which held annual meetings after its reorganization in 1906. [17]

Insisting that it advocated not a project but a policy, the National Rivers and Harbors Congress favored regular annual appropriations

[16] Joseph E. Ransdell, "Legislative Program Congress Should Adopt for Improvement of American Waterways," *Annals*, American Academy of Political and Social Science, XXXI (January, 1908), 38–39. Hereafter this publication will be cited as *Annals*, AAPSS.

[17] For more information concerning the Atlantic Deeper Waterways Association and the National Rivers and Harbors Congress and their continuing activities, see, in addition to their own publications, Arthur Maass, *Muddy Waters: The Army Engineers and the Nation's Rivers* (Cambridge, Massachusetts, 1951), pp. 41–43, 45–51, *et passim*. Senator Ransdell briefly explained the purpose of the Rivers and Harbors Congress in 1917, in response to the question: "Is not the object, or one of the chief objects, of the organization to coerce Congress into making appropriations for rivers and harbors?" "No, sir," he answered, "the objects of the . . . Congress are, in every proper way by publicity, to overcome the remarkable ignorance which seems to possess the American people and many Senators in regard to waterway transportation and, having overcome that ignorance, to try to induce Congress to make proper and reasonable appropriations for every worthy watercourse in this land." *Congressional Record*, 65th Congress, 1st Session, p. 5467.

for the development of waterways. Composed of individuals, including various congressional leaders, corporations, commercial organizations, and waterway associations from 33 states, it sought to "unite all friends of waterways in an effort to have Congress adopt a definite policy that will provide for the complete improvement within ten years of every worthy and deserving water course on our seaboards, lakes, and interior." President Ransdell described the program of the organization and the need for immediate legislation fostering waterways in an issue of the *Annals* of the American Academy of Political and Social Science devoted to this subject. He asserted his belief that freight movements by water not only were faster than those by rail but also cheaper: "From the best information I can get after a careful study of the subject, I am convinced that *waterway transportation in this country, under favorable conditions, costs only about one-sixth as much as the average cost by rail.*" He declared that waterway expenditures were sound investments, and recommended three courses of action for the United States Congress at its next session: the prompt passage of a rivers and harbors bill appropriating at least $50,000,000; the creation of a national waterways commission to study waterways here and abroad, and to advise Congress thereon; and the creation of a department of transportation for the control and coordination of all matters relating to highways, railways, and waterways. These steps were not taken by Congress immediately, but the National Waterways Commission was appointed in 1909 and the proposal for a department of transportation, with its secretary to have cabinet rank, recently has been adopted.[18]

In addition to the so-called booster organizations, certain other developments stimulated the growth of the waterways movement. New York's decision in 1903 to spend $101,000,000 to convert the Erie Canal into a modern barge canal demonstrated the faith of the people of that state in their historic but antiquated waterway, and President Roosevelt recognized the pressing need for adequate waterways elsewhere. Believing that rivers and canals were necessary to meet the transportation demands of the country, Roosevelt in March, 1907, appointed the Inland Waterways Commission to study the problem in all its forms — navigation, irrigation, reclamation, and conservation. The nine-man group, with Senator Theodore E. Burton of Ohio as its chairman, was to draw up a comprehensive plan for the

[18] Ransdell, "Legislative Program," pp. 37, 39, 47.

improvement and control of the waterway system of the nation. Reporting early in 1908, the commission announced that the time was at hand "for restoring and developing such inland navigation and water transportation as upon expert examination may appear to confer a benefit commensurate with the cost, to be utilized both independently and as a necessary adjunct to rail transportation." It recommended the systematic improvement of inland waterways, the collection of more adequate statistics concerning domestic commerce, and the creation of a National Waterways Commission. Established in 1909, this commission in its final report in 1912 made specific recommendations designed to aid water transportation and to encourage greater cooperation between rail and water carriers.[19]

The movement for a Chesapeake and Delaware ship canal was bolstered by the revived interest in waterways nationally. The Casey Commission report of 1894, recommending the line of the Chesapeake and Delaware Canal as the best route for the new canal, however, had failed to settle the question. According to General Agnus, "there remained open enough difference of opinion to influence the government in making another investigation." Moreover, no appraisal of the value of the existing canal had been made. Consequently a joint resolution authorizing the appointment of a new three-man commission to restudy the matter and to appraise the canal was introduced. Referred to the House Committee on Railways and Canals, the resolution was enthusiastically supported. In its report in 1901, the committee briefly outlined the history and usefulness of the canal, especially during the Civil War, and concluded by reviewing the movement originating in the 1870's for a ship canal, which had led to numerous surveys by government engineers. The committee estimated that the larger canal would result in annual savings on coastwise transportation charges of at least $1,500,000, but it stressed the point that until the present value of the canal was ascertained the previous reports on the subject were of little real value. Therefore, in view of the benefits which would accrue to domestic interstate commerce and in order to make "more available" the existing reports and estimates on "this important sub-

[19] Bureau of Railway Economics, *Economic Survey*, pp. 39–40; Locklin, *Economics of Transportation*, pp. 750–751. See also Theodore Roosevelt, "Our National Inland Waterways Policy," *Annals*, AAPSS, XXXI (January, 1908), 1–11; "Preliminary Report of the Inland Waterways Commission," *Senate Documents*, No. 325, 60th Congress, 1st Session (Washington, 1908); "Final Report of the National Waterways Commission," *Senate Documents*, No. 469, 62nd Congress, 2nd Session (Washington, 1912).

ject," the committee recommended immediate action. In the press of business, however, the matter was not taken up. Reintroduced the following year and accompanied by the same committee report and recommendation, it was again bypassed.[20]

Although the movement was a cumulative one, unquestionably the most important single factor in leading to eventual congressional action was the ship canal convention held in Wilmington in January, 1904. Described as "the most notable gathering of men ever assembled in Delaware," the meeting was sponsored by the Wilmington Board of Trade and featured addresses by prominent men from Philadelphia, Wilmington, and Baltimore. It was attended by congressmen and business leaders from each of the five states bordering the Chesapeake and Delaware bays. George Gray, a distinguished Delaware jurist and son of Andrew C. Gray, a former president of the Chesapeake and Delaware Canal Company, was toastmaster at the evening banquet. The Board of Trade had recently established a Delaware Ship Canal Executive Committee, and the ship canal banquet helped publicize its activities. The 45-page pamphlet containing a verbatim report on the proceedings there, from invocation to benediction, also included additional information about the executive committee, whose stated object was the following: "An open, free Ship Canal connecting Delaware River and Chesapeake Bay; to be built by the United States Government, for national defense and commerce." [21]

The sole subject discussed at the dinner was the proposed ship canal along the route of the present lock canal as recommended to Congress in 1894. It was pointed out that, far from its being a local work, the project had engaged the interest, for commercial reasons, of states up and down the Atlantic coast, as well as interior states having an outlet for their products on the Atlantic coast, and that the entire nation would benefit from the ship canal as an aid to the defense of the country. Judge Gray, in his introductory remarks, ob-

[20] "Ship Canal between Chesapeake and Delaware Bays," *House Reports*, No. 2947, 56th Congress, 1st Session (Washington, 1901), pp. 1–3; "Ship Canal between Chesapeake and Delaware Bays," *House Reports*, No. 2610, 57th Congress, 1st Session (Washington, 1902), pp. 1–3.

[21] Wilmington Board of Trade, *Delaware Ship Canal to Connect Delaware River and Chesapeake Bay: Speeches at Celebrated Inter-State Banquet* (Wilmington, [1904]), p. 2. Among the members on the executive committee were Thomas H. Savery, president of Pusey & Jones Company; Alfred D. Warner, president of Charles Warner Company; T. Coleman du Pont, president of Du Pont Powder Company; William W. Lobdell, president of Lobdell Car Wheel Company; and Howard T. Wallace, president of Diamond State Steel Company.

served that no other bays or estuaries on the American coast "minister to the wants of a population so dense, so varied, so marked and distinguished by its industrial and economic conditions, and by the aggregate of its wealth, as do the great bays and rivers upon whose shores and watersheds the most of us have our homes." To increase the benefits from these waterways, however, not only did the rivers need to be deepened but the Chesapeake and Delaware Canal needed to be "made wide enough and deep enough to accommodate our ships of war and all of our merchant marine, so that there may be a safe and secure inland waterway for steamers of the larger size from Norfolk, Washington, Baltimore, and so on to Philadelphia and to New York. . . . I do not think," Gray concluded, "the national government can much longer ignore it. There have been three expert surveys and reports that are now in the archives at Washington, all recommending the project, and all showing how feasible and necessary it is." [22]

Four major addresses were delivered during the course of the evening. Anthony Higgins, former United States Senator from Delaware, spoke on the military importance of the ship canal. Comparing it to Germany's Kiel Canal connecting the Baltic and the Atlantic, Higgins pointed out that a Chesapeake and Delaware ship canal would double the effective force of the navy at a cost of less than that of a single battleship. He concluded by repeating his conviction that adequate defenses, on land and on sea, were the surest deterrent to war. Charles Emory Smith of Philadelphia, formerly a member of President McKinley's cabinet, also spoke on the canal as "an aid to national defense." [23]

Turning from national and strategic considerations to commercial ones, Alfred O. Crozier of the Wilmington Board of Trade described Delaware's economic interest in the project. He considered the Delaware and Chesapeake bays linked by a ship canal "as one great harbor with two entrances," and predicted that Wilmington, blessed with this and other natural advantages, would become "the greatest industrial center on the American continent." Blanchard Randall of Baltimore, president of the National Board of Trade, also emphasized the commercial importance of the canal and announced that Baltimore, contrary to the general impression, now was strongly in favor of the canal at its northern location. [24]

Remarks from the floor followed the four speeches. Two con-

---

[22] *Ibid.*, pp. 5–7.   [23] *Ibid.*, pp. 8–13.   [24] *Ibid.*, pp. 24–25.

gressmen from Virginia and one from New Jersey voiced support for the project, and finally John Cadwalader, president of the Ericsson Line as well as a member of the board of the Chesapeake and Delaware Canal Company, made a few remarks. He informed the group of the little-known fact that the federal government was a sizable stock-holder in the canal company, having considered nearly a hundred years ago that its project was of national importance. He believed that this might more readily induce the government to carry out the present project. That it was sorely needed Cadwalader readily admitted. Re-cently the Baltimore and New York Transportation Line had aban-doned its fifty-year-old route through the canal for the outside route because of inadequate canal accommodations.[25]

Immediately following this meeting, another bill calling for the appointment of a board to recommend a route and appraise the exist-ing canal property was introduced in Congress, and an enthusiastic new report by the committee to which it was referred was made. It noted that the ship canal project had been before Congress in one form or another "almost continuously" for twenty-five years. "Its necessity has been widely recognized both in and out of Congress, and as time passes the reasons for urging its construction multiply." Naval economy alone would have justified it, but there were equally com-pelling commercial considerations. The two bays, with a shore line of 2,500 miles and 10,000 registered vessels, carried a commerce estimated at from 50,000,000 to 90,000,000 tons annually, an amount far in excess of the total foreign commerce of the United States and ten to twenty times as much as carried on the Suez Canal. Current traffic on the lock canal between the bays was approximately 700,000 tons annually, even though the average rate of toll was four cents a ton-mile, an almost prohibitive charge. At the committee hearings on the bill, attended by "large delegations of prominent business men from various states," much information was submitted to the commit-tee, including the report of the Delaware Ship Canal Executive Com-mittee on its banquet. The House committee was particularly impressed by the railroads' attitude towards the project; there was "no opposition" from them, and "none from any quarter" in the hearings, while "sentiment for the canal has appeared to be wide and influ-ential."[26]

[25] *Ibid.*, pp. 35–36.
[26] "Waterway Connecting the Chesapeake and Delaware Bays," *House Reports*, No. 2725, 58th Congress, 2nd Session (Washington, 1904), pp. 1–11.

This was the third strong committee recommendation in four years, but again there were delays. Lewis M. Haupt castigated the government's policy as being shortsighted and wasteful. Writing in 1905, he observed that the Chesapeake and Delaware Canal had been "urged upon the Government for enlargement by its most competent officials, and by various commercial bodies, to no effect, for more than a score of years," and added:

This work would cost less than the price of one battleship, and would increase the efficiency of a whole fleet at least two-fold. It would save $1,000,000 on the coal bills of the New England consumers of this commodity, and enable coastwise tonnage to avoid the dangerous detour around Cape Charles, of about 400 miles, with its doubled rates of insurance and loss of time. Yet the measure cannot get farther than a unanimous report from the House Committee having it in charge, on the plea of "economy"; and yet large appropriations are still made for battleships. In consequence of the failure to legislate, this toll-gate continues to restrict interstate commerce, as its capacity is sufficient to pass only three per cent. of the coastwise vessels, which have outgrown the draft of its locks.

While the Government is proposing to expend over $200,000,000 for a canal connecting the two oceans, which will be used by our foreign competitors carrying American products far more than by ourselves, it does not see the wisdom of removing the obstacles to the interchange of nearly 90,000,000 freight-tons of produce tributary to this single, short canal, which could be done in a few years at a cost not exceeding $7,500,000. The whole traffic of the Panama Canal, it was estimated, would not exceed about 7,000,000 tons for the year 1909, and most of that would be foreign. Considering the cost, the Chesapeake and Delaware Canal is one of the most promising canal propositions on the globe.[27]

At length the ceaseless agitation brought results. The joint resolution authorizing President Roosevelt to appoint the long-desired commission was reintroduced in January and approved in June, 1906. A three-man group, to consist of an officer of the Corps of Engineers, an officer of the United States Navy, and one person from civilian life, was to "examine and appraise the value of the works and franchises of the Chesapeake and Delaware Canal" with reference to the desirability of their purchase by the United States and the construction over the same route of "a free and open waterway having a depth and capacity sufficient to accommodate the largest vessels afloat at mean low water." Insofar as possible, using extant surveys and staying within the $10,000 appropriation, the commission was also to investigate the feasibility of the Sassafras River route for such a waterway.

[27] Haupt, "Urgent Need," p. 426.

Its report was to offer conclusions on the probable cost, commercial advantages, and the military and naval uses of each route, and was to be made to the next session of Congress.[28] Considerable attention along the Atlantic seaboard was focused on the work of the commission during the latter half of 1906; its findings and recommendations were eagerly awaited by the canal proponents.

[28] *Agnus Report*, p. 17.

Plans for a Ship Canal

13

In accordance with the legislation, President Roosevelt promptly named General Felix Agnus (retired) of Baltimore as the civilian chairman of the ship canal commission; Major C. A. F. Flagler of the Corps of Engineers and Lieutenant F. T. Chambers of the United States Navy were its military members. As Chambers was later to point out, the commission labored under a considerable handicap to a full investigation: "It was limited not only in time and money, but more particularly in the requirement of a canal to accommodate the largest vessel afloat." Many people, convinced that the canal should be taken over by the government, favored converting the lock canal into a ship canal by stages, according to the traffic demands. Because of its instructions, however, the Agnus Commission could not make estimates on an intermediary barge canal. It did, nevertheless, along with submitting estimates for both 30- and 35-foot canals, "record the public pressure for gradual deepening."[1]

Convening for the first time on July 30, 1906, the commission visited the canal area and conducted public hearings in Baltimore, Wilmington, and Philadelphia. Wide publicity was given to the Agnus

[1] Chambers made these comments in his discussion of an engineering report on the enlargement of the Chesapeake and Delaware Canal in the 1920's. See Earl I. Brown, "The Chesapeake and Delaware Canal," *Transactions*, American Society of Civil Engineers, XCV (1931), 764–765. Hereafter this publication will be cited as *Transactions*, ASCE.

Commission and almost unanimous support for the ship canal was recorded in each of the three cities visited. The public hearings were held on consecutive days beginning September 25 in Baltimore. Only one man there opposed the canal, on the ground that Philadelphia would get Baltimore's trade, but no opposition was found elsewhere. The Delaware newspapers expressed themselves in favor of the ship canal, and urged that "men of influence" attend the Wilmington hearing so that the commission would be "duly impressed." No less than fifteen commercial organizations in Philadelphia had representatives appear before the commission to endorse the project. Congressmen, members of the judiciary, and city and state officials also testified. The commission reported that in "these great cities" and elsewhere they found "a remarkably efficient and practically unopposed demand for the ship canal." The remarks of Judge George Gray, one of those who spoke in Wilmington, were included in the report "because of his well-known conservatism and his standing with the American people." Gray stressed the antiquity of the original canal scheme, its proven usefulness once accomplished, and the "immense importance" to the nation of now having a ship canal along the same route.[2]

The Chesapeake and Delaware Canal Company also lent its full support to the Agnus Commission, supplying it with all the information possible concerning the company's business, finances, property, and employees. A letter from President Neall to General Agnus listed twenty items forwarded to the commission in August. Some of the material had been requested, in order to permit an appraisal of the canal, but "in view of the National character of your Commission . . . [and] of the fact that the United States Government is a stockholder in the Canal to the extent of [14,625] shares or say over thirty-eight per cent (38%) of the total outstanding stock," the company "volunteered certain information" and offered to supply more if needed.[3]

In addition, the company later endeavored to have the merits of its route properly placed before the commission. Charles Chauncey recommended that both a "written statement" and a "proper advocate

---

[2] *Sunday Star* (Wilmington), September 23, 1906; *Agnus Report*, pp. 10–11.

[3] President Frank L. Neall to General Felix Agnus, Philadelphia, August 31, 1906, Board Minute Book. Among the items sent to Agnus, many of which were specially compiled, were a condensed general balance sheet, showing the company's business and financial structure since 1830, a summary of the laws passed in Maryland, Delaware, and Pennsylvania relative to the canal, an atlas recently completed showing all of the company's property along the canal line, a list of canal company employees, current toll sheets, a copy of the rules and regulations governing navigation through the canal, and recent copies of the *General Reports*.

be used" to plead the case, and meet the arguments in the brief presented by the advocates of the Sassafras route. An eloquent address, drafted principally by new board member Lewis M. Haupt, pointed out the greater physical, financial, commercial, and engineering objections to the Sassafras route as compared with the other, greatly superior route. Special counsel for the company was hired, and a private hearing before the Agnus Commission was requested. J. Southgate Lemmon, "an able representative of the Bar and occupying high special position in the community, also a personal friend of General Agnus," agreed to represent the company, and on December 10, he, President Neall, Haupt, and three other board members met with the commission and again presented arguments "on behalf of the large and important property interest" they represented.[4]

The commission was dissatisfied only by the board's refusal to set a sale price upon its property. All that the company did was to state the "cost" of the property, although the figure given, $4,019,137.02, actually represented the combined cost of original construction, subsequent improvements, regular maintenance, and accumulated profit and loss, with nothing charged off as depreciation. Its inadequacy as a basis for a valuation of the property is evident.[5] The company also estimated the probable cost of reconstruction (over $5,000,000), and gave the figures concerning current financial structure ($1,903,238.50 in stock, $2,602,950 in bonds).

The board considered it was beyond its authority to set a price on a property owned by 340 stockholders and 531 bondholders. Consequently, the commission, in appraising the value of the canal, simply used the par value of the bonds, less the current value of the negotiable securities in the contingent fund, and arrived at the figure of $2,514,289.70. As no dividends on the stock had been declared since 1876, it was deemed valueless.

The Agnus Commission submitted its report to the Secretary of War on January 1, 1907. It concluded that the construction of a

[4] Board Minute Book, October 4, 1896, November 13, 16, December 11, 1906.

[5] For an analysis of the company's general balance sheet and an informed though disinterested valuation, see Wilfred H. Schoff, "Notes on the History of the Chesapeake and Delaware Canal Company, with Statistics of its Finances and Operation Compiled from the Company's Annual Reports, 1804–1913," typescript, Free Library of Philadelphia. Mr. Schoff was secretary of the Commercial Museum in Philadelphia and served several years in a similar capacity for the Atlantic Deeper Waterways Association. In 1914 he suggested $2,100,000 as a fair value for the canal, basing this upon its value as a "going concern" as determined by capitalizing its net earnings at the time.

Chesapeake and Delaware ship canal was justifiable according to commercial, military, and naval considerations, and recommended that it be located along the line of the existing canal. Although the advantages of both it and the Sassafras route were about the same, the former route was selected because it was less expensive, was better defended, had fewer bridges, and was a developed property with earning capacity. The entire cost of converting the Chesapeake and Delaware Canal was set at $20,621,323.70 for a 35-foot channel and $17,312,064.70 for a 30-foot channel. The comparable costs of the Sassafras route would be $21,143,470 and $18,414,639, plus $2,150,000 to move the present defenses of the Delaware. Nothing was considered due any corporation or individual for works and franchises on the lower route.[6]

The lack of adequate commercial statistics on domestic movements was deplored, but from the limited amount available, the commission determined that the canal would be of "very great advantage to commerce." An annual output of $2,000,000,000 in southern raw materials, most of which sought a northern market, would be aided. It was estimated, for example, that 2,000,000 tons of coal would go through an enlarged canal each year. Most of the coal then being shipped north went via the outside route, although coal vessels often had to remain "at Hampton Roads ten days to two weeks awaiting a shift of wind" in order to begin the trip northward. The canal was deemed "the most important link in the proposed waterway from the Gulf to the City of Philadelphia for barge traffic, and its purchase and improvement by the Government would be a benefit of extraordinary value." Agnus and his colleagues also considered at length the military and naval uses of a ship canal, and decided it would be "of great strategic value as an adjunct to our land and naval forces."[7]

Shortly after the report was transmitted to Congress, a bill authorizing purchase of the canal was introduced, although the price of purchase inexplicably was set at not more than $2,500,000. The canal company, already disappointed in the commission's appraisal of the canal's value, was even more upset by the reduced purchase price named in the bill. A lengthy statement on the "value of the Chesapeake and Delaware Canal and the advantages to the United States of its purchase" was prepared and sent to all the members of Congress. In it the board reviewed the company's history and the value of the canal to the country since 1829: "On account of the demand for increased

[6] *Agnus Report*, p. 2.
[7] *Ibid.*, pp. 11–16.

means of transportation, by water especially, it is now more valuable than for many years, and promises to increase in value to its owner, [for] its business is steadily increasing." It continued:

The reports of the several Commissions, the last especially, set forth such convincing reasons, both from a scientific and practical point of view in favor of the purchase of the present canal, that it is useless to enlarge on them here. There can be no question that the present Chesapeake and Delaware Canal is the proper route and that its immediate acquirement by the United States Government will be a very great saving in time, a saving which in regard to the commerce and industry of the Country is now important, and which the course of events, should this Country become involved in war, may cause it to be of inestimable importance, greater even than several battleships. The water way which effects this saving, moreover, will possess a permanent value, which no battleship can have.

Then the board discussed the matter of price:

The owners of this property ask nothing but a reasonable compensation. The value of their property, stated in the report of the Chesapeake and Delaware Canal Commission, is below its real value to them, and the bill before the House of Representatives has cut down without any explanation the sum named by the Commission.

A property which cost over $4,000,000, which in the year ending May 31st 1906, paid all its expenses, 4% interest on $2,602,950, and had a surplus of $9,486, whose business is increasing, on which large sums have been expended within the past few years to put it in the condition in which it now is, a better one for transaction of its operation than ever before, and which if Government Canal building were not proposed, could be improved to great advantage, is certainly worth more than the amounts fixed by the Commission and still more than that named in the bill.

The owners of this property, the large majority of whom have held their interests for many years, assert that the slightest examination will show that the value they set on their property is moderate, and that the most searching investigation on every ground will fail to show that it is not.[8]

Opposed by the canal company, the bill of purchase in 1907 was not adopted and a similar bill in 1909, with the price increased to the amount recommended by the Agnus Commission, also failed. The demand for the ship canal was growing but still lacked the necessary strength.

It was at this point that the Atlantic Deeper Waterways Association, a waterways booster organization established in 1907, entered the scene. It became the chief advocate of the Chesapeake and Delaware Canal improvement as a part of its project to have an inland waterway along the Atlantic coast constructed.

[8] Board Minute Book, February 12, 1907.

The president of the association, from the time of its organization until three years prior to his death in 1950, was J. Hampton Moore. A congressman from Pennsylvania from 1906 to 1920 and twice thereafter mayor of Philadelphia, Moore was a very able, genial, and effective leader in the waterway movement.[9] He was an excellent organizer and administrator, personally indefatigable and capable of inspiring others with an enthusiasm almost equal to his own for the association's work. A strong Republican himself, he enlisted bipartisan support up and down the coast as well as in Washington for the intracoastal waterway. President Roosevelt voiced his approval of the association's work, and President Taft attended some of the annual conventions of the association. Its publications contain invaluable information on waterway development in the twentieth century.

Formation of the association was important in the eventual development of the Atlantic Intracoastal Waterway because one of the main reasons for the lack of success of its advocates before 1907 had been their failure to coordinate their activities. The government, faced with a variety of conflicting claims, resorted to delay or at best piecemeal appropriations. Following the organization of the waterway association, however, a plan for the systematic construction of, first, an inland waterway capable of accommodating the barges ordinarily used in bay and river navigation between Boston and Beaufort, North Carolina, was adopted. Moore and John H. Small, a leader in the association second only in importance to its president, introduced in Congress in 1908 resolutions calling for army engineering surveys of the Boston-Beaufort and the Beaufort–Key West routes. Authorizations for the surveys were included in the Rivers and Harbors Act of 1909, and reports made in 1912 and 1913 recognized the feasibility of the projects, except for the section across New Jersey. The first portion of the waterway to be constructed by the government ran from Norfolk to Beaufort, North Carolina, Congressman Small's home state, but the Chesapeake and Delaware Canal was the second. By 1941 the association could boast of having obtained the construction of eleven of the twelve links or sections in its 2,000-mile waterway. The "missing link" remains a ship canal across New Jersey.[10]

[9] Moore's political career has been examined by Robert Edward Drayer, J. Hampton Moore: An Old Fashioned Republican (unpub. diss., University of Pennsylvania, 1961). Only slight notice has been taken of Moore's waterway activities in this study.
    [10] "Report on the Intracoastal Waterway — Boston, Mass., to Beaufort, N.C., Section," House Documents, No. 391, 62nd Congress, 2nd Session (Washington, 1912); "Intracoastal Waterway: Beaufort, N.C., to Key West, Fla.,

Because of its central location, the Chesapeake and Delaware Canal was widely discussed at the association's first few conventions. Following the group's organization in Philadelphia in November, 1907, its first annual meeting was held in Baltimore in November, 1908. Delegates from the Philadelphia area journeyed en masse to the convention by steamboat, a practice subsequently followed. While passing through the Chesapeake and Delaware Canal aboard an Ericsson Line vessel, the association's flag was unfurled for the first time, an event pictured on the back cover of the published report of the convention. According to the editor of the volume, "The trip through the canal was extremely interesting to those who have never before seen this waterway, destined to be one of the most important links in the chain along the coast. The big steamboat 'Penn,' which carried a party of nearly 300, was barely able to get through the locks, the need for enlargement being made evident at a glance. At the same time the value of the communication between the Delaware and Chesapeake bays was demonstrated." [11]

During the well-attended and enthusiastic convention which followed, most speakers promised support for improving the Chesapeake and Delaware Canal. As R. J. MacLean, president of the Wilmington Board of Trade, expressed it, "We are with [the association] on the entire proposition for waterways from Maine to the Gulf of Mexico, but, gentlemen, we must make a start, and we ask you to start where we are now ready, for all we need is the money from Congress, and we expect to get that the next session." Resolutions adopted at the convention called for the chain of waterways along the Atlantic coast, the improvement of certain rivers and harbors, and specifically requested purchase and reconstruction of the Chesapeake and Delaware Canal. [12]

At its Norfolk convention the following year, the association reiterated its appeal for the construction of the coastwise canals. Noteworthy progress had been made during the past year, but more was demanded. It was pointed out by Moore in his presidential address that the coastal canals were insufficient to pass four torpedo boats recently sent from the Philadelphia to the Charleston navy yard, and that on their outside passage the boats were damaged and several sailors

Section," *House Documents*, No. 229, 63rd Congress, 1st Session (Washington, 1913). See also Corps of Engineers, U. S. Army, *The Intracoastal Waterway. Part I: Atlantic Section* (Washington, 1951), and Corps of Engineers, U. S. Army, *The Intracoastal Waterway: Gulf Section* (Washington, 1961).

[11] ADWA, *Proceedings* (1908), p. 7.
[12] *Ibid.*, pp. 57, 180–182.

injured. He also mentioned that the association had intended to exhibit in Norfolk models of the *Clermont* and the *Half Moon* built for the Hudson-Fulton celebration, but it was found impossible to pass them through the Delaware and Raritan Canal. The 300-year-old ship had too much draft, the 100-year-old boat too much beam.[13]

President Taft addressed the Norfolk meeting and committed himself to support the construction of waterways of demonstrated utility, for which plans had been approved by the United States engineers. Taft stated that he had heard Speaker of the House Joseph G. Cannon question the usefulness of the inland waterway

when it was only a biscuit throw over into the ocean; but that is because he came from Illinois. If in the discharge of his duty it had been his fate, as it has been mine, to go around this neighboring Cape Hatteras, he would understand the difference in a biscuit throw. He would know that there is something in quiet water. If he does not believe it, let him get on the "Sylph" or the "Mayflower" and travel up from here when there is a good strong wind blowing in Hampton Roads, and tell the difference between Chesapeake Bay and the Potomac River. (Laughs himself.) He would tell it in his stomach.[14]

Perhaps Cannon's beliefs were once representative of the country, but by the time of the Providence convention in 1910, Addison B. Burk, secretary of the association, commented that the idea of interior waterways was developing in a promising way. In 1907 there was only a vague general idea that waterways were a good thing, but in 1910 knowledge on this subject was more exact: "Today we know their value; we know the routes they should follow, the depth of water they should be given and what is required in the nature of water terminals to make the canals effective and useful." Burk also remarked that the delegation from Norfolk, after a rough trip via the outside route to Providence, had become the "most enthusiastic advocates of an inside route."[15]

While the promising revival of interest in waterway transportation during the first decade of the twentieth century was taking place, the Chesapeake and Delaware Canal Company was directly affected but very little. The company was struggling to avoid a mortgage foreclosure until, it was hoped, the government would purchase its property. Deficits were experienced in six of the ten years between 1901 and 1910, and for a time it was feared that only 3 per cent interest

[13] ADWA, *Proceedings* (1909), pp. 34–35.
[14] *Ibid.*, pp. 192–193.
[15] ADWA, *Proceedings* (1910), pp. 5–6, 9.

on the mortgage loan could be paid, but borrowings from the contingent fund and an upturn in business after 1905 averted that embarrassment. The lack of money for maintenance, however, caused the canal property to deteriorate so much that by 1906, $60,000 was required to restore it to minimum operating standards — decayed lockgates were renewed, sunken banks were repaired, and sorely needed new equipment was purchased. As another way to improve its service, towing by mules trudging along the towpath was discontinued in 1902. Thereafter steam tugs performed all the necessary towing through the canal; stationary steam engines were used at the locks.

TABLE 7. TOLLS AND TONNAGES, 1891–1919[a]

Year Ends June 1	Tolls Received	Total Tonnage
1891	$157,733	625,652
1892	153,138	594,138
1893	150,578	648,342
1894	149,463	664,761
1895	140,187	626,475
1896	155,691	675,226
1897	152,978	726,582
1898	149,215	752,537
1899	135,523	617,793
1900	150,096	639,548
1901	133,919	539,490
1902	129,274	663,016
1903	127,778	615,045
1904	142,861	671,292
1905	149,665	699,924
1906	176,354	759,866
1907	144,933	591,066
1908	160,626	658,948
1909	163,079	730,352
1910	174,104	842,821
1911	175,742	862,206
1912	164,856	802,471
1913	187,051	908,594
1914	177,222	958,378
1915	183,534	1,000,744
1916	187,301	995,549
1917	175,568	836,382
1918	175,137	734,714
1919	192,474	686,810

[a]Source: "Comparative Statement showing Receipts, Expenses, percentages and Tonnage of Mdze.," 1830–1919, C & D Papers, HSD.

The company also made a major effort in 1903–06 to obtain the right to charge a passenger toll. Sixty years before, under railroad sponsorship, this right had been expressly denied the company by the Delaware legislature for a certain period of time, and thereafter attempts to levy a direct passenger toll had been resisted successfully by the Ericsson Line. In 1903, however, a committee was appointed to restudy the subject. It discovered that the state of Maryland had passed a law back in 1846 authorizing the company to charge passengers at a rate not to exceed 37½ cents a person, but one third of the said toll was to be paid to the state. The law, of course, was to be of no effect until accepted by the company. Unable to find any record of acceptance, the committee asked its Maryland counsel if the company could now formally accept the act of 1846 and thereafter collect a toll in Maryland only. If this was illegal, they inquired as to the proper course to be taken to get the desired amendment to its charter.[16]

The Maryland lawyers made a lengthy reply to the inquiry. Because of the contractual nature of the company's charter among the three incorporating states, as explained in the Supreme Court case of *Perrine* v. *the Chesapeake and Delaware Canal Company*, it was their opinion that the only method of obtaining the charter alteration was to have the necessary legislation passed in the three states of Maryland, Pennsylvania, and Delaware. One state alone could not authorize a new toll. Accordingly, the committee presented to the board a draft of the bill it desired enacted into law. In addition to granting a passenger toll not exceeding 50 cents a person, the bill was to give the company the right to operate its own line of boats upon the canal. A grant of transportation powers had been received in 1877 only from the state of Delaware.[17]

It was decided to apply first to the Maryland legislature, and in December, 1903, the committee was authorized to employ an "agent" to sponsor the bill. Austin L. Crothers, an attorney of Elkton soon to become governor of Maryland, accepted the appointment and introduced the bill in the House of Delegates in January, 1904. Crothers and Coleman L. Nicholson, secretary-treasurer of the company, appeared before the House committee studying the bill and made "a clear and forcible statement of the reason and justice of the application." Representatives of the Ericsson Line also addressed the com-

[16] Board Minute Book, June 9, 1903; Hood Gilpin to Gans & Haman, Philadelphia, July 23, 1903, *ibid*., September 8, 1903.
[17] Gans & Haman to Hood Gilpin, Baltimore, n.d., *ibid*., September 8, 1903.

mittee in opposition to the measure, stating that the Chesapeake and
Delaware Canal Company was a bankrupt corporation whose application, if granted, would destroy the business of their company, a Maryland corporation which had been of great benefit to Baltimore and
Maryland. They charged that the canal company had driven business
away by exorbitant tolls, and that the Ericsson Line had lost over
$80,000 on its freight business through the canal. This was made up
from the profits on its passenger traffic which the canal company now
proposed to tax.[18]

Apparently these arguments were convincing to the legislative
committee, for it made an adverse report on the bill to the House. In
reporting this defeat to the board, the canal company committee
commented on the motivation of the Ericsson Line officials:

The hostile action of the Baltimore & Philadelphia Steamboat Company was not unexpected, and their reasons for it are plain; they intend
to retain, if they can, the practical monopoly of passenger traffic on the
canal, which for years they have enjoyed, and to pay the Canal Company
nothing for it. The new boats, finer, faster and larger than those heretofore
used, can carry but little freight, since if loaded they draw too much water
to pass through the canal, [and] their passage through it, by reason of
their large size, is very injurious to the banks of the canal on account of
the great wash they cause.

They complain that last year they lost $80,000. on their freight busi-
ness; quite a number of persons and Corporations have for years been
doing a similar business at a profit, but whatever the result of the operations
of the Baltimore & Philadelphia Steamboat Company this company cannot
afford to make good any loss they may suffer no matter from what cause.
We are doing this on the present basis of their passenger traffic.

The committee concluded that its efforts, if successful, would have
increased the earning power of the company and strengthened its
credit.[19]

The following year the company authorized the committee to try
again to obtain the new legislation. Crothers was again retained to
sponsor the measure, and "a program" for promoting it at the next
session of the legislature was agreed upon. Literally hundreds of hand-
outs presenting and defending the company's case — letters, pamphlets,
reprints of editorials, statistics, and maps — descended upon the members of the legislature. In addition, a powerful memorial to accompany
the bill was distributed. It pointed out that the tolls then being charged
were far below the amounts authorized in the company's charter, with

[18] *Ibid.*, April 12, 1904.
[19] *Ibid.*

the result that earnings for the past eleven years had not equaled expenses by $11,687.31. The company had continued to operate the canal in spite of decreased tonnages, low tolls, and actual deficits, but this could not continue indefinitely:

. . . it naturally feels that it is unjust that it should be longer deprived of the right to receive any revenue from a large part of the important services it renders. The Company has always believed that it was entitled to charge tolls for the transportation of passengers, and that if this right is not specifically mentioned in its charter, it is, nevertheless, a logical deduction therefrom. It believes that this right can only be contested by private, selfish interests, who may desire a monopoly, and who might, otherwise, deprive the public of the opportunity for cheap local and through transportation which this waterway should assure them.

A canal is a water turnpike. Its receipts are from tolls. It differs from the ordinary road turnpike in that the operation of its gates, and the maintenance of its way, are vastly more expensive. It also differs in that tolls are charged not on the vehicle and power, say the wagon and horse, as in land pikes, but on the commodities carried through: consequently, if part of the load is exempt from tolls while the service rendered by the canal remains the same, the tolls received are diminished in exact proportion to the amount so exempted, and this may be so great as to reduce the receipts of the canal below the cost of the service rendered, not only to the detriment of the canal, but an unjust discrimination against freighters, no part of whose cargo is exempt. Now, under our present limitation, this is exactly what takes place in the case of all passenger vessels that use the canal.

Is it either *just* or *equitable* that the Canal Company should longer be denied the right to make a reasonable toll charge on passenger traffic transported over its waterway?

The memorial also pointed out that the Ericsson Line's passenger traffic often produced a larger net revenue per vessel than did its freight business. The company believed the right to charge passenger tolls was denied to it "only by an unintentional oversight on the part of those who framed the original legislation," and requested that Maryland act to uphold the integrity and usefulness of the canal. Certain statistics accompanying the petition listed the total number of vessels through the canal since its opening (708,000) and the total tonnage carried through the canal (46,000,000 tons).[20]

John Cadwalader, president of the Ericsson Line and also a

[20] Chesapeake and Delaware Canal Company, *The Chesapeake and Delaware Canal: Its Purpose, Its Needs, Its Possibilities* ([Philadelphia], 1905), pp. 4, 7–9. See also the collection of Chesapeake and Delaware Canal Company "Literature in Connection with Proposed Maryland Legislation, 1906," in the library of the Bureau of Railway Economics, Washington, D.C.

board member of the canal company, had objected to the proposal to seek the new legislation. He thought it inimical to the best interests of the canal company, for, if obtained, it would destroy the business of the Ericsson Line. He asserted the line "could not possibly" pay more toll than the present contract called for, and stated that if more were demanded, it would either have to adopt the outside route or abandon its business. Cadwalader reiterated these statements when the subject was discussed in March, 1906, and a heated argument among the board members developed. At one point R. Dale Benson asked Cadwalader, since all the subjects he had presented and the movements he had proposed were against the canal, how in his judgment it was to be maintained. What method did he suggest? Cadwalader replied that he had little to say on that, but when pressed for a more definite answer, he said, "Go on as before. Keep what you have." [21]

In the meantime, despite the objections of Cadwalader, who was soon to lose his seat on the board, the company vigorously worked to get its bill through the Maryland legislature. Two other Maryland lawyers were employed to assist Crothers within the legislature, and President Neall, Secretary Nicholson, Chesapeake City Collector Waitman Smithers, and others visited Annapolis several times to present their case. Considerable difficulty was experienced in getting the bill introduced into the Senate, because Senator Joseph I. Price of Cecil County, where the canal was located, was opposed to it, although, as reported by the committee,

he gave no good reason for this hostility, nor did he ever attempt to controvert the reasoning which showed the justice of our claim. It was not until over one thousand of his constituents petitioned the Legislature in favor of our application, that he would even bring in "by request," at the same time stating that he did not approve it, our bill. He bitterly opposed it before the Senate Committee, and amended it to our great disadvantage, although voting for it when taken up on the floor of the Senate after an adverse report of the Committee. The bill failed on third reading in the Senate by a vote of 13 to 14.

Much of the blame for its failure was laid with the Baltimore and Philadelphia Steamboat Company:

Their agents circulated among the people of Cecil and Kent Counties, and the members of the Legislature, grossly misleading representations as to the scope and purposes of the bill, and the design of its promoters, among whom they asserted was the Pennsylvania Railroad Company. By such means they created an opposition, none the less bitter that it was selfish

[21] Board Minute Book, March 13, 1906.

and unjust, supported by irrelevant reasoning and appeals to mean prejudice; as, for instance, that the Baltimore and Philadelphia Steamboat Company was a Maryland corporation, owned in Maryland, paying heavy taxes there, while ours was not at all so, especially in the last particular.

Before the Senate Committee the Counsel of the Baltimore & Philadelphia Steamboat Company, and Mr. John Cadwalader, its President, argued against the Canal Company bill, the latter going into a history of the defalcation or fraudulent issue of loan in 1886, which had nothing whatever to do with a fair decision of the matter under consideration, and could have been introduced for no other reason than to create prejudice against the management of the affairs of the Canal and the justice of its application for additional power to raise revenue, and to throw suspicion on the motives of those pressing this application.

The committee ended its report by remarking on the heavy expenses incurred in the proceedings, but it believed that its efforts were justified and knew, "and indeed have been assured by outsiders, that nothing was neglected which should have been done to attain their object by fair and honorable means." Success would have made the attempt worthwhile; in the past year 39,000 passengers had been carried through the canal by the Ericsson Line. Nevertheless, having twice failed, the attempt to obtain the right to charge a direct passenger toll was not made again.[22]

In consequence, the canal remained toll-free to passengers, and relations with the Ericsson Line worsened. Trouble had always been experienced in trying to arrange mutually satisfactory rate agreements between the canal company and the steamboat company, in 1904 the only transportation line regularly trading through the canal. In the 1890's a percentage on the total freight receipts of the Ericsson Line had been paid to the canal company, plus an additional $1,000 for "the unlimited right to carry passengers through the canal." The canal company was dissatisfied, however, and recommended in 1896 that certain adjustments be made. It was believed that the transportation line should pay, instead of a fixed amount for the passenger concession, 10 per cent of its total passenger receipts, as well as a higher percentage on its freight business. As an inducement to the transportation line to increase its languishing freight traffic, the canal company recommended a rate of 25 per cent on all freight until receipts equaled the average for the past seven years ($34,000), after which a charge of 15 per cent was to be made.[23]

The Ericsson Line countered with an offer to pay 15 per cent on

[22] Ibid., April 10, 1906.
[23] Ibid., January 7, 1896.

both freight and passengers. If receipts for any year failed to meet the average received since 1889, it would make up the difference. The committee handling the negotiations opposed the adoption of this proposal, because it was tantamount to "leasing your Canal for the average amount paid by the Steamboat Company in the past seven years," and it obtained the support of the board for the original proposal, with a single alteration. Payment of a fixed sum for carrying passengers was continued, but the amount was raised from $1,000 to $2,500. The Ericsson Line accepted the terms presented to it, and the agreement ran until 1898, when it was renewed upon the same terms for five more years.[24]

In 1903, because the previous arrangements were no longer "satisfactory to either party," a new three-year contract was made. A flat payment of $42,500 was agreed upon, and the Ericsson Line was to run only the seven boats named in the contract through the canal; their total passages in any one year were not to exceed 774 without the additional payment of $30 per passage. The idea of merging the two companies was briefly considered in 1903 but rejected. Still there was dissatisfaction, and when the 1903 agreement expired new terms could not be reached immediately. Eventually a charge of $55 per trip was levied upon the Ericsson steamers; after 800 trips in any one year, subsequent passages would cost only $45. Although the exact terms of later contracts varied somewhat, the line continued to pay a toll based upon the number of passages made by its vessels rather than one based upon the freight or passengers carried. The "long controversy . . . between the managers of the canal company and officers of the Baltimore and Philadelphia Steamboat Company (Ericsson Line)" mentioned by the Inland Waterways Commission in 1908 lasted as long as the canal company existed.[25]

In addition to trouble with the Ericsson Line, the canal company was involved in various lawsuits which, although eventually decided in favor of the company, added to its expenses. One case instituted in 1902 concerning the right of the company to regulate towing through the canal dragged on for eight years. Litigation less drawn out involved the applicability of Maryland's law prohibiting work on Sunday to canal company employees. In October, 1905, on two successive Sundays, a total of 45 persons were arrested for an alleged breach of the law, and the magistrate at Chesapeake City imposed fines of $5.00

[24] *Ibid.*, February 11, 1896, December 12, 1898.
[25] *Ibid.*, April 14, May 12, 1903, September 11, 1906; "Preliminary Report of the Inland Waterways Commission," p. 280.

and costs in each case. The superintendent of the canal paid the fines the first week but an appeal was taken to the Circuit Court at Elkton; payment of the later fines was delayed pending outcome of the appeal. Austin L. Crothers again represented the company, and witnesses were obtained to testify to the necessity of opening the canal on Sundays.[26]

When the case was decided the following spring, the court based its decision upholding the company on the fact that the canal was, by its charter, a public highway:

> If when the Sunday law does not forbid the navigation of vessels engaged in commerce upon navigable public highways, such vessels must have the right to use such highways upon Sunday, and as this use cannot be enjoyed without opening and closing the locks, and this can only be safely and properly done under the direction of the Canal Company, and by its agents and employes under their control, it must logically follow that the opening and closing of the locks on Sunday for such purpose, is not forbidden by the Sunday law, but is a work of necessity within the exception of the act.

Two changes did occur as a result of the lawsuit. Thereafter arrangements were made so that an employee at the canal line worked only on alternate Sundays, and the rate of pay for Sunday work was increased.[27]

As the end of the first ten years of the present century, the decade which saw a marked renewal of interest in waterway transportation, drew to a close, the future of the Chesapeake and Delaware Canal Company was clouded. Towards the end of the decade traffic on the canal had increased slightly, and the canal property was once again in reasonably good repair. R. Dale Benson, who retired from the board in 1907 after serving more than twenty years as a director of the canal company, declared at the annual meeting of the stockholders in June, 1909, that he had recently visited the canal and found it "in the best condition" he had ever seen. Similarly Walter Hall, the secretary-treasurer of the company, stated in 1912, that the canal and its works were "being kept in the highest state of improvement."[28] Nevertheless, the only real hope of the company lay in government purchase of its property. The canal was gradually filling up — vessels of 9-foot draft occasionally had trouble passing the canal supposedly capable of accommodating boats drawing 10 feet. Moreover, the

[26] Board Minute Book, November 14, 1905.
[27] Ibid., August 14, 1906.
[28] Stockholders' Minutes, June 7, 1909; [Walter Hall], "The Chesapeake and Delaware Canal," typescript in the C & D Papers, HSD.

newer barges then in use would not fit into the outdated locks. But the company, basically because of the insufficient original financing which plagued it throughout its history, was unable to modernize its waterway by building the desired ship canal. It was perhaps symbolic that the company in 1909 joined the Atlantic Deeper Waterways Association, the loudest voice then calling for federal construction of the Atlantic coastal waterway.

Government Purchase
of the Canal

14

The final nine years in the 116-year life of the Chesapeake and Delaware Canal Company were no less stormy than the years before. A rather continuous increase in traffic in the canal after 1900 caused tonnage to reach the 1,000,000 mark in 1915, something which had not happened since 1884, but a steady decline set in after that time. In 1919 annual tonnage was down to 686,810 tons. Even the increased demand for transportation during World War I had failed to halt the decline, although it did give added impetus to the movement for government purchase and improvement of the canal.

The main reason for the decreasing trade on the canal was limited accommodations. An "official statement" on the extent of its "present ability . . . to meet the demands of the Coastwise Trade" prepared by the company for use in Washington stated the problem succinctly:

The effort to meet the demand for economy in transportation, by increasing the size of single shipments, has so changed the character of the vessels carrying low grade heavy goods, as to eliminate the old style of canalboat, carrying at most 200 tons, to be replaced by Barges, with a Capacity of from 1500 to 2000 tons. With every effort on the part of the Chesapeake and Delaware Canal Company to accommodate the trade, and of the builders of barges, to conform their construction to existing conditions, the limit of size for a barge to trade through the present Canal, has been reached at 750 tons of Cargo; which, it will be noticed is not half the capacity of the modern economical Coal barge. This handicaps the Canal to an extent beyond the mere half of the trade unable to pass its locks, by driving to other less economical routes, not only this half, but all the balance of the trade of the same shippers, who, naturally in making their contracts seek and use "the line of least resistance" for all they have to ship.

Instead of a canal with a draft of 9 feet, and 60 feet wide at the surface, the company deemed a draft of 20 feet and a surface width of 150 feet necessary to accommodate 2,500-ton barges. This they believed would treble the tonnage through the canal.[1]

But to maintain, let alone enlarge, the small lock canal was almost beyond the capabilities of the company. Despite the increased tonnage through 1915, expenses climbed so much that net income failed to rise. Between 1906 and 1917, the average expenses of operation and maintenance increased 56 per cent, while average gross receipts increased only 23.6 per cent. In three of the last six years the company operated the canal, deficits were reported. The contingent fund had been built up to $86,672 by 1916, almost the amount necessary before the company would resume paying 5 per cent interest on its mortgage loan, but the deficits caused the fund to drop to $25,060 by 1919. Three years previously the loan originally due in 1886 but extended for thirty years had been extended again for ten years. As Charles Biddle, attorney for the company, explained to the loanholders, there were only two alternatives — foreclosure or extension — and there were decided disadvantages to foreclosure. Using basically the same arguments that were used in 1886, Biddle pointed out that the loanholders already controlled the company, that there were large expenses involved in reorganization, and that elimination of the stockholders would be unwise: destroying the state of Maryland's interest in the canal might lead to taxation; destroying the United States' interest might jeopardize the future purchase of the canal by the government. Extension seemed "to be the only proper course"; additional security for the bondholders was provided in the new mortgage and, assuming sale of the property, payment of the principal could be anticipated at any time.[2]

One reason for the low revenues and occasional deficits lay in the continuous preferential treatment given the Ericsson Line company. In 1910 four of the line's steamboats were being used on the

[1] "Official Statement of the extent of the present ability of the Chesapeake and Delaware Canal to meet the demands of the Coastwise Trade," n.d., C & D Papers, HSD.
[2] Board Minute Book, June 13, 1916, March 13, 1917; *The Fitch Bond Book* (New York, 1918), p. 192; *One Hundredth General Report* (1919), p. 6.

canal route. Two, the *Anthony Groves, Jr.* and the *Ericsson*, ran year-round and carried both passengers and freight. "This service," according to an Ericsson Line publication, "became so popular, the two large and fast new steamers, 'Penn' and 'Lord Baltimore,' became necessities. These boats embody speed, safety and comfort. They have four Almy water tube boilers developing 2200-horse power, four cylinder triple expansion engines developing 25 miles per hour and accommodate 800 passengers." The latter two boats had been designed primarily for the passenger trade and ran only during the summer season. All four were large, "strangely constructed boats" especially built to fit the Chesapeake and Delaware Canal locks — "these boats look like freaks," said J. Hampton Moore in 1918, "but they deliver the goods" — and were the largest vessels using the canal. Annually the Ericsson Line steamers accounted for approximately one third of all the revenue-producing passages through the canal (empty vessels returning within thirty days after paying tolls upon a cargo passed free of charge), but they contributed less than one fourth of the canal company's total revenue from tolls. In 1917, when the average canal toll was 21 cents per ton, the Ericsson Line paid only an average of 11.13 cents per ton, "one half of the rate now paid on a much lower class of freights by other carriers." [3]

Not only did the line fail to pay its full share of tolls, but frequent complaint was made about injuries to the canal banks caused by its speeding steamers. Reported a canal company committee in 1913: "The injury to the banks of the canal from the swell and suction they cause, even at the speed to which they are restricted is serious; if they exceed this rate of speed, which frequently they do, the damage is proportionately increased. The 'Lord Baltimore' and 'Penn' draw usually over 10 feet: if fully loaded they would draw 12 feet. They always draw more than 9 feet, the extreme depth offered by the canal." Nevertheless, in 1913 when it was necessary either to extend or make a new contract with the line, despite a committee recommendation to the contrary and a warning that continued preferential treatment "might well constitute the basis of a prosecution against the Canal Company for discrimination," the rates to be paid were reduced slightly. A clause was inserted in the new agreement, however, which

[3] Board Minute Book, January 14, 1913, March 13, 1917; *Ericsson Line by River, Lock and Bay* (Philadelphia, [1909]), p. 2; *Hearings on the Subject of the Purchase and Improvement of the Chesapeake and Delaware Canal, held before the Committee on Rivers and Harbors, House of Representatives*, December 16, 1918 (Washington, 1918), p. 13.

exonerated the canal company from liability in case of damages or injuries resulting from the excess draft of the steamers. Attempts to raise the contract rates in 1917 and 1918, when increased expenses made it "imperatively necessary" for all tolls to be increased, also failed.[4]

The concessions granted to the Ericsson Line can only be accounted for by the fact that the canal board feared their discontinuance would drive the line away. Since the turn of the century one transportation line already had abandoned the canal, and loss of the $35,000 to $40,000 annually received from the remaining line, it was feared, might prove fatal. The Ericsson Line, for its part, considered it was paying the canal company all that was possible. It was proud of its route and featured the canal portion of the trip in advertising the daily run between Philadelphia and Baltimore. A small illustrated brochure listing fares and times contained several pictures of the canal, its locks and bridges, and described the picturesque water route:

This trip furnishes the pleasures of a sail on the river and bay, with its extended views and salty air, also the novelty, to most people, of a trip through one of the most beautiful deep-water canals, with its attending interest of passing through the locks. To secure a trip that furnishes all this, as well as the delights of the country, which this does during the passage of fourteen miles through the canal, is possibly not offered elsewhere in America.

. . . we reach Delaware City and the entrance to the canal, forty-five miles from Philadelphia. The operation of locking is distinctly seen by the passengers; the boat is gradually raised to the level of the canal, it then glides on its placid surface through lovely glades or dense silent forests, with here and there a clearing; farther on we see well-kept farms and picturesque villages. This run of fourteen miles through the canal forms a delightful portion of the trip, offering an ever-changing and delightful panorama.

In going through the canal we use three locks — at Delaware City, St. George's and Chesapeake City.

Shortly after passing St. George's we reach Lorewood Grove, a beautiful picnic ground, where dancing, bathing, boating and fishing are much enjoyed; fine black bass and pickerel, some weighing four or five pounds, are frequently caught.

Chesapeake City is at the end of the canal, and is a very popular resort for Baltimoreans. Here the excursionists can enjoy a sail, bathing, fishing, or the dance, as preferred, and return after a day's enjoyment in good time to either Baltimore or Philadelphia.

[4] Board Minute Book, January 14, March 28, April 8, 1913, March 13, 1917, June 11, 1918.

During the summer, special excursion rates to Lorewood Grove on the canal were offered.[5]

In addition to the passengers, on which no direct tolls were paid, and the assorted cargo carried by the Ericsson Line, wood products and coal were major items of traffic. The single most important commodity carried through the canal during its last years of private operations was wood taken in various forms from the southern forests to Delaware River markets. Sawed lumber, mine props, railroad ties, and pulpwood were carried in large quantities; lumber and timber products accounted for 43 per cent of the total traffic in 1913. In this traffic, more so than with coal, the barge companies operating via the canal offered strong competition not only to vessels operating on the outside route but also to the New York, Philadelphia, and Norfolk division of the Pennsylvania Railroad, whose principal traffic was lumber and timber products. George F. Sprouls, testifying before the House Committee on Rivers and Harbors in 1914, estimated that of the 212,107,867 feet of lumber received on the Delaware in 1913, 125,684,801 feet came via the Chesapeake and Delaware Canal "at rates of freight greatly below those paid by the outside passage." However, should the canal be enlarged, the rates would go down even more.[6]

In 1889, a new type of sailing vessel, called the sailing ram, had been developed to carry lumber and timber through the Chesapeake and Delaware and the Chesapeake and Albemarle canals. With its overall dimensions governed by the size of the Chesapeake and Delaware locks, the ram was a long, narrow, shallow-draft vessel equipped with either three or four masts. Some 30 of them were in use in 1911. The principal carrier of this traffic, however, was the Southern Transportation Company, with offices in Norfolk, Baltimore, and Philadelphia. It had 14 tugs and 38 barges in use exclusively on the inland waterways, and 42 "combination barges" used in either the inland or coastwise waters. Eleven other barges were too wide to use on the inland waterways. Loaded to the maximum draft permitted by the depth of the Chesapeake and Delaware Canal, the first two classes of barges carried approximately 600 and 800 tons respectively. Because this company did its own towing through the canal, the Canal and

[5] *Ericsson Line*, pp. 4, 9–10. The brochure also included a panoramic map of the company's "picturesque route, Philadelphia to Baltimore," which pictured various cities and other noteworthy points of interest along the way, including views of Delaware City, St. Georges, Lorewood Grove, Summit Bridge, and Chesapeake City. See Plate, following p. 50.

[6] "Atlantic Intracoastal Canals," *Senate Documents*, No. 279, 65th Congress, 2nd Session (Washington, 1918), pp. 91–92.

Back Creek Towing Company ceased its operations in 1912. The remaining business did not justify a continuation of service, although the canal company itself was forced to acquire one of the company's tugs and the steam towing apparatus installed at the locks to handle the small amount of towing still required.[7]

In 1914 the Southern Transportation Company provided more revenue to the canal company than did the Ericsson Line, with the northbound cargoes "consisting of lumber, piling, mine props, and other forest products, and the southbound cargoes consisting of coal, cement, gravel, plaster, steel rails, fertilizer, and fertilizer material." R. C. Moore, traffic manager of the company, pointed out in 1918 that improvement of the Chesapeake and Delaware Canal would not only permit economies through carrying greater tonnages in each unit but also in permitting greater speed in handling tows. "At the present time, tugboats proper, for use on Chesapeake Bay or on the coast, can not be used through the inland waterways, which means the use of smaller and lighter-powered tugs in the inland waterways, which in turn means a change in the tows at Norfolk and Baltimore. The improvement of these conditions, together with the abolition of tolls, will necessarily result in a material reduction in the freight rates on this traffic moving via the inland waterways."[8]

The major development during the decade, of course, was the culmination of the movement for government purchase and enlargement of the canal. This was a slow and laborious process, because strong opposition to including a clause in a rivers and harbors bill authorizing purchase of the Chesapeake and Delaware Canal came from the West and Midwest. The Atlantic Deeper Waterways Association continued to call for immediate action in regard to the project, and report after report, each invariably recommending purchase on the twin bases of aid to commerce and national defense, piled up in the government archives, but still there was delay.

J. Hampton Moore, president of the Atlantic Deeper Waterways Association, opened the debate anew in 1911 by urging exertions at home equal to those being made on the Panama Canal. He referred to the much greater tonnage carried in the coastwise than in the interoceanic trade, but yet there was no Cape Cod Canal, the 1834 Delaware and Raritan Canal was still being used, and, between Philadel-

[7] James E. Marvil, *Sailing Rams: A History of Sailing Ships Built in and near Sussex County, Delaware* (Laurel, Delaware, 1961); Board Minute Book, April 9, 1912.

[8] "Atlantic Intracoastal Canals," pp. 94–95.

phia and Baltimore, "we continue to employ, though feebly, the Chesapeake and Delaware antiquity of 1829." But there was much more than commercial considerations at stake. Between 1900 and 1909 more than 5,700 disasters to shipping along the Atlantic coast occurred, in which 2,200 lives were lost and property damages exceeded $40,000,000. The most dangerous area was around Cape Cod, but an average of 10 lives a year were being lost between Cape Charles and Cape Henlopen. The vessels on which these men sailed had been engaged in the coastwise trade, and might have used the Chesapeake and Delaware Canal had it been available.[9]

Despite little tangible progress, Moore was encouraged by the "gradual increase of sentiment in favor of improved waterways along the Atlantic coast" among the members of the House of Representatives since 1907. He was even more encouraged when the report by the Corps of Engineers on the intracoastal waterway system from Boston to Beaufort, submitted to Congress early in 1912, strongly recommended the immediate purchase of the Chesapeake and Delaware Canal for $2,514,290 and its gradual conversion to a tide-level canal 25 feet deep. It was estimated that this would cost an additional $9,910,210, and that $3,000,000 should be made available at once. The canal was deemed an essential part of the through waterway, and important to the commercial and military needs of the country. In order to interfere as little as possible with existing traffic, the corps suggested that a depth of 12 feet at mean low water, with removal of the locks, be attained before going on. In fact, final estimates on the work of deepening the 12-foot barge canal into a 25-foot ship canal were not completed and submitted until the following year. One minor change in the route of the canal was recommended. In order to provide more ready access to deep water in the Delaware River, as well as to eliminate a sharp curve in the canal line, it was decided to locate the eastern terminus at Reedy Point, almost two miles below Delaware City, "retaining the Delaware City arm as a branch channel for the use of light draft boats."[10]

[9] ADWA, *Proceedings* (1911), p. 79; "Atlantic Intracoastal Canals," p. 89. See also J. Hampton Moore, "A Free Seaboard Safety Line," *Congressional Record*, 61st Congress, 3rd Session, Appendix, pp. 35–44, a speech in which he described recent maritime disasters on the Atlantic coast and again pointed out the need for an intracoastal waterway.

[10] ADWA, *Proceedings* (1911), p. 149; "Report on the Intracoastal Waterway," pp. 4–5, 274. This report was made by Colonel W. M. Black, Colonel Frederic V. Abbot, Lieutenant Colonel J. C. Sanford, Lieutenant Colonel Mason M. Patrick, and Major R. R. Raymond, and was submitted, in accordance with procedures adopted in 1902, to the Board of Engineers for Rivers and Harbors

The engineers estimated in their original report that not less than 2,537,622 tons of freight "could and would" use a free Chesapeake and Delaware ship canal to advantage. The saving which would thereby be effected in tolls, at the current average rate of 23¾ cents per ton, would amount to $577,309, while a further saving of 21¾ cents per ton on general freight, it was believed, would result from the economy afforded in using larger vessels. This would amount to an additional $551,933, making the direct annual saving in the transportation of goods immediately available $1,129,242. This was based upon current traffic, and did not take into account the increase in traffic which could be expected following completion of other links in the waterway.[11]

These estimates were based upon reports filled out by the traffic managers and other officials of various companies doing business on the two bays. Among these items was a statement from F. S. Groves of the Ericsson Line. Besides giving exact figures on the business in passengers and freight of his company, Groves predicted that the amount of tonnage which would use the canal, if enlarged, "would be very great in both directions. All eastbound vessels would use the canal or inside route to save the sea risks via Cape Henry. A great deal of trade would use the canal via Cape May to and from the East, which would save them from the long haul and sea risk." From Groves' point of view, "the present canal is in a deplorable condition as well as unreliable in operation. The rates charged for tolls are prohibitory, restrict trade and prevent competition." These statements were challenged by Walter Hall, secretary-treasurer of the canal company, in testimony before a Senate committee, but it was true that no major expenditures for betterments had been made since 1887. The extensive

for review and recommendation. This board concurred in the recommendations of the report, as did the chief of engineers. Much information concerning the Chesapeake and Delaware Canal, including the specifications for the new project, can be found in this report and its full appendix.

For explanations of the complicated process involved in getting a waterway improvement authorized, see John H. Small, "Legislative Status of the Atlantic Inland Waterways Project," ADWA, *Proceedings* (1908), pp. 61–63; William Stull Holt, *The Office of the Chief of Engineers of the Army: Its Non-Military History, Activities, and Organization* (Baltimore, 1923); C. H. Chorpening, "Waterway Growth in the United States," *Transactions*, ASCE, CXVII-A (1953), 976–1041. See also Haywood R. Faison, "Some Economic Aspects of Waterway Projects," *Transactions*, ASCE, CXX (1955), 1480–1549, which is in part a rebuttal to the criticisms leveled at the Corps of Engineers and its public works projects in Maass, *Muddy Waters*.

[11] "Report on the Intracoastal Waterway," pp. 97–98.

repairs needed in 1906 were considered as delayed maintenance work rather than capital improvements.[12]

J. B. Blades, president of his own lumber company in New Bern, North Carolina, also predicted great savings if the Chesapeake and Delaware Canal were enlarged. The mills with which he was connected shipped from 15,000,000 to 20,000,000 feet of lumber per year, 90 per cent of which went by the Chesapeake and Delaware Canal. The water rate on it to Philadelphia was $2.75 per 1,000 feet, compared to a rail rate of $5.25, "so you see that with the present water facilities the saving to us is very great." If sea-level canals between the North Carolina sounds and Chesapeake Bay and between Chesapeake Bay and the Delaware River were built, however, the savings would be increased:

we would not only save the amount of the toll, which is about $45,000, but we would be able to ship in larger barges, and by this means saving at least 50 cents per thousand, or $75,000. This does not take into account the mills that we are interested in at Elizabeth City, with an output of about 12,000,000 feet of lumber per year, which is all shipped almost wholly by rail, but with the improved and free waterways would move largely by water, and the amount of business done by us is only a small part of the whole amount.

Blades added that another "wonderful saving" would result in building their barges, because inside route vessels "do not need to be built too expensively to stand the work, and it is safe to use them almost twice as long as if they were trading in the ocean." Already his lumber barges were used to carry coal, fertilizer, and general merchandise on the return trips. "The merchandise shipments," he stated, "with free water rates, would be greatly enlarged and I believe a regular steamer line would be established." [13]

The Rivers and Harbors Act of 1912, although it provided for government acquisition and improvement of the Chesapeake and Albemarle Canal as part of the intracoastal waterway, did not authorize similar action for the Chesapeake and Delaware Canal. According to J. Hampton Moore, "the desire to keep down the total appropriations and the pressure from the Mississippi Valley were too strong to be overcome." This was particularly annoying to Moore because he considered improvement of the Chesapeake and Delaware Canal vital to the entire intracoastal waterway system: "It is the most feasible link of the entire chain and is substantially the vital link."

[12] Ibid., p. 248.
[13] Ibid., p. 249.

As presently conducted, however, the canal, with tolls almost equal to the railroad charges, hindered rather than encouraged commerce. Every official report, he recalled, had been favorable to the project and additional examinations were a waste of time. The route, the cost, the advantages were known; he hoped that the Atlantic Deeper Waterways Association in 1912 would urge immediate action here. As John H. Small observed, the last Congress had recognized one link in the Atlantic chain of waterways, the Norfolk to Beaufort section; now "our insistent demand" for the next link, the Chesapeake and Delaware section, "is necessary." [14]

When President Taft attended the Atlantic Deeper Waterways Association's convention in New London, Connecticut, in 1912, he too added his support to the Chesapeake and Delaware Canal project. "We have there a little canal that is hardly big enough for a canal boat, between those two great waterways, the Delaware and the Chesapeake," he stated. "It can easily be made a great waterway, and it ought to be made a great waterway." The association's resolution in this regard was unusually strong: "We demand of Congress at its next session an act acquiring the Chesapeake and Delaware Canal, one of the most essential links in the whole intracoastal chain, one of the most feasible to improve for modern requirements, and the next in logical order of progress northward, all of which is fully shown by the recent report of the United States Army Engineers." If no satisfactory purchase contract could be made with the company, the association favored immediate condemnation proceedings or construction of a canal over an alternate route. [15]

After provision for the improvement of the Chesapeake and Delaware Canal was again omitted from the Rivers and Harbors Act of 1913, the association adopted substantially similar resolutions calling for its inclusion in the next bill. Small again endorsed the project, saying in connection with a story about the high price of liquor in a dry city, "whatever it costs, it is worth the price." Congressman J. Charles Linthicum of Maryland made the telling point that, "under the present restrictions incident to its operation, the Chesapeake and Delaware Canal has lagged so far behind what a canal in its commanding position should be that it is nearly open to the charge of enjoying a title without an office." But he hastened to add that, once widened and deepened, "and made a broad avenue of navigation in this proposed chain of intracoastal canals, it will prove a valuable

[14] ADWA, *Proceedings* (1912), pp. 47–48, 82.
[15] *Ibid.*, pp. 273–274, 286–287.

link in this route of our inland commerce." This concurred with the Corps of Engineers' final report on the Chesapeake and Delaware section of the intracoastal waterway, submitted to the Secretary of War on August 9, 1913. Again the Board of Engineers for Rivers and Harbors and the chief of engineers stated that it was advisable for the United States at once to buy the canal and enlarge it to a sea-level canal 12 feet deep and 90 feet wide. A decision concerning further enlargement, it was believed, should await new investigations into the "commercial changes resulting from the first increase in canal depth and especially the release from canal tolls."[16]

A factor which complicated the problems of those seeking to promote this, however, was the government's suit against the canal company begun in 1912. The government claimed that its share of the stock dividends declared in 1873, 1875, and 1876, amounting in all to $51,187.50, had not been paid. This fact had been discovered in 1900, when the absence of adequate vouchers for the payments was noticed. John E. Wilkie, chief of the Treasury Department's secret service division, examined the canal company's records in June, 1900, and became convinced that the government claim was a valid one. No action was taken immediately, although the government ceased to pay the canal company's claims for toll on government vessels on the basis of its larger claim. Apparently the canal company directors were secure in the belief that the dividends had been paid, or felt that the statute of limitations offered adequate protection, for they continued to press for payment of the tolls. Consequently, following a letter dated November 17, 1911, from Secretary of the Treasury Franklin MacVeagh seeking payment of the unpaid dividends "because the Canal Company have denied the right of the United States to set off the same against tolls charged Government vessels for the use of the Canal," suit was filed in April, 1912, in the United States District Court at Wilmington, Delaware.[17]

The government sought to recover only the unpaid dividends on its stock, amounting to $51,187.50, plus interest from November 17, 1911, the date when formal claim for payment was made. The case

[16] ADWA, *Proceedings* (1913), pp. 86, 231; "Intracoastal Waterway — Boston, Mass. to Beaufort, N. C.: Final Report on Sections from New York Bay to Delaware River and from Delaware River to Chesapeake Bay," *House Documents*, No. 196, 63rd Congress, 1st Session (Washington, 1913), pp. 5–6. See also the remarks of Eugene W. Fry, treasurer of the Southern Transportation Company, at the convention of the waterway association in ADWA, *Proceedings* (1913), pp. 224–228.

[17] Board Minute Book, June 12, 1900, January 9, 1912.

was heard originally in March, 1913, before Judge Edward G. Bradford. Charles Biddle and Andrew C. Gray represented the canal company; the government's case was presented by District Attorney John P. Nields, who was assisted by Chapman Maupin. The canal company pleaded, in answer to the charges, *non assumpsit*, release, and the statute of limitations, but Judge Bradford upheld the government's demurrer. In announcing his decision against the company, however, Judge Bradford gave "leave to the defendant to plead over." In the second trial, held in October, 1914, the government presented its case simply and quickly. After ownership by the government of 14,625 shares of stock in the canal company and the fact that stock dividends had been declared in 1873, 1875, and 1876 were established, testimony was presented to the effect that the government had not received its share of the dividends. A deposition taken from J. A. L. Wilson, the aging and nearly blind former secretary of the canal company who had served five years in prison after confessing to embezzlement in 1886, and who was one of the men suspected of having stolen the government's dividends in the 1870's, was not introduced into evidence because of Biddle and Gray's objections.[18]

These attorneys, on behalf of the company, admitted that the government owned the shares in question, but stated that proof of nonpayment of the dividends had not been established. The main defense, however, was the application of the statute of limitations. Biddle dwelt upon the point that if the complainant has allowed a claim to rest for twenty years or more without making any attempt to collect it, then it is presumed that the claim has been paid. "Time," he said, "runs against the government with the same force as it does against the individual." It was Nields' position, however, that the government is never limited by time in such cases; it "shall not suffer because of any negligence on the part of the servants of the government." The court, in its charge to the jury, also gave the opinion that Biddle's argument could not stand: "The Government was charged with such a multiplicity of duties that it would be unfair and against public policy to enforce the statute of limitations in such a case." Instructed to bring in a verdict for the plaintiff, the jury did so, and a judgment of $60,111.19 against the canal company was entered.[19]

Biddle immediately filed an exception to the instructions to the

[18] *United States* v. *Chesapeake and Delaware Canal Company*, 206 *Federal Reporter* (1913), 964–969; *Wilmington Morning News*, October 12, 1914.
[19] *Wilmington Morning News*, October 12, 1914.

jury and asked that reasonable time be granted for appealing the case
to a higher court. The appeal was heard in the Circuit Court of Appeals
in June, 1915. This court reversed the decision and awarded a new
trial to the company on the grounds that sufficient evidence to warrant the verdict had not been presented. At the third trial in the district
court, held in January, 1916, the government presented its case much
more carefully and thoroughly. Official records from the Treasury
Department were used to show the absence of dividend receipts for
1873, 1875, and 1876, although receipt of the previous 14 dividends
declared by the canal company was recorded. More importantly, Wilson's deposition was accepted as evidence in this trial. The former
secretary, then deceased, had admitted in his statement that the dividends in fact had not been paid to the government — "the money
had been used by Mr. Lesley and myself, for other purposes, but
without the knowledge of the company." Judgment for the government, by this time amounting to $63,924.66, again was rendered,
and again the case was appealed.[20]

This time, however, the Circuit Court of Appeals upheld the
lower court's decision. "That the money was stolen by the company's
trusted servants is its grievous misfortune," the court declared in
March, 1917, "but this is undoubtedly the fact, and the loss must
rest where it has fallen." No reversible error had been committed in
the conduct of the trial, "and the judgment must therefore be affirmed."
A final appeal was carried to the Supreme Court, where judgment for
the government was affirmed once more. "We agree," wrote Associate Justice John H. Clarke in May, 1919, "with the Circuit Court of
Appeals that the evidence introduced carries clear conviction that
the dividends were never paid, and that the request of the Canal Company for an instructed verdict in its favor was properly denied." By
that time, happily for the company, condemnation proceedings to
fix the purchase price of the canal had been concluded, except for
the final executive approval, so the claim was never paid. Nevertheless, knowledge that the government's dividends had been withheld
and that there had been a fraudulent overissue of $609,200 in bonds
damaged the company's reputation. Both thefts were effectively used
against the company during the long debate concerning government
acquisition of the canal. J. Hampton Moore exclaimed in exaspera-
tion early in 1917 that "every time we come before a committee some-

[20] *Chesapeake and Delaware Canal Company* v. *United States*, 223 *Federal
Reporter* (1915), 926–933; printed transcript of the 1916 trial, p. 122, C & D
Papers, HSD; ADWA, *Bulletin*, VIII (January, 1916), 7.

body wants to know who stole that $600,000. And that is not the question at all."[21]

A strenuous effort to have the Chesapeake and Delaware project included in the 1914 rivers and harbors bill was made, but there were two obstacles. In the first place, it proved exceedingly difficult to set a price on the property acceptable to both parties. Second, the outbreak of World War I led to a drive for governmental economy, and postponement of many public works projects occurred. It was ironic, however, that a canal so vitally important to national defense as the Chesapeake and Delaware was omitted from the bill on grounds of wartime economy. At the beginning of the year, it seemed inclusion of the canal was certain. A hearing was conducted "on the subject of the purchase of the Chesapeake and Delaware Canal" by the House Committee on Rivers and Harbors in January, 1914. J. Hampton Moore and other Atlantic Deeper Waterways Association members were prominent among those appearing before the committee. Testimony given by Wilfred H. Schoff, secretary of the association and perhaps the most knowledgeable person in the country on the history of the canal, excepting only a few company directors, explained the national character of the work as a central part in the Atlantic intracoastal waterway. General Felix Agnus and others from Maryland, Delaware, Pennsylvania, and New Jersey testified as to the past importance of the canal, the series of engineering reports unanimously recommending its improvement, and the present commercial need for such an improvement.[22]

The following month the committee introduced a bill authorizing purchase of the canal for not more than $1,300,000. It had been learned from the Agnus Commission report of 1907 that some of the canal bonds in 1906 were sold at $48 or $49. Agnus had pointed out that this was an isolated instance and could not serve as a basis for valuation, but the committee nonetheless recommended purchase for less than half the bonded indebtedness of the company. The company directors considered the price as "entirely inadequate," one they would not consider, and they notified the loanholders that they would

[21] *Chesapeake and Delaware Canal Company* v. *United States*, 240 *Federal Reporter* (1917), 903–910; *Chesapeake and Delaware Canal Company* v. *United States*, 250 *United States Reports* (1919), 123–129; *Hearings on the Subject of the Purchase and Improvement of the Chesapeake and Delaware Canal, held before the Committee on Rivers and Harbors, House of Representatives*, January 6, 1917 (Washington, 1917), p. 20.

[22] *Hearings on the Subject of the Purchase of the Chesapeake and Delaware Canal, held before the Committee on Rivers and Harbors, House of Representatives*, January 15, 1914 (Washington, 1914).

continue to watch carefully over their interests. Members of the Senate also deemed the price unrealistic. Consequently, in March, 1914, a subcommittee of the Committee on Coast and Insular Surveys conducted hearings expressly for the purpose of determining ownership and control of the canal and its fair value. Senator Willard Saulsbury of Delaware, a newcomer to the Senate and a recent convert to the movement for a Chesapeake and Delaware ship canal, was chairman at the hearings, which put the complete details of the Chesapeake and Delaware Canal Company's financial status and ownership into the public record. Walter Hall, the secretary-treasurer of the company, supplied the committee with most of this information. The board members were identified, the salaries of all the company officers and employees were given, the names, addresses, and amount of stock or bonds held by each investor were listed, and traffic statistics since the time of the *Agnus Report* were furnished. Hall stated that the "canal never was in as good condition as it is today" — "we are passing through the canal to-day tows of barges of capacity of 25 carloads each behind a single tug, equivalent to a train of 100 cars, and we are doing it with less trouble than we ever have had." Information was also supplied concerning the two largest users of the canal, the Ericsson Line and the Southern Transportation Company; the final 11 pages in the transcript of the hearings contained the company's itemized toll sheet, giving the tolls in force since May, 1913.[23]

As a result of Saulsbury's investigation, valuation of the canal was raised to $2,250,000, still slightly below the appraisal by Agnus in 1907. Provision was made in the bill for condemnation proceedings if the Secretary of War could not purchase the canal for that price. This was likely, for although the canal directors still refused to name a definite price (motions to set the figure at $2,798,489 and at $3,708,186 were rejected), the Senate committee had been informed in April that the board could not "recommend to the stockholders and loanholders less than the par value of the bonds and a sufficient amount for the stock to induce their favorable action."[24]

Between the time these preliminary discussions over the price were taking place and the time the rivers and harbors bill came up for debate in the Senate in September, war had engulfed Europe. A filibuster against all new projects in the bill was led by Senator Theo-

[23] Board Minute Book, March 10, 1914; *Hearings before the Subcommittee of the Committee on Coast and Insular Surveys, United States Senate, March 21, 24, 28, 31, 1914* (Washington, 1914), *passim*.
[24] Board Minute Book, April 6, 1914.

dore E. Burton of Ohio and Senator William S. Kenyon of Iowa. Eventually, instead of a $53,000,000 rivers and harbors bill, one making a lump sum appropriation of $20,000,000 to the Corps of Engineers for use on previously authorized projects was made. Senator Saulsbury remarked afterwards that initiation of the Chesapeake and Delaware project was "possibly prevented at the last session of Congress by the physical ability of one Senator [Burton] to vocalize for a week or so and to do this at a critical time for twenty-four hours on a stretch." Wilfred H. Schoff, editor of the Atlantic Deeper Waterways Association publications, was another who placed primary responsibility for defeat of the project on Senators Burton and Kenyon. He was particularly angered by their unjustified and unfair criticisms of the Chesapeake and Delaware Canal, and charged that they used out-of-date reports and estimates in referring to it. In a lengthy article replying to the senators, Schoff corrected certain of their obvious misstatements and made an effective appeal for reconsideration. He stated that "the imposition of tolls on a waterway, connecting great courses of water traffic such as the Chesapeake and Delaware Bays is a monopolistic privilege and an unreasonable hindrance to commerce under present conditions," and that "the anachronism of a private toll canal" there should be done away with once and for all.[25]

Burton defended his filibuster on the grounds that many unworthy items were in the bill, but his opposition indiscriminately extended to all new projects. Even opinion in Burton's state was divided on the Chesapeake and Delaware issue. An editorial in the *Cleveland Plain Dealer* expressed disappointment that the appropriation for it was eliminated from the 1914 bill. "In the general satisfaction over the achievement of Senator Burton," the paper said, "many will feel a little regret that this measure to advance the Atlantic inland waterway has been necessarily postponed." Its acquisition was the "one most important step under contemplation" for promoting the waterway, but it "suffered, probably, because of being in bad company." Schoff too was disappointed with the bill, but he was pleased that Senator Saulsbury's resolution calling upon the Secretary of War to ascertain the price at which the Chesapeake and Delaware Canal could be purchased, and to prepare a summary of all the official reports relative to the canal, was adopted. Schoff believed the advan-

[25] ADWA, *Bulletin*, VII (December, 1914), 10; VI (September, 1914), 14–20. For information on Senator Burton's career, see Forrest Crissey, *Theodore E. Burton: American Statesman* (Cleveland and New York, 1956), particularly chapter 18, "Senate Filibuster."

232]   Government Purchase of the Canal

tages of this resolution were obvious — Congress at its next session
would have the facts, and ancient reports, giving the wrong dimensions
or using estimates based on outdated methods of work, would not be
cited. "This is," he declared, "a proposition which will withstand
any fair attack if the facts are fully and fairly presented." [26]

The 1914 convention of the Atlantic Deeper Waterways Association, with meetings held at various points along the Hudson River,
happened to coincide with the Senate filibuster on the rivers and
harbors bill. The association took the position "of reasonable acqui-
escence in any measures of economy proven to be temporarily necessary, owing to abnormal conditions, but of vigorous protest against
exploitation of such economy in the interest of a general attack on
water transportation, which was the form taken by the filibuster. The
feasibility and desirability of the Atlantic Intracoastal Waterway, as
set forth in previous Conventions of the Association, were reaffirmed,
with added emphasis on its great importance to the national defense
in time of war." Particular regret was expressed at the New York
convention that the Chesapeake and Delaware project was under attack. President Moore pointed out that almost 1,000,000 tons of
freight had passed through the canal in 1914 and paid tolls "to the
existing canal monopoly," and said that "ten times that tonnage would
use the canal if it were improved and made free. Even the Panama
Canal does not offer a better immediate prospect than this." Moore
was anxious to resign as president of the association in 1914, a post
he had held since 1907, but he accepted renomination in order to
carry on the current fight for the Chesapeake and Delaware project
without its having to "swap horses" in mid-stream. He hoped that
by next year the canal would be acquired by the government, "and
if that is done, then I may rightfully and properly ask that this high
office that you have confided to me for so many years may be taken
over by someone else." [27]

With Moore remaining in office, the association kept up its fight
for the Chesapeake and Delaware appropriation. The preparedness
issue was stressed throughout 1915 and 1916; indeed, the entire

[26] Cleveland Plain Dealer, quoted ADWA, Bulletin, VI (November,
1914), 7; ibid., VI (October, 1914), 8. See also Theodore E. Burton, "The
Truth about Our Waterways," Munsey's Magazine, LVI (January, 1916), 550–
561. For an example of an attack, in the muckraking tradition, on rivers and
harbors legislation, see Judson C. Welliver's comments about the "Water Power
Trust" in "The Pigs and the Pork," Pearson's Magazine, XXXII (November,
1914), 547–557.
[27] ADWA, Proceedings (1914), pp. 8, 36, 285–286.

Atlantic intracoastal waterway was declared to be "economically sound, commercially necessary, and strategically invaluable," but improvement of the Chesapeake and Delaware Canal should be the government's first step. Points along either of the two bays it joined were likely targets in case of enemy attack, as they had been in 1776 and 1812, but the canal, "geographically . . . the Kiel Canal of the United States," had the same dimensions given it by its original builders in 1829; "strategically, in its present condition, it would be as serviceable in time of war as a raft against a battleship." Secretary of Commerce William C. Redfield informed the association in 1915 that the government used the inland waterway frequently — "we are constantly sending through the Delaware and Chesapeake Canal and the Raritan Canal such vessels as can go through those somewhat damp places" — and Rear Admiral A. W. Grant, addressing the association on the subject of "Submarines and the Inside Passage," declared that he regarded the "Cape Cod and the Chesapeake and Delaware Canal as being the two of greatest strategic value at this time." He hoped that soon they would be of battleship size. General William L. Marshall, chief of engineers in 1910, had already pointed out the essentially military nature of such works as the Panama, the Delaware and Raritan, the Chesapeake and Delaware, and the Chesapeake and Albemarle canals, "all now under construction or survey."[28]

Strong endorsements of the Chesapeake and Delaware project were also offered in newspaper editorials. A Philadelphia editor captured the gist of their statements in these words:

Whether the Federal Government shall take over the Chesapeake and Delaware Canal by purchase or condemnation proceedings or whether it shall be in response to the universal popular demand for military preparedness or in recognition of the importance of the inland waterway as a means of promoting the nation's commerce, is immaterial. The important point is that the Government shall at the earliest moment take over the canal, deepen it and make it an integral part of the national facilities for commerce as well as for defense. The waterway has for many years served a useful purpose, but it has long been made obsolete by the demands of modern shipping, and its sole value now lies in the potentialities it possesses for a greater service in the future.

These advocates of the Chesapeake and Delaware project were heartened in December, 1915, by the favorable report from the War De-

---

[28] *Ibid.* (1915), pp. 78, 185, 253; William L. Marshall, "River and Harbor Work from a Military Point of View," *Professional Memoirs,* Corps of Engineers, United States Army, and Engineer Department at Large, II (July–September, 1910), 394–395.

partment on its military and naval value, but little action was taken by Congress during 1916 in spite of the preparedness campaign of that year. Hearings were conducted by the House Committee on Rivers and Harbors on the entire Atlantic intracoastal waterway, north and south, after which five bills to provide for the acquisition of the Chesapeake and Delaware Canal were introduced. Before the rivers and harbors bill came up for discussion, the committee members, accompanied by several other congressmen, were escorted through the canal in July, but after conferring with President Wilson, the committee again decided to omit all new projects in the bill.[29]

Major debate on the question of acquiring the Chesapeake and Delaware Canal came in 1917, after the Atlantic Deeper Waterways Association's "Delaware River Convention" in the fall of 1916, during which successive meetings were held in eight different cities along the river. On September 13, the association held an afternoon session in Wilmington, Delaware, after which the group traveled by steamer to Delaware City, where an evening session was held within sight of the canal lock there. General William H. Bixby, former chief of engineers and the man who directed the original surveys for the Atlantic intracoastal waterway authorized in 1909, was among the speakers in Delaware who unanimously called for action; three days later, following formal adjournment of the convention, General Bixby explained various engineering features included in the proposed improvement of the canal to a large number of association members who inspected the canal aboard an Ericsson Line steamer.

An appropriation for the purchase of the canal was belatedly written into the 1917 rivers and harbors bill, after an impromptu hearing by the Committee on Rivers and Harbors on January 6, 1917, to determine the value of the canal. J. Hampton Moore was the only person who appeared before the committee, and because of the short notice he was unable to supply all of the detailed information requested, but he reiterated his support of the project and urged action during the current session. Again only $1,300,000 was the price recommended by the committee to be paid to the canal company for its property, but even this small appropriation was strongly opposed.

[29] *Philadelphia Ledger*, quoted in ADWA, *Bulletin*, VIII (December, 1915), 18; *ibid.*, VIII (February, 1916), 1. See also "Letter from the Secretary of War, transmitting certain information relative to the proposed acquisition of the Chesapeake and Delaware Canal, the probable cost thereof, and as to the advantages and disadvantages, commercial, naval, and military, of the acquisition of the said canal by the United States," *Senate Documents*, No. 14, 64th Congress, 1st Session (Washington, 1915).

After a "hard fight" both in the committee and on the floor of the House, the bill was passed. Because the amount of the appropriation was deemed insufficient to purchase the canal, the Senate committee considering the bill substituted for the specific amount a clause providing for condemnation proceedings, but then the entire rivers and harbors bill was lost in the Senate in March.[30]

A month later the United States entered the war. When this happened, Moore introduced a bill in the House authorizing President Wilson "to take over the Chesapeake and Delaware Canal for war purposes," and to improve and develop it in accordance with the recommendations of the army engineers, and to operate it as an adjunct to national defense. Reasonable compensation, as determined through condemnation proceedings, was to be paid to the owners of the canal. This bill was tabled, and a later attempt by Senator Saulsbury, the chief advocate of the Chesapeake and Delaware project in the upper house, to get an authorization for the purchase of the canal into a naval appropriations bill also failed. His maneuver was blocked on a point of order by Senator Kenyon of Iowa.[31]

A new rivers and harbors bill, drawn up in June, included the Chesapeake and Delaware project and carried an appropriation of $5,000 for the conduct of negotiations by the Secretary of War to purchase the canal or to acquire it by condemnation. Acceptance of a condemnation award, however, would be subject to future congressional ratification and appropriation. The entire rivers and harbors bill was subjected to close scrutiny, both because of its supposed association with "pork barrel" legislation and because of the war. As Senator Kenyon remarked at one stage in the debate, "We are admonished by Mr. Hoover to have meatless and wheatless days in this country. Let us start out by having some porkless bills in Congress." The new rivers and harbors bill, however, contained appropriations only for the maintenance of existing projects, which otherwise would deteriorate; for the continuance of work on projects underway, which otherwise would waste the expenditures already made; and for new projects of undoubted military value to the country.[32]

Moore led the fight for the bill, particularly the Chesapeake and Delaware section, in the House, as did Saulsbury in the Senate. As Moore noted at the outset of the debate, it was the "one item in the

[30] *Hearings on the Chesapeake and Delaware Canal*, January 6, 1917, *passim*; ADWA, *Bulletin*, IX (February, 1917), 1.

[31] ADWA, *Bulletin*, IX (April, 1917), 4, 8.

[32] *Congressional Record*, 65th Congress, 1st Session, p. 5444.

Government Purchase of the Canal

bill that will probably be more contested than any other." Not only was it a new project, but much misinformation about it had been circulated. Consequently, when this section came up for consideration, Moore asked for extra time to explain the project, its relation to the intracoastal waterway, and its relation to national defense to his colleagues. Representatives James A. Frear of Wisconsin and Martin B. Madden of Illinois, the chief opponents of the bill, repeatedly asked for clarification of certain points during Moore's presentation, and finally almost managed to exclude the Chesapeake and Delaware section from it on a technicality. On a point of order, Madden raised the question of proper referral of the section. He contended that the old and nearly defunct Committee on Railways and Canals, rather than the Committee on Rivers and Harbors, should have jurisdiction over legislation dealing with canals. An appeal from the decision of the chair upholding Madden, however, was sustained and the bill eventually passed the House intact.[33]

The Senate, working closely with the War Department, then considered each item of the bill with reference to the existing national emergency. Secretary of War Newton D. Baker had already stated that he favored immediate acquisition of the Chesapeake and Delaware Canal. The primary opposition to this came from senators Kenyon of Iowa and Smoot of Utah. Kenyon stated that this was no time "to be unloading on the government a defunct and bankrupt canal," and made the grossly misleading statement that the canal company was indebted to the government for some $600,000 to $700,000. He was replied to in part by Senator Boies Penrose of Pennsylvania, who said in his opinion "the Chesapeake and Delaware proposition is one of the most meritorious in the measure." Saulsbury, however, made the most informed and effective reply to the project's critics. After giving the correct amount of the government's judgment against the canal company, then on appeal in the circuit court, he gave the oft-repeated military and commercial reasons for government improvement of the canal. He also read into the record a portion of a letter he had recently received from former Senator John D. Works of California,

[33] *Ibid.*, p. 3718; ADWA, *Bulletin*, IX (June–July, 1917), 1. See also the extension of Moore's remarks on June 25, 1917, printed under the title of "Producing the Evidence in the Case of the Chesapeake and Delaware Canal," *Congressional Record*, 65th Congress, 1st Session, Appendix, pp. 444–451. This contains a summary of reports on the canal between 1872 and 1913, and more than two pages of endorsements of the ship canal project by leading statesmen, military authorities, and businessmen.

one of the three men on the subcommittee that investigated the financial and physical condition of the canal in 1914:

I had known nothing about the Chesapeake and Delaware Canal before that time. The investigation by the subcommittee was a very interesting one to me, and, as you remember, I attended the hearings quite regularly throughout. I will probably not be in the Senate when the question of the purchase of the canal is finally considered, and I would like to say to you now, if it will help you in any way to bring about what you desire in this matter, that I was thoroughly and completely convinced by the hearings before our subcommittee that the Government should acquire this canal and make it free. . . .

Saulsbury reminded the Senate that both the Secretary of War and the Secretary of the Navy had recommended acquisition of the canal, and stated his belief that this was "one of the greatest projects which the Government can perform."[34]

Kenyon remarked at the end of Saulsbury's defense of the project that Congress might as well capitulate and take the canal. "The Senator has proposed it as an amendment to most of the bills that come along and has been very diligent in the matter. . . . I am always impressed by the argument the Senator from Delaware makes on this canal. I have heard it a good many times, and it is pretty hard to resist it." Other senators found it equally hard to resist, for on July 26, the bill was passed by a 50–11 margin. President Wilson signed it in August.[35]

Although condemnation proceedings were authorized in 1917, little headway in the matter was made until the war ended. Immediately thereafter, however, a meeting between government and company representatives was arranged for the purpose of agreeing, if possible, upon a price for the canal. The conference was held on November 14, 1918, at which time Walter Hall, president of the canal company, agreed to accept the price recommended in 1907 by the Agnus Commission, $2,514,289.70, although for various reasons it was deemed desirable to handle the transfer through actual condemnation proceedings.

Shortly before this meeting took place, another strong endorsement of the Atlantic intracoastal waterway had come from the Department of Commerce. Secretary Redfield, in transmitting a report from the Bureau of Foreign and Domestic Commerce on the commercial and military advantages of sea-level ship canals at Cape Cod,

[34] *Congressional Record*, 65th Congress, 1st Session, pp. 5444–47.
[35] *Ibid.*, p. 5447.

across New Jersey, and between the Delaware and Chesapeake bays, summarized its findings in these words:

> The direct saving in the cost of transportation would doubtless be much greater than the cost of construction and operation, and the whole country would benefit, directly or indirectly, as a result of the consequent reduction in the costs of manufactured goods. The military and naval value of the canals would seem, of itself, to warrant the expenditure required for their construction.
>
> The engineering and operating problems are in no sense experimental. The Nation which has built and operated the Panama Canal need not hesitate at the lesser task. He would be bold, indeed, who after full study of the subject in all its bearings would assert the Panama Canal to be of greater present and future value to all the Nation than the waterway system now discussed.
>
> The conclusion is reached that the commercial and other advantages of this system of canals would be so great and so far-reaching as to warrant the early acquisition by the United States Government of the Cape Cod and the Chesapeake & Delaware Canals and their prompt improvement as deep sea-level canals, as well as the early construction across New Jersey of a sea-level canal of a minimum depth of 25 feet. In the opinion of this department the time for action has come.

These conclusions were borne out in a hearing by the Committee on Rivers and Harbors in December, 1918. John H. Small, one of the leaders in the Atlantic Deeper Waterways Association and a congressman from North Carolina, was chairman of the committee and conducted the investigation. The difficulties Philadelphia had experienced during the war in getting supplies because of railroad congestion and inadequate waterways in the Philadelphia–New York area, in what Bernard Baruch had called the "red flag district," were described by George S. Webster, director of wharves, docks, and ferries in Philadelphia. Wilfred H. Schoff supplied the committee with accurate, detailed, up-to-date information regarding the canal company, especially its financial history.[36]

Shortly after this hearing, the necessary appropriation for the purchase of the canal was included in the rivers and harbors bill enacted in March, 1919; in April the district court in Wilmington made the condemnation award: $2,514,289.64 went to the Fidelity Trust Company of Philadelphia, substituted trustee under the mortgage loan of 1856, on behalf of the bondholders of the company; 6

[36] "Atlantic Intracoastal Canals," p. 6; *Hearings on the Chesapeake and Delaware Canal*, December 16, 1918. See also Wilfred H. Schoff, "Chesapeake and Delaware Canal," ADWA, *Bulletin*, XI (December, 1918–January, 1919), 16–21, which is a substantial repetition of his testimony before the House committee concerning the canal company's financial history.

cents went to the canal company, representing the stockholders. Only executive approval of the proceedings, to come from the Attorney General's office, was necessary before the final decree could be entered. In the meantime, the canal company held a new election in June, 1919, as usual. President Hall informed the new board that the award failed to meet the amount of the outstanding bonds by $88,660.36. Consequently the trust company had called upon the board to turn over all the securities in the contingent fund, which amounted to only $13,597.31. This was done, but the interest payment on the mortgage loan due July 1, 1919, was delayed "until such time as the Canal is finally acquired by the United States Government and the money paid under the award." Formal transfer of the property to the government was made on August 13, 1919; on October 29, 1919, at a special and final meeting of the board, President Hall was authorized to liquidate all assets of the company and to pay the net proceeds to the trust company, "on account of the interest and principal due" on the mortgage.[37]

After an existence of 116 years, the Chesapeake and Delaware Canal Company disappeared from the scene, but its legacy, a ninety-year-old canal, remained. The movement to transform the ancient lock canal into a modern ship canal, begun in 1871, was finally assured of success. A series of official reports and investigations, beginning with the *Craighill Report* of 1872 and culminating with a fourth congressional hearing on the subject of the purchase of the canal in 1918, had at last brought about the desired result. To paraphrase the remarks of Representative Albert F. Polk of Delaware in 1917, if ever the spotlight of publicity and investigation had been turned upon any proposed government project, it was this one. Senator Penrose agreed: "I do not think the government ever went through a more honest transaction than this." Many persons and groups, of course, were responsible for the eventual success of the Chesapeake and Delaware project, but none more so than J. Hampton Moore or the association he headed. He happily announced the August 13 transaction to the membership of his organization in September: "The Chesapeake and Delaware Canal has been taken over by the Government — that's the big thing. The Association has to its credit now the key to the entire Atlantic coastal situation." Next it was up to the government to make the long-awaited improvements.[38]

[37] ADWA, *Bulletin*, XI (December, 1918–January, 1919), 21–22; XI (April–May, 1919), 8; Board Minute Book, April 9, June 10, October 29, 1919.
[38] *Congressional Record*, 65th Congress, 1st Session, p. 5444, Appendix, p. 339; ADWA, *Bulletin*, XI (August–September, 1919), 1.

Government Operation
of the Canal

15

On August 13, 1919, the Chesapeake and Delaware Canal became a toll-free waterway. Official ceremonies in connection with government acquisition of the canal, however, were held in Delaware City on October 11, under the auspices of the Atlantic Deeper Waterways Association. Delegations from Philadelphia, Chester, Wilmington, and other nearby cities attended the celebration, where speeches from both Delaware senators, the governor, the chief of engineers, and other public officials were heard. A map and folder distributed by the waterway association contained a summary of the canal's history, beginning with the first surveys made 150 years before. The long legislative struggle for federal aid and the eventual completion of the canal in 1829 were described. Its years of operation as a private canal demonstrated, declared the ADWA publication, "a record of continuous service far superior to that of any other American waterway, except the Erie Canal," and foreshadowed "a largely increased business when freed from tolls and modernized as a federal waterway."[1]

Only limited improvements in the canal were made in 1920 and 1921, using the balance of the initial $3,000,000 appropriation, although studies necessary in planning the enlargement were undertaken. In 1922, when funds became available, work on a large scale

[1] ADWA, *Bulletin*, XII (March, 1920), 13.

began immediately. Colonel Earl I. Brown of the Corps of Engineers, the district engineer at Wilmington, Delaware, was put in charge of the project. The new lock-free canal was to be 12 feet deep and 90 feet wide at the bottom at mean low water. It was to have a new eastern entrance, and five new bridges, four highway and one railroad, were to be built. More than 16,000,000 cubic yards of earth had to be excavated. The task was complicated by the fact that it was to be carried on with as little hindrance as possible to the trade of the canal, then consisting of from 30 to 50 vessels a day, or to the overland traffic using the bridges over the canal.

In planning the work, consideration was also given to future enlargements of the canal. "The Federal Engineers," Brown informed an Atlantic Deeper Waterways convention, "regard this [12-foot] channel as being merely a construction stage, of probably limited duration, in the progress to an ultimate ship canal of probably 250 feet in width and 30 to 35 feet in depth. With that end in view, all permanent structures such as bridges and breakwaters have been designed and constructed." It was originally expected that the first enlargement would be completed in 1926, but the army engineers, just like the private contractors almost a century earlier, ran into unforeseen difficulties in the marshy eastern and deep cut sections of the canal.[2]

While an embankment approximately one mile long between the canal channel and the marsh east of St. Georges, "a very soft and treacherous place for a structure of any kind," was being constructed, it settled "as fast as built up. Its final completion was, however, consummated after all the soft material had been displaced by harder and firmer material for depths varying from 10 to 40 feet." Westward in the deep cut, "slides of greater or lesser magnitude have occurred," which required additional dredging before the water in the upper level could be lowered. By keeping the locks on the canal in use until the dredging was completed, the engineers insured that these slides and shoalings did not interfere with traffic because the canal was actually 30 feet deep in the upper level.[3]

Not only increased excavation work but the loss of a large dredge intended for use in doing the final cleanup work, as it attempted to make the journey from New York to Delaware by sea, caused delay in completing the enlargement. J. Hampton Moore, in reporting that

[2] ADWA, *Proceedings* (1926), p. 110.
[3] *Ibid.*, pp. 110–111.

this incident would delay the completion ceremonies planned by the Atlantic Deeper Waterways Association, told why the dredge was lost:

In the absence of a canal across the State of New Jersey . . . there was no other way . . . except to take the risk on the outside of the New Jersey coast. What has happened in numerous other instances, to vessels not intended for the open sea, happened in this case. Under tow the dredge got along all right until . . . it struck a storm against which it could not sustain itself. The dredge, valued at $500,000, went down and only by a miracle were the lives of the men on board saved. The government loss in delay will probably run up to $100,000.[4]

A replacement dredge was secured in August, but because those using the canal protested closing it for the purpose of removing the locks until the winter season, Brown decided to delay converting the canal into a sea-level waterway until February, 1927. Accordingly, announcements were made in January that the canal would be closed, beginning at midnight on January 31, for at least two weeks in order to permit the change-over. A small group of representatives from the government and Atlantic Deeper Waterways Association witnessed the actual union of the waters of the Chesapeake and the Delaware on February 1, and by February 25 the impediments to navigation in the canal — slides, shoals, locks, and a sunken barge — were sufficiently removed to permit limited navigation through the waterway. The new bridges, all of the vertical lift type, had already been completed. Each bridge afforded a minimum vertical clearance of 140 feet, a minimum horizontal clearance of 175 feet. The total cost of the initial enlargement, including purchase of the old canal, was $10,060,000.[5]

A thorough report on the project from an engineering point of view was made by Colonel Brown in an address to the American Society of Civil Engineers in 1931. The problems met during the reconstruction of the Chesapeake and Delaware Canal frequently had been described by others as being small-scale replicas of those encountered during the construction of the Panama Canal, and there was a great deal of interest in the work. "The more this work advances the greater it appears," reported J. Hampton Moore in 1925, "and it is said by engineers to be the most important canal work thus far done by the Federal Government in the United States."[6]

[4] ADWA, *President's Letter* (May 1, 1926), p. 1.
[5] Brown, "The Chesapeake and Delaware Canal," pp. 717, 720, 732–733. See also ADWA, *President's Letter* (March 1, 1927), pp. 2–4, for a description of the February conversion.
[6] ADWA, *President's Letter* (June 1, 1925), p. 1.

Brown included in his report some remarks on the economic value of the enlarged canal. "Antagonists of waterway improvements have declared it a waste of public funds," he noted, but he maintained this was not true: "Assuming that a public work like this is for public good, for public convenience, and for public economy, this canal makes an excellent showing for the funds expended on it." After omitting all consideration of pleasure boats, passengers, and empty vessels, he estimated in 1926 that the canal afforded a direct savings of $1.25 per ton on the transportation costs of the 600,000 to 700,000 tons of freight then using it. He concluded, however, that another enlargement of the canal was needed at once for safety reasons. Variations in the water level and the current through the canal caused by the tides on each bay were detrimental to navigation: "The detriment lies not so much in their effect on speed and time of transit, but on safety to the vessel. If a large and heavily laden vessel grounds and gets athwart the channel, as it may readily do under action of currents, a fall in the tide may break the vessel in two. Tows approaching closed bridges with a fair wind and tide, and having to check their speed on account of failure of the bridge to open, are particularly exposed to having one or more vessels in the tow grounded."[7] The truth of these observations has been demonstrated repeatedly.

The sea-level waterway was completed to project dimensions by the end of May, 1927, although it had been opened on February 25 during daylight hours to boats drawing not more than 9 feet. New permanent regulations adopted by the War Department relative to the canal placed all vessels using it under the supervision of the district engineer. A speed of 6 miles per hour in the canal was permitted, but vessels with an overhanging deckload were barred, as were tows and rafts unless special permission for their passage was received. By mid-April conditions had improved to the extent that Brown permitted vessels drawing up to 12 feet to use the canal "at all hours of the day or night." Vessels with a vertical height of more than 64 feet were still barred, however, and tows were limited to one barge "until further notice."[8]

While the final touches were being made, the Atlantic Deeper Waterways Association went ahead with its plans for a great celebration marking the completion of the project. The day selected for the big event was May 14, 1927, and hundreds of people were on hand

[7] Brown, "The Chesapeake and Delaware Canal," pp. 757–758, 763.
[8] Ibid., p. 733; ADWA, President's Letter (April 1, 1927), pp. 3–4; ADWA, President's Letter (May 1, 1927), pp. 7–8.

to watch scores of boats parade through the waterway and to hear formal dedicatory exercises at Reedy Point Bridge, at the eastern end of the canal. President Coolidge participated in the celebration to the extent of pressing a button in Washington to open the waterway officially. J. Hampton Moore described the scene:

The procession of boats through the waterway was an imposing one. They had assembled at Delaware City and were led by the "Nenemoosha," belonging to Alfred I. du Pont, of Wilmington. Following the flagship came the "City of Chester," a large Delaware River boat carrying a thousand members of the Atlantic Deeper Waterways Association and their friends. Decorated craft belonging to the Army and Navy, to the State of New Jersey, to the City of Philadelphia, to the yacht clubs, and to numerous private owners, followed in line. There were about 50 in all. The trip through the 13 miles of new waterway was marked by the waving of flags, the bursting of bombs, the blowing of whistles, the singing of children and the salutations of the people along the banks. Demonstrations were particularly noticeable at Reedy Point, St. Georges, and Chesapeake City. At the latter hundreds of school children, waving flags and singing patriotic songs, stood in the rain as the boats passed by.

Unfortunately, as at a previous opening celebration (on July 4, 1829), rain dampened the participants, but their spirits were unaffected. The formal exercises observing the barge canal opening, however, were held aboard the *City of Chester* as it returned from Delaware City to Wilmington rather than at Reedy Point Bridge. Various persons, including Governor Robert P. Robinson of Delaware, Colonel Earl I. Brown of the Corps of Engineers, and Congressman J. Charles Linthicum of Maryland, took part in the program, although J. Hampton Moore, speaking on behalf of the Atlantic Deeper Waterways Association, made the featured address. He described the early history of the canal and the efforts, spearheaded by the association, made since 1907 to convert the canal into a sea-level waterway. He reminded his listeners that what they had just inspected was only a 13-mile stretch of a far greater and larger waterway reaching 600 miles from Trenton, New Jersey, to Beaufort, North Carolina:

It is a big National business that brings you here today . . . a business important to commerce in times of peace and important to the Nation in the event of war. The President of the United States, who pressed the button which officially opened this new sea level waterway between the North and the South, is to be congratulated upon the relief it will bring to commerce and to the country. The members of Congress . . . who voted for the project, are to be commended for their support; and the War Department is to be commended for the engineering skill employed in its construction.

And you, members of the Atlantic Deeper Waterways Association, together with your distinguished and honored guests: You are to be congratulated that you are participants in an historic event which will be memorable as a National achievement. You inspired this work. You labored long and earnestly to accomplish it. I rejoice with you in the success which today crowns your unselfish and public-spirited efforts.[9]

J. Adam Bede, a former congressman from Minnesota and a leading advocate of the St. Lawrence Seaway, had taken notice of the forthcoming Chesapeake and Delaware celebration in the May issue of his waterway publication, *Bede's Budget*:

After twelve years of politics and four years of construction work, the new sea level Chesapeake and Delaware Canal . . . will be formally opened with a grand celebration on the site Saturday, May 14. The building of this bigger, better and deeper canal . . . is a notable achievement, and means much to the Atlantic sea-board states. J. Hampton Moore, president of the Atlantic Deeper Waterways Association, former member of the Congress and recent mayor of Philadelphia, will feel the ocean tide swell his proud and patriotic breast and could float home without a life preserver.

Indeed, much of the credit for the waterway belonged to Moore, but neither he nor others along the Atlantic coast were satisfied with only a 12-foot channel. Calls for the further deepening of the canal to 25 or 35 feet were made with increasing frequency from 1927 to 1935, when such a project was authorized. As Moore pointed out in his presidential address to the association in the fall of 1927, "it is already apparent that a greater depth than 12 feet must be provided; and this Convention should discuss it and, if agreeable, approve of immediate steps to induce Congress to authorize a new channel at least 25 feet deep."[10]

During the first years of government operation, even the limited dimensions of the canal prism (12 feet by 90 feet) were not always available. Brigadier General Herbert Deakyne reported on the current status of the canal in 1928:

I visited that canal in July and went all the way through it for the purpose of finding out just how it stood as to the difficulties that have developed since the canal has been opened. We had a great deal of trouble with some of the bridges and with the sliding of the banks. I found in July that all these difficulties with the bridges had been overcome and the bridges were in good condition. We are working as fast as we can to get a full depth of twelve feet in that canal. With respect to the slides we are working with them along the same lines that General Goethals did with respect to

[9] ADWA, *President's Letter* (June 1, 1927), pp. 1–2, 4–5.
[10] Quoted *ibid.*, pp. 10–11; ADWA, *Proceedings* (1927), p. 67.

the slides in the Panama Canal, and I think it is only a question of time when the difficulties that are experienced there at present will be completely eliminated.

The slides, however, continued to occur at frequent intervals, necessitating additional dredging operations to clear the channel. "No method of controlling the slides is known," said Colonel Brown in 1931, "drainage would have no effect." He predicted that soon the banks would reach a state of equilibrium, but until then it would be expensive to keep the canal free of obstructions, and "navigation will experience the hazard of occasional interruption." [11]

Despite the problems attendant to maintaining the new channel, there was a promising and steady increase in traffic through the canal. In 1920 only 481,000 tons of freight were carried through the toll-free lock canal, but in 1928, the first full year of operations as a tide-level canal, tonnage slightly exceeded 700,000 tons, and grew rapidly thereafter. It exceeded 1,000,000 tons in 1932 and remained well above that figure throughout the decade. New, enlarged vessels for use in the coastwise trade were soon trading regularly through the canal. The Ericsson Line built a new 1,500-passenger steamer, the *John Cadwalader*, described as the "biggest and best" of the new boats built for use on the canal. Its maiden voyage down the Delaware came on April 16, 1927, and on April 18 its first regular trip through the canal to Baltimore was made.[12]

In December, 1927, a barge grounded in the canal and later sank, under circumstances as described above by Colonel Brown, completely blocking the canal for several days. "As traffic is increasing in this waterway," Moore reported, "the incident was embarrassing to a large number of shippers and vessel owners, but in due course the obstruction was removed. . . ." In time occasional shallow-draft ocean-going vessels began to use the canal. The Atlantic Deeper Waterways Association reported the passage in August, 1930, of the *West Galoc*, a 3,200-ton steamer being towed to Baltimore, and early in 1931 the first foreign steamer to use the canal, the British *Myrtis*, passed through the canal en route to Baltimore from Wilmington. Later in the year other foreign vessels used the canal, and some 20 ocean steamers, many of them over 400 feet long, were towed through from Philadelphia to Baltimore, where they were to be scrapped. In addition, of course, a great number of barge lines regularly used

[11] ADWA, *Proceedings* (1928), p. 56; Brown, "The Chesapeake and Delaware Canal," p. 737.
[12] ADWA, *President's Letter* (May 1, 1927), p. 4.

TABLE 8. CHESAPEAKE AND DELAWARE CANAL TRAFFIC, 1920–65[a]

Calendar Year	Short Tons	Calendar Year	Short Tons
1920	481,000	1943	7,450,000
1921	490,000	1944	5,354,000
1922	797,000	1945	3,690,000
1923	771,000	1946	3,698,000
1924	683,000	1947	5,388,000
1925	727,000	1948	5,597,000
1926	610,000	1949	6,362,000
1927	608,000	1950	7,298,000
1928	700,000	1951	8,636,000
1929	709,000	1952	6,748,000
1930	867,000	1953	8,897,000
1931	990,000	1954	8,816,000
1932	1,017,000	1955	9,151,000
1933	1,191,000	1956	10,709,000
1934	1,039,000	1957	9,808,000
1935	1,061,000	1958	9,146,000
1936	1,300,000	1959	8,852,000
1937	1,437,000	1960	8,899,000
1938	2,223,000	1961	8,830,000
1939	3,035,000	1962	9,250,000
1940	3,795,000	1963	10,500,000
1941	4,062,000	1964	11,168,000
1942	10,827,000	1965	12,250,000(est.)

[a]Compiled from the records of the U.S. Army, Corps of Engineers, Philadelphia District.

the canal, and a new commodity — oil — was carried through the canal in 1931 in tankers made as large as possible for use on the canal route. "That is going to be a great business," said Colonel R. P. Howell, Colonel Brown's successor as the district engineer at Wilmington. Howell also called attention to the "perfect stream" of boats through the canal on weekends: "All kinds of pleasure boats are going through that canal, not only the bigger boats from New York and Philadelphia which go down to the South in the wintertime, but also a great number of smaller boats."[13]

The increasing traffic not only strengthened the demand for an enlarged waterway but also necessitated the inauguration of a traffic control system. A central dispatching office was established at Chesapeake City, and patrol boats were stationed at either end of the canal. These boats, as well as each of the bridges, were equipped

[13] *Ibid.* (January 1, 1928), p. 16; (September 1, 1930), p. 10; (February 1, 1931), p. 9; R. P. Howell, "The Chesapeake and Delaware Sea Level Waterway," ADWA, *Proceedings* (1931), pp. 74–79.

with two-way radiophones, enabling them to keep in constant communication with the chief dispatcher. As vessels entered and left the canal they were reported to the dispatcher, and their progress through the canal, moreover, was reported by the bridgetenders. In this way the dispatcher knew at all times the exact number of boats in the canal and their approximate location. The patrol boats were also used to collect data concerning the dimensions and cargoes of vessels transiting the canal. Substantially the same traffic control system is employed today.[14]

In 1931 the Corps of Engineers reported on a project to improve the Delaware City branch canal, about two miles long, connecting Delaware City with the main canal along the original canal route. By that time the branch had deteriorated considerably, but local interests were calling for a 12-foot by 90-foot channel, one equal in size to the main channel and one that might restore to the city its former prosperity. Such a project would cost an estimated $343,000, however, and was economically unjustifiable in the eyes of the engineers. They did recommend that a channel 8 feet deep and 50 feet wide be provided, which would cost only $67,000 and would meet the needs of Delaware City so far as its business with pleasure craft transiting the canal was concerned.

At a hearing on the subject, the older inhabitants recalled the days of the lock canal, when Delaware City was a regular port of call for Ericsson Line steamers and other vessels, and painted a rosy picture of the former bustle along the waterfront. They were inclined to place the blame for the dearth of such activity solely on the fact that the government had purchased the canal and reconstructed it, leaving Delaware City off the main line. They believed that if their channel were made equal to the main one the city's former business would return, although this was undoubtedly a vain hope. As the district engineer stated in his report, "the change from a lock canal with its forced halting of craft at Delaware City into an open waterway which allows boats to go through without stopping . . . has been the main cause of whatever damage Delaware City has suffered."[15]

[14] Corps of Engineers, United States Army, *The Chesapeake and Delaware Canal: An Inland Waterway from Delaware River to Chesapeake Bay, Delaware and Maryland* (rev. ed., Philadelphia, 1941), p. 21; Interview with B. H. Brown, Marine Traffic Control Officer at the Chesapeake and Delaware Canal, April 4, 1958.

[15] "Report on the Delaware City Branch of the Chesapeake and Delaware Canal," *House Documents*, No. 201, 72nd Congress, 1st Session (Washington, 1931), pp. 2–4, 9–10.

A more legitimate claim of the Delaware City residents was that the reconstruction of the canal, by lowering the water level in the old lock canal, had destroyed the beauty of their city, and the engineers suggested that "the project for the branch channel should provide for reestablishing the sightliness of the waterway at Delaware City as far as is practicable under the new conditions." This project was adopted in 1935 as part of the program to enlarge the main canal.[16]

As a result of the growing demand for a wider and deeper channel on the main line, the House Committee on Rivers and Harbors, on January 7, 1932, requested the Board of Engineers for Rivers and Harbors to make a review report on the existing waterway "with a view to determining if any improvement is necessary to protect and facilitate commerce, both existing and prospective." Colonel Earl I. Brown, once again the district engineer at Wilmington after temporary service in Texas, recommended in his report to the board that the project be modified to provide for a ship canal with a navigable depth of 25 feet and a bottom width of 250 feet, at an estimated cost of $9,788,000. Although the division engineer in New York did not agree with these recommendations, and instead recommended that a deeper barge canal be constructed at a cost of $2,978,761, the Board of Engineers not only agreed with Brown that a ship canal was called for, but recommended that its depth be 27 rather than 25 feet.[17]

When conflicting reports were received from the district and division engineers by the review board, it conducted its own special hearing to hear the views of interested parties. Evidence submitted at the hearing, particularly that presented by the Baltimore Association of Commerce, indicated that the present dimensions of the canal were grossly inadequate to meet the needs of the existing traffic, and that there were frequent delays to vessels using the canal as well as occasional accidents resulting in material losses to shipping interests and complete interruptions of canal traffic for extended periods of time. The evidence also indicated that enlargement of the channel to permit its use by ocean-going vessels would result in sufficient economies in time and costs to justify the expenditure. It was esti-

[16] *Ibid.*, p. 16.
[17] "Letter from the Chief of Engineers, transmitting Report of the Board of Engineers for Rivers and Harbors on Review of Reports heretofore submitted on Inland Waterway from Delaware River to Chesapeake Bay, Del. and Md., with 13 Illustrations," Committee on Rivers and Harbors, *House Committee Documents*, No. 24, 73rd Congress, 2nd Session (Washington, 1933), pp. 2–3.

mated that a ship canal would result in annual savings of at least $970,000, and that it would accommodate more than 90 per cent of the ships likely to use such a canal if available. The board concluded that a 27-foot channel for the accommodation of vessels drawing up to 25 feet was called for, and that its bottom width through the land cut between Reedy Point and the Elk River should be 250 feet; its width down the Elk and through Chesapeake Bay to deep water in the bay should be 400 feet. It was estimated that the cost of the project would be $12,500,000, and that the annual maintenance and operation charges on the waterway would be increased by $200,000.[18]

G. H. Pouder, executive vice-president of the Baltimore Association of Commerce, described the work of his organization in promoting the deeper channel to the Atlantic Deeper Waterways Association convention in 1933. The Baltimore group made a careful analysis of the port's trade for the six months ending August 31, 1933, and learned that 1,035 of the 1,079 vessels calling at Baltimore during that time could have used a 25-foot canal, with resulting savings amounting to several hundred thousand dollars. It was these figures, in fact, upon which the Board of Engineers for Rivers and Harbors had based its recommendations for the ship canal.

The testimony of practical ship operators, port representatives, and other technical witnesses at the hearing [stated Pouder], demonstrated that these were sound and conservative figures. It was most gratifying at the hearing to have had the written and oral support of official representatives of the ports of Boston, New York, Philadelphia, Camden and Wilmington, and last but certainly not least, the support of a number of substantial commercial organizations led by the representatives of the Atlantic Deeper Waterways Association. Your Mr. Small's remarks were most forceful and timely, as were Mr. Bernard's; your President's letter was of great value for the record, and the testimony of several of your affiliated members was highly vital in the composite picture. We, of Baltimore, appreciate this support.[19]

The project as recommended was adopted by Congress in 1935, when $5,107,000 was appropriated under the Emergency Relief Appropriation Act to initiate the enlargement. Since one of the purposes of the act was to provide employment for persons on relief, it was specified that the contractors had to obtain at least 90 per cent of their workers from the relief rolls. Work was begun immediately, with the 35,000,000 cubic yards of material to be removed handled

[18] *Ibid.*, pp. 4–8.
[19] ADWA, *Proceedings* (1933), pp. 66–71.

both by dry excavation and dredging. In spite of the planning for future enlargements when the original government work was undertaken in the 1920's, two bridges across the canal had to be substantially altered. This was done to prevent restricted channels at those points, which would have created increased and treacherous currents there.[20]

As on previous projects, the greatest difficulties were experienced in the deep cut area, where more slides developed. Studies to find a method of stabilizing the banks were conducted at laboratories in Ithaca, New York, and Wilmington, Delaware. Their findings indicated that a flatter slope and more thorough drainage of the banks were needed, and in April, 1939, a program of bank stabilization was instituted.[21]

In 1939, before the new project was completely finished, the bridge at St. Georges was demolished when it was struck by the *S. S. Waukegan.* The lift span of the bridge was knocked into the canal, and navigation was interrupted for several days. Rather than rebuild a vertical lift bridge, a type rapidly becoming outmoded, the engineers were authorized to replace it with a high-level four-lane bridge which was completed in 1941. This was the first modern highway bridge constructed across the canal, but two others have been erected since then. Plans for modernizing the remaining vertical lift highway bridge at Reedy Point have been approved.

There was a sudden and substantial increase in traffic through the canal as a result of its conversion from a barge to a ship canal. Even during the period of transition from 1935 to 1940, annual transits rose from 9,034 to 14,154, an increase of 57 per cent, and tonnage carried through the canal jumped from 1,061,207 tons to 3,794,999 tons, almost a fourfold increase. In the single month of March, 1938, 32 ships in both the coastwise and overseas trade moved to and from Baltimore through the partially completed ship canal. According to the Baltimore *Port Bulletin,* among the shippers using the canal route were A. H. Bull and Company; Dichmann, Wright, and Pugh; Furness, Withy, and Company; Merchants and Miners Transportation Company; Moore and McCormack, Inc.; Procter and Gamble Manufacturing Company; and the Terminal Shipping Company. The principal commodities being transported in 1940 were petroleum products, fertilizer, coal tar, chemicals, lumber, woodpulp, iron and

[20] Corps of Engineers, *The Chesapeake and Delaware Canal,* pp. 13, 15–17.
[21] *Ibid.,* pp. 17–19.

steel products, refined sugar, canned goods, seafood, and miscellaneous manufactured items.[22]

The usefulness of the canal in times of national emergencies was proved once again during World War II. Completed as a ship canal just prior to the outbreak of the war, it provided a protected passage for ships, boats, and barges between the two bays. It was particularly useful in 1942, when no less than 10,827,162 tons of freight passed through the waterway. Major General Eugene Reybold of Delaware City, Delaware, who became chief of engineers in 1942, spoke to a group in Philadelphia about the utility of the canal in wartime: "Many vessels are now using this canal as the more secure route. I recall that just such a development was foreseen by some of the early proponents of the canal and the prospect was used in their arguments for authorizations and funds. At the time many people scoffed at the idea — but now, those farsighted men are entitled to take a bow." [23]

Submarines operating just off the Atlantic coast sank 127 vessels there between December 7, 1941, and April 12, 1942, and drove to the canal as many ships as could possibly use it. It also became part of a widely used all-water route from South to North, over which makeshift wooden tank barges transported oil. A perceptive journalist described in April, 1942, the advantages of the Atlantic intracoastal waterway:

> Once the voyaging ground of the pleasure-boat owner, the Atlantic Intracoastal Waterway is gaining an unexpected importance as a result of the war. . . . Travel along it is tortuous and slow . . . but there are more dangers than storms off the Atlantic coast these days, and though ship-routings are secret it's a safe assumption that those portions of the waterway deep enough for sea-going ships now are in constant use.
>
> Moreover, because of ship shortages, the possibilities of moving freight or oil by barge tow through the canal are being studied. Barges can be built quickly of wood or can be snatched from inland rivers, though most river barges are pretty busy already. This is no negligible means of transport; 20,000-ton barge tows are not unknown on some rivers. But such transport needs sheltered water.[24]

Joseph B. Eastman, appointed by President Roosevelt as director of the Office of Defense Transportation on January 2, 1942, quickly became well aware of the advantages of America's inland waterways. With most ocean-going vessels being used in overseas service and with the railroads overcrowded, the inland rivers and

[22] *Ibid.*, p. 26; quoted in ADWA, *President's Letter* (April 1, 1938), p. 5.

[23] ADWA, *President's Letter* (April 1, 1942), p. 5.

[24] "Inside Passage," *Business Week* (April 11, 1942), p. 18.

canals, as well as the Gulf and Atlantic intracoastal waterways, were utilized to the fullest possible extent. He described, in an address to the Mississippi Valley Association entitled "The Debt to Inland Water Transportation" and delivered in October, 1943, the steps taken the previous year when an emergency in petroleum developed in the eastern seaboard territory. Over 100 dry-cargo barges in use on the river system were converted into tank barges, and 500 new wooden tank barges, each with a capacity of 6,000 barrels, were constructed for use primarily on the intracoastal waterways. These craft answered the demand; as Eastman remarked at the time, "The inland and intracoastal barge operations have demonstrated their value." [25]

The heavy traffic through the canal in 1942 was interrupted for almost two weeks after an accident in which a second bridge was demolished. On July 28 the tanker *Franz Klasen*, being assisted through the canal by three tugs, crashed into the south tower of the bridge at Chesapeake City, dropping the lift span into the channel, displacing both towers, and wrecking both approach spans. According to B. H. Brown, marine traffic control officer at Chesapeake City, this incident was caused chiefly by an inexperienced pilot. Conditions of wind, water, and weather were ideal for navigation, but the pilot, who had guided a ship through the canal only once before, relied too heavily on the tugs to get him through and the accident occurred. On August 8, the canal was clear for limited navigation and a week later full depth was restored. The vertical lift bridge was not repaired, but instead a high-level two-lane bridge across the canal, not completed until after the war, was erected.[26]

After the record year for tonnage in 1942, when more than 10,000,000 tons of freight were carried through the canal, traffic declined gradually through 1945, when it amounted to 3,689,537 tons. Since 1945, however, there has been a steady increase in tonnage, which by the mid-1950's amounted to nearly 10,000,000 tons of freight passing through the canal annually. Traffic slumped slightly in the late 1950's but then moved upwards again. The increased trade on the canal once more led to a movement for its enlargement. A review report on the existing project was called for by the Senate

[25] G. Lloyd Wilson, ed., *Selected Papers and Addresses of Joseph B. Eastman, Director, Office of Defense Transportation, 1942–1944* (New York, 1948), pp. 185, 308–315.
[26] "Inland Waterway from Delaware River to Chesapeake Bay, Del. and Md.," *Senate Documents*, No. 123, 83rd Congress, 2nd Session (Washington, 1954), p. 18; *Wilmington Morning News*, August 8, 1942; Interview with B. H. Brown.

Committee on Commerce on March 28, 1939, but the final report was not submitted to Congress until May, 1954. At that time the Corps of Engineers recommended that a substantial enlargement of the waterway be made.

The chief of engineers, Major General S. D. Sturgis, in transmitting the report to the Secretary of the Army, emphasized that "the volume of traffic far exceeds the safe capacity of the waterway, and long delays, groundings, and vessel accidents occur frequently. Hazardous conditions arise primarily from inadequate bridge clearances, sharp bends, inadequate depths, and from channel widths which are inadequate for the safe passage of vessels." The district engineer's report contained many details concerning the hazards of navigating the 27-foot by 250-foot channel. Eight bridge collisions occurring between 1938 and 1950 were described, and information concerning 209 other accidents — collisions and groundings — was provided.[27]

There was even more recent evidence which might well have been included in the report. A particularly costly and tragic accident occurred in 1952 when the *F. L. Hayes*, a tanker laden with 640,000 gallons of high-octane gasoline, collided with a freighter, the *Barbara Lykes*. Richard K. Smith, a member of the freighter's crew, recorded the events of the day in his diary:

> Shortly after midnite, May Fifteenth, while transiting the Chesapeake-Delaware Canal, enroute to New York from Baltimore, at a sharp curve in the narrow ditch, a small tanker . . . came cruising out of the dark ahead on a collision course.
>
> Our pilot blasted on our whistle, and almost swung our ship into the steep canal bank in an effort to miss the smaller ship — but she came on! At the last minute the *Hayes* began to veer away, but too late! Too late for them, but in time to save us!
>
> She struck us on the port bow, glanced off and scraped down our side and passed astern of us. . . . 300 yards astern of us she exploded! — went sky high! Gasoline flowed from her shattered tanks onto the water and in seconds the narrow canal had become a raging inferno.[28]

Four crewmen on the tanker were killed, and two members of the crew on a third ship, abreast of the *Hayes* when her tanks exploded, were badly burned. The ruptured tanker settled to the shallow bottom of the canal within a few mintues, but "her cargo continued to

[27] "Inland Waterway from Delaware River to Chesapeake Bay," p. ix.

[28] Diary of Richard K. Smith of Chicago, Illinois, May 15, 1952. The diary remains in Mr. Smith's possession; he transcribed the portions relevant to the collision for me.

burn for seventeen days," and it was several weeks more before the channel was cleared of the wreckage.[29]

During this time the canal was closed to all but small craft. This necessitated use of the "outside route" by all ships calling at the Port of Baltimore, although normally about 30 per cent of the Baltimore trade passed through the canal. Sailing the longer route added to the time and expense of shipments; less than two months after the closing, it was estimated that the Baltimore ship operators had lost more than a million dollars. The city's Association of Commerce termed the situation "unbearable and disastrous," and asked for emergency demolition of the blockading vessel, rather than repeated salvage attempts which were proving fruitless. "I guarantee you it is criminal," said the representative of one shipping broker. "We are losing hundreds of thousands of dollars," added an official of a large shipping company. Eventually, however, 103 days after the collision, the ship was raised and travel through the canal resumed.[30]

The need for improvements in the canal was obvious, and immediate steps were taken to proceed with plans to increase both its safety and its accommodations. The army engineers recommended deepening the channel to 35 feet, widening it to 450 feet, replacing the movable-span highway bridges with high-level fixed structures, and reducing the curvatures in the canal to not less than a radius of 7,000 feet. "It should be undertaken immediately with a view to providing a suitable facility for the safe passage of large vessels," stated General Sturgis:

It would be inadvisable to recommend work of lesser extent thus leaving some of the hazardous features for many more years after which it would be necessary to remove them with undoubtedly a greater expenditure than if the changes were accomplished at this time. The canal was particularly valuable to the Nation during World War II. The proposed improvement would greatly increase its value in the case of any future emergency. The plan proposed by the Board could be undertaken in steps, and, when completed, would adequately meet the needs of commerce for a long period of time.

[29] *The New York Times*, July 21, 1952.
[30] *Ibid.*; *Baltimore Sun*, August 9, 1952. The dangerous salvage operations were handled by Richard W. Stosch, an imaginative small-scale manufacturer engaged in his first major salvage attempt, after two large firms failed to raise the ship. After bidding for the opportunity to make the attempt, Stosch met the deadline imposed by the Corps of Engineers with days to spare; had he failed, the ship would have been dynamited in order to clear the canal. *Baltimore Sun*, August 26, 28, 29, 1952.

The cost of the improvement was originally estimated at $96,000,000, although revised estimates made in June, 1957, placed it at $126,745,800.[31]

These recommendations were submitted to the Senate Committee on Public Works in May, 1954, accompanied by statements from other federal and state governmental agencies. Authorization of the project was received in September, 1954, but large-scale construction was delayed until 1962, when the necessary appropriations were made. These came following Corps of Engineers testimony giving the most recent calculations on the cost-benefit ratio of the project. The figures showed 30 per cent greater benefits than costs and, in the opinion of the corps, fully justified the work.[32] In the meantime, various small portions of the project were undertaken. By June, 1960, the entire project was about 18 per cent complete, the major item being completion of a modern high-level four-lane bridge at the summit level. The $6,000,000 structure is the fourth bridge erected there since 1826 and, like the original summit bridge, has a fixed span.[33]

At present the Chesapeake and Delaware Canal is a waterway of considerable importance to the ports of Baltimore and Philadelphia primarily, and to a lesser degree to other Atlantic coast ports. Delaware's interest in the canal centers upon the bridges across the canal, the ground water supply in the vicinity of the canal, and the possibility of using some of the canal lands as state parks. The state has little interest in the waterway as a carrier of freight, but it has no objection to its improvement as long as the fresh water aquifers near the canal do not become contaminated with salt water and adequate bridges are provided. Area residents frequently experience exasperating delays at the single remaining vertical lift highway bridge. Elsewhere, particularly in Baltimore, which "is the best friend of the canal today," there is strong support for rapid completion of the current project. Approximately 40 per cent of the ships calling at Baltimore use the canal.[34]

[31] "Inland Waterway from Delaware River to Chesapeake Bay," pp. ix–xi; *Annual Report of the Chief of Engineers, United States Army, on Civil Works Activity, 1956–1957* (Washington, 1958), II, 239.
[32] Colonel T. H. Setliffe, District Engineer, Philadelphia, to author, August 14, 1962.
[33] "McLean Makes 36-Hour Pour on Summit Bridge Footing," *Constructioneer* (June 23, 1958), pp. 18–19; *Annual Report, Chief of Engineers, 1959–1960*, I, 228; *Journal–Every Evening*, August 11, 1960.
[34] Ira Wendell Marine and William Charles Rasmussen, *Preliminary Report on the Geology and Ground-Water Resources of Delaware* (Newark, Dela-

An average of 20,000 vessels pass through the canal each year, carrying a commerce bound for all parts of the world. The waterway is under the supervision of the district engineer at Philadelphia, who maintains the canal at its current project depth and width of 27 by 250 feet. Seventy-two persons were employed in 1960 to operate and maintain the canal; the average annual maintenance charges, 1955 to 1960, amounted to $858,198. Publications issued by the district engineer provide general information about the canal and describe the particular regulations governing its navigation. With its present dimensions, vessels drawing less than 25 feet and having an overall length of less than 275 feet may transit the canal without making prior arrangements, while all vessels over 275 feet long must arrange for their passage with the Chesapeake City dispatcher. Vessels more than 375 feet in length may not pass each other in the canal, and vessels longer than 650 feet are barred from using the canal at all. A "safe speed" is required at all times.[35]

When the present improvement project is completed in 1968 or 1969, the result will be a 35-foot-deep, 450-foot-wide waterway capable of accommodating the largest cargo vessels in continuous, two-way traffic. The huge modernization task involves the removal of some 100 million cubic yards of materials, modifications to the older bridges, and alteration of the channel at the summit level so as to eliminate a particularly sharp, hazardous curve. The project extends 55 miles from naturally deep water in Chesapeake Bay to the shipping channels of the Delaware River.

An account of a recent trip through the canal by the captain of an oil company's huge tanker reveals the limitations of the present canal as well as the potential of an enlarged waterway:

The *Chester* has been utilizing the Chesapeake and Delaware Canal on the run from Baltimore to New York. . . . If the timing is perfect, we can leave the dock in Baltimore, transit the Canal, go down the Delaware River and up to New York in 18 hrs. Going by way of Chesapeake Bay and Cape Henry takes 28 or 29 hrs. In addition to 10 or 11 hrs. saved, there are times when we can escape fog in lower Chesapeake Bay and the shorter distance via the canal (266 vs. 417 miles) saves about 160 bbls. of fuel.

ware, 1955), p. 148; *Wilmington Morning News,* June 15, 1954; Maryland Port Authority (Baltimore), Press Release, December 4, 1964.

[35] See Corps of Engineers, United States Army, Philadelphia District, *Inland Waterway, Chesapeake & Delaware Canal: Rules and Regulations* ([Philadelphia, 1956]), *passim,* and the periodic "Notices to Mariners" issued by the same office.

258] Government Operation of the Canal

The *Esso Chester* is one of the largest type vessels presently permitted through the Canal. Regulations limit a vessel's maximum length to 650′ and the *Chester* is only 22′ less than that. Also, for this type vessel, it is daylight transit only and one way traffic. . . . The Baltimore Pilot takes the con from clear of dock to about 1/3rd through the Canal (to Chesapeake City), where the Delaware River Pilot boards and cons the rest of the way and on out the Delaware River to the breakwater.

The Canal is approximately 18 miles long and the transit takes about 2 hrs. 20 min. as we must go at slow and half speed due to an improvement project underway. . . .

The closest squeeze is the Canal Railroad Bridge where the vessel passes through at very, very close quarters and at the same time negotiates a 30° turn. A new section of Canal being cut at this point and a new railroad bridge will eliminate this hazard. . . . Another tight squeeze is the Reedy Point Bridge near the Delaware River entrance to the Canal but this is a straightaway.[36]

During the ninety-year life of the canal as a privately operated enterprise, more than 57,000,000 tons of commerce transited the canal; in the nearly five decades of its operation by the government, over 215,000,000 tons have passed through; annual traffic has exceeded the 10,000,000-ton mark since 1963. Shipping interests in Baltimore and other Atlantic ports are enthusiastic over the modernizations underway and expect them to result in a much heavier use of the facility. A 50 per cent increase in tonnage is anticipated by the economic analysts of the Corps of Engineers.[37] The future of the Chesapeake and Delaware Canal, an important cog in the eastern seaboard's transportation system since the early nineteenth century and the "central link" in the twentieth-century Atlantic Intracoastal Waterway, is assured. What began as a dream of Thomas Gilpin's in the 1760's has become, by the 1960's, an essential and increasingly significant avenue of commerce.

[36] Captain Edward Crawford's description of his passage through the canal was published in *Fleet News*, a trade publication of the Humble Oil & Refining Company, in late spring, 1965. J. W. Bennett, Acting Manager, Baltimore Branch, Humble Oil & Refining Company, to author, July 26, 1965.

[37] Testimony of General Lipscomb, Corps of Engineers, in *Hearings before the Subcommittee of the Committee on Appropriations*, House of Representatives, 87th Congress, 1st Session (Washington, 1961), pp. 1584–85.

LOCKS IN THE ORIGINAL CANAL

At Delaware City. (*Gulf Oil Corporation*)

At St. Georges. (*Postcard in author's possession*)

J. Hampton Moore, president, Atlantic
Deeper Waterways Association, 1907–
47. (*Free Library of Philadelphia*)

General Felix Agnus, chairman of the
Agnus Commission, 1906. (*Maryland
Historical Society*)

Colonel Earl I. Brown, Corps of Engineers, supervised conversion from lock
to barge canal, 1922–27. (*Corps of
Engineers, Philadelphia District*)

GROWTH OF THE CANAL, 1830–1965

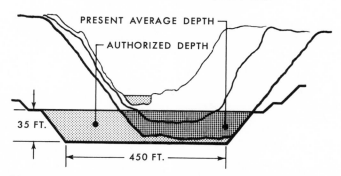

Four stages in canal development. (*Redrawn from Corps of Engineers, U. S. Army*)

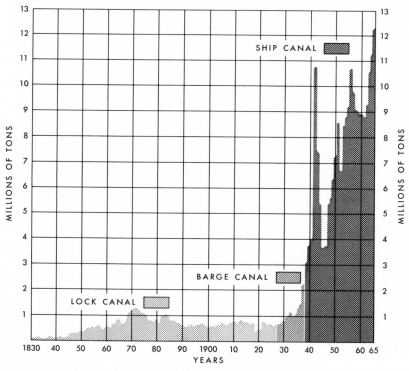

Tonnage carried on the canal, 1830–1965. (*Corps of Engineers, U.S. Army*)

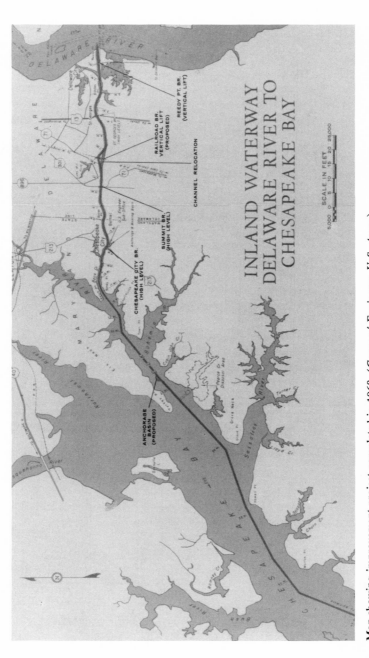

Map showing improvement project completed in 1968. (*Corps of Engineers, U.S. Army*)

The cutoff at the railroad bridge. (*Corps of Engineers, Philadelphia District*)

The Chesapeake and Delaware Canal. (*Gulf Oil Corporation*)

A New Issue Emerges

16

Throughout the 1960s and into the early 1970s, the Chesapeake and Delaware Canal continued to serve as a vital link in the navigation system along the east coast of the United States. During this period, too, work continued on enlarging and modernizing the canal according to the project authorized in 1954. Completion of this project, which included a channel 450 feet wide and 35 feet deep, three new bridges (two highway, one railroad) with vertical clearances of 135 feet, and certain route modifications, was expected before 1970, but for several reasons this was delayed until 1981. The major factor in the delay was the potentially harmful environmental effect of the channel enlargement.

Such environmental concern, relatively new throughout the United States in the 1960s and 1970s, had found concrete expression in the National Environmental Policy Act signed into law on January 1, 1970. Consequently, when the canal contractors were getting ready to "pull the plug"—that is, take the final section of the canal down to its project depth—various individuals and organizations expressed grave concern over the deleterious effect this might have on the water quality and biota in the upper Chesapeake. Congressional hearings followed, the final channel enlargement was postponed, and not until the impact of a thirty-five-foot open channel between the lower Delaware River and the upper reaches of Chesapeake Bay had been carefully studied was construction permitted to resume. In the meantime, however, work on the western portions of the canal project, including the open water areas between Chesapeake City and Poole's Island, many of the land-cut sections, and other aspects of the modernization program proceeded.

Impetus for the channel improvement came from the continuously heavy traffic through the canal, with even more growth limited by the canal dimensions, which were increasingly inadequate as ship sizes and drafts grew. Nevertheless, whereas traffic on the canal averaged just under 10 million tons annually for the decade of the 1960s, up slightly from its average in the 1950s, it grew substantially in the 1970s. For the decade, it averaged 11.5 million tons annually, reaching a new peak of 14.6 million tons in 1978. At that time a normal day's traffic consisted of ten or twelve ocean-going ships and an equal number of tows (barges and tugs), in addition to dozens of pleasure craft. "There are a great number of people," stated canal dispatcher Ed Patterson in 1977, "who don't realize the enormity of traffic this canal has." A few years ago, he continued, a study comparing traffic on the Suez, Panama, and Chesapeake and Delaware canals showed that "this canal had more tonnage than the other two canals combined." Similarly, a traffic-potential analysis completed in 1977, when the controlling depth was still 26.1 feet and vessels longer than 725 feet were barred, estimated that 561 more vessels (all with a draft between twenty-six and thirty-three feet) would use a thirty-five foot canal, saving as much as $7.8 to $9.0 million annually. Such savings would be derived from lowered pilotage and other operating costs. The canal reduces travel time between Baltimore and Philadelphia by sixteen hours, between Baltimore and North Atlantic ports (in New York, New England, Canada) by ten hours, and between Baltimore and northern European ports by seven hours. Over the estimated 100-year life of the project, "the present worth of the benefits would exceed 300 million dollars."[1]

Work on the $100 million project authorized in 1954 had begun with the construction of two high-level highway bridges, a vertical-lift

[1] Quoted in *Wilmington* (Delaware) *Evening Journal,* February 2, 1977; "Chesapeake and Delaware Canal Traffic Potential Analysis," March, 1977, Chesapeake and Delaware Canal Papers, District Engineer Office, U.S. Army Corps of Engineers, Philadelphia (hereafter C. & D. Papers, DEO). This report was prepared for the Corps of Engineers by the engineering firm of Tippetts, Abbett, McCarthy, and Stratton of New York. See also John A. Burnes and Albert T. Rosselli, "Shipping Cost Savings via the Chesapeake and Delaware Canal," a paper delivered at the Second International Waterborne Transportation Conference in New York City, October 5–7, 1977, also in the C. & D. Papers, DEO.

railroad bridge, and a few channel relocations designed to eliminate dangerous bends in the route. Two of the current four high-level highway bridges were already in place, their predecessor lift bridges having been toppled into the canal by ship collisions in 1939 and 1942. These handsome new landmarks, at St. Georges, Delaware, and Chesapeake City, Maryland, were completed in 1941 and 1948 respectively. They were matched in the 1960s by Summit Bridge (1960) and, finally, by Reedy Point Bridge (1968). The Corps of Engineers also constructed a new vertical-lift railroad bridge in the Summit area, topping it off in 1966.[2] The two-leaf bascule bridge spanning the old channel at Delaware City, however, remained in place. The Corps of Engineers had discontinued its lift operations there in the 1940s, and in 1971, during a general rehabilitation and strengthening of the structure, then nearly forty years old, the leaves were welded together.

At the other end of the canal, where a significant modification of the canal channel was undertaken in the 1960s, some extraordinary problems were encountered. A number of homes in North Chesapeake City had to be razed to make room for a widened channel, a venerable Chesapeake City institution—Schaefer's wharf, store, and restaurant—had to be (for the third time) relocated, and a boatyard and a service station on the south bank of the canal were abandoned. The most involved aspect of the channel-enlargement project in this area, however, concerned the Methodist church and its adjoining cemetery at Bethel, a small south-bank community just east of Chesapeake City.

Given the project requirement of 7,000 feet for the minimum radius of curvature in the new channel, all of the land containing the Bethel Methodist Episcopal Church cemetery and part of an older Bethel cemetery had to be acquired by the Corps of Engineers. (The only alternative would have taken many more buildings in Chesapeake City and required large additional expenditures for bank-stabilization work.) It was expected that 505 bodies in the two cemeteries would have to be reinterred, and the necessary approvals and permissions were obtained from church officers and, when known, the next of kin. The Corps hired a local minister, the Reverend William O. Hackett, to

---

[2]For details (and photographs) of the bridges constructed in the 1960s, particularly the easternmost Reedy Point Bridge, see Frank E. Snyder and Brian H. Guss, *The District: A History of the Philadelphia District, U.S. Army Corps of Engineers, 1866–1971* (Philadelphia, 1974), pp. 102–108. Much additional information on the highway bridges across the canal is in the Bridge Inspection Reports, C. & D. Papers, DEO. It should be noted that both the railroad bridge and Summit Bridge received awards from the American Institute of Steel Construction for their superior designs and appearances.

undertake these delicate negotiations and to oversee all aspects of the work.

Following acquisition of the land (1.56 acres, through condemnation proceedings in federal court) on April 12, 1965, Reverend Hackett arranged for a local mortuary to disinter, transport, and reinter the remains encountered. (The most famous person whose remains were moved was Joshua Clayton, a Federalist politician and the first governor of Delaware.) Not 505 but rather 1,137 bodies were discovered, most of whom were unknown and for whom no cemetery records existed.[3] The work was completed, nevertheless, early in 1966, and a dedication service at the new gravesites was held on May 1, 1966.

Another change, one which provides an example of Corps of Engineers' responsiveness to the sensibilities and desires of the local populace in the 1960s, was its decision to preserve the huge steam-powered lifting wheel and the "pumphouse" in which it was located. Initial plans had called for the removal of this engineering marvel, which, according to newspaper reports, Henry Ford had attempted to purchase in 1927 for his museum in Dearborn, Michigan, but it was decided in 1964 that, by building a steel bulkhead near the building, the structure could be saved and converted into a canal museum. Although this displeased some North Chesapeake City residents, whose property had not been given similar consideration, the majority of residents had responded favorably to a drive spearheaded by the Cecil County Historical Society not only to preserve the unique lifting wheel, steam engines, and building but also to give them wider recognition. In 1965, largely through the efforts of the historical society, the "Old Lock Pumphouse" at Chesapeake City was officially designated as a Registered National Historic Landmark, under the provisions of the Historic Sites Act of 1935.[4]

Robert M. Vogel, curator of heavy machinery at the Smithsonian Institution in Washington, D.C., called the pumphouse machinery "absolutely unique," "the only one of its sort in the country," and was amazed to find it "still preserved and intact." The wheel, housed in a "Port Deposit granite" building erected in 1837, remains the largest piece of machinery of its kind dating back to the mid-nineteenth century, and its two 175-horsepower "walking beam" steam engines, sim-

[3]The removal contracts with the mortuary were adjusted accordingly, increasing from $87,586.70 to $138,373.20 for disinterment, from $68,745 to $149,593 for reinterment; Rev. Hackett's compensation was $2,750. "Final Report. Cemetery Relocation. Bethel Methodist Episcopal Cemetery and Bethel Cemetery. January 1966," C. & D. Papers, DEO.

[4]*Baltimore Sun*, October 11, 1965.

ilar to those used on side-wheeler steamboats, are the largest still in existence.[5] Some three years later, on July 4, 1968, the Corps of Engineers' Canal Museum opened its doors to the public. In anticipation of this event, the Chesapeake City Lions Club expressed its appreciation to the Philadelphia District Engineer, Colonel William W. Watkins, Jr., and to the Corps of Engineers for their combined efforts in preserving the pumphouse and other "historical, esthetic and recreational features of the canal." Colonel Watkins responded, in accepting a citation from the Lions Club in May, 1968, that the Corps hoped to make the museum into one of the "prime attractions in the Chesapeake City area."[6]

In the meantime, work on deepening and widening the channel continued throughout the 1960s as improvements in other areas were also under way. New fishing piers were constructed for public use, while many private landowners whose property along Back Creek or Elk River abutted the canal erected summer homes, docks, and beaches along the waterway. During the summer months hundreds of pleasure craft swarmed through the canal, and picnicking along its banks was a popular pastime. Occasionally, the "wash" from a deep-draft commercial vessel caused problems for the revelers and the property owners. As explained by local historian Edward Ludwig,

Back Creek is wide at many points but there are shelves or flat stretches that extend out to the dredged part of the waterway. As large vessels draw a considerable amount of water, this underbody, pushing through the restricted channel of the canal, caused much of the water to draw off the shallow flats as the vessel passed, and then the effect of this action was to send a large volume of water at right angles to the shoreline rushing back to fill the original space and sweeping up over the dry beaches washing everything from its path. Many a picnic party has broken up after the passage of a freighter in Back Creek.[7]

There were also frequent complaints from property owners in Elk Forest, along Back Creek, and elsewhere that some of the large vessels

---

[5]*Ibid.*

[6]Edward J. Ludwig III, *The Chesapeake and Delaware Canal: Gateway to Paradise* (Elkton, Md., 1979), pp. 39–41; *Wilmington Evening Journal,* May 24, 1968. John Trush, a long-term employee of the Corps of Engineers at Chesapeake City, served as guide and unofficial curator of the canal museum for a number of years. A native of Cecil County, Maryland, with thirty-six years on the canal as a dredger, bridge tender, and traffic-control officer, he brought intimate knowledge of the waterway and enthusiasm for its history to the position. See Ludwig, *Chesapeake and Delaware Canal,* pp. 40–41.

[7]Ludwig, *Chesapeake and Delaware Canal,* p. 42.

traveled at excessive speeds and caused considerable damage to the soft banks on their property. The Wrangs of Elk Forest were particularly upset by this situation and, following their numerous complaints, by what they considered harassment by passing ship captains, pilots, and sailors (prolonged blasts of the foghorn, obscene calls and gestures). The Wrangs at least had the satisfaction of a feature story in a Wilmington, Delaware, newspaper detailing their problems. And the *Cecil Whig,* published in Elkton, Maryland, carried reports of a similar nature under headlines charging that "large ships" were sailing the waters of Cecil County "at speeds above those set by law. Valuable real estate is being reduced to marshlands by the greed of these speeding [ship operators]."[8]

It is the responsibility of the Corps of Engineers, in conjunction with the U.S. Coast Guard, to see to it that passages through the canal and its approaches are made safely and legally, although vessel owners and operators are ultimately responsible for the safe operation of their craft. There was, however, contrary to the statements in the *Cecil Whig,* no fixed maximum speed limit in effect during the period; the regulations governing navigation through the canal required a "safe speed" at all times and the avoidance of damage "by suction or wave wash to wharves, landings, riprap protection, or other boats, or injury to persons." A Corps publication warned violators of the speed regulation, noting that their privilege of transiting the canal could be suspended and that repeat offenders would be cited by the Coast Guard for "reckless navigation." At the same time, however, owners and operators of other craft were cautioned that "large, deep-draft ocean-going vessels and other large commercial vessels ply the canal," and that small craft should moor or anchor well away from the main ship channel with moorings and lines of sufficient size and strength.[9]

During its first decade of operating the canal after its enlargement into a true seaway in 1927, the Corps of Engineers began operating patrol boats in the canal and its approaches in order to improve the traffic-control system. At that time there were restrictive widths in the channel and at the five bridges, all of which were of the vertical-lift type. Moreover, some dangerous bends remained in the route, particularly at the summit area, and there were no reliable communications between vessels transiting the canal and the dispatcher's office at Chesapeake City. Patrol-boat crews transmitted messages between vessels

[8]*Ibid.*, p. 43; *Wilmington Evening Journal,* February 22, 1976.
[9]U.S. Army Corps of Engineers, Philadelphia District, *Inland Waterway. Chesapeake & Delaware Canal. Rules and Regulations* (Philadelphia, 1972), p. 2.

in transit and the dispatcher, enforced regulations governing navigation on the canal, and were on hand in cases of emergency. They also collected required statements about cargo and destination and other commercial statistics. By the end of the 1960s, however, given the improvements in channel alignment, the new high-level highway bridges, and advances in communications technology, coupled with the requirement that all vessels longer than 375 feet had to have operable two-way radios, the Corps decided that the patrol boats were no longer needed. Their elimination represented an immediate annual savings of $75,000. Some canal employees protested the decision, as did the pilot associations for both the Chesapeake Bay and the Delaware River and Bay (who shared the task of steering ships through the canal, the changeover occurring at Chesapeake City). They expressed their concern about the continued safety of operations without patrol boats, particularly during times of fog and bad weather.[10] Both groups may have believed their views were vindicated a few years later, when a disastrous ship-bridge collision occurred early one morning on the fog-shrouded canal, but that event led to more modernizations and procedural changes in traffic control rather than a return to patrol boats. Indeed, it was laxness in the operation of the new system rather than defects inherent in it that led to the accident. In January, 1969, shortly after the new radio-control system had been installed, a Philadelphia District Office news release reported on its efficiency. It quoted thirty-year employee John Fears, who was also president of Lodge 902 of the American Federation of Government Employees, which represented canal employees, as saying, "In all the time I've been associated with the (Chesapeake and Delaware) Canal I've never seen it operated more safely."[11] At the time of Fears's statement, some 1,500 radio-dispatched vessels had passed through the canal without incident, and all parties were satisfied with the arrangement. The collection of traffic statistics, which had become the primary function of the patrol boats during their final years, has since been handled by mail.

At the time of this news release, the District Office also announced the imminent completion of the Canal Modernization Project, which had been authorized in 1954 and begun in earnest in 1962. The work was in its final phase, and the Corps had just closed its construction field office at Summit, Delaware. The remaining work was to be directed from a consolidated office at the permanent installation in Chesapeake City. A rude surprise, however, awaited the Corps.

[10]*Wilmington Morning News,* November 28, 1968.
[11]News Release, January 27, 1969, C. & D. Papers, DEO.

In February, 1970, the Corps of Engineers in Washington, D.C., received a complaint from Congressman Gilbert Gude of Maryland, in whose district the Maryland portion of the Chesapeake and Delaware Canal was located, about the potential harmful effect of the canal enlargement upon marine life in Chesapeake Bay. Simultaneously, Congressman Gude released a statement to the press warning of an "environmental disaster" for the entire upper bay area if the canal project were completed according to the original plans. He believed that a device of some type, perhaps a tidal lock, to prevent a "massive flow" of fresh water from the Chesapeake into the Delaware was needed. An unchecked interchange of bay waters, he warned, would endanger the entire ecology of the bay.[12]

This action by the Maryland congressman, whose information about possible harm to the bay had come from a small group of environmental scientists at Johns Hopkins University in Baltimore, set in motion a complex series of responses, including hearings on the situation by the House Committee on Public Works, a number of environmental studies by scientists at Johns Hopkins, the University of Maryland, the University of Delaware, and elsewhere, and a decade-long delay in completion of the modernization program.

When Congressman Gude's letter came in, Louis G. Feil, Chief of the Planning Division, Civil Works Directorate, in the Office of the Chief of Engineers in Washington, referred the matter to both NAD (North Atlantic Division) and the subordinate District Engineer Office in Philadelphia for comment and draft responses. Staff engineers in Washington considered the initial drafts received in early March to be weak and potentially troublesome; the NAD letter implied that the Corps would wait until the canal enlargement was complete before it would undertake a long-term bio-engineering investigation. "We should be more responsive than that," commented an unknown staff member, "particularly in the light of a 'preservationist' attitude by conservation groups & by [the Department of the] interior."[13] Other staff members in Civil Works suggested the immediate implementation of a modest proposal by the Waterways Experiment Station in Vicksburg, Mississippi, for a 5,000-dollar, four-week study of the canal using NAD construction funds. The study embraced a computer analysis of

---

[12]Congressman Gilbert Gude to Major General Charles M. Duke, February 5, 1970, Chesapeake and Delaware Canal Papers, Historical Division, Office of the Chief of Engineers, Fort Belvoir, Virginia (hereafter cited as C. & D. Papers, OCE). See also the UPI teletype report of February 6, 1970, based on a news release by Gude, in the same file.

[13]Internal memorandum, March 12, 1970, *ibid.*

the water flow through the canal, for which a computer program already existed, and the "Corps could get a lot of mileage from this study, both at the OCE [Office of the Chief of Engineers] level & in the field, & in Planning, Operations & Engineering."[14]

In the meantime, while the Corps' formal response was being developed, John B. McAleer, an engineer in the Civil Works Division, OCE, had authorized a consultant to estimate the net diversion of water from the Chesapeake that an unobstructed 35-by-450-foot channel would cause. This was to be handled by Clarence F. Wicker, who had made similar calculations in 1938 regarding a 27-by-250-foot channel. "Wick," a former employee of the Corps in Philadelphia, made his report on February 13, 1970. He determined that the net diversion would not exceed 2,100 cubic feet per second (cfs), if the basic assumption that the tides at either end of the canal were the same in 1970 as in 1938 was valid. He was "reasonably certain" this was true on the Delaware end, and that a discharge on the order of 2,100 cfs would have no appreciable effect, but he was "not at all certain" this would be the case on the Chesapeake side, at Elk River. He concluded, however, that if there was a change, it would "principally show up in a lowering of the plane of mean tide level [and] . . . there will be less net eastward discharge than 2,100 cfs." Wicker also pointed out that the water in the Chesapeake at Courthouse Point "is not fresh, although its salinity is less than that of the Delaware"; consequently, "the loss of fresh water . . . is not as great as the net discharge." His final point was the reminder that about 1,000 cfs had been transferred via the existing canal for many years, and the additional net flow eastward was about 1,100 cfs.[15]

If this limited response—promises of new studies once the enlargement was made and an updated calculation of the net outflow from the Chesapeake—was expected to satisfy the Maryland congressman and his constituents, it soon became clear that much more would be required.[16] On March 23, 1970, Congressman Gilbert Gude

[14]*Ibid.*

[15]Clarence F. Wicker to John B. McAleer, February 13, 1970, *ibid.*

[16]On March 4, 1970, the results of Wicker's calculations were forwarded to Gude, along with expressions of shared concern for preserving the resources of Chesapeake Bay. It was pointed out that a lack of complete information regarding "the complex hydraulic-biological interactions of the area prevents any precise assessment at this time of the impact the channel improvement may cause." In other words, the necessary data for completing a meaningful environmental impact statement was unavailable. Given the small canal outflow in comparison with the large Susquehanna inflow, however, the Corps' spokesman suggested that no significant impact was likely except during periods of extreme low water in the Susquehanna. Meaningful data on

was joined by a House colleague from Maryland, Rogers C. B. Morton, in a formal request to the House Committee on Public Works. They sought a feasibility study from the Corps of Engineers "as quickly as possible" regarding the installation of "some kind of barrier" to prevent an outflow of fresh water from the upper reaches of the Chesapeake Bay through an enlarged canal. George B. Fallon, also from Maryland and chairman of the Public Works committee, promptly scheduled hearings on the subject for April 7 and 8, and asked the Corps of Engineers to be ready to present full information to the committee at that time.[17]

The hearings opened with a brief statement from the chairman on the canal's history, its economic and military value to the nation over the years, and its current status. Characterizing the waterway as both "vital" to national defense and a "major lifeline of the Nation's economy," Fallon pointed out that the project authorized in 1954 was then about 77 percent complete but that there was grave concern over the effect the canal construction would have on the Chesapeake Bay's environmental stability. He also pointed out that more than ten years ago the Committee on Public Works had secured authorization for the construction of a hydraulic model of the entire Chesapeake Bay Basin, which would have permitted a sophisticated, multidisciplinary estuarine study, but that budgetary constraints prevented it. Reauthorized by the House in 1969, despite total estimated costs of $15 million for the model, the bill was then pending in the Senate.[18]

The first testimony came from J. Millard Tawes, Secretary of the Maryland Department of Natural Resources and former governor of the state of Maryland. He presented an eloquent statement of his long-standing concern, and the concern of the state, over the anticipated loss of fresh water from the upper Chesapeake, which he feared would eventually damage the entire ecosystem of the bay. In the absence of precise information about these points, however, he urged both that engineering safeguards be incorporated into any projects modifying the bay's hydrological-biological systems and that construction of the

this point, however, would have to await completion of the Chesapeake Bay model then under construction at the Corps' Waterways Experimental Station (WES) in Vicksburg, Mississippi. Edwin D. Patterson to the Hon. Gilbert Gude, March 4, 1970, C. & D. Papers, OCE.

[17]Congressman George H. Fallon to Major General F. P. Koisch, March 26, 1970, *ibid.*

[18]*The Chesapeake and Delaware Canal. Hearings before the Committee on Public Works, House of Representatives,* 91st Cong., 2d sess. (Washington, D.C., 1970), pp. 1–2. A copy of the "Chesapeake Bay Study and Hydraulic Study," prepared by the Baltimore District of the Corps of Engineers, along with portions of two other reports

Corps' hydraulic model of the bay be expedited. At the same time, he professed sympathy for those interested in economic development and, in particular, in strengthening the competitive stance of the Port of Baltimore. Accordingly, given the advanced stage of the construction project, he favored having the Corps begin immediately to study ways to control the interchange of waters between the bays while permitting construction on the current project to continue.[19]

Congressman Gude of Maryland was the second witness before the committee. He repeated his warnings about possible harmful effects of the enlargement "upon the physical, ecological, and biological profile of the bay," and his disappointment that the project was scheduled for completion before the hydraulic model would be operable: "This is an alarming state of affairs." Some 600 million pounds of fish and shellfish, valued at $30 million, were harvested from the bay in 1966, and some 3.5 million people lived within a day's drive of the "boating, swimming, fishing, and scenic pleasures of the bay." Gude expressed particular concern over increased salinity in the bay and its impact upon commercial and sport fishing if a two- or three-fold increase in net outflow from the Chesapeake occurred. Shellfish, especially oysters, are sensitive to even relatively slight changes in salinity levels, and any alteration in such levels was fraught with danger. A net outflow of 2,000 cfs, the Corps estimate (compared to 2,700 cfs estimated by Johns Hopkins University scientist J. R. Pritchard), translates to 1,350,800,000 gallons a day. In Gude's view, this meant the potential for serious damage to one of Maryland's greatest commercial and recreational resources was obvious, and Gude rejected what he called the "counsel of complacency" offered by the Corps of Engineers. Rather than wait, therefore, until the bay model was ready while permitting the canal-enlargement project to continue, Gude repeated his and Congressman Morton's call for a halt, or at least a pause, in construction activities: "However, if we could act to prevent further diversion of fresh water by means of some type of barrier, lock, or gate system, completion of the canal could proceed without

on the bay prepared by the Federal Water Pollution Control Administration and the Fish and Wildlife Service of the Department of the Interior, were inserted into the record of the proceedings, occupying pages 5–77 of the published *Hearings*. Chesapeake Bay is the largest estuary in the United States, its water surface in Virginia and Maryland covering 4,300 square miles, its drainage basin covering 69,170 square miles. The Susquehanna River, a major tributary of the bay, supplies 49 percent of the fresh water entering the bay. Among the research problems that use of the bay model was expected to answer was "the effects of navigation projects and channel geometry changes on currents and salinities." *Ibid.*, pp. 6–8.

[19]*Ibid.*, p. 79.

delay. There must be a pause to permit full analysis of existing information and consideration of steps to offset the diversion."[20]

"The burden," Gude continued, "should be upon the Corps of Engineers to show that the risk of damage is too slim to justify remedial steps," and that finding should be accompanied by an opinion on the matter from the newly constituted Environmental Advisory Board.[21] "In a case involving such critical questions," Gude believed both the House committee and the Corps should have the benefit of the new advisory board's counsel. Too often, he concluded, research has taken a back seat to construction, but with today's technology and our greater ability to "insult" the environment, the priorities had to be reversed. Under questioning, Gude indicated that he was "wholeheartedly" in support of the canal project, but that it ought not be at the expense of the Chesapeake Bay.[22]

This position was supported by a statement from Congressman Rogers C. B. Morton, presented by William O. Mills, administrative assistant to the Maryland congressman. Morton opposed further construction work on the canal project until its effects on the Chesapeake were more fully known. No one doubts, he conceded, the economic value of the canal. It has always had heavy traffic, and with its planned improvement, "it will be one of the most, if not the most, extensively used canals of its kind in the world." The issue was, however, whether another boost to the economy was worth the risk of an irremediable change in the ecology of the bay. "Industry and technology," Morton believed, have flourished too long at the expense of our environment. . . . Economically we are booming, but ecologically and environmentally we are falling fast." He used the analogy of the canal as a "hole in the wall" of the bay, with the effects of enlarging that hole unknown and potentially disastrous. "We have let too many areas be

[20]*Ibid.,* pp. 85–87.

[21]*Ibid.,* p. 88. For an account of the EAB's first decade of activity and an assessment of its influence, see Martin Reuss, *Shaping Environmental Awareness: The United States Army Corps of Engineers Environmental Advisory Board, 1970–1980* (Washington, D.C., 1983). Gude's early expression of confidence in the still-untested Environmental Advisory Board is noteworthy.

[22]*Chesapeake and Delaware Canal Hearings,* pp. 88–89. Gude appended to his statement a copy of HJR 74, adopted by the Maryland legislature, recording its objections to further enlargement of the canal without a lock or other devices to prevent losses of fresh water from the Chesapeake, its worries about the lack of a plan for the proper deposit of "the massive amounts of spoil material" being dredged from the canal, and its congratulations to the Maryland congressional delegation, specifically Congressmen Gude and Morton, for their efforts to protect the environmental quality of Chesapeake Bay. *Ibid.,* pp. 89–90.

spoiled by man and I do not wish to see the Chesapeake Bay and the Maryland blue crab go the same route. . . . If man does not protect his natural surroundings, who else will?"[23]

After hearing repeated calls for delays or at least modification in the canal project, the committee listened to a statement from the Corps of Engineers, presented by Brigadier General Richard H. Groves, Deputy Director of Civil Works; he was accompanied to the table by Colonel James A. Johnson, District Engineer at Philadelphia, and Rodney Resta, Assistant Chief of the Engineering Division at the Baltimore District Office. General Groves reviewed the construction progress on the 1954 project, nearly 80 percent complete. The major tasks remaining were enlarging the channel in the easternmost section of the canal, removing the old highway bridge at Reedy Point now that a new high-level bridge there was in place, and relocating a jetty extending into the Delaware River at Reedy Point.

As General Groves pointed out, an interchange of water between the Chesapeake and the Delaware had existed since 1927. Given the tidal differentials, approximately 5.4 feet in the Delaware, 2.2 feet in the Chesapeake at the entrance to the canal, as well as a ten-hour time lag in the tidal peaks, the mean level of the Chesapeake at Turkey Point was approximately 0.3 feet higher than the mean level of the Delaware at Reedy Point. This resulted in an average net flow of from 700 to 900 cfs into the Delaware, as had been the case since 1938, when the canal achieved its present dimensions. General Groves then gave detailed information on the kinds of water involved—the well-mixed (not stratified) nature of the water in the upper Chesapeake, the Delaware, and the canal itself—and the variation in the flow stemming from changes in tides, winds, and runoffs. The Susquehanna River's annual flow of about 40,000 cfs of fresh water into the Chesapeake, he stated, "seems large in comparison with a diversion of 2,200 cfs of mixed (not fresh) water through an enlarged canal"; however, during periods of extreme low water on the Susquehanna, when its flow drops

[23]*Ibid.*, pp. 97–98. It is interesting to note that Morton was sounding themes here he would develop more fully during his tenure as Secretary of the Interior during parts of both the Nixon and Ford administrations. He predicted in October, 1971, for example, that the dominant world power in the future would not necessarily be the one with the most military hardware but the nation "that does the best job of managing its environment and extending the life of its fixed resources." Three years later he repeated his call for "balanced" development. The choice facing policy-makers was not either conservation or development, but rather one of balancing the two strategies. Alan F. Pater and Jason A. Pater, eds., *What They Said in 1971: The Yearbook of Spoken Opinion* (Beverly Hills, Calif., 1972), pp. 129–130; Pater and Pater, eds., *What They Said in 1974*, p. 112.

below 5,000 cfs (about 5 percent of the time), the diversion "could be significant."[24]

Based upon the Corps' review of the biological effects of the canal upon the Chesapeake and Delaware estuaries over the past twenty years, General Groves reported that no harmful effects had been found. During the past five years, the results of even more intensive study of the ecological effects of shallow-water spoil disposal associated with the enlargement project proved "generally favorable" and failed to indicate a need to modify the project: "Indeed, they show that the canal and its Chesapeake approach are becoming one of the best fishing and spawning grounds for striped bass in the bay area."[25]

General Groves concluded his prepared statement with comments on the Corps' plans to develop mathematical models at its Waterways Experiment Station for determining changes in net flow through the canal under various tidal conditions and channel configurations. Results from these calculations would be known long before the canal was dredged to its project depth in September, 1972. Until then, a "partial plug" would prevent increases in the flow, and the Corps would confer with its ecological consultants before removing the plug. "If it is determined that serious adverse effects are likely," he announced, "we will defer that action until remedial measures, such as tidal gates or submerged weirs, can be taken."[26]

In his subsequent informal testimony, the general reported an average of about 100 transits of the canal a day, about 15 of which were cargo vessels carrying about 10 million tons of goods annually. The estimates for an enlarged canal, which have proved to be conservative, were 15 million tons a year. General Groves reported a benefit-cost ratio of 2.2; in dollar figures, the total annual benefits were estimated to be $9.5 million to navigation, $260,000 to recreation. Most of the canal traffic (62 percent) was domestic, the principal items of cargo being petroleum and petroleum products, coal and iron ore, steel and steel products, acids and chemicals, and general cargo. When Congressman Cramer of Pennsylvania suggested that the Corps should become "ecology oriented," General Groves replied simply, "Sir, we are, really," and, in response to a request from the chair, subsequently supplied a listing of eight specific and twelve general studies by the Corps of Engineers concerning environmental effects on the Chesapeake Bay Basin. He agreed with Congressman Cramer's observation that the

[24]*Chesapeake and Delaware Canal Hearings*, pp. 99–100.
[25]*Ibid.*, p. 100.
[26]*Ibid.*, p. 101.

Corps was to some extent "straitjacketed" by benefit-cost ratio considerations, which precluded giving adequate consideration to adverse ecological effect. "My observation is," concluded Cramer, "that it is time to take off the straitjacket and to put proper input of benefits to the environment into the cost-benefit ratio, and therefore the adequate cost needed to protect that environment in the total cost of the project. . . ." [27]

The first day of testimony before the committee concluded with an informal statement from Dr. Gordon Gunter, an ecologist at the Gulf Coast Research Laboratory in Ocean Springs, Mississippi, who began serving as a consultant to the District Engineer at Philadelphia in 1964. He confirmed the statements about the canal being a new and congenial host to the eggs of the striped bass, and expressed his lack of fears about ecological harm resulting from the canal-enlargement project.

Additional testimony during the second day of hearings, on April 8, reinforced several of the general views presented earlier. A group of scientists from the Fish and Wildlife, Parks and Marine Resources Division, U.S. Department of the Interior, the Federal Water Pollution Control Commission, the Bureau of Commercial Fisheries, and the Chesapeake Biological Laboratory at the University of Maryland appeared first. Dr. Leslie L. Glasgow, a fish and wildlife specialist in the Department of the Interior, headed the group and testified that the problem of placing spoil material dredged from the canal had been managed with minimum damage. The Corps had refrained from depositing spoils on areas of high value to fish and wildlife, such as Lum's Pond in Delaware, an area once scheduled for destruction, and overboard disposal of the spoils in open water was being carefully monitored. Dr. Glasgow expressed grave concern, however, over the ecological changes an enlarged canal would bring, the extent of which could not be predicted, and he concluded that construction on the canal should be halted until more environmental information could be obtained and analyzed: "There is just too much at stake for us to proceed without having the necessary information upon which to evaluate the effects the project would have on these most important water bodies." [28]

[27] *Ibid.*, pp. 105–106, 108.
[28] *Ibid.*, p. 116. In part, Dr. Glasgow's testimony reflected the Fish and Wildlife Service's nationwide concern over the potentially harmful effects of overboard dredge-disposal methods. A case in point involved the Atchafalaya Basin in Louisiana, where an ongoing "channelization" project prompted a vigorous protest from environmental-

Chairman Fallon chided Dr. Glasgow and his colleagues initially for not having come forward sooner—the project was sixteen years along and nearing completion, $80 million had been expended on it, and many environmental and ecological reports had already been made. In reply, the point was made that the earlier studies had focused upon dredge-disposal problems rather than any associated with a net outflow of fresh water from the Chesapeake. When this matter was addressed, environmental scientists began "to feel considerable apprehension." This position clearly irritated Congressman Ray Roberts of Texas, who was unwilling to see the $80 million already expended diluted in any way. "I may be the only [one] in this committee," he announced, "but I am going to vote to continue the project."[29]

Another representative from the Department of the Interior, Reinhold W. Theime, Assistant Secretary for Water Quality and Research, followed up on Dr. Glasgow's remarks. Theime presented detailed information on the ecological effects of the canal's enlargement, based on a number of studies using mathematical models (one-dimensional only), and he also recommended delay in completing the canal project until additional calculations regarding salinity and water-quality changes could be made. There was in his view, however, no need to delay completion until the physical model of the bay basin was completed. If his division's ongoing water-quality monitoring revealed adverse effects in either the Chesapeake or Delaware bays, remedial measures such as locks could be incorporated into the canal design.[30]

Clearly the chief witness of the day was Dr. Donald W. Pritchard of Johns Hopkins University, a professor of oceanography and director of the Chesapeake Bay Institute who had been studying the Chesapeake Bay Basin for over twenty years. He reported on the anticipated effects of an enlarged canal upon the physical and chemical hydrography of the upper Chesapeake. The differences in estimated net outflow from the Chesapeake—Wicker's 2,100 cfs, his own 2,700 cfs—he considered as inconsequential, given the much greater volume of waters moving eastward, then westward, according to tidal and other influences. In his calculations for the committee, he used a median figure as the basis for a computer-generated analysis of Chesapeake Bay salinity over an eleven-year period (1958–68). The results indicated that salinity differences over that period varied only slightly, and

ists, particularly fish and wildlife groups. See Reuss, *Shaping Environmental Awareness*, pp. 26–27.
[29]*Chesapeake and Delaware Canal Hearings*, pp. 117–118, 122.
[30]*Ibid.*, pp. 125–128.

that there would be similarly small and probably inconsequential variations following enlargement of the canal. Dr. Pritchard recognized that absolute estimates were impossible, but he considered it "unlikely that there will be significant or even measurable detrimental effects on the ecology of the bay if this diversion . . . is made," and he believed that work on the canal should continue while further engineering and environmental studies were also continuing. Pritchard explicitly endorsed the Corps' position, as stated by General Groves, of pursuing the construction and research projects simultaneously.[31]

The director of the Chesapeake Biological Laboratory at the University of Maryland, Dr. L. Eugene Cronin, supported both Dr. Pritchard's call for additional research and the installation of "control structures" for water flow and salinity regulation while construction proceeded. He noted that the biological effects of the enlargement would be substantial, but it was impossible at that time to know if the changes would be "favorable or unfavorable." There was a "very large supply of small fish, of a wide variety of species [and many] small shrimp on which the young fish feed and on which they are dependent. It is a very rich area for these small shrimp for reasons that we do not yet understand, but it is a very productive addition because of the creation of the canal." Moreover, a principal species of fish in Chesapeake Bay is the striped bass, of which 8 to 10 million pounds a year are produced; "we caught more striped bass in the canal than any place else in the whole upper bay series."[32]

If the environmental scientists gave a reluctant nod of approval for continuing the project, in part because definitive study results were still many years away, unequivocal direct support for continuation came from representatives of a number of business and labor organizations in Baltimore and Philadelphia—the International Longshoreman's Association, the National Maritime Union, the Steamship Trade Association, the Association of Maryland Pilots and other maritime pilots' groups, the Chamber of Commerce of Metropolitan Baltimore, and a committee for the development of the Philadelphia Port Authority. Each representative, by his presence, acknowledged his organization's approval of a statement prepared by the Maryland Port Authority (MPA), presented by Henry T. Douglas. Not only would halting work then jeopardize thousands of jobs, but it would have widespread, if

---

[31]*Ibid.*, pp. 181–189. In addition to Pritchard's statement to the committee, four papers he had prepared for presentation elsewhere on the same subject were inserted into the record. See *ibid.*, pp. 189–252.

[32]*Ibid.*, pp. 263–265.

more subtle, deleterious consequences on the economic lives of both Baltimore and Philadelphia. When the MPA learned of the proposal to halt construction, it had conducted its own investigation of the situation. Port authority officials met with various Maryland congressmen as well as Doctors Pritchard and Cronin, "the two scientists whom we felt knew more about the hydrography and ecology of the Chesapeake Bay than anyone else." They sought information from Dr. Pritchard about anticipated salinity changes and from Dr. Cronin about the effect of those changes "in terms of marine biology, in other words, the effect on the Bay's crabs, fish, oysters and clams."[33]

"We came away from that meeting," Douglas stated, "with the distinct impression that the changes in salinity and the corresponding biological effects would be relatively minor and not of sufficient magnitude to justify halting work on the Canal." The group was in "complete sympathy" with the idea of additional studies and monitoring, but in view of the economic considerations, which were "very substantial indeed," they also favored rapid completion of the project. Its potential benefits would not be realized until the canal had been enlarged throughout its entire line.[34]

After hearing from one more witness, Dr. Irvin Eugene Wallen, director of the Office of Environmental Sciences at the Smithsonian Institution, who endorsed the consensus that had developed over the two days, the committee adjourned. Subsequently, additional statements were added to the record. William V. Roth, Jr., the lone Delawarean in the House of Representatives, expressed great concern over the potential ecological damage, not only to the upper Chesapeake but also to the Delaware River, and he called for an "immediate and thorough" study of such effects, studies which should have been conducted ten years ago, before the enlargement project was undertaken. In view of the work then under way, however, he did not favor interrupting it in order to await the studies; with eighteen months of dredging work still required, there was ample time for the necessary ecological questions to be answered before permitting the Corps to "pull the plug."[35]

The Delaware River Port Authority and a committee for the im-

---

[33]*Ibid.*, pp. 276–278.

[34]*Ibid.*, p. 278.

[35]*Ibid.*, pp. 285–287. Roth appended to his statement a copy of a resolution from the Delaware House of Representatives urging that, if a lock facility for the canal proved necessary, careful consideration be given to placing it in the old branch channel through Delaware City. This proposal, however, would require expanding the channel, removing several buildings, and erecting another high-level highway bridge; it deservedly received no serious attention. *Ibid.*, p. 287.

provement of the Port of Philadelphia also urged speedy completion of the authorized improvements. These groups recognized the "vital need" to protect natural water resources, but argued that the economic worth and equally "vital need" of the canal project had been clearly established. On the other hand, there was no information indicating that the canal enlargement would have any significant adverse effects on the ecology of the region. They expressed shock at the thought of a construction moratorium, which would jeopardize a $100 million investment in Philadelphia-area ports as well as comparably large investments in the Port of Baltimore:

. . . over sixty per cent of general cargo moving between ports in the North Atlantic range of the United States and Europe is being carried in container vessels, with higher percentages expected in the future; . . . the key to further usefulness of the Chesapeake and Delaware Canal can only be found when the final stage of the present project is completed. Containerships carrying the dominant share of the world's general cargo trade will not be able to utilize the canal and the savings it was designed to offer, until the final stage of the project is complete. To further delay the project is to jeopardize an investment running into the hundreds of millions of dollars.[36]

These comments advocating continuation were balanced by three lengthy statements by William W. Jeanes, an environmentalist from Villanova, Pennsylvania, who was also a landowner along the Elk River in Maryland and a spokesman for the Cecil County Anti-Pollution League. He expressed his alarm over the changes that had occurred in the approaches to the land-cut areas the canal. Prior to the enlargement in 1938, the water was clear, teeming with fish, and safe for swimmers and small craft anchored in the Elk River. Since the enlargement of the 1930s, however, great changes had occurred—all of them for the worse. Large ships, often traveling at speeds from twelve to eighteen miles per hour, produced wakes that churned the bottom of the channel, caused high waves and damage to the shore, and left the water "turbid" year round. Consequently, he urged the committee to continue the ecological studies, to design a barrier to prevent fresh water from passing from the Chesapeake to the Delaware, and to keep the canal and the upper Chesapeake free from pollution. He also appealed for the continued development of lands along the canal for recreational purposes: boating, fishing, picnicking, and, perhaps eventually, swimming. There was a great need, in Jeanes's view, for recreational facilities in the eastern United States, and, para-

[36]*Ibid.,* p. 289. These comments are contained in a statement presented for inclusion in the record by Willis Jackson, chairman of the Joint Executive Committee for the Improvement and Development of the Philadelphia Port Area.

doxically, he pointed to the potential for a "magnificent" national park along both sides of the canal.[37]

There was a final interesting, if not unique, statement from Albert H. Oshiver, a long-distance swimmer who previously had swum the twenty-five-mile length of Gatun Lake in the Panama Canal. He requested that the Chesapeake and Delaware Canal be opened to recreational swimmers like himself, something Corps of Engineers regulations at the moment prohibited.[38]

From the Corps' point of view, the hearings had gone satisfactorily. According to an internal memorandum drawn up the day after the hearings closed, General Groves's testimony had been "very well received," and most of those who testified had subsequently supported the basic Corps position of simultaneous action: continuing the canal improvement while making intensive studies of hydraulic and ecological effects. Only the Department of the Interior, through Dr. Glasgow, had recommended that construction be stopped, and his position was weakened by the long time that would be required to study possible ecological damage, and by the fact that there was no money for such research. As a result of the hearings, two overriding points—beyond the immediate fate of the canal project—were clear: the acute need for the long-delayed Chesapeake Bay hydraulic model, and the necessity for the Corps to give full information on environmental effects in the planning and pre-construction phases of waterway projects. As Chairman Fallon admitted in his summation, the committee in the past had been more concerned with economic development than with ecological matters, but this was going to change. In the future, he pledged, environmental effects will be considered to be every bit as important as any other feature of a project.[39]

In keeping with this new concern on the part of the committee, General Groves appeared before it again in May, 1970, spelling out in detail the Corps of Engineers' comprehensive study proposal for the canal project. It consisted of six phases, the first four of which involved further data collection on tides, currents, and salinities in the canal area; the Corps also planned to modify its hydraulic model of the Chesapeake Bay Basin (in order to include the canal) at the Waterways Experiment Station in Vicksburg, and to perform both physical and mathematical model analyses. At the same time, preliminary designs for flow-control structures in the canal would be drawn up and a

[37]*Ibid.*, pp. 290–295.
[38]*Ibid.*, pp. 295–297.
[39]*Ibid.*, p. 285.

new contract for a long-term ecological study would be drafted. The combined cost of these studies was estimated at $1 million, with the first five phases completed within one year.[40] Congressman Fallon closed the brief hearings by again commenting on the Public Works committee's new emphasis. "We are," he said, "basically concerned with development and environment," issues that are in the minds of some "diametrically opposed." "We know, however," he added, "that to provide the food, water, transportation, and economic well-being necessary for our growing population that development is necessary. We take as our approach that reasoned development is essential—development which considers environmental values in relationship with public need." He then pledged the committee's support for continuation of the canal project while the proposed environmental studies were being made, noting that the committee would call upon the Corps from time to time for progress reports.[41]

Congressman Gude also kept track of the Corps' promise to have a preliminary report on ecological effects ready within a year. He wrote to General Groves exactly one day short of a year after the report had been promised, asking not only about the studies but also if there were any plans in the works for enlarging the canal beyond its 35-by-450-foot dimensions. Tankers of "very substantial tonnage" and requiring channels in excess of sixty feet deep were in the planning stages, and he wanted to know if a further enlargement of the canal to accommodate ever larger ships was being contemplated. General Groves admitted that the non-biological studies were six months behind schedule, the biological studies were eighteen months behind, and that construction progress was also behind schedule. He assured the congressman, however, that no canal-enlargement studies were under way or being planned.[42]

The construction difficulties, if not the delayed environmental reports, were welcomed by some. There had been an outcry over the Corps', and the committee's, decision to continue the construction work while trying at the same time to assess its ecological impact. A typical report, summarizing the view of concerned citizens as well as environmental scientists, appeared in the *Baltimore News-American* for August 2, 1970, under the title of "Susquehanna's Waters Essential to Life in Bay," although the report repeatedly referred to the C. & O.

[40]*Ibid.*, pp. 299–302.
[41]*Ibid.*, pp. 317–319.
[42]Congressman Gilbert Gude to Brigadier General Richard H. Groves, May 20, 1971, and Groves to Gude, June 9, 1971, C. & D. Papers, OCE.

(Chesapeake and Ohio) Canal, rather than to the C. & D. Canal, as the offending project. Concluding that it would cause "dramatic changes" in the basic character of the Chesapeake, the writer predicted that the canal nevertheless would be enlarged: "Involved . . . are huge profits for shipping interests as well as allied interests in the Port of Baltimore," and, "as usually is the case, money applied in the proper places speaks louder than all considerations for non-renewable natural resources." The Maryland press also gave considerable attention to the ecological research being conducted by Johns Hopkins University and University of Maryland Professors Pritchard and Cronin, publicizing their oft-expressed concerns for preserving the environmental quality of the upper Chesapeake and its tributary streams, but most reporters accepted their hypothesis that, with proper safety precautions, damage to the bay resulting from the canal project would be minimal.

It was an obvious but shrewd decision on the part of the Corps of Engineers to issue an environmental studies contract in November, 1970, to the organizations directed by Professors Pritchard and Cronin. Under its terms, the Chesapeake Biological Laboratory at the University of Maryland was to "investigate the biological conditions in the canal and its approaches, collect information on phytoplankton, the spawning of various species of fish, the movements of fish (using tagging methods and net counts) and also check, by laboratory means, the effects of changing environments on the fish." At the same time, the Chesapeake Bay Institute at Johns Hopkins University was to "study current velocities and gather and analyze salinity samples in the canal and its western approaches." The studies, contracted for at $800,000, were to be completed within three years, but preliminary analyses and reports were expected within two years.[43]

In the meantime, the Corps of Engineers encountered unanticipated construction delays, caused by various factors including necessary emergency repairs following extensive damages inflicted upon the upper Chesapeake basin in June, 1972, by Hurricane Agnes, one of

[43]J. Perry Stirling, "Modernizing the C & D Canal," *Baltimore Engineer*, July, 1971, 9.

[44]For a report on the massive impact of the hurricane, which took more than 100 lives, caused upwards of $3.1 billion in damages, and led to the evacuation of some 387,000 people, see "Hurricane Agnes!" *Annual Report of the Chief of Engineers, 1972*, I, 3–7. In the Chesapeake Bay drainage basin, one of the hardest hit areas, the flood waters carried "record loads of silt, debris, chemicals, bacteria, and sewage into the upper reaches of the Bay and its tributaries and caused abrupt changes in salinity, oxygen, temperature, tidal circulation and sediments." *Ibid.*, p. 7. See also Paul K. Walker, *The Corps Responds: A History of the Susquehanna Engineer District and Tropical Storm Agnes* (Baltimore, Md., 1974).

the greatest natural disasters in U.S. history.[44] These delays, coupled with growing environmental concerns and the fact that the scientific studies called for would soon be available, finally did what the congressional hearings of 1970 had not done—postponed completion of the canal-enlargement project. And, once delayed, it proved difficult to obtain the appropriations necessary for large-scale "new work" operations to resume. This finally occurred in 1978, and virtual completion of the project first authorized in 1954 was celebrated in 1981.

In the meantime, the environmental scientists submitted their report, complete with fourteen volumes of appendices, in September, 1973. Professors Pritchard, Cronin, and others concluded that there would be various, but probably minimal, environmental effects resulting from the canal enlargement under contemplation. Their findings indicated that the net flow eastward from the Chesapeake into the Delaware would increase from about 900 cfs to 2,450 cfs, with a resulting slight change in the salinity levels in both bays; that tidal-flow velocities would increase about 15 percent; that some sixty-two species of fish inhabited the canal, and that no adverse effects on adult fish populations would occur; that additional fish eggs and larvae would be carried into the Delaware; that some anadromous migrating fish might be attracted to the Delaware River by the increased flow; and that the canal was of "exceptional importance" as a haven for striped bass, of "value" for alewives and perch, and of "some use" for approximately twenty other species.[45]

This report enabled the Corps to complete the Environmental Impact Statement (EIS) required by the National Environmental Policy Act, but it had to be recognized that there were limitations to the university studies resulting from outside circumstances. First of all, the period of the studies, from late 1970 to early 1973, coincided with continued dredging work, with unusually heavy fresh-water flows coming in from the Susquehanna, and with other "massive impacts" on the region stemming from Hurricane Agnes. These and other problems left some of the questions supposedly addressed in the studies unanswered and, "at this time, unanswerable." In its review of the EIS early in 1974, the Maryland Department of Natural Resources concluded, therefore, that until more definitive knowledge was acquired

[45]"Hydrographic and Ecological Effects of Enlargement of the Chesapeake and Delaware Canal" (15 vols., September, 1973), C. & D. Papers, DEO. These volumes were prepared by staff members of the Chesapeake Biological Laboratory, University of Maryland; the Chesapeake Bay Institute, Johns Hopkins University; and the College of Marine Studies, University of Delaware.

TABLE 9. CHESAPEAKE AND DELAWARE CANAL, ANNUAL EXPENDITURES, 1965–85[a]

Year	Expenditures ($000,000)	New Work Maint. ($000,000)		Dredging (000,000 cy)	Percent Complete ('54 Proj.)	Total Cost (thru FY) ($000,000)
1965	16.0	14.4	1.6	6.0	43	82.1
1966	17.0	15.9	1.1	7.1	57	98.1
1967	15.1	14.0	1.1	7.5	67	115.1
1968	10.7	9.6	1.1	3.1	80	129.1
1969	4.2	4.2	0.0	4.2	86	133.3
1970	6.1	5.0	1.1	2.2	87	139.4
1971	6.8	5.6	1.2	2.2	88	146.2
1972	11.6	5.8	5.8	4.4	88	157.7
1973	7.1	4.4	2.7	1.9	88	164.8
1974	3.5	1.2	2.3	.03	88	168.4
1975	5.8	2.8	3.0	1.0	89[b]	174.1
1976	3.2	0.9	2.3	0.8	89	177.8
1977	4.2	0.0	4.2	0.8	89	182.1
1978	9.2	0.0	9.2	2.8	89	191.3
1979	13.3	0.0	13.3	7.7	89	204.6
1980	7.2	0.0	7.2	4.8	89	211.8
1981	9.5	0.0	9.5	6.4	89	221.3
1982	6.8	0.0	6.8	2.8	87	228.1
1983	12.2	0.0	12.2	6.4	87	240.3
1984	10.7	0.0	10.7	5.4	87	251.0
1985	11.9	0.0	11.9	5.2	87	263.2

[a]Sources: "Chesapeake and Delaware Canal Data Consolidation Report," C. & D. Papers, DEO; *Annual Report of the Chief of Engineers, 1965–1984, passim,* Public Affairs Office, U.S. Army Corps of Engineers, Philadelphia District.
[b]At this point, the project of channel enlargement was essentially complete; although stated as only 89 percent finished, the remaining authorized work relates to an anchorage in Elk River (for which the need has not yet been demonstrated) and protective fenders for the bridge piers. Since 1975 work categorized as maintenance has constantly improved and deepened the channel, thus permitting larger ships to use the canal and tonnages to grow. See Table 10 below.

about the environmental effects of the canal project, it would not sanction its completion unless "flow moderating structures (such as locks) were installed."[46]

It should be pointed out that, in the same year as the C. & D. Canal hearings, the Corps of Engineers established an Environmental Advisory Board. Lieutenant General Frederick J. Clarke, Chief of En-

[46]Herbert M. Sachs, Director, Water Resources Administration, Maryland Department of Natural Resources, to Worth D. Phillips, June 20, 1974, C. & D. Papers, DEO.

gineers, in an admittedly risky undertaking, created a panel of six outstanding environmentalists to assist the Corps in planning and developing its civil-works projects. Such assistance was important as the Corps attempted to redirect its energies (and its reputation as "irrepressible and irresponsible builders") to meet, in General Clarke's words, "both the environmental and developmental needs of the nation for the future."[47] Although there was some resistance within the Corps to this new emphasis, and although criticism of the Corps by outsiders continued, there was a broad acceptance of the need for altered procedures and the consideration of new factors when civil-works projects were under evaluation. According to General Clarke, the people in the Corps of Engineers realized that their job "was to do what we always had done: do what the people of the country wanted." If environmental concerns were now important to the general public, they were also important to the Corps.[48]

Colonel Clyde A. Selleck, Jr., reflected upon this change, what he called a "new awareness" of the environment, during his exit interview from his position as District Engineer in Philadelphia in 1975. Twenty years earlier, during an earlier tour of duty in Philadelphia, there had been no such concern. In the 1970s, however, the job required, in addition to being "an operator carrying out projects," serving as a "regulator . . . determining whether other agencies and other individuals" may do certain things and "whether they are in the public interest," which is often "very difficult, very challenging" to determine. Another major change by the 1970s was the extent of public participation in the decision-making process. Hearings were generally well attended, with often a "considerable organized opposition to some of the things that we do."[49] If, however, environmental issues were uppermost in the minds of the public during the early 1970s, an event in 1973 served to shift it away. The new concern focused on the way in which the canal was operated, a concern that was triggered by a tragic collision in February, 1973, when a large freighter, the *Yorkmar,* rammed the Penn-Central Railroad bridge in its down position.

[47]Reuss, *Shaping Environmental Awareness,* pp. 1–6; the quotations appear at pp. 1 and 6.

[48]Quoted in *ibid.,* p. 6.

[49]Transcript of an interview with Colonel Clyde A. Selleck, July 11, 1975, Oral History Collection, OCE. Selleck was District Engineer at Philadelphia from June 29, 1973, to July 11, 1975, and had previously served in the Philadelphia District Office in 1955–56.

Preparing for the
Twenty-first Century

17

It had appeared, as the decade of the 1970s arrived, that the canal was going to enter its most important decade in terms of service to the maritime interests and the recreational needs of the general public while at the same time its guardian, the Corps of Engineers, would focus on environmental concerns and improving operations and maintenance. In 1971, seen perhaps as an augur of things to come, a giant aircraft carrier, the U.S.S. *Monterey*, safely transited the canal—all other traffic, of course, being stopped during the five-hour passage of the big ship.[1] The following year traffic was again stopped for fourteen hours, this time to permit environmental scientists from Johns Hopkins University to make careful flow measurements in the canal channel through a complete tidal cycle. For the most part, however, increasing amounts of traffic moved through the canal year after year without incident.

The most significant activity in the early 1970s was the preparation, according to guidelines set forth in the National Environmental Policy Act of 1969, of an Environmental Impact Statement. A long document, the final version of which contained the responses of some twenty government agencies in Pennsylvania and Delaware, but especially in Maryland and Washington, D. C., its findings served to give much greater particularity to earlier environmental studies and to ex-

[1] *Wilmington Evening Journal*, June 11, 1971.

plore several new questions, but its conclusions were in agreement
with those previous reports. As indicated in the congressional hearings
of 1970, analyzed in the preceding chapter, there would be both positive and negative effects to the canal-enlargement project, but none of
the findings indicated that the canal project should be abandoned
or even substantially modified. Even the issue of barriers, which the
EIS examined thoroughly by reporting on six different types of flow-
control structures (ranging from a standard navigation lock to an in-
flatable underwater barrier), dissolved under close scrutiny and none
was deemed necessary at the moment.[2] Instead, the minimal environmental impact, compared to the economic impact anticipated and the
enormous investment already made in the waterway, including the current improvements under way, seemed to indicate that continuation of
the project would be approved. Efforts also continued to improve the
traffic-control system in place at the canal; in 1971, television cameras
were installed along the land-cut portion of the canal, and (except for
those times when fog blanketed the region) the new system seemed to
be working well.

All such feelings of satisfaction and confidence in the safe and
secure operation of the canal, mingled perhaps with a touch of com-

[2]The findings of the environmental study group, reported to the Corps of Engineers in September, 1973, are discussed in the preceding chapter. See also the
Final Environmental Impact Statement, based in large part upon these studies, in the
C. & D. Papers, DEO. The preliminary draft, circulated in the summer of 1972, drew
some harsh criticisms, particularly from the Environmental Protection Agency administrator in Pennsylvania, but the Corps responded to his concerns and comments, as
well as to all others, in its much expanded final version in late 1973. Among the
subjects examined for environmental impact were soils, water quality and flows, fish,
wildlife, recreation, and the tranquility of rural areas adjacent to the canal. The Corps
reported a 2.4:1 benefit-cost ratio, using interest rates mandated by Congress but ones
which were, nonetheless, challenged by one agency. Even it conceded, however, that
given the closeness of the project to completion, it should go forward.

For examples of the critiques about the Corps of Engineers and its civil-works
programs in general current during the heady early days of environmentalism, see John
Noble Wilford, "Corps of Engineers Caught Up in Battle of the Builders against the
Preservers," *New York Times,* February 20, 1972, 1, 65; and Elizabeth B. Drew, "Dam
Outrage: The Story of the Army Engineers," *Atlantic,* April, 1970, 51–62. Both speak
of the "eighteen steps to glory," the steps spelled out by the Corps for seeing a water
resources project from conception to completion, and the way in which benefit-cost
ratios had been manipulated in the past. For a statement of the Corps' position, see
"The Corps and Our Environment," *Annual Report of the Chief of Engineers, 1971,* I,
5–8. The highlights of the National Environmental Policy Act were summarized in the
first volume of the annual report for 1970, p. 6. The "eighteen steps to glory," later
amended to twenty-two steps but then reduced to six (with various substeps), are
spelled out and discussed in "Planning of Water Resource Developments," *Annual Report of the Chief of Engineers, 1976,* I, 5–13.

placency, were shattered like the bow of the *Yorkmar* when that ship collided with the railroad bridge. Only moments before, at 8:47 A.M. on February 2, 1973, the last cars of a southbound Penn-Central freight train had cleared the bridge. Less than a minute later, the westbound *Yorkmar* slammed into the still-lowered lift section of the bridge: "The lower chords of the bridge swept the forward decks of the freighter clear, killing one crew member and seriously injuring another. The bridge of the *Yorkmar,* located aft, came to rest against the east side of the railroad bridge at almost exactly mid-span." [3]

In the space of a few seconds, both the canal and the railroad had been rendered inoperable, and several months would be needed for making the necessary repairs. In addition to the death and injuries caused, huge economic losses were involved. The entire Delmarva Peninsula lost its only rail link to the outside, and all ships requiring a vertical clearance in excess of forty-seven feet were forced to sail the lengthy, hazardous outside route between Baltimore and Philadelphia and other North Atlantic ports (an additional 286 miles). Between Baltimore and various European ports, the additional sailing distance was approximately 115 miles. It was estimated that the Port of Baltimore lost $1.5 million for every day the canal remained closed, and that the economic losses and hardships encountered in the Delmarva Peninsula were incalculable. As many as twelve trains a day, each with from 75 to 100 cars, then used the railroad bridge over the canal. Similarly, a large proportion of Baltimore trade, perhaps as much as 40 percent of the total, used the canal. By mid-February, some 800 workers in the canal area had been laid off, the jobs of 7,000 more were in jeopardy (nearly 10 percent of Delaware's work force), production at the oil refineries near Delaware City was severely limited because of the rail service restrictions, and farmers in the peninsula lost access to northern markets completely. [4]

Governor Sherman W. Tribbitt of Delaware organized a tri-state emergency board to deal with the transportation crisis. The board's first priority was to see to it that the railroad bridge was repaired promptly, and in the meantime to expedite the establishment of alternate shipping routes, especially the use of rail-car barges for carrying goods between Norfolk and Cape Charles, Virginia. The Penn-Central Railroad, bankrupt since 1970, was unable to pay for the bridge re-

---

[3]Colonel Carroll D. Strider and Captain Thomas R. Zappacosta, Jr., "Shipwrecked Bridge," *Military Engineer,* January–February, 1974, 31–33.

[4]*Ibid.; Wilmington Evening Journal,* February 3, 1973; *Philadelphia Inquirer,* February 25, 1973.

pairs and disclaimed all responsibility for the accident anyway; consequently, the Corps of Engineers was ordered to proceed with the repairs immediately, estimated at $400,000 for emergency measures designed to reopen rail connections; the cost of permanent repairs to the bridge was estimated to be $1,600,000. Penn-Central was to be billed for the repairs later.[5]

This led, of course, to the need for assessing responsibility for the crash. There was some immediate criticism of the Corps of Engineers for having replaced men with machines in its traffic-control system only two years before. John M. Fears of Summit, Delaware, now retired from his job as a "canal checker," contradicted his statement of 1969 regarding the extraordinary safety of operations under the new system. He stated that he had warned the Corps, and anyone else who would listen, about the dangers inherent in replacing human "canal checkers" stationed at each end of the canal with closed-circuit television cameras. Fears pointed out that the new cameras, located at Reedy Point (near the Delaware River) and Town Point (in Chesapeake Bay), could not detect ships during a fog, and said he had long believed "it was just a matter of time until a wreck of this nature happened."[6] The Corps of Engineers declined immediate comment on the matter, as did the shipowner (Calmar Lines), captain, pilot, and, for the railroad, the bridge tender.

All of these principals testified during a prompt U. S. Coast Guard investigation of the incident. The 315-page transcript of the Coast Guard hearing, conducted in Baltimore before Administrative Law Judge Richard K. Gould, is valuable not only for its role in determining responsibility for the accident but as a report on the customary practices and procedures followed in the day-to-day operations of the canal at that time. In his initial findings, Judge Gould criticized the Corps for its "poor canal management," including carelessly kept counts of vessels transiting the canal at any one time, but he found both Captain Benjamin Edelheit and Pilot John Sundling "guilty of negligence" for the way in which they operated the *Yorkmar* on the morning of February 2, 1973. The pilot's mistake was in permitting the ship to "proceed at excessive speed under conditions of fog and reduced visibility," and in approaching the railroad bridge "without ascertaining the position of the lift span"; the captain's error was in acquiescing to the pilot's conduct. Both were suspended from duty—

[5]*Philadelphia Inquirer,* February 17, 1973.
[6]*Cecil Whig* (Elkton, Md.), February 7, 1973.

Edelheit for two months, Sundling for six months, plus twelve months more on probation.[7]

A newspaper reporter who analyzed the Coast Guard hearings for the *Wilmington Morning News* called the story "a tale of maritime blundering that rivals those found in fiction," and he suggested that any one of at least nine persons could have prevented the accident. Clearly there was a general lack of communications between the canal dispatcher in Chesapeake City and radiomen on vessels seeking to transit the canal, and between the dispatcher in Maryland and the bridge tender in Delaware; there were, moreover, no standard procedures among the involved parties regarding the issuance of permission to enter and transit the canal, no notification to the dispatcher's office when the railroad bridge was to be in its down position; and only loose, verbal reports were made by dispatchers regarding transits under way when shift changes occurred. The dispatchers, moreover, conversed with vessel pilots and with bridge tenders on different radio frequencies. Two major complicating factors in the case under litigation were that the *Yorkmar*'s radio was malfunctioning, and that a heavy fog, limiting visibility at the time of the crash to only a few hundred feet, was blanketing the canal on the morning in question.[8]

Canal dispatcher Frank H. Briscoe, Jr., was on duty until 7:15 A.M. on February 2, 1973, and he had given the *Yorkmar* permission to enter the canal, following four other ships, by speaking to the *Yorkmar* via telephone through the Wilmington marine operator. When Briscoe was relieved by Harry J. Longacre, he failed to make it clear to Longacre that the *Yorkmar* had been cleared for passage (and no written records to that effect were then kept or required). Neither was Leon Biggs, the Penn-Central's bridge tender on duty that morning, notified of the number of ships cleared for passage, but such notifications were not the usual practice. Instead, the ship pilots usually called the bridge operator to say they were en route, "hanging back" as necessary when the bridge was lowered for trains to pass. Pilot John Sundling, a veteran of more than a thousand passages through the Chesapeake and Delaware Canal, however, said the usual procedure was for the canal dispatcher to notify him if the railroad bridge was down; Captain Edelheit, who had made only four or five trips through the canal previously, said he had never seen the bridge lowered, and in

[7]*Wilmington Morning News* and *Wilmington Evening Journal*, April 6, 1973. A copy of the U.S. Coast Guard report is in the library of the Wilmington News-Journal Company.

[8]*Wilmington Morning News*, May 29, 1973.

Two freighters pass on a misty day at the Chesapeake and Delaware Canal.

Chesapeake City Bridge unites the north and south sections of Chesapeake City, Maryland. Canal operation headquarters and the Canal Museum are on the right side of the canal just above the bridge.

Tug and tow pass under the Summit Bridge. More than 11,000 commercial transits are made through the canal each year, making it one of the busiest in the world.

Lights and shadows play on the water near Chesapeake City Bridge, adding a touch of beauty at nightfall.

The freighter *Yorkmar* sits wedged under the canal's only railroad bridge, then used by the Penn-Central Railroad, during heavy fog February 2, 1973. The accident cut off all rail traffic between the northern and southern portions of the Delmarva Peninsula.

Dispatchers at the operations center in Chesapeake City, Maryland, guide commercial vessels through the canal with the aid of sophisticated electronics equipment.

Sign of the times: The advent of the container ship has added a new dimension to canal traffic. Conrail Bridge is in the background.

Reedy Point Bridge, approximately 10,000 feet long, carries Delaware State Route 9 across the canal. Dedicated in 1968, its deck was rehabilitated in 1985 at a cost of $1.9 million.

fact was unaware that it ever came down. Both men also testified that their speed was about 8 knots, a rate which was not excessive but rather was necessary to keep the ship under control in the often strong currents of the canal. The U. S. Coast Guard, based on the time logged between bridges, estimated the *Yorkmar*'s speed at about 11.8 knots. "It seems clear," concluded reporter Milford,

that procedures on the canal will change radically when it re-opens this summer. Testimony suggests that radio communications among dispatchers, bridge tenders, and ships crews all will have to be received and transmitted on a common frequency.

In addition, both written and oral procedures will have to be developed to inform each shift at the Corps of Engineers center in Chesapeake City and at the bridge tenders' office at Summit whether the canal is open for traffic and in what direction; which ships have actually upped anchor and entered; which have passed under the railroad bridge, and what position the railroad bridge is in at all times.

Ships also will have to be notified of the canal and bridge status constantly; and in turn ships will have to notify officials of their positions.

Detailed procedures also must be worked out for ship officers, stating clearly which tasks must be performed at which points to insure safety.

It is clear that the television camera system is inadequate in foggy weather and that mere use of a "traffic light" at the canal ends is not an adequate safeguard.[9]

There was also a civil action in the federal courts, filed on behalf of Mrs. Jaqui Brazil, widow of Philip J. Brazil, the forward lookout aboard the *Yorkmar* who had stayed at his post and vainly tried to warn the ship's officer of the danger. This litigation, consolidated with other claims and counterclaims among the principals and concluded in 1977, also affords another perspective on the events of February 2, 1973. Most important for the participants, the judge's Solomonic decision allocated responsibility for the tragedy among all three parties.[10]

The litigation also brought forth certain basic facts concerning events leading up to the accident and information regarding customary practices at the canal at that time. In a masterful narrative and analysis of events on the fateful day, Judge Joseph H. Young of the federal district court in Baltimore described events, step by step, from the time the *Yorkmar* sailed from Port Newark, New Jersey, on January 31 until the moment of the crash. He also noted the customary procedures

[9]*Ibid.*
[10]Judge Joseph H. Young, "Memorandum Opinion and Order [re SS *Yorkmar* Collision]," U.S. District Court, District of Maryland. A copy of this 44-page document is in the C. & D. Papers, DEO.

and practices being followed by those involved with the supervision and safety of ships transiting the canal.

At the outset, Judge Young pointed to "an amazing lack of organization" in canal operations, which permitted a "hit-or-miss" procedure for calling the dispatcher and receiving permission to enter the canal. Whereas formerly patrol boats had served as the intermediary between dispatcher and pilot, now direct contact between the two was both possible and essential, if only to give information to the pilot about other vessels in the canal. If this contact was occasionally haphazard, that between dispatcher and bridge tender was virtually nonexistent. According to custom, the position of the bridge was a matter between the railroad and the ship. In practice, the only responsibility exercised by the dispatchers for the safe operation of the canal was to monitor the width of vessels in the canal and be certain that adequate clearance margins existed. The bridge tenders kept the lift span in its raised position, lowering it only in times of heavy sleet, for routine maintenance, and to allow for the passage of trains. The time required for raising or lowering the bridge was twenty to twenty-five minutes; if the bridge tenders were aware of a ship entering the canal from the Delaware River side, only a short distance from their location, they would not lower the bridge until the ship had passed.[11]

Having taken note of the "varied background of rules and regulations" governing canal and bridge operations, the judge turned his attention to the *Yorkmar* and its situation. As it approached the eastern canal terminus, the pilot had been unable to raise the Chesapeake City dispatcher by radio. This fact, coupled with fog and weather problems, prompted the decision to drop anchor shortly after midnight. The captain and the pilot (Edelheit and Sundling) then retired for the night, but were awakened at 6:30 A.M. on February 2 with the information that the canal was open and that they had been advised to follow the fourth vessel into the canal. Sundling attempted to verify the clearance with the dispatcher by telephone, and he testified that the following conversation took place:

Sundling: "*Yorkmar* calling, have UHF radio problem, can we get clearance, have channel 13 receiver."

Dispatcher: "Okay, follow other ships."

Sundling: "Can't give a call as we enter breakwater, can we have an obstruction-free channel?"

Dispatcher: "Okay."

[11]"Memorandum Opinion and Order," pp. 11, 14–15.

Dispatcher Frank Briscoe, however, had no recollection of the request for an obstruction-free passage and did not recall having given any clearance other than permission to get under way. Vessels then entering the canal were required to call in at Reedy Point, as did the ships passing through prior to the *Yorkmar.* Turning then to a discussion of the law applying to allisions generally, and the *Yorkmar* specifically, the judge attempted to allocate responsibility for the accident and to determine "relative degrees of contributory fault" of each of the three parties involved.[12]

In the case of the Penn-Central Railroad, Judge Young ruled that its responsibility was slight but that, according to the general law of torts and given the probability of accident at the bridge location, "the magnitude of the harm" which would result, and the relatively slight cost of additional warning devices, "a prudent bridge owner" might have installed such a device. Failure to do so Judge Young considered a fault, but a minor one compared to the "gross derelictions of the Corps and the *Yorkmar.*" He found the railroad's degree of liability to be 10 percent.[13]

In terms of the Corps of Engineers and its degree of fault, the issue came down to the content of the communications between the dispatcher and the *Yorkmar* via the Wilmington marine operator. Both parties agreed on the time of the conversation—6:45 A.M.—and that a clearance of some sort had been given. Dispatcher Briscoe considered it merely permission to get under way, and expected a second call from the vessel when and if it reached Reedy Point. Consequently, he did not tell his relief dispatcher that the *Yorkmar* had been cleared to enter the canal, but he did mention its radio problem to him. Although the major fault for the accident was with the *Yorkmar,* the judge believed, again given the magnitude of possible harm and the ease with which corrective steps could have been taken, that additional actions should have been taken at the time. On a broader level, he also ruled that the Corps of Engineers in general did not "adequately . . . supervise navigation in the Canal." He faulted the Corps for "ambiguity" in its published rules and regulations (citing specifically the need to clarify the concept of clearance and when the required radio contacts were to be made), the lack of regular communications with the bridge tenders, and inadequate procedures by which dispatchers going off duty communicated relevant information to their replacements. He termed

[12]*Ibid.,* pp. 16–17. An allision is a collision between a moving object and a stationary one.
[13]*Ibid.,* pp. 20–23.

the existing system "slipshod" and said the Corps' entire operation of the canal "lacked due care." He concluded that the Corps was 40 percent at fault.[14]

In assessing the *Yorkmar*'s degree of fault, Judge Young examined the issue of "unseaworthy personnel and equipment" and general operational negligence. He found the *Yorkmar* "unseaworthy" on several grounds—its failure to have an operable radio and to maintain a "listening watch" at the time it entered the canal being the most serious. He also faulted Pilot Sundling for his failure to have sufficiently precise knowledge regarding the customary law of the canal, and cited several examples of "operational negligence" on his part: "the decision to enter the waterway with no channel 13 transmitter, failure to obey the traffic light, failure to respond immediately to the train whistle and operation at excessive speed under the existing conditions." His conclusion was that the *Yorkmar* was 50 percent at fault.[15]

The Corps and its employees were chagrined at the severity of Judge Young's criticism of the way in which they operated the canal, but it is also true that the accident and resultant litigation transformed canal operations. New, more careful procedures were instituted immediately, and substantial modernization in all phases of the operation, featuring computers and other sophisticated electronic equipment, occurred as soon as possible. The most recent steps in this movement came in 1985, with the installation of a computer console at the dispatcher's office.

Disappointment with the court decision, however, was offset in 1978 when full-scale construction at the canal resumed once more. Authorized in 1954, the enlargement project was then nearly a quarter-century old, but the basic purposes and clearly demonstrable need, now greater than ever, were the same. By April, 1981, when two U. S. hopper dredges, the *Comber* and the *Goethals,* completed dredging the easternmost section of the canal to its project dimensions, a channel approximating the 35-by-450-foot one authorized in 1954 was open for navigation. The canal's new dimensions meant that the depth of the waterway was about the same as the bottom width of the original canal in 1829, and its width was nearly seven times greater

[14]*Ibid.,* pp. 23–25.
[15]*Ibid.,* p. 37. Judge Young also decided other related suits and their financial settlements. He exonerated the several principal defendants, however, from damages suffered by General Foods Corporation by having its railroad access to its facilities in southern Delaware cut off by the ship-bridge accident. C. & D. Papers, 1978, DEO.

TABLE 10. CHESAPEAKE AND DELAWARE CANAL TRAFFIC, 1964–85[a]

Year	Tonnages (000,000)	Passages
1964	11.2[b]	16,738
1965	10.7	15,303
1966	10.3	15,351
1967	10.3	14,756
1968	9.6	9,723
1969	9.9	9,772
1970	10.5	9,858
1971	10.3	9,622
1972	11.0	9,709
1973	9.0[c]	9,219
1974	12.5	10,218
1975	10.8	9,158
1976	11.3	9,595
1977	10.8	10,798
1978	14.6[d]	14,259
1979	14.4	11,207
1980	16.0	11,424
1981	16.0	10,502
1982	17.0	11,245
1983	17.4	9,438
1984	17.6	10,064
1985	17.8	11,597

[a]Sources: *Waterborne Commerce of the United States,* an annual publication, and the Public Affairs Office, U.S. Army Corps of Engineers, Philadelphia District.
[b]This figure marked a new record tonnage, the previous peak tonnage having come in 1942, during World War II.
[c]The canal was closed to large-ship traffic for four months during 1973.
[d]Possible explanations for the increased tonnages after 1977 are the fuel shortages of the late 1970s and the improvement in channel dimensions throughout the entire length of the canal after 1975.

than the initial width. Most significantly, the long-anticipated increase in traffic materialized at once.

It is too much to say that the problems of the Chesapeake and Delaware Canal are now behind it. There is a constant need for maintenance work—keeping the channel at project dimensions, stabilizing the canal banks (an age-old problem), upgrading the traffic-control components (navigation lights, radio and telecommunications systems), and, perhaps most significant in terms of non-navigational interests, improving the bridges which carry ever-increasing amounts of truck cargo and passenger traffic across the canal—and doing everything possible to continue operating the canal in a safe and efficient manner. Related problems include the development of adequate, esthetically acceptable, and environmentally safe dredge-disposal sites, additional recreational sites and facilities for the general public, and continued good will on the part of visitors, area residents, and users of the canal.

No major accidents have occurred in the canal since 1973 and the establishment of improved operational procedures following the *York-mar* incident. There have, however, been occasional mishaps, usually resulting from equipment malfunctions, which cause minor delays and damages. There were collisions in 1979, 1981, and 1982, a small toxic spill in 1982, and two vessels brushed against the bridges at either end of the canal at different times in 1984.[16] Occasionally, too, cars or trucks have toppled into the canal—dispatcher Ed Patterson refers to operators of such vehicles as "water drivers"—and, although swimming in the canal is prohibited, drownings have occurred there from time to time.[17] During this same period, traffic through the canal increased significantly after the enlargement project was completed early in 1981, and larger and larger ships are utilizing the expanded waterway. In 1971, when the U.S.S. *Monterey* transited the canal, all other traffic was barred. In the latter 1980s, however, huge container ships up to 886 feet long—nearly three football fields in length—are regularly admitted to the canal. This step was taken after careful observation of repeated trial passages of various Maersk Line ships of this class, all of which occurred without incident.[18]

Increasing use of large container ships and the so-called RO-RO vessels (roll-ons, roll-offs, much like the TOFCs [trailers-on-flatcars] or "piggy-back" railroad cars) will mean, however, that the project depth of thirty-five feet must be maintained. Such near-continuous dredging is expensive, with $4.6 million budgeted for this purpose in FY 1986, and $8.0 million for FY 1987. In places of rapid shoaling, overdredging by as much as two feet is performed so that at least the project depth will be available longer.[19] The 886-foot Maersk Line

[16]Lieutenant Colonel Ralph V. Locurcio, Philadelphia District Engineer, to Senator William V. Roth, August 20, 1985, C. & D. Papers, DEO.

[17]*Wilmington Evening Journal*, February 10, 1975, and May 15, 1982. At least two suicides have occurred at the canal too, the victims jumping from a high-level bridge into the water 135 feet below.

[18]*Wilmington Morning News*, April 7, 1985; "C & D Canal Opens to 886-Foot-Long Vessels," *Port of Baltimore Magazine*, January, 1986, 13–15.

[19]Interview with James R. Tomlin, Project Officer, Corps of Engineers, Chesapeake City, August 15, 1986.

ships, for example, require a minimal channel depth of thirty-two feet. These 52,000-ton vessels, used in a weekly Baltimore–Far East service, can accommodate as many as 3,000 twenty-foot containers and operate at speeds up to twenty-three knots. Using the canal reduces sailing time on these behemoths by from four to ten hours, depending upon ultimate destination, thereby saving a portion of their $50,000-per-day operating expenses. There is also a savings in fuel consumption for all commercial vessels resulting from canal transits. The fuel crisis in the mid-1970s was a factor in causing canal usage to increase dramatically at that time, even before the enlarged dimensions were available in the 1980s.

Dredging expenses are usually the largest single item in the Corps' "operations and maintenance" budget for the canal. This activity is also one of the most troublesome undertakings for the Corps, given the growing concern over the environmental effects of the canal in all of its ramifications. According to engineer James R. Tomlin, superintendent of the canal at Chesapeake City, dredging activity in the canal and its approaches "fouls up" the shellfish for about a year afterward, but by the third year after such operations the shellfish population has increased. There is also concern about the disposal of dredging spoil, either in designated land areas along the canal or overboard, again in designated and prepared areas. Most of the dredging in recent years has been done by private contractors, particularly after an "Industry Capability" policy from the federal Office of Management and Budget mandated such practice whenever possible. At the present time, only a single dredge, the *McFarland*, is operated by the Philadelphia District Engineer Office.[20]

As part of its bank-stabilization program and canal-lands reclamation program, the Corps of Engineers in 1981 began permitting the disposal of treated sewage waste or sludge from the city of Baltimore along the canal banks in Delaware. The project, carried on by a Maryland company known as Enviro-Gro, was carefully monitored by the Corps as well as the Delaware Department of Natural Resources. It was found that there were no harmful effects from the program, either in terms of heavy metals leaching into the groundwater or damage to fish and wildlife in the area. Indeed, coupled with a phragmite-grass control program, intended to make the area habitable to wildlife and thereby advantageous to hunters in season, the program was considered a major success. When the Corps attempted, in 1985, to utilize

[20]*Ibid.;* Interview with Roy A. Pirritano, Public Affairs Officer, DEO, August 14, 1986.

sludge-disposal sites in Maryland as well, however, there was an enormous outcry from the Maryland public, condemning both the program and the Corps of Engineers in equal measure. A public meeting to consider the issue was held in the Bohemia Manor High School gymnasium in March, 1985. An audience estimated at more than 500 crowded the gymnasium, shouted down government officials, including Maryland Congressman Roy Dyson, when they called for more study before making a decision, and demanded an immediate end to the disposal program. Many viewed the situation as a battle between tiny Chesapeake City and two arrogant, overgrown organizations, the Corps of Engineers and the Enviro-Gro Corporation of Baltimore, and they considered it a victory when the Corps announced, shortly after the meeting, its decision not to deposit sludge at any site along the canal banks in Cecil County, Maryland.[21]

Perhaps the intensity of this meeting, and the opposition of Chesapeake City residents to the Corps, reflected past resentments. Not only had the city been permanently divided when the last low-level bridge connecting the two halves of the community was replaced by a high-level structure requiring a trip of several miles in order to cross, but more recently the city had experienced severe water problems and related financial difficulties because of the canal and its appurtenances. In the 1960s, when the canal had been widened and deepened in the Chesapeake City vicinity, not only were thirty to forty residences and half that many businesses razed, because the land on which they were located was to be removed, but also an underground waterline was excavated and never replaced. Instead, the Corps erected a second water tower for the city on the south side of the canal. This meant, however, that the city now needed two complete water-treatment systems. "I feel like we were duped," stated Thomas L. Mercer, an official of the Cecil County Historical Society and Planning Commission, during a special meeting of the town council with representatives from the federal government. When an aide to Senator Paul Sarbanes commiserated, suggesting that the Corps was not "overgenerous" but that, if proof of the damages sustained could be offered, it "might feel a moral obligation to help," Mercer added: "I don't think the Corps has been moral, I don't think they ever have been." An officer from the

[21] See the account of the meeting, which the paper labeled "emotional" and "unruly," in the *Wilmington News-Journal*, March 27, 1985; see also Lieutenant Colonel Ralph V. Locurcio to Senator William V. Roth, April 4, 1985. A Philadelphia District Office official, in the course of a discussion of this and other events, called the Chesapeake City people "strange" and "hostile." Interview, August 14, 1986.

Corps of Engineers responded, saying they were unaware of any anti-Corps sentiment in the town, and that no correspondence on the matter had been received. He suggested that the town seek federal funding for the necessary water-treatment plant, either a block grant from HUD or a loan from the FHA. In any case, water bills in Chesapeake City rose and resentment against the Corps continued. This attitude has tempered in recent years, especially following the new openness of the Corps in dealing with the public, the development of the canal museum at Chesapeake City, and the Corps' support of the annual Canal Days celebration. This event, initiated in 1979 to mark the sesquicentennial of the original lock canal's completion, has continued and grown in popularity. Few people, it appears, remain bitter about the way in which the canal divides the town—it is, as one resident suggested, "part of the price paid for progress."[22]

Except for Baltimore, the attitude of Maryland in general, however, is more hostile to the canal. There is continuing concern over the environmental effects of the enlarged canal, particularly on the upper Chesapeake, and frustration over the fact that detailed information on those effects is still not known. In 1984, William Jeanes, a director of the Upper Chesapeake Watershed Association, recalled Brigadier General Richard H. Groves's statement in 1970 that the Corps of Engineers, if it made mistakes, "fix[ed] them," and he called upon the Corps to fix its mistake of "unlocking" the Chesapeake and Delaware Canal in 1927, and of considerably enlarging the gateway between the bays in later projects. As a result, according to a Baltimore newspaper reporter, "at peak tidal flows, water roars through the 12-mile-long cut at a rate greater than the normal spring freshet of the Susquehanna . . . the East Coast's largest river." Part of the time the flow "is on the order of 150 billion gallons a day. Marker buoys 15 feet high can be pulled completely underwater. To weight their metering devices in place, the oceanographers working here have had to replace 200-pound boxcar wheels with 900-pound locomotive wheels." Most of the time, of course, the water simply sloshes "back and forth between the two bays at each turn of the tide," but critical data on the extent of the net flow eastward is not known. Whatever this figure is, even if there is in fact a net inflow from the Delaware River, "the Chesapeake," according to University of Delaware marine biologist Robert Biggs, "probably loses something either way. . . . If the Chesapeake

[22]*Wilmington Morning News,* December 11, 1979; Interview with James R. Tomlin, August 15, 1986.

is getting Delaware water, that's bad . . . and if the Chesapeake is losing fresh water, that can have real impacts upon the [aquatic systems] there in times of low river flow from the Susquehanna."[23]

Jeanes and his association were particularly annoyed that the multi-million-dollar Chesapeake Bay hydraulic model (subsequently dismantled by the Corps) had been unable to provide the answers sought: "The problem was that the model couldn't take into account the effects of the wind and changes in atmospheric pressure on the bay; and as scientists have learned in the last few years, the wind is the dominant influence on the bay's circulation so much of the time that attempts to understand it on the basis of tidal effects alone are virtually meaningless."[24] Clearly, additional information on the water flows, changes in salinity, the influence of the current upon fish eggs and larvae, and other vital matters is needed, and the Corps of Engineers should attempt to be more responsive to environmental issues and values while remaining sensitive to the burdens upon taxpayers of additional construction costs. A restraining system of some type, designed to inhibit if not eliminate completely water from flowing between the two bays without causing substantial interference to ship traffic, may be required. This was promised by the Corps in 1972; evidently its experiences with the canal have convinced the engineers it is not essential, but in view of the uncertainty regarding water flows and their impact and the continued expressions of concern or outright fear about irreversible damage to the upper Chesapeake, a reconsideration probably is in order. The barrier to water transfers might also serve to slow traffic down in its transits of the canal, particularly in the narrow land-cut portions, and further ameliorate the situation.

Relations between the canal and the state of Delaware are, like Maryland's, mixed but on the more positive side. There was a temporary disruption in the rapport between the two when a Corps contractor inadvertently but inexcusably bulldozed a portion of an important geological study site, a 70- to 80-million-year-old resource uncovered in the 1820s in the Deep Cut area of the canal. The Delaware Nature Education Society characterized it "a unique natural area in Delaware," and the state geologist said he was "outraged" by the action but

[23]Quoted in Tom Horton, "C. & D. Canal Suspected of Fouling Upper Bay," *Baltimore Sunday Sun,* November 11, 1984, D, 1, 5. See also the statement by William Jeanes, shortly before his death, in the June, 1986, issue of the Upper Chesapeake Watershed Association's *Newsletter,* "The Chesapeake & Delaware Canal: A View from the Upper Bay," pp. 1–4.
[24]Horton, "C. & D. Canal Suspected," p. 5.

conceded that "an honest mistake" had been made.[25] The Corps immediately halted its excavation work in the area, intended to be part of its ongoing bank-stabilization program, apologized for the error, and subsequently constructed access routes and a bridge over the "fossil area."[26]

As if to make further amends for its bulldozing mistake, the Corps of Engineers has continued to do much to provide recreational opportunities, including boating, fishing, hunting, and camping facilities, to the people of Delaware. Besides thirteen fishing piers erected along the entire route of the canal, major attention has been focused in the 1980s upon the development of new fishing sites within Delaware. The water area of the canal itself within Delaware approximates 545 acres, three times the size of Lum's Pond, the largest such fishing spot in the state, and the need is acute for additional sites. New Castle County contains approximately 70 percent of the state's population, but the county has only 16 percent of its public park acreage. The old State Pond no longer exists, having been filled with dredge spoils some years earlier, but an abandoned section of the canal, the "cut-off" at the railroad bridge created when the channel was straightened in the 1960s, represents an impoundment of thirty-two acres. Only one-sixth the size of Lum's Pond, it is, nevertheless, deeper than most other ponds and lakes in Delaware and was already well stocked with bass, bluegill, and catfish. Its depth and available baitfish made the so-called Canal Pond well suited for introducing exotic game fish not found elsewhere in Delaware.[27]

Eventually the pond project matured into plans for a large, 600-slip marina at the Summit North Recreation Area; the necessary construction permits were issued to the state by the Corps of Engineers in December, 1982, with construction to begin within four years. Initially the construction of only 250 slips was authorized, pending an evaluation of the impact of the marina upon canal traffic. The Corps also imposed various other safety and environmental requirements. The state was to keep search-and-rescue vessels in service at the marina twenty-four hours a day, develop comprehensive emergency procedures, and install both sewage pumps and oil-spill barriers at the facility. The Summit North Recreation Area, located on a scenic ridge overlooking the canal at its historic Deep Cut, was already a popular picnic spot, and rapid development of the new marina was anticipated.

[25]*Wilmington Morning News,* February 23, 1982.
[26]*Ibid.*
[27]*Wilmington Evening Journal,* May 25, 1980, and September 26, 1982.

The project was put on hold, however, in 1986, after some $700,000 had been expended. There was a shortage of state money, and an unanticipated silting problem at the site had caused the total cost of the project to escalate by 33 percent.[28]

The continuing problem between the Corps of Engineers and the state of Delaware remains highways, and highway bridges, over the canal. Unlike Maryland, which has Port of Baltimore interests to consider, Delaware has little interest in the canal as a canal; its interest is in not having its north-south highway traffic interrupted or the access of northern Delawareans to the ocean beaches in the southern part of the state impeded. A complicating aspect of the problem is that, contrary to its usual pattern and to its preference, the Corps owns and has maintenance responsibilities for the four high-level bridges there, three of which are in Delaware. The oldest bridge, moreover, carries U. S. Route 13 and the heaviest traffic, and frequent repairs, accompanied by unavoidable delays in traffic, are required. In the summer of 1983, for example, when traffic between populous New Castle County and Delaware's ocean beaches in the southern part of the state was picking up, the *Wilmington Evening Journal* reported that St. Georges Bridge traffic was "restricted again" to one lane southbound while bridge-expansion joints were being replaced, and that congestion over the weekend was expected to be heavy. The state police suggested detours to either Summit Bridge or Reedy Point Bridge. Unfortunately, however, no convenient roads near the canal were suitable for a detour route, and the problem continued. Similarly, in 1985, all three Delaware bridges over the canal underwent repairs and improvement (including a newly developed latex-concrete surface for the Reedy Point Bridge).[29]

Given the increasingly heavier trucks operating along U. S. 13, bridge-maintenance work along its route would be required often. Indeed, St. Georges Bridge, dating from 1941, was unsuited for traffic demands of the 1980s, even with truck-weight restrictions imposed, and plans by the state of Delaware were drawn up in 1985 to construct a "relief route" for U. S. 13. This route includes a new bridge a few hundred feet west of the existing one. The cost of the new bridge was estimated to be $135 million, and the total cost of the entire project was set at between $446 and $552 million, with tolls on the bridge

[28]*Ibid.*, March 11, 1986.
[29]*Ibid.*, June 17, 1983; News Release, Corps of Engineers, Philadelphia District, June 20, 1985, C. & D. Papers, DEO.

likely.[30] The new relief route would also make it possible to close other bridges across the canal for extended periods during repair work, thereby reducing both maintenance costs and safety hazards.[31]

The St. Georges Bridge project symbolizes a new spirit of cooperation (or at least toleration) between state and federal agencies in the canal region. It also reflects an acceptance of the canal, in reality an inland waterway of immense significance to the nation, and a willingness of the people to tolerate its presence and, whenever possible, take advantage of its facilities. Delaware Congressman Tom Carper is particularly outspoken regarding his own, and his state's, "ambivalence" toward the canal. Though vital to the nation's transportation system, the canal is, in Carper's view, of "scant economic benefit" to Delaware, and is frequently mentioned more in terms of its undesirable attributes than in terms of "its positive economic benefits for our neighbors." Not only is highway and rail traffic disrupted significantly by the inadequacy of the bridges, particularly for the increasingly heavy truck and beach traffic on U. S. 13, but the canal has encouraged feelings of "social division" between Delawareans on opposite sides of the waterway and serves to emphasize "different lifestyles supposedly led on the different sides of the canal." According to Carper, Delawareans are also troubled by possible adverse environmental problems—dredge spoil and municipal sludge deposits along the canal banks in Delaware worry many citizens, despite the careful monitoring of both practices by the Delaware Department of Natural Resources and Environmental Control. Nevertheless, the congressman concludes, there is little outright antagonism toward the canal:

Most Delawareans accept the Canal as a fact of life, one which differentiates our state from almost every other in the nation. We realize that we might be better off without it, but that some of our neighbors would be worse off if it did not exist. The Canal is not likely to go away, and with the help of the Corps of Engineers and our neighbors, we in Delaware will just have to do the best we can with this particular hand we've been dealt.[32]

[30]Wilmington *Morning News,* November 9, 1985. More recently Senator William V. Roth of Delaware, whose alarm over burgeoning federal budget deficits is well known, has acknowledged the bridge problem. Although he recognizes the economic importance of the canal to the Port of Wilmington and to other Delaware businesses and favors keeping it "operating properly," he is concerned about the amount of vehicular traffic over the canal on a daily basis, and worries that the existing bridges over the canal in Delaware might be "insufficient to meet future traffic demands." Senator William V. Roth, Jr., to author, Washington, D.C., July 1, 1987.

[31]*Wilmington Morning News,* November 6, 1986. The Corps released new, slightly lower cost estimates for the bridge-highway project at this time. The revised figure set the total cost at approximately $400 million.

[32]Congressman Tom Carper to author, Washington, D.C., July 15, 1987.

Toward this end, both Delaware City and Chesapeake City now
have Canal Days celebrations which capitalize upon the unique "arti-
fact" at their doorstep. They recognize that the C. & D. is both a relic
from the early nineteenth-century canal era and an ultramodern waterway capable of accommodating all but the very largest ships in the
world's oceanic fleet. In 1983, the Delaware Section of the American
Society of Civil Engineering designated the canal as a Delaware Historic Civil Engineering Landmark, and a bronze plaque affixed to the
old lock at Delaware City reminds visitors that the canal remains the
only one "built during the early 1800's which is still a major commercial shipping route."[33]

That the Port of Baltimore now has the most direct economic
interest in the modern waterway does not detract from its value to
Delawareans or other Delaware Valley residents. At the same time,
Baltimore's maritime interests have retreated from an earlier position
of demanding an even larger waterway, one that would correspond in
its accommodations to the deeper (up to fifty feet) channels and harbors under construction in or near the Port of Baltimore. Most responsible observers recognize that the C. & D. Canal, given its singular
qualities as a conduit between two major drainage basins as well as its
distinct ecological systems, cannot be enlarged further without the risk
of ecological disaster. Additional widening, moreover, would be enor-
mously expensive and disruptive to residents along the canal. Port of
Baltimore officials, consequently, disavowed their call in 1984 for an
enlarged C. & D. channel ("the lifeline of the port"). Instead, in
March, 1986, Maryland Port Authority officials announced their belief
that the thirty-five-foot channel was adequate for current needs. They
emphasized, however, that increased dredging, sufficient to maintain a
channel depth of thirty-five feet at all times, was essential, and that
other improvements (straightening the channel, improving approaches
and overhead clearances) should be made.[34]

Baltimore clearly recognizes the value of the canal to its overall
prosperity, and that the savings enjoyed by ships en route from Baltimore to the northeastern United States or North Atlantic ports are substantial. Increased tonnages through the canal, noticeable immediately
upon completion of the thirty-five-foot channel, have contined to rise
during the decade of the 1980s. Prior to 1981, a large amount of cargo

---

[33]News Release, May 7, 1983, C. & D. Papers, DEO. Two years later, the canal
was also named a National Civil Engineering Landmark.

[34]"C & D Canal Channel Maintenance Urged," *Port of Baltimore Magazine,*
April, 1986, 20–21.

Bibliographical Essay

There is an abundance of primary material, in print and in manuscript, relating to the history of the Chesapeake and Delaware Canal, but the secondary works on the subject are both few in number and incomplete. Not since Joshua Gilpin's promotional *Memoir on the Rise, Progress, and Present State of the Chesapeake and Delaware Canal* (Wilmington, 1821) appeared prior to the construction of the canal has a book on this waterway been published, and more recent general treatments of American canals have either ignored the Chesapeake and Delaware or relegated it to an undeserved minor position. A brief account of its history is given in James Weston Livingood, *The Philadelphia-Baltimore Trade Rivalry, 1780–1860* (Harrisburg, 1947), but it is told within the framework of intercity competition for trade with the interior, deals with the period prior to 1860, and is not based on an examination of the company records. Similarly, in *Old Towpaths: The Story of the American Canal Era* (New York, 1926), Alvin F. Harlow's popular treatment of this subject, only brief mention is made of the Chesapeake and Delaware Canal.

Consequently, this study is based upon three general categories of primary material: (1) the records of the Chesapeake and Delaware Canal Company, organized in 1803 and dissolved in 1919, the bulk of which is located in the Historical Society of Delaware, Wilmington; (2) published reports issued by congressional committees, presidential commissions, or, more recently, the Corps of Engineers, United States Army, under whose jurisdiction the canal has been since its acquisition by the federal government in 1919; and (3) the publications of various waterway organizations, particularly those of the Atlantic Deeper Waterways Association.

The original Chesapeake and Delaware Canal Company materials in the Historical Society of Delaware consist of letter books, board minute books, ledgers, stock subscription books, survey books, and receipt books, as well as ten folders of loose papers — correspondence, maps, toll sheets, and miscellaneous items, including photocopies of significant papers in other depositories. The Gilpin Papers in the H. F. Brown Collection, the separate collection of Henry Dilworth Gilpin Papers, and the Latrobe Papers (transcriptions of the originals in the Library of Congress) are useful supplements to the company records. The society's collection of Delaware newspapers, beginning with issues of the late eighteenth century, is also helpful.

Many of the canal company's publications, especially the annual *General Report of the President and Directors of the Chesapeake and Delaware Canal Company* (100 volumes, Wilmington and Philadelphia, 1804–06, 1824–1919), are in the collection of the Historical Society of Delaware. Other particularly useful company publications available there are *A Collection of the Laws Relative to the Chesapeake and Delaware Canal; Passed by the Legislatures of the States of Maryland, Delaware, and Pennsylvania, subsequent to the Year 1798* (Philadelphia, 1823; rev. ed., Philadelphia, 1840); *Address of the Board of President and Directors of the Chesapeake and Delaware Canal Company, to the Stock and Loanholders of that Company* (Philadelphia, 1845); and *The Chesapeake and Delaware Canal: Its Purpose, Its Needs, Its Possibilities* ([Philadelphia], 1905). Various company petitions to Congress, some of which are accompanied by Senate and House committee reports upon them, appear in *American State Papers*, ed. Walter Lowrie and Walter S. Franklin (Washington, 1834), Miscellaneous, volumes I and II. This publication also contains the highly significant Gallatin "Report on Roads and Canals," I, 724–921.

Other manuscript sources utilized in this study were the records of the Supreme Executive Council of Pennsylvania, as well as the small body of Chesapeake and Delaware Canal Papers at the Pennsylvania Historical and Museum Commission, Division of Public Records, Harrisburg. This material is revealing about Pennsylvania's early efforts to build the canal; the William Irvine Papers at the Historical Society of Pennsylvania, Philadelphia, are also helpful on this subject. A particularly illuminating series of letters, relating to the revival of the canal company, 1821–23, is in the Carey Collection at the Library Company of Philadelphia. Here is preserved the correspondence between the directors of the dormant canal company and a group of Philadelphia merchants anxious to revitalize the company. Other important Carey material, as well as copies of his numerous writings on the Chesapeake and Delaware Canal and internal improvements in general, is in the Historical Society of Pennsylvania. Reports and correspondence of the United States Army Engineer Department, in the War Records Division of the National Archives, tell of the service rendered by that body in locating the canal route in 1823–24. This story is summarized in Forest G. Hill's instructive book, *Roads, Rails, & Waterways: The Army Engineers and Early Transportation* (Norman, Oklahoma, 1957). Miscellaneous manuscript items of value were used at the following places: American Philosophical Society, Philadelphia; Delaware State Archives, Dover; Eleutherian Mills Historical Library, Wilmington, Delaware; Hall of Records, Annapolis, Maryland; Library of Congress; National Archives; New York Public Library; and the libraries at the universities of Delaware, Illinois, Virginia, and Pennsylvania (Mathew Carey's diary is here).

The second general type of source material used in this study was government publications. This includes such standard sources as the *Congressional Record* and its predecessors, which reveal the outward struggles to obtain federal assistance for, and then federal purchase of, the canal. Of more significance, however, are the some thirty special congressional committee reports or hearings on the canal made between 1806 and 1954. These items, almost all of which were available at the University of Illinois Library, were used extensively; exact citations are given in the footnotes. In addition, there were two presidential commissions, appointed in 1894 and 1906, which made thorough investigations of the existing canal and the need for improved transportation facilities between the Chesapeake and the Delaware. Their reports, known respectively as the *Casey Report* and the *Agnus Report*, are among the most valuable printed sources on the history of the Chesapeake and Delaware Canal Company. See "Letter from the Secretary of War, transmitting the Report of the Board appointed under the River and Harbor Act of August, 1894, to examine and determine, from surveys heretofore made, the most feasible route for the construction of the Chesapeake and Delaware Canal," *House Executive Documents*, No. 102, 53rd Congress, 3rd Session (Washington, 1894), and "Report of the Commission appointed by the President to Examine and Report upon a Route for the Construction of a Free and Open Waterway to Connect the Waters of the Chesapeake and Delaware Bays," *Senate Documents*, No. 215, 59th Congress, 2nd Session (Washington, 1907).

For more recent information, particularly on current operations and improvements, the publications and personnel of the Corps of Engineers, United States Army, have been of enormous help. Interviews were granted the author by the Philadelphia District engineer, under whose general supervision the canal is operated, by the resident engineer in Chesapeake City, Maryland, and by the marine traffic control officer, also in Chesapeake City. The most helpful publications are *The Chesapeake and Delaware Canal: An Inland Waterway from Delaware River to Chesapeake Bay, Delaware and Maryland* (rev. ed., Philadelphia, 1941); *Inland Waterway, Chesapeake & Delaware Canal: Rules and Regulations* ([Philadelphia, 1956]); *The Intracoastal Waterway. Part I: Atlantic Section* (Washington, 1951); and *Rules and Regulations Relating to the Navigable Waters of the United States* (Washington, 1939); see also the *Annual Reports* of the chief of engineers, Corps of Engineers, 1868 following, and the annual publication, *Waterborne Commerce of the United States*, 1920 following. A critical account of rivers and harbors legislation and the role played by the Corps of Engineers is Arthur Maass, *Muddy Waters: The Army Engineers and the Nation's Rivers* (Cambridge, Massachusetts, 1951).

The third general category of primary material is waterway association publications. In 1907, the Atlantic Deeper Waterways Association was organized to promote the construction of an enlarged intracoastal waterway from New England to Florida. One of the chief objects of the association was the improvement of the Chesapeake and Delaware Canal as a necessary link in the system. The association took the leadership in calling for federal acquisition of the canal and when this was done, it began a rather continuous campaign seeking improvements so as to render the tiny lock canal into a modern ship channel. Consequently, hardly an issue in three series of association publications — the *Bulletin*, the *President's Letter*, and the fuller *Reports of the Proceedings of the Annual Conventions of the Atlantic Deeper Waterways Association* — fails to mention and provide information about the canal. The publications of the National Rivers and Harbors Congress also contain information on this project. Although the absence of monographs on these and similar booster organizations is to be deplored, William R. Willoughby's study, *The St. Lawrence*

Waterway: A Study in Politics and Diplomacy (Madison, 1961), supplies some general information on the phenomenon of waterway
associations in the early twentieth century. J. Hampton Moore, president of the Atlantic Deeper Waterways Association for almost forty
years, has been the subject of a doctoral dissertation by Robert Edward
Drayer — J. Hampton Moore: An Old Fashioned Republican (University of Pennsylvania, 1961) — but this study does not elaborate on
Moore's waterway activities. In recent years, Baltimore has succeeded
Philadelphia as the city most intimately concerned with the canal, and
numerous Baltimore publications, especially the *Port of Baltimore
Handbook, 1965/1966*, are useful sources of information.

Descriptions of the old lock canal may be found in travel accounts by the following persons: J. E. Alexander, C. D. Arfwedson,
J. S. Buckingham, E. T. Coke, Basil Hall, J. C. Myers, Alexander
Randall, Francis Trollope, and Henry Tudor. See also Davison's
The Fashionable Tour (4th ed., Saratoga Springs, 1830) and the
*Eleventh General Report of the President and Directors of the Chesa-
peake and Delaware Canal* (Philadelphia, 1830). Later in the century
advertising material distributed by the Ericsson Line, the principal
steamboat line using the canal, contained descriptions of the route.

Articles on the Chesapeake and Delaware Canal have appeared
infrequently. Colonel Earl I. Brown's paper, "The Chesapeake and
Delaware Canal," *Transactions*, American Society of Civil Engineers,
XCV (1931), 716–765, is primarily concerned with describing the
enlargement of the canal, 1922–27. Robert Rossiter Raymond's short
essay, "The Chesapeake and Delaware Canal in the Civil War," *Pro-
fessional Memoirs*, Corps of Engineers, and Engineer Department at
Large, III (1911), 267–269, adds little not readily found elsewhere.
More useful is Lewis M. Haupt, "The Chesapeake and Delaware
Canal," *Journal of the Franklin Institute*, CLXIII (February, 1907),
81–107, and the special waterways issue of the *Annals of the American
Academy of Political and Social Science*, XXXI (January, 1908).

Among the secondary literature, the best treatments of the de-
velopment of transportation in the United States are by George Rogers
Taylor, *The Transportation Revolution, 1815–1860* (New York and
Toronto, 1951), and Caroline E. MacGill and others, *History of
Transportation in the United States Before 1860* (Washington, 1917).
The best studies of individual canals in America are Walter S. Sander-
lin, *The Great National Project: A History of the Chesapeake and
Ohio Canal* (Baltimore, 1946), Christopher Roberts, *The Middlesex
Canal, 1793–1860* (Cambridge, Massachusetts, 1938), and the recent

Erie Water West: A History of the Erie Canal, 1782–1854 (Lexington, Kentucky, 1966), by Ronald E. Shaw. On related subjects, see Julius Rubin, *Canal or Railroad? Imitation and Innovation in the Response to the Erie Canal in Philadelphia, Baltimore and Boston* (Philadelphia, 1961), and David Budlong Tyler, *The Bay & River Delaware: A Pictorial History* (Cambridge, Maryland, 1955). Carter Goodrich and others, in *Canals and American Economic Development* (New York, 1961), have analyzed the considerable economic impact of the canal era. Previously Goodrich studied the role of federal assistance in internal improvements in his *Government Promotion of American Canals and Railroads, 1800–1890* (New York, 1960).

Another very important source for historical research and documentation is physical remains. Unfortunately in this respect, the successive enlargements of the canal have obliterated most examples of the original canal company's work. When the canal was converted to a sea-level waterway, however, the eastern entrance was relocated. A portion of the original canal through Delaware City consequently was spared of extensive enlargement, and is used today as a branch canal for small craft. At the opposite end of the canal, the waterwheel and steam pumping unit installed in the 1850's may still be seen at Chesapeake City. Evidences of the feeder canal, nearly completed in 1804 and 1805 but then permanently abandoned, can be seen in the vicinity of Glasgow, Delaware.

The major sources for the second edition, like those of the first, consist of various types of primary material—government records, especially Corps of Engineers files in both Philadelphia and Washington; newspaper and magazine articles, particularly the daily press in Wilmington, Delaware (the *News-Journal* publications) and Elkton, Maryland (the *Cecil Whig*), and the *Port of Baltimore Magazine*; and, finally, interviews and correspondence with current Corps of Engineers employees involved with the canal, interested parties residing in the vicinity of the canal, Maryland Port Authority officials in Baltimore, and members of Congress and their staffs. No major secondary accounts on the history of the canal have appeared during the past twenty years since this study first appeared, but the congressional hearings in 1970, the Environmental Impact Statement of 1973, and the judicial reports stemming from the ship-bridge accident in 1973 add much to the written record about the canal. Commercial statistics as well as other information about significant waterway developments appear in the annual reports of the Chief of Engineers of the Corps of Engineers and the annual publication, *Waterborne Commerce of the United*

States. There are, however, in the category of secondary works, at least two works which deserve mention here: Martin Reuss, *Shaping Environmental Awareness: The United States Army Corps of Engineers Environmental Advisory Board, 1970–1980* (Washington, D.C., 1983) provides valuable context for the specifics relating to the Chesapeake and Delaware Canal during the 1970s; and Frank E. Snyder and Brian H. Guss, *The District: A History of the Philadelphia District, U.S. Army Corps of Engineers, 1866–1971* (Philadelphia, 1974) is a useful history through 1970 of the district office with responsibility for the Chesapeake and Delaware Canal. Additional references to both primary and secondary materials appear in the chapter notes.

Index